On the Trail of Capital Flight from Africa

On the Trail of Capital Flight from Africa investigates the dynamics of capital flight from Angola, Côte d'Ivoire, and South Africa, countries that have witnessed large-scale illicit financial outflows in recent decades. Quantitative, qualitative, and institutional analysis for each country is used to examine the modus operandi of capital flight; that is, the 'who', 'how', and 'where' dimensions of the phenomenon. 'Who' refers to major domestic and foreign players; 'how' refers to mechanisms of capital acquisition, transfer, and concealment; and 'where' refers to the destinations of capital flight and the transactions involved. The evidence reveals a complex network of actors and enablers involved in orchestrating and facilitating capital flight and the accumulation of private wealth in offshore secrecy jurisdictions. This underscores the reality that capital flight is a global phenomenon, and that measures to curtail it are a shared responsibility for Africa and the global community. Addressing the problem of capital flight and related issues such as trade misinvoicing, money laundering, tax evasion, and theft of public assets by political and economic elites will require national and global efforts with a high level of coordination.

Léonce Ndikumana is a Distinguished Professor of Economics and Director of the African Development Policy Program at the Political Economy Research Institute at the University of Massachusetts Amherst. He is an Andrew Carnegie Fellow, a member of the Independent Commission for the Reform of International Corporate Taxation, and an Honorary Professor of Economics at the University of Cape Town and the University of Stellenbosch in South Africa. He held senior positions at the African Development Bank and the United Nations Economic Commission for Africa. His previous books include Africa's Odious Debts: How Foreign Loans and Capital Flight Bled a Continent (with James K. Boyce, Zed Books, 2011), and Capital Flight from Africa Causes, Effects, and Policy Issues (with S. Ibi Ajay, OUP, 2014).

James K. Boyce is a senior fellow at the Political Economy Research Institute at the University of Massachusetts Amherst. His previous books include Economics for People and the Planet (Anthem, 2019), Africa's Odious Debts: How Foreign Loans and Capital Flight Bled a Continent (with Léonce Ndikumana, Zed Books 2011), Investing in Peace: Aid and Conditionality after Civil Wars (OUP 2002); The Philippines: The Political Economy of Growth and Impoverishment in the Marcos Era (Macmillan, 1993), and Agrarian Impasse in Bengal (OUP, 1987).

Praise for *On the Trail of Capital Flight from Africa*

"This important book should be read widely by anyone interested in African political economy as well as the global mechanisms of capital flight. While most work on capital flight focuses on aggregate figures, Ndikumana, Boyce and their co-authors provide cutting-edge analysis of three major African countries as well as of the destinations for stolen funds. Marrying the best available work on the economics of capital flight with insightful case studies, the book shows the importance of fine-grained qualitative analysis for an understanding of the consequences of capital flight for Africa and the global economy more broadly."

Ricardo Soares de Oliveira, Oxford University

"Under the right conditions, external capital can help lift people out of poverty in poor, capital-scarce, places. However, the social benefit from capital inflows can largely vanish if local elites syphon-off the capital and park it elsewhere for themselves. Earlier Ndikumana-Boyce calculations exposed the alarming extent of illicit capital flight from Africa. Their new edited volume provides three detailed country case studies, pointing to better data for monitoring and better policies globally. The volume provides a welcome foundation for both further research and effective action to help assure that global capital flows reduce global poverty."

Martin Ravallion, Georgetown University

"Many developing countries continue to suffer significant resource outflows, largely due to illicit capital flight. On the trail of capital flight from Africa: The Takers and the Enablers—edited by Léonce Ndikumana and James Boyce—studies this blight in sub-Saharan Africa. The world has much to learn from their forensic analysis. . . The West's piecemeal approach to sanctions targeting individuals is recognized as costly, time-consuming and ineffectual. Instead, the editors recommend a pre-emptive, across-the-board effort to undermine transnational networks enabling illicit financial flows. This should begin with closing financial system loopholes."

Jomo Kwame Sundaram, former assistant secretary-general, United Nations Department of Economic and Social Affairs

"Léonce Ndikumana and James Boyce have been at the forefront of research on illicit financial flows since before that term was even coined, and this book confirms it once again. But where Ndikumana and Boyce are most well known for their comprehensive quantitative analyses, here they have edited a volume that focuses deliberately on the experience of specific countries suffering illicit flows. The result, part investigative journalism and part academic analysis, is to bring the damage done to countries' governance into sharp focus. The book contributes powerfully to the case to understand illicit financial flows, facilitated by rich countries as they are, as a continuation of imperial extraction which robs people not only of resources but ultimately of the right to effective statehood."

Alex Cobham, Tax Justice Network

On the Trail of Capital Flight from Africa

The Takers and the Enablers

Edited by

LÉONCE NDIKUMANA

and

JAMES K. BOYCE

OXFORD
UNIVERSITY PRESS

Great Clarendon Street, Oxford, OX2 6DP,
United Kingdom

Oxford University Press is a department of the University of Oxford.
It furthers the University's objective of excellence in research, scholarship,
and education by publishing worldwide. Oxford is a registered trade mark of
Oxford University Press in the UK and in certain other countries

First published 2022
First published in paperback 2023

Published in the United States of America by Oxford University Press
198 Madison Avenue, New York, NY 10016, United States of America

British Library Cataloguing in Publication Data
Data available

Library of Congress Cataloging in Publication Data
Data available

ISBN 978-0-19-885272-8 (Hbk.)
ISBN 978-0-19-888313-5 (Pbk.)

DOI: 10.1093/oso/9780198852728.001.0001

Contents

Acknowledgements

We owe a sincere debt of gratitude to the many individuals and institutions who contributed directly and indirectly to bring this book to completion. We especially appreciate the valuable contributions from experts and policy makers in Angola, Côte d'Ivoire, South Africa, and elsewhere—notably Portugal, France, and the UK—who donated their time and knowledge, as well as providing valuable data and qualitative information to the authors of the case studies. Their assistance is greatly appreciated.

We are grateful to the Open Society Foundations (OSF) for a grant that supported this project, and to the Freidrich Ebert Stiftung in Berlin and the Political Economy Research Institute at the University of Massachusetts Amherst for valuable additional support.

Léonce Ndikumana and James K. Boyce
Amherst, Massachusetts
January 2022

List of Figures

List of Tables

List of Acronyms

ACE	Audit Contrôle et Expertise
ADM	Archer Daniels Midland Company
AMCU	Association of Mineworkers and Construction Union
AML	Anti-money laundering
ANAPROCI	Association Nationale des Producteurs de Café-Cacao de Côte d'Ivoire [National Association of Coffee and Cocoa Producers of Ivory Coast]
ANC	African National Congress
API	American Petroleum Institute
B/L	bill of lading
BAI	Banco Africano de Investimentos
BASIC	Bureau for the Appraisal of Social Impacts for Citizen Information
BCEAO	Banque Centrale des États de l'Afrique de l'Ouest [Central Bank of West African States]
BdP	Banco de Portugal
BEE	Black Economic Empowerment
BES	Banco Espírito Santo
BESA	Banco Espírito Santo Angola
BIS	Bank for International Settlements
BNA	Banco Nacional de Angola
BNI	Banque Nationale d'Investissement [National Investment Bank]
BoP	balance of payments
BWIs	Bretton Woods Institutions
CAA	Caisse Autonome d'Amortissement [Autonomous Amortization Fund]
CAISTAB	Caisse de Stabilsation et de Soutien des Prix des Produits Agricoles [Stabilization and Price Support Fund for Agricultural Products]
CBS	Statistics Netherlands
CCC	Conseil Café-Cacao [Cocoa-Coffee Council]
CCHA	Compagnie Commerciale Hollando Africaine
CD	Certificate of Deposit
CEO	Chief Executive Officer
CFA franc	Communauté financière d'Afrique franc [franc of the Financial Community of Africa]
cif	cost, insurance and freight
CIF	China International Fund
CIU	Customs Inspection Unit
COD	Country of Destination
COMD	Crude Oil Marketing Department
COO	Country of Origin

CPC	Customs Processing Center
CSA	Coal Supply Agreement
DN	Debit Note
DOTS	Direction of Trade Statistics
DPR	Department of Petroleum Resources
DRC	Democratic Republic of Congo
DTI	Data Transmitting Interface
DUS	Droit unique de sortie [Single exit duty]
ECOWAS	Economic Community of West African States
EFCC	Economic and Financial Crimes Commission
EIR	Equipment Interchange Report
EU	European Union
FCPA	Foreign Corrupt Practices Act
FDI	Foreign direct investment
FDPCC	Fonds de Développement et de Promotion des Activités des Producteurs de Café et de Cacao [Fund for Development and Promotion of the Activities of Coffee and Cocoa Producers]
FGCC	Fonds de Garantie des Coopératives Café et Cacao [Guarantee Fund for Coffee and Cocoa Cooperatives]
FILOCOM	Fichier des Logements par Communes [Housing Records by Commune]
FN	Forces Nouvelles [New Forces]
fob	free on board
FPI	Front Patriotique Ivoirien [Ivorian Patriotic Front]
FPSO	Floating production, storage and offtake platform
FRCC	Fonds de Régulation du Café et du Cacao [Regulatory Authority for Coffee and Cocoa]
FT	Financial Times
GDP	Gross Domestic Product
ICCO	International Cocoa Organization
ICIJ	International Consortium of Investigative Journalists
IDC	Investissement Développement Conseil
IMF	International Monetary Fund
IMTS	International Merchandise Trade Statistics
IOC	Independent oil company
IIP	international investment position
IP	Intellectual property
ISO	International Organization for Standardization
ITIC	International Transportation and Insurance Cost
JSE	Johannesburg Stock Exchange
JVs	Joint ventures
KYC	know-your-customer
LSE	London Stock Exchange
MPLA	Movimento Popular de Libertação de Angola
NBER	National Bureau of Economic Research
NCS	Nigerian Customs Service

NEPC	Nigerian Export Promotion Council
NIMASA	Nigerian Maritime and Safety Administration Agency
NNPC	Nigerian National Petroleum Corporation
NPDC	Nigerian Pipeline Development Corporation
OCM	Optimum Coal Mine
OECD	Organisation for Economic Co-operation and Development
OPEC	Organization of the Petroleum Exporting Countries
OPM	Other People's Money
PAAR	Pre-Arrival Assessment Report
PDCI	Parti Démocratique de la Côte d'Ivoire [Democratic Party of Ivory Coast]
PEPs	Politically Exposed Persons
POS	point of sale
PwC	PricewaterhouseCoopers
R&D	Research and development
RDA	Rassemblement Démocratique Africain [African Democratic Party]
RDR	Rassemblement des Républicains [Republican Party]
SADC	Southern African Development Community
SAIE	Société Africaine d'Importation et d'Exportation [African Import-Export Association]
SARB	South African Reserve Bank
SARS	South African Revenue Service
SEC	US Securities and Exchange Commission
SGD	Single Goods Declaration
SIFCA	Société Financière de la Côte Africaine [Financial Corporation of the African Coast]
SITC	Standard International Trade Classification
SSA	Sub-Saharan Africa
SVDP	Special Voluntary Disclosure Program
SYNAP-CI	Syndicat National Agricole Pour Le Progrès [National Agricultural Union for Progress]
TAIS	Trans Africa Investment Services
TDO	Terminal Delivery Order
UAE	United Arab Emirates
UN Comtrade	United Nations International Trade Statistics Database
UNCTADstat	United Nations Conference on Trade and Development Statistics
UNDP	United Nations Development Programme
UNITA	União Nacional para a Independência Total de Angola

List of Contributors

Adam Aboobaker, Lecturer in Economics, University of the West of England, Bristol, UK

Melvin Ayogu, Professor, Department of Economics, Emory University, USA

James K. Boyce, Senior Fellow, Political Economy Research Institute, University of Massachusetts Amherst, USA

Jean Merckaert, Director of Action and Advocacy, Secours Catholique-Caritas, France

Karmen Naidoo, Doctoral candidate, Department of Economics, University of Massachusetts Amherst, USA

Léonce Ndikumana, Distinguished Professor, Department of Economics, University of Massachusetts Amherst, USA

Nicholas Shaxson, Writer, Journalist, and Investigator, Tax Justice Network, Berlin, Germany

1

Introduction

Why Care about Capital Flight?

Léonce Ndikumana and James K. Boyce

For Africa, the beginning of the twenty-first century marked a turn from a history of economic stagnation to an era of growth acceleration on the back of an unprecedented commodity boom. Until the boom was checked by the 2008 global economic crisis, Africa emerged as the world's fastest-growing region, its economies branded as "lions on the move" by McKinsey & Company.[1] Following that crisis, the Sub-Saharan Africa (SSA) region rebounded and continued to grow robustly in the century's second decade at an annual rate of more than 4%.[2] Many African countries saw substantial improvements in human development outcomes, with rising literacy and declining child mortality.

Yet even as African countries witnessed these economic improvements, they continued to suffer from major outflows of resources, much of it in the form of illicit capital flight. The problem is not new, but ironically it has accelerated even as African economies embarked on growth acceleration. We have estimated that capital flight from African countries since 1970 amounted to $2 trillion, of which almost $600 billion exited after the turn of the century. If we include the interest income that would be earned from these outflows, the cumulative amount of private wealth held offshore stood at $2.4 trillion by 2018. This was more than three times higher than the stock of external debts owed by the same countries, making Africa a "net creditor" to the rest of the world (Ndikumana and Boyce 2021).

The phenomenon of capital fleeing from the continent at a time when it is experiencing a renaissance defies common logic and economic theory, which suggest that capital should move across borders in pursuit of higher returns to investment. Growth acceleration and improvements in macroeconomic and political stability in Africa, as seen in the past two decades, should encourage domestic investment while reducing incentives for moving private capital abroad. The fact that capital

---

[1] McKinsey Global Institute (2010).
[2] IMF, World Economic Outlook database, April 2020 edition, available at https://www.imf.org/external/pubs/ft/weo/2020/01/weodata/index.aspx (accessed on July 21, 2021).

Léonce Ndikumana and James K. Boyce, *Introduction*. In: *On the Trail of Capital Flight from Africa*. Edited by Léonce Ndikumana and James K. Boyce, Oxford University Press.
© Léonce Ndikumana and James K. Boyce (2022). DOI: 10.1093/oso/9780198852728.003.0001

nevertheless seems to flow upstream, fleeing Africa towards lower-return markets abroad, suggests that wealth holders are motivated not by conventional portfolio choice considerations, but by a desire to keep their assets out of sight of the authorities in their own countries. Indeed, empirical research shows that annual capital flight is not responsive to differentials in risk-adjusted interest rates between African countries and the rest of the world (see, among others, Ndikumana et al. (2015) and Ndikumana and Boyce (2003)), implying that capital flight is driven by other factors.

One key motive behind capital flight from Africa may lie in the fact that the wealth itself was acquired illegally, and therefore needs to be shielded from prosecution for the predicate crimes that generated it. In addition, some of the capital flight may originate from legally acquired wealth that the owners illicitly transfer abroad, in contravention of capital controls and foreign exchange regulations, in order to evade tax on capital gains and interest income or to avoid the risk of asset capture or nationalization in countries with high political instability.

Capital flight is widespread across the African continent, but it varies significantly from country to country, with resource-rich countries being typically more exposed than their less well-endowed counterparts (Ndikumana and Sarr 2019). Two key mechanisms of capital flight are the misinvoicing of commodity exports and the embezzlement of export revenues in state-owned mineral and oil companies. The association of capital flight with natural resources is one manifestation of what is sometimes called the "resource curse." This association appears to be particularly pronounced in the case of oil-rich countries, which in Africa tend to be more poorly governed.

The issue is not resource endowments per se, but the quality of governance in the concerned countries. Lamenting the inadequacy of economic progress in her country, Liberia's president Ellen Sirleaf Johnson remarked:

> I've often said that Liberia is not a poor country, but rather a rich country that has been poorly managed. The same is true for most of sub-Saharan Africa. Africa's crisis was a failure of leadership and management. Sub-Saharan Africa is rich in resources, talent, and energy and spirit. But it has not been rich in leadership. It is made up of countries that were poorly managed, and the results have been disastrous.
>
> (Sirleaf Johnson, 2010, p. 5)

Capital flight can be understood as a result and symptom of an environment that incentivizes and facilitates the smuggling of domestic assets to offshore havens.

But capital flight is not only a domestic phenomenon "pushed" by features of the local economic and political order. It is also a global phenomenon "pulled" and facilitated by institutions and actors in the international economic order. Within Africa, capital flight is enabled by the failures of legal and regulatory systems to enforce the rule of law in acquisition of wealth and the transfer of wealth across borders. Internationally, capital flight is enabled by systematic defects in the global trading and financial systems that allow transactions and wealth to be shielded from scrutiny, and facilitated by an elaborate transnational network that includes banks, lawyers, accountants, and consulting firms. Tackling the problem will require a global strategy with committed engagement by national, regional, and global stakeholders.

Why Care about Capital Flight?

Capital flight should be a matter of concern not just for Africans but for the world at large. In Africa, capital flight undermines domestic resource mobilization by eroding the tax base. It undermines government finances directly when the capital comes from embezzled externally borrowed funds—through the "revolving door" that links debt and capital flight—and by theft of government revenue from state-owned enterprises and natural resources (Ndikumana and Boyce 2011). These leakages come at a heavy cost in terms of poverty reduction and public investments in health care, education, water and sanitation (Ndikumana 2014, Nkurunziza 2015). The negative impacts on public services fall disproportionately on the poor who cannot afford privately provided services at home or abroad. Meanwhile, the fact that offshore wealth goes untaxed means that the burden of taxation falls disproportionately on the middle class and domestic businesses that are unable to hide their assets abroad. These effects exacerbate inequality, fueling social and political instability arising from the resentment of ordinary citizens against a system they perceive, with good reason, to be working in the interest of the economic and political elites in collusion with international actors operating in an opaque global financial system. As African countries attempt to design strategies to sustain inclusive economic growth and reduce inequality, they must integrate combating capital flight as a central element of their efforts.

The countries that are destinations for flight capital bear serious costs, too. In the real estate markets of New York, Paris, London, and other global cities, capital flight inflates prices and rents for the residents. The loopholes and defects in the international financial architecture that are exploited by capital flight also facilitate tax avoidance and tax evasion by corporations and wealthy individuals in rich countries. Transnational corruption crosses national borders, corroding democratic governance and undermining legitimate economic activity wherever it goes. For countries on the receiving end of African capital flight, too, efforts to combat capital flight are in the interests of everyone apart from enablers who are on the take.

Why Case Studies?

There is sufficient evidence today to make a compelling case that capital flight is a problem that deserves serious attention given its magnitude, its deleterious developmental effects on African economies, and the fact that it seems to be worsening over time (Ndikumana and Boyce, 2011, 2015; Ndikumana and Boyce, 2021). But the existing evidence remains inadequate as a basis for formulating effective policies to prevent further capital flight and induce repatriation of past capital flight. First, aggregate macroeconomic evidence does not furnish fine-grained, country-specific information on the mechanisms of capital flight, the institutional contexts in which it occurs, and the players involved in facilitating it. Second, the existing literature on capital flight has not paid adequate attention to the destinations of private wealth accumulated and held offshore and the roles of the banking sector and public institutions in the destination territories. Third, the literature has not sufficiently delved into the effects of national and international institutions and governance on the magnitude and mechanisms of capital flight and the possible reverse effects of capital flight on governance.

This volume seeks to address these gaps with detailed analysis at the country level. It aims to provide evidence that can help guide effective policy formulation on how to combat capital flight from Africa as well as to advance policy-relevant research on the issue. To do so, the book first presents a quantitative analysis of capital flight and its drivers in Angola, Côte d'Ivoire, and South Africa. This is followed by qualitative and institutional analysis for each country to examine the *modus operandi* of capital flight; that is, the "who," "how," and "where" dimensions of the phenomenon. "Who" refers to major domestic and foreign players; "how" refers to mechanisms of capital acquisition, transfer, and concealment; and "where" refers to the destinations of capital flight and to the bilateral transactions involved.

Why Angola, Côte d'Ivoire, and South Africa?

South Africa and Angola come in second and third position respectively (after Nigeria) among countries with the biggest outflows of capital flight in Sub-Saharan Africa; Côte d'Ivoire ranks seventh (Ndikumana and Boyce 2018). These countries share the common feature of high natural resource endowments that is often correlated with capital flight, but they are heterogeneous in terms of history, economic structure, and institutions in ways that reflect the heterogeneity of the continent.

With the fifth largest economy in Sub-Saharan Africa, Angola is known not for what it has done with its vast natural resource endowment, but what it has failed to do with it. The country features prominently in the literature on the "oil curse" (Hammond 2011, Shaxson 2007), as the discovery and exploitation of petroleum has suffocated the development of other economic sectors while profiting the national elite and multinational oil companies. This has been accomplished notably through establishment of a powerful parastatal to manage oil, Sonangol, which observers have described as "an island of competence thriving in tandem with the implosion of most other Angolan state institutions" (Soares de Oliveira 2007). Angola's natural resources also played a critical role in motivating and financing the country's devastating civil war (Frynas and Wood 2001). Angola's "paradox of plenty," as a country with rich resources and poor development outcomes, makes it ideal for the study of capital flight.

Côte d'Ivoire was "long touted as an island of political stability and (relative) economic prosperity in West Africa," wrote Boubacar N'Diaye (2005, p. 89), but since the turn of the century the country "has joined the more common category in the sub-region: praetorian states mired in political uncertainty and unending turbulence." Klass (2008, p. 109) echoed the sentiment, saying "Once touted as the 'Ivorian miracle,' Côte d'Ivoire has become a development nightmare." In the past decade, the country has recovered to the point of regaining its status as one of "Africa's most rapidly expanding economies, with significant oil, gas and mineral reserves; a major agriculture sector; and a growing, youthful population driving the country forward" (Oxford Business Group 2020). But the country is still struggling to recover from its troubled past and the failure to harness its natural resources, notably as the world's top producer of cocoa, for the benefit of its people. Instead, the cocoa sector has been the scene of complex and often corrupt schemes of "rent-seeking" by domestic political elites in collusion with global business partners (Losch 2002). The case study of Côte d'Ivoire focuses on the cocoa sector to illustrate the interplay between capital flight and the plunder of the country's resources.

South Africa, a member of the elite G20 club of rich countries, is the second largest economy in Sub-Saharan Africa after Nigeria, and the most integrated in the global economy, with a sophisticated financial system. Owing to its diversified economy, it is less dependent on its natural resources than Angola or Côte d'Ivoire. But its mineral sector has been an arena for massive export misinvoicing and tax evasion by politically well-connected private individuals and corporations. In the post-apartheid era, the country witnessed both concerted liberalization of the economy and an explosion of capital flight. Again, transnational networks have played a key role in enabling illicit outflows of wealth to the detriment of the vast majority of the country's people.

Structure of the Book

The book comprises five chapters besides the introduction and the conclusion. Chapter 2 presents updated estimates of capital flight and one of its important elements, trade misinvoicing, for the three case-study countries. The results indicate that all three have experienced substantial capital flight over the past four decades, amounting to $103 billion (in constant 2018 dollars) for Angola, $55 billion for Côte d'Ivoire, and $329 billion for South Africa.[3] Misinvoicing, especially in primary commodity exports, has been an important mechanism of capital flight. The fact that unrecorded capital outflows have persisted over a long period suggests that they are driven by systemic structural and institutional factors pertaining to both the source countries and the global financial system. Capital flight has led to the accumulation of massive offshore wealth belonging to the economic and political elites of these countries, even as their populations continue to face deprivation in access to basic services. In all three African countries, capital flight is a major obstacle to development financing that needs to be tackled through coordinated national and international strategies.[4]

In Chapter 3, Nicholas Shaxson examines how Angola has failed to take advantage of its vast oil reserves to transform its economy and improve the lives of its people. During its "golden decade," between the end of the civil war in 2002 and the oil price crash of 2014–2015, Angola exported massive amounts of oil under a patronage system that kept the benefits in the hands of the president's family and a narrow elite. Today the country faces the depletion of its oil reserves with very little to show in terms of development outcomes beyond the country's capital, Luanda. Shaxson poses the question: where did the money go? He explains how a large chunk of Angola's wealth ended up overseas in the hands of a relatively small number of individuals, enabled by a transnational network of intermediaries. This giant money drain is a tragic story that Angola shares with many other resource-rich African countries.

In Chapter 4, Jean Merckaert tells the story of capital flight from Côte d'Ivoire, focusing on the cocoa sector. He describes how the impressive economic growth fueled by cocoa exports after independence, once hailed as the "Ivorian miracle," evaporated after the collapse of cocoa prices and the explosion of foreign debt. As the country plunged into an economic crisis, followed by a political crisis that culminated in civil war, the primary commodity sector continued to be highly vulnerable to illicit financial flows. The chapter documents large and persistent discrepancies between Côte d'Ivoire's export statistics and the import statistics of its major partners in the cocoa trade, indicative of substantial capital flight through export misinvoicing. Merckaert traces the continuities and changes across political regimes since independence in the mechanisms of resource rent capture and personal enrichment and the roles of the key national and foreign players. The patronage nexus linking state power to market power contributed to large-scale

---

[3] The estimates for Côte d'Ivoire and South Africa refer to the period 1970 to 2018; for Angola they refer to the period 1986 to 2018 owing to insufficient data for earlier years.

[4] See UNCTAD (2020) for an analysis of the implications of illicit financial flows for sustainable development in Africa.

capital flight and the failure of the country to take full advantage of its natural resource endowments.

Chapter 5 turns to the case of South Africa. Adam Aboobaker, Karmen Naidoo, and Léonce Ndikumana examine the mechanisms, actors, enablers, and institutional environment that have facilitated capital flight from South Africa and the attendant accumulation of offshore private wealth. While capital flight is not a new phenomenon in South Africa, it accelerated during the modern era of economic liberalization and rapid integration into the global economy. The financial hemorrhage deepens the country's financing gaps, multidimensional poverty, inequality, and unemployment. The chapter describes the systematic failure of the country's regulatory system, which has been compromised by "state capture" orchestrated by an intricate network of private enablers with deep connections within the government and the global economy. It illustrates the phenomenon with the story of the Gupta family, which built its fortune by forging connections with key figures in government and parastatal companies in the mining and energy sectors, and used a complex network of opaque transactions to move money out of the country.[5] The authors discuss the adverse effects of capital flight on economic development, state institutions and governance, and call for urgent attention to prevent even more devastating consequences for the country's political and social instability.

In Chapter 6, Melvin Ayogu examines the double-edged role of governance in capital flight. Poor governance enables capital flight and undermines the fight against it. Capital flight, in turn, erodes the quality of governance and weakens the regulatory system. Focusing on international trade and trade-related financial transactions, Ayogu demonstrates that "the sword of governance has been wielded to cut predominantly one way—to facilitate capital flight—in key African countries." He argues that "getting governance right" will require reforms in the management and oversight of international trade data to enhance quality, consistency, and transparency in data reporting and the exchange of information. The chapter describes the complexities governing import and export transactions, with a view to understanding how political, social, and economic arrangements facilitate corruption in general, and capital flight in particular. Changing the rules of the game in international trade will be an important step in building a global constituency in the fight against capital flight.

The issues analyzed in these case studies are by no means unique to these three countries. We hope that the evidence presented in this book will help sow the seeds for more detailed investigations of the economic and institutional mechanisms of capital flight in Africa, so as to provide input into the design and implementation of better-targeted policies to combat this scourge. Increasingly, addressing the

---

[5] The dealings of the Gupta family and key former government officials are the subject to ongoing investigation by the Office of the Public Protector South Africa (2016) and investigative journalists.

problem of capital flight is considered as a central pillar of the agenda of mobilizing financing for sustainable development in Africa (UNCTAD 2020).

The evidence presented in this volume on the complex network of actors and enablers involved in orchestrating and facilitating capital flight, and in the accumulation of private wealth in offshore secrecy jurisdictions, underscores the point that capital flight is a global phenomenon, a shared responsibility for Africa and the global community. Addressing the problem of capital flight and related issues such as trade misinvoicing, money laundering, tax evasion and theft of public assets by political and economic elites will require national and global efforts with a high level of coordination.

References

Frynas, J.G., and Wood, G. 2001. Oil & war in Angola. *Review of African Political Economy*, 28(90), 587–606.

Hammond, J.L. 2011. The resource curse and oil revenues in Angola and Venezuela. *Science & Society*, 75(3), 348–378.

Klass, B. 2008. From miracle to nightmare: An institutional analysis of development failures in Côte d'Ivoire. *Africa Today*, 55(1), 109–126.

Losch, B. 2002. Global restructuring and liberalization: Côte d'Ivoire and the end of the international cocoa market? *Journal of Agrarian Change*, 2(2), 206–227.

McKinsey Global Institute. 2010. Lions on the move: The progress and potential of African economies. New York: McKinsey & Company, June 1, available at https://www.mckinsey.com/featured-insights/middle-east-and-africa/lions-on-the-move# (accessed on September 29, 2020).

N'Diaye, B. 2005. Not a miracle after all... Côte D'ivoire's downfall: Flawed civil-military relations and missed opportunities. *South African Journal of Military Studies*, 33(1), 89–117.

Ndikumana, L. 2014. Fuite des capitaux et paradis fiscaux: impact sur l'investissement et la croissance en Afrique. *Revue d'Economie du Développement*, 22(2), 113–141.

Ndikumana, L., and Boyce, J.K. 2003. Public debts and private assets: Explaining capital flight from sub-Saharan African countries. *World Development*, 31(1), 107–130.

Ndikumana, L., and Boyce, J.K. 2011. *Africa's Odious Debts: How Foreign Loans and Capital Flight Bled a Continent*. London: Zed Books.

Ndikumana, L., and Boyce, J.K. 2015. Strategies for addressing capital flight. In S.I. Ajayi and L. Ndikumana (Eds.), *Capital Flight from Africa: Causes, Effects and Policy Issues* (pp. 393–417). Oxford: Oxford University Press.

Ndikumana, L., and Boyce, J.K. 2021. Capital Flight From Africa, 1970–2018: New Estimates with Updated Trade Misinvoicing Methodology. Amherst, MA: Political Economy Research Institute, May.

Ndikumana, L., Boyce, J.K., and Ndiaye, A.S. 2015. Capital flight from Africa: Measurement and drivers. In S.I. Ajayi and L. Ndikumana (Eds.), *Capital Flight from Africa: Causes, Effects and Policy Issues* (pp. 15–54). Oxford: Oxford University Press.

Ndikumana, L., and Sarr, M. 2019. Capital flight and foreign direct investment in Africa: An investigation of the role of natural resource endowment. *Resources Policy*, 63(101327) (October).

Nkurunziza, J.D. 2015. Capital flight and poverty reduction in Africa. In I. Ajayi and L. Ndikumana (Eds.), *Capital Flight from Africa: Causes, Effects and Policy Issues* (pp. 81–110). Oxford: Oxford University Press.

Office of the Public Protector South Africa. 2016. State Capture. Report No. 6 of 2016/2017, available at https://www.sahistory.org.za/sites/default/files/2019-05/329756252-state-of-capture-14-october-2016.pdf (accessed on November 14, 2019).

Oxford Business Group. 2020. The Report: Cote d'Ivoire 2020. London: Oxford Business Group, available at https://www.oxfordbusinessgroup.com/c%C3%B4te-divoire-2020 (accessed on September 23, 2020).

Shaxson, N. 2007. Oil, corruption and the resource curse. *International Affairs*, 83(6), 1123–1140.

Sirleaf Johnson, E. 2010. *Introduction*. In S. Radelet (Ed.), *Emerging Africa: How 17 Countries Are Leading the Way* (pp. 1–8). Washington, DC: Brookings Institution Press.

Soares De Oliveira, R. 2007. Business success, Angola-style: Postcolonial politics and the rise and rise of Sonangol. *Journal of Modern African Studies*, 45(4), 595–619.

UNCTAD. 2020. *Tackling Illicit Financial Flows for Sustainable Development in Africa*. Geneva: UNCTAD.

2

Capital Flight from Angola, Côte d'Ivoire, and South Africa

An Overview

Léonce Ndikumana and James K. Boyce

Introduction

This chapter presents an overview of capital flight from Angola, Côte d'Ivoire, and South Africa during the period 1970–2018. It begins with a discussion of the distinction between capital flight and illicit financial flows, two overlapping but different phenomena, although the terms have often been used interchangeably in both technical literature and the media.

The measurement of capital flight follows the methodology used by Ndikumana and Boyce (2010) and Henry (2012), among others, in which capital flight consists of unrecorded capital flows, measured as discrepancies between the inflows and outflows of foreign exchange reported in the country's official balance of payments. Net foreign exchange inflows consist mainly of additions to the stock of external debt and foreign investment. In the absence of capital flight, these capital account inflows would be balanced by the sum of the current account deficit and net additions to foreign exchange reserves. In the presence of capital flight, the discrepancy between recorded inflows and recorded outflows leaves a residual.

Net trade misinvoicing, derived from trading partner data comparisons, is added to this residual to obtain the measure of capital flight. A key innovation in this chapter is that it goes beyond national aggregate measures to examine trade misinvoicing at the bilateral and product levels in order to shed light on possible conduits of capital flight, focusing on major export commodities.

In addition to the flow perspective on capital flight, it is important to recognize that a substantial fraction of the capital that is smuggled abroad is invested offshore in income-generating assets. We therefore present estimates of stocks of private wealth accumulated offshore, drawing on the prior work of James Henry (2012, 2016). The twin processes of unrecorded capital outflows and the accumulation of

Léonce Ndikumana and James K. Boyce, *Capital Flight from Angola, Côte d'Ivoire, and South Africa*. In: *On the Trail of Capital Flight from Africa*. Edited by Léonce Ndikumana and James K. Boyce, Oxford University Press.
© Léonce Ndikumana and James K. Boyce (2022). DOI: 10.1093/oso/9780198852728.003.0002

hidden offshore private wealth are aided and abetted by enabling institutions in the international financial system.

We first present the definitions of the key concepts used in the chapter and describe the methodology and the data used to estimate capital flight.[1] This is followed by the results for Angola, Côte d'Ivoire, and South Africa, respectively. Finally, we discuss the unrecorded offshore wealth resulting from capital flight.

Definitions, Methodology, and Data

Capital flight as a subset of illicit financial flows

Capital flight refers to capital outflows that are illicit by virtue of illegal acquisition, illegal transfer, and/or illegal concealment from tax authorities. It is useful to clarify the relationship between capital flight and "illicit financial flows," concepts that at times have been used interchangeably in recent literature and policy debates.[2] While all capital flight is illicit, not all illicit financial flows are capital flight. Payments for smuggled imports, for example, involve illicit financial flows, but they are not capital flight.

In quantitative studies, capital flight is usually measured as the missing residual in the balance of payments, after making corrections for underreported external borrowing and possibly for trade misinvoicing. Since this measure is based on unrecorded flows, it captures the illegal transfer aspect of capital flight. But it may miss capital flight that is transferred legally but is illicit in other respects. For example, some illicitly acquired funds may be laundered domestically and then sent abroad as recorded transfers.

Mechanisms for *illicit transfer* include the smuggling of bank notes, clandestine wire transfers, and falsification of trade invoices. The motives for these illicit transfers include evasion of judicial scrutiny of the origins of the wealth, evasion of taxes, and fear of extortion or outright expropriation.

In addition to being illicit by virtue of its unrecorded transfer, this measured capital flight is often illicit in other respects. *Illicitly acquired capital* is money obtained through corruption, embezzlement, theft, bribes, extortion, tax evasion, counterfeit, trafficking in illegal goods and services, and other criminal activities. Wealth acquired illicitly is often transferred abroad in an effort to shield it from legal scrutiny and forfeiture risk. *Illicitly held funds* are external assets that are not declared to national authorities of the owner's country. The concealment of foreign assets may be motivated by the desire to evade prosecution for illicit acquisition or transfer of the funds, and to evade taxes on asset earnings.

---

[1] Details can be found in Ndikumana and Boyce (2019).
[2] For further discussion, see Cobham and Jansky (2020), Ndikumana et al. (2015), and Reuter (2012).

Private assets held abroad are a heterogeneous pool that includes legitimate capital associated with normal portfolio allocation, laundered capital that was illegally acquired but legally transferred, smuggled capital that was legally acquired but illegally transferred, and dirty capital that was both illegally acquired and illegally transferred. The measures of capital flight presented in this chapter comprise the latter two categories.

Capital flight and other illicit financial flows share in common the feature that they all involve cross-border movements of money. For the economy of origin, these flows result in net losses of foreign exchange, tax revenue, and capital. At the same time, the corresponding inflows confer costs as well as benefits upon the foreign economies that receive them, as the attendant gains in foreign exchange, tax revenue, and capital are accompanied by adverse effects, including corrosion of the integrity of private and public institutions.

A central theme of this book is that capital flight is enabled by factors and actors both in the countries of origin and in the destination countries. The illicit export of capital from Africa is a manifestation of failures in the international financial system that facilitates and enables it. Former German President Horst Köhler (2015, p. 6) put the matter clearly:

There is an African proverb: "Beware of the naked man who offers you clothes." And my goodness, we Europeans are naked, with our double standards and our comfortable hypocrisy vis-à-vis our past and present contribution to Africa's problems. It is high time we regained our credibility.

We cannot ignore the global kleptocratic model of capitalism that is sucking obscene amounts of capital out of Africa in particular—and certainly more than is being invested in the continent as development assistance. Chief among the beneficiaries of this flight of capital are the European banks where African despots and tax-evading corporations stash their billions. If we finally brought order to the international financial system and allowed the tax havens to wither away, that would be credible!

Because capital flight from Africa is a transnational phenomenon involving shared costs and responsibilities for Africans and the global community, any analysis of its drivers and strategies to prevent it must address both sides of the flows.

Capital flight as a balance of payments residual

Measuring capital flight is a challenging exercise because it is by nature a hidden activity that can be measured only indirectly. Complicating matters further, the underlying data that can be used in such a forensic exercise are themselves imperfect and fraught with imprecision. The original approach to measuring capital flight considered it as consisting of discrepancies between recorded inflows and uses of foreign exchange as reported in the country's balance of payments. This became known as the residual method.

In the wake of the debt crisis of the early 1980s, World Bank economists uncovered that inflows of external borrowing had been substantially underreported in the official balance of payments accounts of many developing countries, as a result of which their accumulated stock of external debt turned out to be much larger than previously assumed. The World Bank's World Debt Tables (WDT), which were reconstructed to track debt flows better than the balance of payments (BoP), were therefore used as an alternative source of data on external borrowing in the computation of capital flight.[3] The WDT were later renamed the Global Finance Development (GDF) database, and subsequently International Debt Statistics (IDS).

To obtain a more accurate measure of resource inflows through external borrowing, three important adjustments have been made to the published debt series. First, given that countries borrow in different currencies and that the stock of debt is reported at the end of the year in a common currency (the US dollar), variations in the exchange rates of the currencies of original denomination of the debt vis-à-vis the dollar may create biases in the debt inflows obtained as simple year-on-year changes in debt stock. The debt stock is therefore adjusted by taking into account the currency composition of long-term debt.[4]

Second, following Henry (2012), an adjustment is made to correct the bias caused by the fact that interest arrears are added to the debt stock in the IDS database even though they do not correspond to inflows of foreign exchange. To obtain an accurate measure of annual debt inflows, net changes in interest arrears are subtracted from the change in debt stock.

Third, the series are adjusted for debt forgiveness and write-offs. Otherwise, the resulting changes in end-of-year debt stocks would give the false impression of a debt repayment and apparent outflow of foreign exchange.

For each country, the annual measure of capital flight by the residual method is computed as follows:

$$KF = CDEBTADJ + FDI + PI + OI - (CAD + CRES) \qquad (1)$$

where CDEBTADJ is the change in the external debt stock, adjusted for exchange rate fluctuations, change in interest arrears, and debt forgiveness; FDI is foreign direct investment; PI is foreign portfolio investment; OI is other foreign investments; CAD is the current account deficit; and CRES is net additions to foreign exchange

[3] For discussion, see World Bank (1985), Erbe (1986), and Lessard and Williamson (1987).
[4] Details of the adjustment algorithm are provided in Ndikumana and Boyce (2010).

reserves. Data on debt are obtained from the World Bank's International Debt Statistics Database.[5] Data for the other variables are taken from the balance of payments.[6]

Adjustment for trade misinvoicing

The BoP data on trade transactions may be subject to erroneous or deliberate misinvoicing of the value of imports and exports. In addition to smuggling, mis-invoicing is a channel of capital flight and money laundering.[7] Attention to trade misinvoicing dates from the 1960s with the pioneering work of Jagdish Bhagwati (Bhagwati 1964, 1967; Bhagwati and Hansen 1973; Bhagwati et al. 1974), and was revived in the 1980s in the context of the research on capital flight motivated by the debt crisis faced by developing countries (Gulati 1987).

In addition to serving as a mechanism for capital flight through the under-invoicing of exports (allowing foreign exchange receipts to be sequestered abroad) and the over-invoicing of imports (allowing foreign exchange outflows in excess of the true cost of imports), misinvoicing can also take the form of import smuggling for tariff evasion. In "technical" smuggling, a false invoice is submitted that under-states the true value of the imported goods and services. In "pure" smuggling, the import is wholly concealed and no invoice is submitted. Of course, imports must be paid for (in foreign exchange) regardless of whether or not accurate invoices are submitted to the authorities. These payments are one type of illicit financial out-flows, but since goods and services are received in return, they are not a transfer of assets and hence not capital flight.

The accuracy of the residual measure of capital flight can be improved by ad-justments for the impacts of trade misinvoicing. The net effect on the magnitude of capital flight can go in either direction. If misinvoicing for purposes of capital flight exceeds smuggling, the adjustment adds to the total; conversely, if smuggling exceeds misinvoicing for purposes of capital flight, the adjustment subtracts from the total since part of the missing money in the balance of payments was used to finance the unrecorded imports.

---

[5] The International Debt Statistics (IDS) database is available at https://databank.worldbank.org/source/international-debt-statistics. For South Africa, the IDS series starts in 1994; hence data for 1970–1993 were obtained from the African Development Indicators (now discontinued), the South African Reserve Bank, and the African Development Bank.

[6] Data on foreign direct investment may also be obtained from the UNCTAD statisti-cal database (UNCTAD Data Center, Investment: http://unctadstat.unctad.org/wds/ReportFolders/reportFolders.aspx).

[7] Estimates of the share of trade misinvoicing in illicit financial flows and capital flight vary across studies due to differences in methodology, data and sample. Spanjers and Salomon (2017) estimate that trade misinvoicing represents up to 87% of total illicit financial flows from developing countries from 2005 to 2014. See, for example, Ndikumana et al. (2015), Kar and Spanjers (2014), and UNCTAD (2016).

Measuring trade misinvoicing

The measurement of trade misinvoicing is based on data from the Direction of Trade Statistics (DOTS) database compiled by the IMF, which reports aggregate imports and exports by partner.[8] Misinvoicing for specific products can be measured using the Comtrade database compiled by the United Nations Statistics Division. Trade misinvoicing can be estimated at three levels: for all trading partners taken together, for trade with individual partners, and for specific products.

Misinvoicing estimates are based on the simple principle that the value of exports reported by country A to country B should match the value of imports reported by country B from country A, after accounting for the cost of insurance and freight (cif).[9] When the data from trading partners can be considered more reliable than the mirror data reported by African authorities, comparisons between the two can be used to estimate the direction and magnitude of net misinvoicing.

In the case of exports, we expect such comparisons to show systematic under-invoicing, motivated by the desire to evade taxes, retain some of the export proceeds abroad (often in violation of controls on foreign exchange outflows), and avoid having to convert them into local currency at the official exchange rate (often less favorable than the market rate). Apart from special circumstances (such as export incentive programs), there is little motive for over-invoicing of exports. In the case of imports, however, the net impact of misinvoicing can go either way: if under-invoicing for smuggling exceeds over-invoicing for capital flight, the value of exports reported by the trading partner will exceed the value of imports reported by the African country (after adding the cost of insurance and freight), whereas if import over-invoicing dominates (as a way to obtain foreign exchange from the central bank and shift it abroad), the discrepancy has the opposite sign. The net trade misinvoicing adjustment in capital flight estimates is obtained as the sum of export misinvoicing and import misinvoicing.[10]

Motivations for trade misinvoicing

Trade misinvoicing thus occurs for a number of reasons, including financial motives, circumvention of foreign exchange controls, and reduction of administrative burdens.[11]

---

[8] The Direction of Trade Statistics database is available at http://www.imf.org/en/data.
[9] This principle was first proposed more than a century ago by Ferraris (1885).
[10] For details, see Ndikumana and Boyce (2019).
[11] See Buehn and Eichler (2011); Buehn and Farzanegan (2012); Patnaik et al. (2012); Storti and de Grauwe (2012); and Kellenberg and Levinson (2016). See also UNCTAD (2016) for further discussion with a focus on primary commodities exports from resource-rich developing countries.

Financial motives: Exporters and importers may engage in misinvoicing to minimize tax liabilities and take advantage of tax incentives. Import under-invoicing enables importers to reduce tariffs, and pure smuggling allows them to avoid them altogether. In addition to the under-reporting of the value of imports, misinvoicing may occur through the misreporting of product types by declaring low-tariff products in lieu of the actual products that face higher import tariff rates.[12]

Similarly, export under-invoicing may result from attempts to avoid export taxes levied on specific products (McDonald 1985). In the presence of tax incentives aimed at promoting exports, exporters may instead resort to over-invoicing, inflating the value of their exports to reap more incentive payments. But when the exporter must surrender the inflated amount of foreign exchange to the central bank, export over-invoicing will occur only if the firm expects the gains from extra subsidies to exceed the costs of the premium on foreign exchange on the black market (Bhagwati 1967, p. 67).

Circumventing exchange controls: Another motive for misinvoicing is to bypass currency controls to get access to foreign exchange and move money abroad. In the presence of strict controls, misinvoicing provides a means to acquire foreign exchange that can be held abroad or traded for a profit on the black market. Such an environment can be expected to encourage over-invoicing of imports (so that importers obtain extra foreign exchange from the central bank above and beyond what is required to pay for the imports), and under-invoicing of exports (so that exporters do not have to surrender all of their foreign exchange earnings to the central bank at the official exchange rate). Empirical studies have found a positive correlation between the black-market premium and the extent of import over-invoicing (see, for example, Bahmani-Oskooee and Goswami 2003; Barnett 2003; and Biswas and Marjit 2005).

Reducing administrative burdens: Perceived or actual onerous administrative procedures can incite firms to underreport the true value of trade. Bureaucratic and regulatory inefficiencies can create costs to importers and exporters and delay the authorization of relevant transactions. Firms may seek to circumvent these hurdles to speed up the inward and outward shipment of merchandise. Such hurdles are most likely to be prevalent in countries with high levels of corruption in the customs service as well as those with low human and technological capacity to process imports and exports. Such an environment is expected to induce more smuggling, a prediction that has been supported by empirical evidence (Fisman and Wei 2007; Berger and Nitsch 2012).

---

[12] Bhagwati (1964) noted that import under-invoicing appeared to be prevalent in the case of products facing high tariffs, and subsequent studies have lent support to this proposition (Buehn and Eichler 2011; Epaphra 2015; Fisman and Wei 2004).

Methodological and data issues

The estimation of trade misinvoicing faces a number of issues related to methodology and data. The first and most general problem is the availability and quality of mirror trade data. Some countries do not report trade data to the IMF, in which case the IMF may impute the numbers reported in DOTS from partner data. In such cases, comparisons of mirror trade data cannot detect misinvoicing. This is the case for Angola; for this reason the estimates of Angolan capital flight presented in this chapter do not include adjustments for trade misinvoicing. In the case of South Africa, the series in the electronic DOTS database starts only in 1998, so the estimates of South African capital flight for 1970–1997 reported here do not include misinvoicing adjustments for those earlier years.[13]

A second issue is the lack of transaction-specific information on the cost of insurance and freight. For any given country, such costs may vary by trading partner, by product, and over time. In the absence of more detailed information, the conventional practice in the literature is to use as a proxy the average cif/fob ratio reported by the IMF. Until 2018, this ratio was 1.1; that is, the costs of freight and insurance were assumed to add 10% to the freight-on-board value of the shipment. In 2018, the IMF DOTS changed this proxy, on the basis of an OECD study that estimated a trade-weighted average of International Transportation and Insurance Cost (ITIC) of merchandise.[14] Since then, the IMF has used 10% for the adjustment through 1999 and 6% from 2000 onward. Accordingly, we use the same ratios to estimate aggregate trade misinvoicing: 10% from 1970 to 1999 and 6% thereafter. For misinvoicing estimates at the partner and product levels, however, we make use of more specific cif/fob ratios reported in the ITIC database.[15]

Angola

Angola experienced substantial capital flight over the period from 1986 to 2018, as shown in Table 2.1. In this period the country experienced cumulative unrecorded net outflows amounting to $103 billion. The estimates for Angola begin only in 1986, due to the lack of earlier data on relevant indicators. Moreover, unlike the other two countries examined here, inadequate data prevents an analysis

---

[13] We do not use the earlier printed DOTS data for this purpose due inconstistencies with the subsequent electronic version.

[14] See IMF (2018) and Marini et al. (2018).

[15] For each product the ratio used is the average estimate over the 2012–2016 period covered by the OECD database. Data and methodological issues are further discussed in Ndikumana and Boyce (2019), Cobham and Jansky (2020), and UNCTAD (2020).

Table 2.1 Capital flight from Angola (billion, constant 2018 dollars)

	1986–89	1990–99	2000–09	2010–18	1970–2018
CDEBTADJ	9.1	10.0	12.4	39.0	70.5
FDI	1.3	8.6	10.1	−23.8	−3.9
PI	0.0	0.0	−8.4	3.0	−5.4
OI	3.3	−1.1	−12.4	16.2	6.0
CA	−0.8	−6.2	30.7	36.1	59.7
CRES	0.0	−0.7	−15.6	−7.4	−23.8
Capital flight	**12.8**	**10.5**	**16.8**	**63.1**	**103.1**
Memorandum: total private capital flows					
(FDI+PI+OI)	4.6	7.5	−10.7	−4.7	−3.4

Source: Authors' computations (for variable key and method, see text).

of trade misinvoicing. (The Angola export and import data reported in the DOTS are based on partner data, so cannot be used to calculate misinvoicing.) As a result, the analysis for Angola omits a potentially important channel of capital flight.[16]

Capital flight from Angola was especially pronounced after the turn of the century, a period that includes the country's "golden decade" of peace and high oil prices as well as the final years of the long-lived dos Santos regime, as described by Nicholas Shaxson in this book.

Several other notable features emerge from an examination of the balance of payments for Angola. The first is massive accumulation of current account surpluses, mainly driven by oil exports. The second is a reversal in capital flows since the past decade: from 2010 to 2018, net foreign direct investment outflows totaled a staggering $23.8 billion. In contrast, the period from 1986 to 2009 saw cumulative net inflows of FDI of $20 billion. In addition, portfolio investment generated net outflows amounting to $8.4 billion over 2000–2009, and other investment recorded a net outflow in the 1990s and 2000s of $13.5 billion, although this was offset by net inflows of $16.2 billion in 2010–2018.

This raises the question of what lies behind these massive recorded net outflows of private capital. In the case of FDI, outflows could arise from foreign firms' repatriation of profits to their home countries. The outflows may reflect investments abroad by Angolan residents as well. In the case of portfolio investment, the net outflows may be driven by speculation by private investors in search of higher risk-adjusted returns. They could also reflect portfolio adjustments by firms with substantial cash balances that they decide to invest or hold abroad. Insofar as the

---

[16] In the case of exports, the Angolan economy is heavily dependent on petroleum and related products, and its top five trading partners account for roughly 80% of the total. Using the limited data on petroleum that is reported in Comtrade for the period 2009–2018, mirror partner data comparison shows minimal discrepancies (see Ndikumana and Boyce 2019).

Table 2.2 Capital flight from Côte d'Ivoire (billion, constant 2018 dollars)

	1970–79	1980–89	1990–99	2000–09	2010–18	1970–2018
CDEBTADJ	14.0	22.2	7.9	0.5	7.5	52.0
FDI	1.6	1.1	3.5	3.9	3.8	13.8
PI	−0.1	0.0	−0.1	0.2	6.6	6.6
OI	8.8	18.7	6.7	−5.5	−17.9	10.7
CA	−11.7	−18.9	−8.8	4.2	−0.8	−36.1
CRES	0.1	0.4	−1.3	−2.3	−3.4	−6.5
BoP Residual	**12.6**	**23.3**	**7.8**	**0.9**	**−4.1**	**40.5**
Trade misinvoicing	7.6	2.5	4.0	0.9	0.0	14.9
Adjusted capital flight	**20.2**	**25.8**	**11.8**	**1.8**	**−4.2**	**55.4**
Memorandum: total private capital flows						
FDI+PI+OI	10.3	19.7	10.1	−1.5	−7.5	31.1

Source: Authors' computations (for method, see text).

recorded outflows were of Angolan capital, rather than foreign capital, the data raise the possibility that they include funds that were illicitly acquired or concealed abroad despite having been transferred through officially recorded channels. This would imply that the measured capital flight reported here understates the true magnitude.

Côte d'Ivoire

Estimates of capital flight from Côte d'Ivoire are summarized in Table 2.2. Over the 1970–2018 period, the residual method from the balance of payments yields a total of $40.5 billion. Overall the country experienced export under-invoicing to the tune of $5.9 billion and net import over-invoicing of $9 billion; adjustment for trade misinvoicing therefore adds $14.9 billion, bringing total capital flight to $55.4 billion.

The pattern changed over time. In the 1970s and 1980s, the country saw substantial capital flight. The outflow diminished in the 1990s, and a phase of reversals began in 1998, leading to net unrecorded capital inflows after the turn of the century (although net outflows resumed in 2015). The reversal period, which included years of civil war, also saw a decline in net external borrowing and net outflows of private capital that were officially recorded in the balance of payments under the heading "other investments."

An analysis of trade misinvoicing in the case of cocoa, Côte d'Ivoire's top export, sheds further light on one mechanism for capital flight. Using partner-specific

Table 2.3 Cocoa export misinvoicing in Côte d'Ivoire, 2000–2018 (million, constant 2018 dollars)

Partner	Ivorian exports	Partner imports	cif factor	Export misinvoicing
Belgium	4463.4	4734.7	1.064	−13.5
Estonia	2292.1	1187.3	1.064	−1252.2
France	5413.3	7798.4	1.062	2051.7
Germany	4522.8	9102.8	1.023	4475.1
Italy	2035.2	2460.8	1.045	334.5
Netherlands	19607.0	17662.0	1.064	−3195.9
Spain	2048.5	2109.3	1.063	−67.8
UK	2252.7	2443.6	1.020	146.3
USA*	12611.7	14156.9	*	1545.2
Total	**55246.7**	**61656.0**		**4023.4**

* USA imports reported at fob value.
Note: Export misinvoicing = (partner imports) − (cif x Ivorian exports). Only years where both parties report data are considered.
Source: Authors' computations using data from Comtrade (SITC 072).

mirror data from Comtrade, available starting in the year 2000, we examine the discrepancy between recorded Ivorian exports and imports recorded by the major trading partners in developed countries, whose trade data are usually assumed to be more reliable. We calculate export misinvoicing as the difference between the two after adjusting for the cost of insurance and freight, which Comtrade reports at the product and partner level.

Overall we find a pattern of export under-invoicing: for the nine leading trading partners as a group, this amounted to $4 billion in the 2000–2018 period as a whole (see Table 2.3). This is equivalent to about 7.3% of the declared value of exports to the same destinations. As we have noted, under-invoicing allows exporters to conceal part of their foreign exchange earnings abroad, rather than reporting the full amount and converting them into local currency at the central bank.

The Netherlands stands out as a notable exception to this pattern. Its reported value of cocoa imports is substantially below the corresponding value of exports reported by Côte d'Ivoire, an unusual case of apparent export over-invoicing. The same anomaly can be seen in cocoa exports to Estonia. This is likely to reflect the role of both countries as trading hubs: companies registered there buy Ivorian cocoa and then on-sell it to other destinations that record it as imported from Côte d'Ivoire. (Transshipments by Dutch firms may also help to explain the unusually high degree of apparent under-invoicing in Germany.) A transparent trading regime based on internationally agreed reporting standards would accurately track and report the origins and destinations of cargoes. Côte d'Ivoire would record the final destinations of its cocoa, and the destinations would record the goods as

Table 2.4 Capital flight from South Africa (billion, constant 2018 dollars)

	1970–79	1980–89	1990–99	2000–09	2010–18	1970–2018
CDEBTADJ	3.9	22.5	10.6	68.2	110.5	**215.7**
FDI	2.5	−4.7	−6.9	44.2	0.4	**35.6**
PI	0.0	−3.6	45.2	33.6	109.4	**184.6**
OI	1.0	−10.5	−10.7	23.8	41.3	**44.9**
CA	−24.5	11.0	−1.0	−81.4	−127.8	**−223.7**
CRES	6.1	−6.2	−9.3	−34.1	−17.6	**−61.1**
BoP Residual	**−11.1**	**8.6**	**27.8**	**54.4**	**116.2**	**196.0**
Trade misinvoicing	*	*	4.9	97.7	30.9	**133.5**
Adjusted capital flight	**−11.1**	**8.6**	**32.7**	**152.1**	**147.2**	**329.5**
Memorandum: total private capital flows						
FDI+PI+OI	3.5	−18.7	27.5	101.7	151.1	**265.1**

* Trade misinvoicing not available for 1970–89.
Source: Authors' computations (for method, see text).

originating in Côte d'Ivoire; third parties like the Netherlands would simply record the goods as being in transit. Jean Merckaert delves into this further in Chapter 3.

South Africa

The magnitude of capital flight from South Africa over the years 1970–2018 is summarized in Table 2.4. Over the 1970–2018 period as a whole, South Africa witnessed an estimated $329.5 billion of capital flight. This includes net trade misinvoicing of $133.5 billion in the years 1998–2018, for which mirror data are available for South Africa in the electronic DOTS database. Given the observed pattern of misinvoicing in these later years, it is likely that our estimates understate the magnitude of capital flight presented for the 1970–2018 period as a whole.

Along with capital flight, the table presents the main elements that enter into the computation of the BoP residual. There are two notable trends in capital inflows over the past two decades. The first is a rapid accumulation of external debt since the turn of the century, reflecting a surge in external borrowing after the end of the apartheid with the resumption of international economic and political cooperation. Second, the country experienced a substantial increase in private capital inflows, especially in portfolio investment, reflecting the development of active equity markets that attracted foreign investors. Capital flight rose substantially, with recorded inflows outpacing recorded uses (outflows) of foreign exchange.

Trade misinvoicing appears to have been an important channel of capital flight from South Africa. Over the period 1998–2018, export under-invoicing totaled

Table 2.5 Non-monetary gold export misinvoicing in South Africa, 2000–2018 (billion, constant 2018 dollars)

Partner	South Africa's exports	Partner imports	cif factor	Export misinvoicing
Hong Kong	2.7	30.3	1.002	27.6
India	0.2	8.4	1.035	8.2
Italy	0.0	9.1	1.021	9.0
Switzerland	0.4	7.2	1.025	6.8
Turkey	0.0	2.8	1.028	2.7
UAE	0.1	2.5	1.023	2.4
UK	0.3	32.5	1.009	32.2
Total	**3.7**	**92.8**		**89.0**

Note: Export misinvoicing = (partner imports) − (cif x South African exports). Only years where both parties report data are considered.
Source: Authors' computations using data from Comtrade.

$185.2 billion, with large shortfalls between South Africa's reported exports and the much higher value of imports reported by its trading partners. Net under-invoicing of imports amounted to $51.7 billion, indicating that smuggling for the purpose of tariff evasion exceeded over-invoicing for the purpose of capital flight. Smuggled imports must still be paid for in foreign exchange, so in our measure of capital flight this reduces the net misinvoicing adjustment to $133.5 billion in the period as a whole.

A substantial fraction of the exports recorded by South Africa was listed as going to "non-specified areas." In principle, the earnings from these exports would be reported in the balance of payments accounts despite the lack of information regarding their destination. In calculating the misinvoicing adjustment we take this into account.[17]

An analysis of misinvoicing in the cases of gold and platinum, two of South Africa's leading exports, sheds further light on the phenomenon. Again using partner-specific data from Comtrade at the commodity level (available from the year 2000), we can examine discrepancies between South Africa's recorded exports and the mirror data on imports reported by major trading partners.

The results for non-monetary gold are presented in Table 2.5.[18] The data reveal what appears to be massive under-invoicing: recorded exports to the United

[17] We apportion reported exports to non-specified destinations between developed and developing countries based on their respective shares in the imports reported by trading partners. For details, see Ndikumana and Boyce (2019).

[18] Gold exports are officially classified into two categories: monetary gold (gold held as reserve assets by central banks) and non-monetary gold. According to data from South Africa's Department of Trade and Industry, monetary gold accounted for over 95% of the country's total gold exports up to 2010 after which the two series were merged. The results presented in here refer to non-monetary gold exports only as Comtrade database does not report monetary gold exports.

Table 2.6 Platinum export misinvoicing in South Africa, 2001–2018 (billion, constant 2018 dollars)

Partner	South Africa's exports	Partner imports	cif factor	Export misinvoicing
China	2.6	24.2	1.026	21.5
Hong Kong	6.6	4.6	1.002	−2.0
Germany	11.6	14.0	1.015	2.2
Japan	45.1	50.7	1.032	4.2
Switzerland	17.9	11.6	1.024	−6.7
UK	19.6	14.2	1.009	−5.6
USA	31.1	38.5	*	7.4
Total	**134.5**	**157.9**		**21.1**

* USA imports reported at fob value.
Note: Export misinvoicing = (partner imports) – (cif x South African exports). Only years where both parties report data are considered.
Source: Authors' computations using data from Comtrade (data are not available for the year 2002).

Kingdom, for example, were only $270 million, while imports recorded by the UK for the corresponding years amounted to more than $32.5 billion. A similar discrepancy can be seen for Hong Kong. For the seven countries in the table, total export under-invoicing amounted to $89 billion.

To some extent, these discrepancies may reflect a failure to record destinations rather than failure to record the exports themselves. In the case of non-monetary gold, in particular, the bulk of exports recorded by South Africa are listed as going to "non-specified areas."[19] Moreover, in some years South African trade data do not record any exports to some countries that recorded imports. China, for example, reported $38 billion in non-monetary gold imports from South Africa over the period, while South Africa recorded no exports there. The results shown in Table 2.5 omit years in which South Africa reported no exports to the partner country.

Estimates for platinum are reported in Table 2.6. Again there is evidence of considerable export under-invoicing, totaling $21 billion for the seven trading partners shown. The apparent over-invoicing in exports to Switzerland are likely to reflect the country's role as a trading hub; similarly, the data for Hong Kong could reflect re-exports to China.

---

[19] A further problem is inconsistencies in the distinction between monetary gold and non-monetary gold before the two were merged in 2011. Prior to that year, according to the South African Reserve Bank, "non-monetary gold was incorrectly classified as monetary gold by the entity responsible for provision of trade statistics to the United Nations." However, the Comtrade data shows that substantial discrepancies between South Africa's data and that of its partners persisted in the post-2011 period. For more on South Africa's gold export data, see Ndikumana and Boyce (2019).

From Unrecorded Outflows to Unrecorded Offshore Wealth

Thus far, we have focused on measuring unrecorded capital outflows. The evidence demonstrated that all the three countries experienced high volumes of capital flight over the past four decades as a whole. The fact that these outflows generally persisted over time suggests that they are driven by fundamental structural and institutional factors in the source countries and the global financial system.

These unrecorded outflows cannot be explained simply as a result of portfolio management decisions by savers seeking to maximize returns to investment. It is not clear that interest rates in destination countries are higher than in African countries. Instead most capital flight appears to be driven by medium- and long-term considerations. In other words, it is flight with intention to stay. As James Henry (2012, p. 23) puts it, "since net outflows from developing countries have continued over sustained periods of time, and since little offshore wealth or the earnings that it produces have been repatriated, the most important factors driving it are not those that drive 'hot money,' but long-term de-capitalization."

In addition to measuring the flows of capital flight, therefore, it is important to assess the corresponding accumulation of private wealth held abroad. The story of capital flight does not end with illicit crossing of national borders.

The concealment of private wealth accumulated through unrecorded capital outflows is facilitated by services offered by offshore financial centers. The term offshore here refers "not so much to the actual physical location of private assets or liabilities, but to nominal, hyper-portable, multi-jurisdictional, often quite temporary locations of networks of legal and quasi-legal entities and arrangements that manage and control private wealth—always in the interests of those who manage it, supposedly in the interests of its beneficial owners, and often in indifference or outright defiance of the interests and laws of multiple nation states" (Henry 2012, p. 9).

African private wealth held offshore has a number of deleterious effects on the source countries and their people.[20] Here we highlight some of the most important.

First, the accumulation of unrecorded private wealth in offshore financial centers erodes the country's tax base. In addition to initial losses in income tax when private savings are concealed and exported abroad, subsequent losses are incurred due to untaxed income from the hidden wealth. This is especially problematic for African countries, which generally have very low tax revenue/GDP ratios and face large and growing financial gaps. Globally, it has been estimated that the lost revenue from unrecorded earnings on wealth stashed offshore is more than twice the total development aid from OECD countries (Henry 2012). This substantially changes the debate on financing for development. Rather than focusing exclusively

---

[20] Destination countries, too, experience deleterious impacts; for discussion, see Shaxson (2011, 2018).

on increasing foreign aid, as is typical in international discourse, the focus should be on helping African countries reduce the tax losses due to base erosion resulting from unrecorded offshore wealth.

Second, the accumulation of unrecorded offshore wealth dramatically changes the picture of wealth inequality both within African countries and between Africa and the rest of the world. Because unrecorded offshore wealth generally belongs to political and economic elites, measures of national wealth inequality based on recorded assets are systematically biased downward.[21] At the same time, the wealth gap between African countries and the rich countries where this wealth is domiciled is likely to be lower than official statistics suggest. In short, African countries may be wealthier than we think, but their wealth is grossly unequally distributed.

Third, the accumulation of offshore wealth by African elites depresses public service delivery, further increasing inequality. The lost tax revenue contributes to suboptimal provision of public health, education and infrastructure, services on which the poor depend most heavily. The poor in Africa cannot 'vote with their feet' to protest poor public service delivery; unlike the rich, they cannot afford education and health care for their families abroad. Meanwhile, as the elites do not suffer as much from poor public service delivery, they have little incentive to improve it.

Finally, the accumulation of offshore wealth undermines institutions of accountability and the regulatory system. The elites who hold offshore wealth do not have incentives for developing the type of institutions that would be needed to stem capital flight, induce wealth repatriation and combat tax evasion; quite the contrary. They are unlikely to promote capital controls, anti-money laundering measures, customs reforms, policies to curb trade misinvoicing and the abuse of transfer pricing rules, and so on. Ultimately, capital flight and offshore wealth accumulation persist because of the incentive structures that make them possible in the first place.

Measurement of hidden offshore wealth

There are several ways to measure private offshore wealth. In 2020 the Global Forum on Transparency and Exchange of Information for Tax Purposes, a recent multilateral initiative based at the OECD, reported that for the year 2019 tax authorities in nearly 100 participating countries had obtained data on 84 million offshore accounts with assets totaling 10 trillion Euros, or about $11.5 trillion (OECD 2020). No breakdown is provided for the portion that is held by Africans. This remarkable number, while impressive, understates total offshore

---

[21] For discussion and examples, see Alstadsæter et al. (2018).

wealth in that not all countries and jurisdictions participate in the information ex-change program, and financial institutions sometimes cannot identify the country of residency of account holders.

One alternative approach to estimating offshore wealth uses cumulative histori-cal capital flight flows, like those reported in this chapter, based on the assumption that some fraction of these flows is saved. A second approach measures "miss-ing wealth" as the discrepancy between recorded liabilities and assets as these are reported in international financial statistics.

Wealth accumulation from capital flight

The first approach was used by James Henry in a study prepared for the Tax Justice Network (Henry 2012, updated in Henry 2016).[22] The premise is that substan-tial amounts of unrecorded capital flight are held offshore for long-term purposes, leading to the accumulation of offshore wealth that earns returns that often are not taxed. Because this wealth is unrecorded, it is difficult to know its precise amount and asset composition, including how much is held in liquid assets as opposed to real estate, art objects, and other valuables. And some capital flight is not saved but instead used for consumption, including the extravagant lifestyles frequently profiled in investigative reports on prominent economic and political figures.[23]

Henry (2012) proposed some working assumptions to address these issues based on information from banks and interviews with informed observers. The first assumption is that 50–75% of capital flight is invested offshore in income-generating vehicles and physical assets. The second is that the earnings on these offshore investments are not taxed. The third is that offshore wealth earns a mod-est interest rate proxied by the rate on six-month CDs. On this basis, he capitalizes past capital flight to arrive at an estimate of unrecorded private offshore wealth. For Sub-Saharan Africa, the unrecorded stock of private wealth accumulated off-shore stood at more than $700 billion in 2014. Table 2.7 presents estimates for our three case study countries, along with regional totals for Sub-Saharan Africa, East Asia, and Latin America.

These estimates imply that, contrary to commonly held beliefs, African coun-tries are not heavily indebted vis-à-vis the rest of the world; rather they are net creditors in the sense that the stock of private wealth stashed abroad exceeds their external debts.[24] The problem is that this offshore wealth contributes little or nothing to Africa's development.

---

[22] The results are available at "Global Haven Industry": http://globalhavenindustry.com/.
[23] For examples, see Ndikumana and Boyce (2012), Boyce and Ndikumana (2012a) and Boyce and Ndikumana (2012b).
[24] For discussion, see also Boyce and Ndikumana (2001).

Table 2.7 Estimates of offshore wealth as stock of capital flight (billion dollars)

Country or Region	Stock accumulated over 1970–2014
Angola	70.4
Côte d'Ivoire	14.0
South Africa	113.5
Top 5 SSA	639.6
SSA	709.8
East Asia (excl. China)	2524.0
Latin America and Caribbean	1969.8

Note: Based on flows of capital flight constructed by Henry (2016) without adjustments for trade misinvoicing.
Source: Estimates are obtained from the Global Haven Industry database (http://globalhavenindustry.com/).

Missing external assets

An alternative approach to measuring offshore wealth starts with anomalies that can be found in the IMF data on international investment positions (IIP), which report external liabilities and external assets—stocks of capital rather than the flows reported in the BoP. Implausibly, these data purport to show that the world as a whole is a "net debtor" (Lane and Milesi-Ferretti 2007). "There is a 'hole'," observes Gabriel Zucman (2015, p. 37), who takes this discrepancy as a measure of hidden wealth: "If we look at the world balance sheet, more financial assets are recorded as liabilities than as assets, as if planet Earth were in part held by Mars." In 2013, the hole amounted to $7.6 trillion (Zucman 2014).

Because the IIP data only refer to financial wealth, other types of hidden wealth are missing from this number. As Zucman (2015, pp. 44–45) explains:

> My method says nothing about the amount of non-financial wealth in tax havens. This includes yachts registered in the Cayman Islands, as well as works of art, jewelry, and gold stashed in freeports—warehouses that serve as repositories for valuables. Geneva, Luxembourg, and Singapore all have one: in these places, great paintings can be kept and traded tax-free—no customs duty or value-added tax is owed—and anonymously, without ever seeing the light of day. High-net-worth individuals also own real estate in foreign countries: islands in the Seychelles, chalets in Gstaad, and so on. Registry data show that a large chunk of London's luxury real estate is held through shell companies, largely domiciled in the British Virgin Islands, a scheme that enables owners to remain anonymous and to exploit tax loopholes. Unfortunately, there is no way yet to estimate the value of such real assets held abroad.

Zucman nonetheless reckons that his method captures the bulk of hidden wealth:

> At the top of the wealth distribution—that is, for fortunes of dozens of millions of dollars and more—on average most of the wealth takes the form of financial securities. It is rare than someone invests all of his wealth in a yacht. It is one of the great rules of capitalism that the higher one rises on the ladder of wealth, the greater the share of financial securities in one's portfolio.

He estimates that hidden wealth amounts to about 8% of total personal financial wealth worldwide, and concludes that this is on the right order of magnitude, although "one might imagine that the true figure, all wealth combined, is 10% or 11%." This would suggest that hidden non-financial assets amounted to another $2–3 trillion, bringing total hidden assets to around $10 trillion.

There are reasons to suspect, however, that this figure errs on the low side. High-net-worth individuals who conceal their wealth behind veils of anonymity may not follow the unwritten rules of capitalism with regard to portfolio allocation any more than they obey its written rules (see Box 2.1).

Box 2.1 Hidden Real Estate

Evidence from the world's "supercities"—global centers like New York, London, Paris, Hong Kong and Singapore—suggest that anonymous real estate holdings account for a substantial amount of hidden wealth.

The Financial Action Task Force, an intergovernmental body that combats money laundering, reported in 2013 that "real estate accounted for up to 30% of criminal assets confiscated in the last two years, demonstrating this as a clear area of vulnerability" (FATF 2013, p. 24).

The *Financial Times,* announcing that "London has become a center for dirty money," reported in 2014 that at least £122 billion (about $200 billion) worth of property in England and Wales is held by shell companies registered in offshore tax havens, most of them in the British Virgin Islands and Channel Islands (O'Murchu 2014).

In the United States, Title III of the Patriot Act, signed into law soon after the September 11, 2001 attack, required banks to report suspicious money transfers from abroad, but it contained an exemption for real estate purchases. This "gaping loophole—and extraordinary growth opportunity for high-end real estate," meant that "foreigners could still buy penthouse apartments or mansions anonymously and with ease, by hiding behind shell companies set up in states such as Delaware and Nevada" (Foer 2019).

Shell companies accounted for 54% of luxury real estate purchases in Manhattan in 2014, 51% in Los Angeles, and 48% in San Francisco in 2014 (*New York Times* 2015). The total value of residential property in Manhattan is estimated at $733 billion (Metrocosm 2015), and luxury properties (those sold for $4 million and up) accounted for about 37% of residential sales in 2014 (CityRealty 2017). Together these figures suggest that the value of hidden wealth invested in residential properties in Manhattan alone exceeds $100 billion.[1]

U.S. government investigations "continue to show corrupt politicians, drug traffickers, and other criminals using shell companies to purchase luxury real estate with cash," Jennifer Shasky Calvery, director of the U.S. Treasury Department's Financial Crimes Enforcement Network, stated in a speech in 2016. "We see wire transfers originating from foreign banks in offshore havens where shell companies have established accounts, but in many cases we also see criminals using U.S. incorporated limited liability companies to launder their illicit funds through the U.S. real estate market" (quoted in Swanson (2016)).

"The real estate market has long provided a way for individuals to secretly launder or invest stolen money and other illicitly gained funds," observes a study by Transparency International (2017, p. 5). "Not only do expensive apartments in New York, London or Paris raise the social status of their owners and enhance their luxurious lifestyles, but they are also an easy and convenient place to hide hundreds of millions of dollars from criminal investigators, tax authorities or others."

---

[1] Calculated as follows: $733 billion x 0.37×0.54 = $146 billion. Note that this excludes all non-residential property holdings as well as all residential properties valued at less than $4 million.

Apart from the non-financial assets mentioned by Zucman—art, yachts, gold, jewelry, and real estate—a considerable amount of hidden wealth takes the form of cash. One-hundred-dollar bills, though not widely used in day-to-day transactions, account for 78% of the $1.5 trillion value of US banknotes in circulation. The €500 note accounts for 30% of the total value of Euros, and the 1000 Swiss franc note—which is especially handy for carrying in a briefcase, being worth more than 20 times its weight in gold—accounts for 92% of the total value of the Swiss currency (Sands 2016). "Rather than being a way of paying for things," the *Economist* (2016) remarks, large-denomination notes serve as a "convenient store of value"—convenient, above all, for wealth holders who prize anonymity.

Furthermore, not even all of the world's wealth that is hidden in the form of financial assets shows up in the IIP discrepancy. To understand why, consider Zucman's (2015, p. 37) explanation for the discrepancy:

Let's imagine a British person who holds in her Swiss bank account a portfolio of American securities—for example, stock in Google. What information is recorded in each country's balance sheet? In the United States, a liability: American institutions see that foreigners hold US equities. In Switzerland, nothing at all, and for a reason: the Swiss statisticians see some Google stock deposited in a Swiss bank, but they see that the stock belongs to a UK resident—and so they are neither assets nor liabilities for Switzerland. In the United Kingdom, nothing is registered, either, but wrongly this time: the Office for National Statistics should record an asset for the United Kingdom, but it can't, because it has no way of knowing that the British person has Google stock in her Geneva account.

(Zucman 2015, p. 37).

Now imagine that this same person holds Google stock in a bank account in the United States, the country that is "by some measures, the world's single most important tax haven" (Shaxson 2011, p. 18). The United States ranked second in the world in the 2018 edition of the Financial Secrecy Index, which measures the volume of foreign deposits and the laxity of transparency rules, between #1 Switzerland and #3 Cayman Islands (Tax Justice Network 2018). In this case, the United States would not record an external liability, and the hidden asset would not lead to a discrepancy in the IIP accounts. Similarly, if capital flight from Africa is routed through a shell company incorporated in Delaware and then invested in US equities, there is no discrepancy to be found.

Moreover, apart from unrecorded assets there also may be misrecorded assets—external assets recorded in the IIP as belonging to country A, but whose beneficial owners are really from country B. This is particularly likely if country A is a financial secrecy jurisdiction. Mauritius, for example, is a haven for capital from African countries, including South Africa and Angola (Fitzgibbon 2017). With a population of only 1.3 million, the country recorded a whopping $423 billion in external assets in the IIP data in 2015, more than $300,000 per person, about 15 times the country's per capita income. By way of comparison, Poland and Turkey, with similar per capita incomes, recorded external assets amounting to about $6000 and $3000 per person, respectively.

For these reasons, while Zucman may be correct that the IIP discrepancy gives the right order of magnitude for the world's total hidden wealth—meaning that it is closer to $7.6 trillion than to either $760 billion or $76 trillion—the total amount may be considerably larger, perhaps by a multiple or two.

The IIP discrepancy provides a useful lower-bound estimate of total hidden wealth, but it cannot tell us how hidden wealth is distributed by source regions or countries. To estimate Africa's hidden wealth one must rely on other data sources. For this purpose, Zucman (2013, 2015) used data on financial assets held in Swiss banks. Since 1998, the Swiss National Bank (SNB—Switzerland's central bank) has reported data on foreign-owned assets held in Swiss banks. These amounted to

$2.3 trillion in spring 2015. About 60% of these assets were held by shell corporations, trusts, and foundations, meaning that the nationality of their beneficial owners was unknown. The SNB data do, however, report nationality for the remaining assets, and Zucman (2015, pp. 31–32) uses this information to impute ownership of the assets held by shell corporations:

> To know who really owns wealth in Switzerland, we need to make some assumptions about who is behind these shell entities. After examining the available evidence, the assumption I retain is that the wealth held through shell companies belongs to American, British, or German citizens in the same proportion as the directly held wealth does, with a correction to take into account that since 2005 Europeans have had greater incentives to use shell companies and Gulf countries have less incentive to do so.

On this basis he concludes that Africa accounted for $150 billion of the nonresident bank accounts in Switzerland, about 6.5% of the total. More than half belonged to Europeans, with Germany, France, and Italy—the three countries that share a border with Switzerland—leading the way, together accounting for $640 billion.

Africa likewise accounts for 6.5%, or $500 billion, in Zucman's estimate of the distribution by source countries of the $7.6 trillion in hidden wealth revealed by the IIP discrepancy. In other words, Africa's share of hidden financial wealth worldwide in his calculations is the same as its share of directly held wealth deposited in Swiss bank accounts.

Is it reasonable to assume that the distribution of wealth held by shell companies in Swiss banks mirrors that of directly held assets? Do Germans and Angolans, for example, have exactly the same incentives to channel funds through anonymous offshore entities, incurring the attendant transaction costs, as opposed to opening Swiss bank accounts in their own names? Or does the incentive to use shell entities vary depending on the provenance of the funds?

If the motive for a British person to put money in a Swiss bank is simply to avoid UK taxes, she may deem it sufficient to open an account in her own name. If the UK government somehow were to learn of the ruse, the most she would face are tax penalties. But if the motive is to conceal wealth that was acquired by fraudulent or questionable means—if the wealth is the proceeds of what is called a "predicate crime" in anti-money laundering legislation—she may decide that more elaborate precautions, including routing the money through a shell company or a web of shell companies, are worth the extra expense. For in this case, the penalty for being caught could be forfeiture of the entire amount and criminal prosecution.[25]

---

[25] To create paper trails that conceal the true origins of illicitly acquired funds, common ruses used by offshore banks include backdated currency trades; opposing bets on stock market that cancel each

Law professor Cass Sunstein (2016), in a review of Zucman's book, alludes to this important point when he writes that "all uses of tax havens are not the same." Noting that Zucman's estimates imply that half of Russia's financial wealth is held offshore, Sunstein suggests that "the extraordinarily high figure for Russia might be best understood as involving money corruptly acquired or invested." The same may be true of Africa: by Zucman's estimates 30% of the region's financial wealth is offshore, compared to 10% for Europe and 4% for the United States (Zucman 2015, p. 53).

In sum, estimates of missing external assets based on the global IIP anomalies, while providing a useful indicator of the overall magnitude of offshore wealth, cannot provide a reliable measure of the quantity or timing of capital flight from individual African countries. For this purpose, our estimates start instead with discrepancies in the country's balance of payments, corrected as described above for external borrowing and trade misinvoicing. When recorded inflows of foreign exchange systematically exceed recorded outflows, we can safely assume that most of the missing money is not sitting under mattresses in Johannesburg, Luanda, or Abidjan. It is leaving Africa, although its departure is not registered in official statistics.

To be sure, there is considerable uncertainty as to how much of the flight capital is accumulated as savings and how much is dissipated in consumption overseas. Extrapolating from outflows of money to stocks of wealth held offshore requires strong assumptions, too. In terms of capital flight's cost to source countries, however, it matters little whether the missing money is saved or consumed. From the standpoint of ordinary people, what matters is not how frugal corrupt elites are with their stolen money, but the simple fact that they stole it.

Conclusion

This chapter estimates the magnitude of capital flight from Angola, Côte d'Ivoire, and South Africa, three African countries that feature prominently in total capital flight from the continent. The chapter also delves into a key mechanism of capital flight, trade misinvoicing, with a focus on primary commodity exports. The results show that all three countries suffered substantial losses of capital over the past four decades, amounting to $329 billion for South Africa, $103 billion for Angola, and $55 billion for Côte d'Ivoire.

The chronic nature of capital flight from these countries suggests that the phenomenon is driven by structural and institutional factors in both the source

other out, producing no real profits, in which the winning bet serves as the ostensible source of the funds; fictitious transactions between offshore companies, such as selling goods held in the Geneva Freeport (or even fictitious items) at inflated prices; and ostensible income from rooms in hotels owned by the shell company that are actually empty. See Bernstein (2017, pp. 85, 104, 193).

country and the global financial systems that facilitate it. The outflows result in accumulation of private offshore wealth, some of which was financed by embezzlement of public resources. The results imply that, like many other African countries, the three are net creditors to the rest of the world in the sense that their assets held offshore exceed the stock of their external debts. The difference is that the debts are a liability on the shoulders of the entire population, while the offshore wealth is private. It follows that strategies to address capital flight must involve measures to curtail new outflows as well as measures to repatriate the wealth hidden in offshore financial centers.

To understand more fully the mechanisms of capital flight and to design strategies to combat the hemorrhage of resources from African countries, it is crucial to examine in detail the actors, conduits, and enablers behind these hidden outflows. With this in mind, detailed country studies of the type presented in this volume represent a potentially fruitful avenue for further research.

References

Alstadsæter, A., Johannesen, N., and Zucman, G. 2018. Who owns the wealth in wealth havens? Macro evidence and implications for global inequality. *Journal of Public Economics*, 162, 89–100.

Bahmani-Oskooee, M., and Goswami, G.G. 2003. Smuggling as another cause of failure of the PPP. *Journal of Economic Development*, 28(2), 23–38.

Barnett, R.C. 2003. Smuggling, non-fundamental uncertainty, and parallel market exchange rate volatility. *Canadian Journal of Economics*, 36(3), 701–727.

Berger, H., and Nitsch, V. 2012. Gotcha! A profile of smuggling in international trade. In C. Costa Storti and P. De Grauwe (Eds.), *Illicit Trade and the Global Economy* (pp. 49–72). Cambridge and London: MIT Press.

Bernstein, J. 2017. *Secrecy World: Inside the Panama Papers Investigation of Illicit Money Networks and the Global Elite*. New York: Henry Holt.

Bhagwati, J. 1964. On the under-invoicing of imports [with application to recent Turkish experience]. *Bulletin of the Institute of Economics and Statistics* (Oxford University), 26, 389–397.

Bhagwati, J. 1967. Fiscal policies, the faking of foreign trade declarations, and the balance of payments. *Bulletin of the Institute of Economics and Statistics* (Oxford University), 29, 61–77.

Bhagwati, J., and Hansen, B. 1973. A theoretical analysis of smuggling. *Quarterly Journal of Economics*, 87(2), 172–187.

Bhagwati, J., Krueger, A.O., and Wibulswasdi, C. 1974. Capital flight from LDCs: A statistical analysis. *Studies in International Economics*, 1, 148–154.

Biswas, A.K., and Marjit, S. 2005. Mis-invoicing and trade policy. *The Journal of Policy Reform*, 8(3), 189–205.

Boyce, J.K., and Ndikumana, L. 2001. Is Africa a net creditor? New estimates of capital flight from severely indebted sub-Saharan African countries, 1970–1996. *Journal of Development Studies*, 38(2), 27–56.

Boyce, J.K., and Ndikumana, L. 2012a. Elites loot Africa as foreign debts mount. In N. Chanda and S. Froetschel (Eds.), *A World Connected: Globalization in the 21st Century*. YaleGlobal Online Ebook (pp. 44–47).

Boyce, J.K., and Ndikumana, L. 2012b. How capital flight drains Africa: Stolen money and lost lives. In N. Pons-Vignon and P. Ncube (Eds.), *Confronting Finance: Mobilizing the 99% for Economic and Social Progress* (pp. 31–34). Geneva: International Labour Office.

Buehn, A., and Eichler, S. 2011. Trade misinvoicing: The dark side of world trade. *The World Economy*, 34(8), 1263–1287.

Buehn, A., and Farzanegan, M.R. 2012. Smuggling around the world: Evidence from a structural equation model. *Applied Economics*, 44(23), 3047–3064.

CityRealty. 2017. Year-End Manhattan Market Report. New York: CityRealty, December.

Cobham, A., and Jansky, P. 2020. *Estimating Illicit Financial Flows: A Critical Guide to Data, Methodology and Findings*. Oxford: Oxford University Press.

Economist. 2016. Cash Talk: High Denomination Bank Notes. *The Economist*, March 3.

Epaphra, M. 2015. Tax rates and tax evasion: Evidence from missing imports in Tanzania. *Business and Economics Journal*, 7(2), 122–137.

Erbe, S. 1986. The flight of capital from developing countries. *Rivista di Studi Politici Internazionali*, 53(3), 504–512.

FATF. 2013. *Money Laundering and Terrorist Financing Vulnerabilities of Professionals*. Paris: Financial Action Task Force, June.

Ferraris, C.F. 1885. *La Statistica del Movimento dei Metalli Preziosi fra l'Italia e l'Estero*. Rome: Ministero di agricoltura, industria e commerci.

Fisman, R., and Wei, S.-J. 2004. Tax rates and tax evasion: Evidence from "missing imports" in China. *Journal of Political Economy*, 112(2), 471–496.

Fisman, R., and Wei, S.-J. 2007. The smuggling of art, and the art of smuggling: Uncovering the illicit trade in cultural property and antiques. NBER Working Paper No. 13446.

Fitzgibbon, W. 2017. Tax haven Mauritius' rise comes at the rest of Africa's expense. *International Consortium of Investigative Journalists*, November 7, available at https://www.icij.org/investigations/paradise-papers/tax-haven-mauritius-africa/ (accessed on February 4, 2018).

Foer, F. 2019. Russian-style kleptocracy is infiltrating America. *The Atlantic*, March, available at https://www.theatlantic.com/magazine/archive/2019/03/how-kleptocracy-came-to-america/580471/ (accessed on February 2, 2018).

Gulati, S. 1987. A Note on Trade Misinvoicing. In D.R. Lessard and J. Williamson (Eds.), *Capital Flight and Third World Debt*. Washington, DC: Institute for International Economics.

Henry, J.S. 2012. The price of offshore revisited: New estimates for "missing" global private wealth, income, inequality and lost taxes. London: Tax Justice Network, July.

Henry, J.S. 2016. The Price of Offshore—Data by Region. The Global Haven Industry: http://globalhavenindustry.com/price-of-offshore-menu. Accessed on July 15, 2021.

International Monetary Fund (IMF). 2018. Direction of Trade Statistics: Introductory Notes. Washington, DC: IMF.

Kar, D., and Spanjers, J. 2014. Illicit Financial Flows from Developing Countries: 2003–2012. Washington, DC: Global Financial Integrity (December).

Kellenberg, D., and Levinson, A. 2016. Misreporting Trade: Tariff Evasion, Corruption, and Auditing Standards. NBER Working Paper No. 22593.

Köhler, H. 2015. On the Impossibility of Speaking of Africa: Essay Based on a Speech at the Africa Days of the German Federal Ministry of Education and Research on March 18, 2014. *Africa Journal of Management*, 1(3), 257–263.

Lane, P.R., and Milesi-Ferretti, G.M. 2007. The external wealth of nations Mark II: Revised and extended estimates of foreign assets and liabilities, 1970–2004. *Journal of International Economics*, 73(2), 223–250.

Lessard, D.R., and Williamson, J. (Eds.). 1987. *Capital Flight and Third World Debt*. Washington, DC: Institute for International Economics.

McDonald, D.C. 1985. Trade data discrepancies and the incentive to smuggle: An empirical analysis. *International Monetary Fund Staff Papers*, 32(4), 668–692.

Marini, M., Dippelsman, R., and Stanger, M. 2018. *New Estimates for Direction of Trade Statistics*. Washington, DC: IMF.

Metrocosm. 2015. A Striking Perspective on New York City Property Values. Metrocosm, June 24, available at http://metrocosm.com/new-york-city-property-values-in-perspective/ (accessed on February 2, 2018).

Ndikumana, L., and Boyce, J.K. 2010. Measurement of capital flight: Methodology and results for Sub-Saharan African countries. *African Development Review*, 22(4), 471–481.

Ndikumana, L., and Boyce, J.K. 2012. Rich presidents of poor nations: Capital flight from resource-rich countries in Africa. *ACAS Bulletin*, 87, 2–7.

Ndikumana, L., and Boyce, J.K. 2019. Magnitudes and Mechanisms of Capital Flight from Angola, Côte d'Ivoire and South Africa. Amherst, MA: Political Economy Research Institute, Working Paper 500.

Ndikumana, L., Boyce, J.K., and Ndiaye, A.S. 2015. Capital flight from Africa: Measurement and drivers. In S.I. Ajayi and L. Ndikumana (Eds.), *Capital Flight from Africa: Causes, Effects and Policy Issues* (pp. 15–54). Oxford: Oxford University Press.

New York Times. 2015. Towers of Secrecy: Piercing the Shell Companies. *New York Times*, May 21, available at https://www.nytimes.com/news-event/shell-company-towers-of-secrecy-real-estate (accessed on February 2, 2018).

O'Murchu, C. 2014. Tax Haven Buyers Set off Property Alarm in England and Wales. *Financial Times*, July 31, available at https://www.ft.com/content/6cb11114-18aa-11e4-a51a-00144feabdc0 (accessed on February 2, 2018).

OECD (2020). Tax Transparency and Exchange of Information in Times of COVID-19. Global Forum Annual Report 2020. Paris: OECD, available at https://www.oecd.org/tax/transparency/documents/global-forum-annual-report-2020.pdf (accessed on September 7, 2020).

Patnaik, I., Gupta, A.S., and Shah, A. 2012. Determinants of trade misinvoicing. *Open Economies Review*, 23(5), 891–910.

Reuter, P. Ed. (2012). *Draining Development? Controlling Flows of Illicit Funds from Developing Countries*. Washington, DC: World Bank.

Sands, P. 2016. Making it Harder for the Bad Guys: The Case for Eliminating High Denomination Notes. Cambridge, MA: Harvard Kennedy School, M-RCBG Associate Working Paper Series No. 52.

Shaxson, N. 2011. *Treasure Islands: Tax Havens and the Men Who Stole the World*. London: Bodley Head.

Shaxson, N. 2018. *The Finance Curse: How Global Finance is Making Us All Poorer.* London: Bodley Head.

Spanjers, J., and Salomon, M. 2017. Illicit Financial Flows to and from Developing Countries: 2005–2014. Washington, DC: Global Financial Integrity, May.

Storti, C.C., and de Grauwe, P. (Eds.) (2012). *Illicit Trade and the Global Economy.* Cambridge, MA: MIT Press.

Sunstein, C.R. 2016. Parking the Big Money. *New York Review of Books*, January 14.

Swanson, A. 2016. How secretive shell companies shape US real estate market. *Washington Post*, April 12, available at https://www.washingtonpost.com/news /wonk/wp/2016/04/12/how-secretive-shell-companies-shape-the-u-s-real-estate- market/ (accessed on September 7, 2020).

Tax Justice Network. 2018. Financial Secrecy Index—2018 Results. London: Tax Justice Network.

Transparency International. 2017. *Doors Wide Open: Corruption and Real Estate in Four Key Markets.* Berlin: Transparency International.

UNCTAD. 2016. Trade Misinvoicing in Primary Commodities in Developing Coun- tries: The Cases of Chile, Côte d'Ivoire, Nigeria, South Africa and Zambia. Geneva: UNCTAD, December.

UNCTAD. 2020. *Tackling Illicit Financial Flows for Sustainable Development in Africa. Economic Development in Africa Report 2020.* Geneva: UNCTAD.

World Bank. 1985. *World Development Report 1985.* Washington, DC: World Bank.

Zucman, G. 2013. The missing wealth of nations: Are Europe and the US net debtors or net creditors? *The Quarterly Journal of Economics*, 128(3), 1321–1361.

Zucman, G. 2014. Taxing across borders: Tracking personal wealth and corporate profits. *Journal of Economic Perspectives*, 28(4), 121–148.

Zucman, G. 2015. *The Hidden Wealth of Nations: The Scourge of Tax Havens.* Chicago, IL: University of Chicago Press.

Fig. 3.1 Angola

Credit: Map by Esra Nur Uğurlu (PhD candidate, University of Massachusetts Amherst).

3

Angola

Oil and Capital Flight

Nicholas Shaxson

Introduction

During Angola's "golden decade," the roughly 12-year period between the end of its civil war in 2002 and the oil price crash of 2014–2015, the country exported more than half a trillion dollars' worth of oil. This money could have transformed Angola's economy for the benefit of its 30 million people, but most Angolans saw few benefits. Now, with oil prices down and the oil slowly running out, there is relatively little to show for it beyond some transport infrastructure and some showy projects mostly in and around wealthier parts of the capital, Luanda. (See map of Angola in Figure 3.1)

Much of the money ended up overseas in the hands of a relatively small number of individuals, enabled by a transnational network of intermediaries. This chapter explores how these outflows happened—the *who, what, why, where,* and *how* of this massive money drain.

I was the *Reuters* and *Financial Times* correspondent resident in Angola from 1993 to 1995, during the civil war, and I continued to visit the country frequently until 2007 while reporting for the *FT*, the *Economist Intelligence Unit*, *Africa Confidential* and *African Energy*, among others. Returning in October 2017 for the first time in a decade, I observed the first days of the new administration of President João Lourenço—and I was struck forcefully by a sense of déjà vu. On one level, much had changed. Luanda itself had been massively transformed by imposing, shiny glass-fronted buildings, impressive new expressways, enormous new shopping centers, and a multitude of glass-fronted bank branches all across town.

Yet it became apparent that the Angolan political-economic system was essentially a bigger, more elaborate and more financially sophisticated version of the same oil-fueled creature I had left a decade earlier, populated in its upper echelons by many of the same people. It was a giant patronage system whose essential contours had proved remarkably immune to both internal and external pressures

Nicholas Shaxson, *Angola*. In: *On the Trail of Capital Flight from Africa*.
Edited by Léonce Ndikumana and James K. Boyce, Oxford University Press.
© Nicholas Shaxson (2022). DOI: 10.1093/oso/9780198852728.003.0003

for reform. Angola was in the throes of dealing with an oil price crash: from an average of nearly $100 a barrel in 2014, the world price had fallen to around $40 in 2016, recovering to around $55 when I revisited in 2017. Angolan oil production had also started to decline.

The price of oil has been of primordial importance for Angola since independence. When I lived there in the 1990s, oil accounted for about 95% of the country's recorded exports; adding diamonds, the share of minerals exceeded 99% (IMF 1997, Tables 18 and 21). The country was emerging from "Afro-Stalinism"—a legacy of the Cold War when Angola's ruling Movimento para a Libertaçao Popular de Angola (MPLA) was supported and influenced heavily by the Soviet Union and its Cuban allies (Hodges 2001). Nearly all of Angola's oil production was offshore— and the western-backed rebel leader, Jonas Savimbi, had decided that it would be geopolitically foolish to attack western oil installations—so the oil pumped almost uninterrupted while the rest of the economy suffered the disruptions of war. Years later, at the close of the "golden decade" of post-war reconstruction and high oil revenues, oil and diamonds *still* accounted for more than 99% of the country's export earnings (IMF 2017, Table 4), despite repeated declarations by politicians, pundits and economic advisers that Angola needed to diversify its economy away from oil, and away from Luanda and the coastal enclaves.

By 2017 the euphoria of the "golden decade" among Angolan elites and the urban middle classes had given way to foreboding. Evidence of a "sudden stop" littered the urban landscape in empty or half-constructed buildings. As José de Oliveira, an experienced oil official in Luanda, sourly remarked, "The golden years have been wasted."[1]

All this raises big questions. Why has Angola not been able to harness that wealth to benefit its citizens? Why has Angola been unable to diversify its economy, so long after the end of conflict? And, most pertinently for this particular study, *where did all the oil money go?*

An important part of the answer comes down to two words: "capital flight." An experienced businessman in Luanda explained:

> Externalizing the money out was always very easy to do because the whole economy was based on trade. There wasn't local industry, with local value added. The real motors were on export of oil and diamonds and on the other side was imports—consumables, building materials: everything.

> So, you have two parts of economy, both of which involved the international community. So, there's money moving in and money moving out, and it's fairly

---

[1] José de Oliveira is former editor of the *Revista Energia* magazine, which was Angola's leading energy newsletter for many years. He is now connected to CEIC. Interviewed in Luanda, October 11, 2017.

easy to take your share. Your starting point is that money is already flowing internationally.[2]

In what follows I first discuss the "resource curse," of which capital flight is a major component. I then trace Angola's history starting with the era of Portuguese colonial rule that ended in 1975, moving from José Eduardo dos Santos' accession to the presidency in 1979, through the years of civil war and bouts of shaky peace and renewed war that finally ended in 2002, before turning to the "golden decade" that began in 2002. The story extends to 2017, when dos Santos stepped down after 38 years in power, handing over the presidency to João Lourenço.[3] This, then, is mainly a study of the dos Santos years.

Oil and the Resource Curse

The resource curse has two variants: a weak one in which a country fails to harness its mineral riches effectively for development, and a stronger version in which the country is *even poorer* (and worse off in other dimensions of development) than it would have been without the minerals.[4] There is no doubt that Angola has suffered the weak version, and there are good grounds for concluding that it has been afflicted by the strong version too. The war certainly helps to explain the country's dismal performance, but oil and diamonds also contributed greatly to the severity and duration of the conflict. So, the war itself can be understood as one element of Angola's resource curse.

Oil was first produced in Angola in 1956, and by the time independence in 1975 production had reached 100,000 barrels per day (bpd), rising to more than 500,000 bpd by the early 1990s. New deep-water oilfield discoveries then propelled production steadily higher, peaking around 2 million bpd in 2010, before declining to around 1.3 million by 2020.

In *The Scramble for Africa's Oil*, journalist John Ghazvinian recounts a dinner at the 18th World Petroleum Congress in Johannesburg in 2005:

The evening would not have been the same without the desserts. The organizers had decided to give us each a little chocolate mousse and sponge cake carefully moulded into the shape of Africa. It was hard not to admire the artistry involved, but as I looked round the Dome, I wondered: was I the only one to pick up on the

---

[2] Interview with a European businessman.
[3] In an October 2020 state of the nation address, President Lourenço put the scale of looting under his predecessor at a minimum of $24 billion and stated that "it is likely that much bigger numbers will be announced later" (Cotterill 2020).
[4] See for example Sachs and Warner (1999) and Collier and Goderis (2012).

symbolism of 3,500 drunken oil executives devouring the Dark Continent, bite after dribbling, chocolaty bite?[5]

To some this is the essence of the resource curse: western corporations devouring Africa's treasure, depriving the continent of its chance for development. This frame is apt for Angola's history, but it muddies a more complex story.

In pure revenue terms, Angola hasn't done all that badly out of its oil. The country's independence came at a time of rising resource nationalism and the flexing of OPEC's muscles, and Angola historically has obtained a respectable share of its oil revenue by regional standards: at times as much as 60% of the value of each barrel produced, with much of the rest going to pay for the costs of deep-water oil platforms and equipment. Yet in 2017 Angola's under-five mortality rate stood at 81 per thousand children, compared to 49 in Ghana (where per capita income was only half as much) and 32 in Bangladesh (where per capita income was even lower) (United Nations 2018, pp. 30–32).

The literature on the resource curse, sometimes called "the paradox of poverty amid plenty," identifies three main adverse effects of mineral wealth on a nation's economy.

The first is economic volatility. Enormous swings in world oil prices play holy havoc with Angola's economy. Forecasting and government budgeting become exercises in fantasy accounting, planning goes out of the window, and neither the government nor the private sector can effectively absorb the surging inflows of money during the booms or the sudden collapse of revenues during the busts. Borrowing tends to worsen the picture, as bankers—famously, the people who will happily lend you an umbrella when the sun is shining but want it back when it is raining—prefer to lend when oil prices are high, and then play hardball in crashes.

The second element is the so-called "Dutch disease." Large inflows of foreign exchange lead to appreciation of the nation's currency, making imports cheaper and its exports more expensive. Sectors producing tradable goods or services, like agricultural or industrial products, find it harder to compete against imports and harder to sell abroad. They are crowded out by oil. This is exacerbated by a brain drain as high salaries in the oil industry tend to attract the country's best and brightest, depriving other sectors of talented and educated people. Conversely, non-oil sectors pick up when the world oil price crashes.[6]

The third main element of the resource curse involves governance. This is the most complex, involving political, economic and even cultural elements, and it is the aspect most relevant for our study of capital flight. A starting point for understanding the governance problems in nations like Angola is to consider the

---

[5] See Ghazvinian (2007, p. 5), cited in Ovadia (2016, p. 6).
[6] See Shaxson (2021, Figure 2).

contrast between an economy highly dependent on oil extraction and a more normal economy. Putting it simply, in the latter much of the wealth is usually generated by the citizenry interacting with each other in horizontal relationships based on productive activities. Governments tax the income, and citizens demand public goods and services in return.

In an economy like Angola's, by contrast, oil revenue enters from a point source at the top of the political system and flows downwards from there in a patronage system. Those in positions of power allocate wealth, or access to it, in exchange for political support and loyalty. The government has little need to depend upon the majority of the country's people for either tax revenue or political support, and the economic damage that oil inflicts on other economic sectors reinforces this "rentier-state" structure.[7]

Picture Angola's oil-dominated economic system as a mighty river, descending from a single source in the mountains. It splits, splits again and again, then fans out into a broad, sandy delta as it approaches the sea. Toll keepers operate at each branch, taking a cut before letting the rest flow downstream, and often sending their takings offshore. Nearest to the source, the biggest players divert the biggest flows. Further downstream a more sizeable fraction of the country's population—car-owning urbanites and others—operate close to the beach, where the multiple flow channels are smaller and individual pickings thinner. Meanwhile a much larger fraction of the country's population, living predominantly in the agricultural and subsistence hinterlands, function largely outside this river system.

The economic linkages are vertical, top-down relationships. The attention of policy makers turns away from challenges of nation-building and economic development towards schemes to get access to the flows of wealth. The oil wealth can be used to buy off those who pose a threat and pay for paramilitary forces to suppress malcontents.

But before hasty "corruption" judgement is passed on the petty bureaucrats and other less well-remunerated participants in the patronage system, consider this:

In March 1995, when salaries were almost at their lowest point, with a director earning $11 a month and the minimum monthly wage at less than $1, the National Statistics Institute calculated that the minimum basket of goods and services for the survival of an urban household of eight persons was $187. During the 1990s, therefore, households have had to diversify their sources of income.

(Hodges 2004, p. 79)

---

[7] For a critical review of the social science literature on rentier states, noting that these effects are not necessarily inherent in oil and mineral resource abundance but rather outcomes of country-specific histories, see Di John (2007). See also Natural Resources Governance Institute (2015).

At its crudest, the patronage system may involve members of a ruling family cap-turing oil revenues before they even reach the national treasury and diverting them into their personal offshore accounts. This chapter outlines many slightly less crude examples: the allocation of a controlling stake in companies, or control over sovereign wealth funds, or participation in joint ventures with the state oil company, or control over items of the budgetary process mediated by government ministries. The number and variety of tollbooths is remarkable, as the examples presented below illustrate.

The system has had several predictable effects. One is authoritarianism based on the simple formula of allocating oil wealth downwards in exchange for political support, albeit from a narrow stratum of the population. Another is the fragmen-tation of political structures beneath the presidency: dos Santos exercised power through multiple competing networks, keeping all players in a permanent state of anxiety as they seek to stay in the president's favor for fear of losing positions and privileges. A good example, relevant for the study of capital flight, is the fluctu-ating influence of the Ministry of Finance vis-à-vis other ministries, such as the Ministry of Planning. The Finance Ministry "has gone from super-ministry to ir-relevancy more often and faster than anyone can keep track of," observed Ricardo Soares de Oliveira (2015, p. 44), a leading scholar of Angolan affairs. "The erstwhile influential minister can be sacked for no reason. The result is a muddle."

The main power blocs in this network have been the ruling MPLA party, with a large footprint across the policy-making apparatus; the state oil company, So-nangol; the central bank (*Banco Nacional de Angola*, BNA); power centers at the presidency (notably the *casa civil*, dealing with civil affairs, and the *casa militar*, dealing with the armed forces); an overlapping coterie of "generals" in the armed forces, many with private interests; separate and often competing intelligence ser-vices; and former president dos Santos's own family, notably his daughter Isabel dos Santos, who amassed large or controlling stakes in multiple sectors of the An-golan economy and further afield. Smaller power centers include parastatal firms, the state diamond company Endiama, private banks (whose profits depend heavily on state contracts), and individual ministries.

This divide-and-rule strategy militates against joined-up thinking and ham-pers coherent policymaking. It favors secrecy, not only because transparency and openness would require better co-ordination but also because each node in the power structure constitutes an opportunity for well-connected individuals to profit, shielded from public view.

Independence and Its Aftermath

Prior to the 1900s, Portuguese colonialists controlled only the coastal enclaves of Luanda and Benguela and a thin corridor along the Kwanza river. Yet their economic power "eventually extended across great areas of Central Africa and may have sucked into captivity, in alliance with inland kingdoms, a larger percentage of the African population than in any other catchment area on the continent" (ibid., p. 6). These geographical zones remain the epicenter of Angola's oil-dominated economy, with Luanda the dominant player by far.

António Salazar, the Portuguese dictator, encouraged poor Portuguese to settle in Angola, and by the eve of independence Angola's white population had reached about 330,000 people—roughly five percent of the population. The settlers helped develop an extensive agricultural sector and even the beginnings of an industrial sector. In the 1960s and early 1970s Angola was self-sufficient in all main food crops except wheat, it was vying with Côte d'Ivoire for the role of Africa's top coffee exporter, and oil production was slowly rising.

One legacy of the colonial era is that a significant percentage of the Angolan population, particularly in the coastal urban centers, is mixed-race or white. Many Angolans—perhaps a quarter—speak only Portuguese (Hodges 2001, p. 25). Angola's elites have always been relatively outward-looking—more so than those of most African countries—and this has reinforced the effect of oil in shaping a cultural, political, and economic orientation of the upper and middle classes towards global markets, along with a turning away from the larger indigenous rural populations, again even more so than in most other African countries.

Independence movements had sprung up from the 1950s and were brutally suppressed. But when a coup in Portugal in 1974 led to chaotic decolonization, the lid of the Angolan pressure cooker came off. Full-scale war erupted within weeks, pitting the *Frente National de Libertação de Angola*, strongest among Bakongo-speaking people in northwestern Angola, against Jonas *Savimbi's União Nacional para a Independência Total de Angola* (UNITA), which had backing among Ovimbundu peoples of the central highlands and southern Angola, and the *Movimento Popular de Libertaçao de Angola* (MPLA), strongest in the coastal enclaves and especially in Luanda, with backing from Kimbundu speakers of northern Angola and, crucially, the influential mestiço and white sections of the population. The MPLA would emerge victorious in the long wars ahead.

As the economy collapsed there was one sector—oil—that took a different trajectory. The MPLA had declared before independence that "all those [oil] companies which... operate offshore or inland will be chased from our national territory and all their equipment and assets seized."[8] But when they came to power, they dramatically changed tack, accommodating the western oil companies at the same time as they set about creating a national oil company, Sonangol, destined

---

[8] MPLA statement issued 12 February 1974. Reprinted in *The Complex of United States-Portuguese Relations: Before and After the Coup. Hearings Before the Subcommittee on Africa, Committee on Foreign Affairs, House of Representatives, Ninety-third Congress, Second Session.* Washington, DC: US Government Printing Office, 1974, p. 433.

to become a fortress of technical competence carved out from the economic chaos and mismanagement all around it.

The MPLA reached an agreement that persuaded Portuguese employees of the state oil company Angol, founded in the colonial era, to remain when Sonangol was formed in 1976. Angola also secured advice from the Algerian state oil company Sonatrach, the Italian oil company ENI, and US auditors and consultants Arthur D. Little. In 1983 Sonangol opened its first international office, in London, with Lloyds Bank as their main bankers.[9] As Soares de Oliveira (2007, p. 610) remarks, "There was a general perception that the oil sector was a matter of life-or-death, ensuring the viability of the MPLA state." A top western oil executive described Sonangol as "the Angolan miracle" (Soares de Oliveira 2015, p. 36).

Sonangol remained firmly under the control of President dos Santos, however, serving as "the pivotal tool for the interests of the presidential clique" (Soares de Oliveira 2007, p. 606). Sonangol also provided an anchor for securing international loans—so much so that it was used as a vehicle for implementing all manner of special projects outside the oil sector, including large-scale arms purchases that were financed by borrowing via Sonangol. Sonangol was also a key player when it came to capital flight, as described below.

In the fighting that followed Angola's independence from Portugal in 1975, the ruling MPLA held Luanda and some urban centers and coastal areas, while UNITA reigned in large parts of the countryside. UNITA leader Savimbi never tired of telling his supporters that the downtrodden "real Africans" were fighting against an effete, corrupt gang of globalized, wealthy elites clustering in coastal enclaves and in league with foreign wealth extractors. (It is worth noting, in passing, the similarities with the divisions that roil the United States and other western countries today.)

Each side exploited Cold War rivalries to gain advantage. The Soviet Union backed the oil-rich MPLA and Fidel Castro sent thousands of Cuban troops in support, helping to secure a famous victory over apartheid South Africa's army and its UNITA allies at Cuito Cuanavale in southern Angola in 1987–1988. The Cold War delivered the irony of Cuban troops protecting American oil installations in the northern enclave of Cabinda on behalf of a Soviet-backed regime fighting rebels backed by the United States. Later, in the 1990s, Angolan military officials and UNITA forces sometimes mined almost side-by-side in the country's diamond zones under local non-aggression pacts that allowed uninterrupted trading across the frontlines.[10]

---

[9] Sonangol CEO Manuel Vicente has been quoted as saying that Sonangol set up an account with Lloyds TSB on the Channel Island of Jersey in 1983 (Van Niekerk and Peterson 2002).

[10] In the besieged town of Kuito in the early 1990s, embattled residents told me of a football match between UNITA and MPLA soldiers under a brief local truce, after which they set about killing one another again.

Nearly all the oil was produced offshore, and military operations hardly dented production. Savimbi, a master manipulator, won widespread support in the West by portraying himself as a staunch anti-communist freedom fighter, whereas in reality he ran a tightly controlled military-political machine based on fear. An account in the *New York Review of Books* gives a good sense of the man's opportunism:

> Over the past fifteen years he has been able to switch to whatever rhetoric he feels will best suit the moment. At first, Mao seemed the master. As late as 1976, when South Africa was already his chief supplier, he still used some Maoist jargon. Last year, Savimbi was presented to a Conservative group in the British Parliament as "the black Mrs. Thatcher."
>
> (Smiley 1983)

If one had to identify a single reason for the Angolan war's exceptionally long duration, it was Savimbi's sociopathic political genius and his burning desire to gain power at any and all costs. But the war was also fed, in terms of both materials *and* motivations, by mineral wealth: oil supporting the MPLA and diamonds supporting UNITA.

After the fall of the Berlin Wall, the United States, Portugal, and Russia joined together to help craft the Bicesse peace agreement of 1991. This led to elections in 1992 that dos Santos and the MPLA won. Savimbi rejected the result, plunging Angola into its bloodiest conflict yet. The new war lasted until the signing of the Lusaka protocol in 1994, but in 1998 this, too, collapsed, leading to a new phase that ended only after Savimbi was killed in eastern Angola in 2002.

Capital Flight amid War

A few examples, some more licit than others, illustrate how state wealth was appropriated by small numbers of people in wartime.

The exchange-rate merry-go-round

Perhaps the biggest legal mechanism involved Angola's multiple exchange rates. At the official rate, kwanzas were worth a lot more than on the black market. However, only privileged people could access goods at the privileged rate. For most Angolans imported goods remained expensive, while the small but politically crucial urban elite lived comfortably, buying flights to Lisbon for the black-market price of a few cases of beer, and those who were able to work the system on a large enough scale could make out like bandits. Of course, those privileges could always be withdrawn: it was not just officially sanctioned corruption, as some might describe it, but a useful instrument of political control.

In the 1990s (and still to a degree today) Angola's consumer imports were dominated by a few giants, the best known at the time being Angoalissar, Arosfram, and Golfrate. Many smaller-scale importers existed alongside them, including individuals, but most had weaker political connections and fewer opportunities to prosper. The large firms typically were operated by low-profile members of Lebanese and Indian diasporas who sourced goods from wide international procurement networks. Like anything of significance in Angola's non-oil economy, they relied on "silent partners" for the necessary political connections, who put up little capital themselves but took a generous cut of the profits.

Given the devastation that the war wreaked on local production, imports could be immensely profitable. A mid-level Lebanese businessman who first arrived in Angola in 1992 told me how he had imported goods to sell in Luanda's huge *Roque Santeiro* open-air market:

> Nobody else wanted to come here; the market was very thirsty. [From 1992 to 1996] it was like the old Wild West. If you brought in 100 containers, you would lose 20. But when you got your containers out, you were rich.[11]

Stolen goods, he added, were "the secret of Roque" in the war years: the most profitable items of all.

The importers were generating large volumes of kwanzas from their sales. They converted these into foreign currency in two main ways. The first was to use black-market currency traders called *kinguilas*, usually women, who sat on street corners with fat wads of kwanza notes that they would exchange for dollars with passers-by at rates far above the official rates. Their rates moved in sync, all across town, often within minutes. It was a mystery to most Angolans as to who controlled the *kinguilas* and kept the police and the robbers off their backs, but it was assumed they were closely networked with the presidentially-sanctioned import firms that supplied the kwanzas. The Lebanese businessman explained:

> You'd receive kwanzas from the market, and change them with the kinguilas, and take the dollars to the airport … Or you would exchange diamonds for the dollars. You give the guy here diamonds. He arranges for dollars to be transferred overseas to your account.

---

[11] Interview with a mid-ranking Lebanese importer, Luanda, 2004.

The latter transfers, he said, often involved deals between Shiite Muslim Lebanese merchants and Israeli operators in the diamond sector.

The second, bigger way for importers to obtain dollars—in this case, at the more favorable official exchange rate—was through the central bank. For those with access, this opened the possibility for large additional profits. Say, for example, that the official exchange rate was 100 kwanzas to the dollar, while the black-market rate was 300.[12] A well-connected import firm could sell a container of goods in the *Roque* market for, say, 300 million kwanzas in cash. It could take these kwanzas along with its import license from the Ministry of Commerce to the BNA and exchange them for dollars to import more goods. The BNA would then supply the importer with $3 million based on the official rate. The importer could then sell the $3 million worth of goods in *Roque* at the black-market exchange rate, receiving 900 million kwanzas in cash, effectively tripling its money, less transport costs, taxes, bribes, and so on. It could then take *this* money to the BNA, with the right paperwork, and do it all again.

The importer could also stash some of the dollars overseas, over-invoicing the value of the goods they then imported, using political connections and pay-offs to ensure the ruse went unchallenged. The resulting capital flight would have escaped measurement, since at the time Angola did not report import data to the IMF. If the firm imported enough to recoup its original kwanza investment, it could return to the BNA and repeat the operation, again stashing the excess dollars offshore—another variant of the exchange rate merry-go-round.

In theory, the profits were boundless, but there were limits. For one thing, the BNA only had limited foreign exchange for this purpose, so there was intense political competition for access at the official exchange rate. As one account put it:

> The foreign currency sold at this artificial rate had to be rationed. However, there was no rational, transparent way of doing this. In practice, the political authorities simply informed the banks which individuals should receive the foreign exchange on offer.
>
> (Hodges 2001, pp. 115–116)

Moreover, since the declared aim of the multiple exchange-rate system was to provide cheap imports to consumers, the importers were sometimes politically constrained to sell below full market prices. But while some urban consumers benefitted from the system, much of the subsidy was captured by the large importers and their political protectors. A 1995 IMF report noted "evidence that the exchange rate policy which has actually been implemented benefits in practice

---

[12] At times the discrepancy was even bigger. The IMF (1997, p. 9) reported that "the differential exceeded 1,000% during 1992 and 1993" before shrinking to 100% in 1994 and to less than 50% by 1996.

well-connected persons and/or businessmen at the cost of substantial financial losses for the central bank."[13] In addition, the most favored clients were able to borrow kwanzas at negative real interest rates and convert them into foreign exchange at the generous official exchange rate.[14]

Oil-backed loans and the Bermuda Triangle

In the era of shaky peace and renewed conflict, the Angolan budgetary process suffered gaping holes stemming from the interactions between oil, civil war, external finance, and the ways President dos Santos exercised power. The syndrome was sometimes dubbed the "Bermuda Triangle"—a place where money could disappear without a trace, located somewhere between Sonangol, the Finance Ministry, and the BNA.

The Bermuda Triangle was rooted in a system of oil-backed loans, initially seeded in the late 1980s as a way to finance Sonangol's share in oil developments off the Cabinda enclave. Sonangol did not always have the money readily available to pay for its share, and international bankers were unwilling to lend on reasonable terms to a Marxist-Leninist regime amid a civil war. So, an arrangement called the Cabinda Trust was set up, whereby (initially) the proceeds from the first four of every 16 oil cargoes shipped quarterly from the oilfields were earmarked to an offshore trust managed by Lloyds Bank in London, in return for which banks would supply loans. These flows bypassed the Finance Ministry and BNA, and that was part of the appeal from a lender's point of view: Sonangol was viewed as a far more competent and trustworthy partner.[15] These arrangements worked efficiently (in their own terms), and Angola developed a good track record of repayments over time at relatively high interest rates. New loans came rolling in, and an additional facility called the Soyo-Palanca Trust was established for oil cargoes from outside Cabinda.

The government soon began to use these loans to finance projects and spending outside the oil industry. The oil-backed loan arrangements continued after the trusts were discontinued, with Sonangol as the anchor. After the war resumed in 1992, the government found that it could deploy these "pre-financing" arrangements for weapons purchases and other state priorities, compensating for

---

[13] Quoted by Hodges (2003, p. 132).

[14] A 1996 World Bank report stated: "The credit allocations mirror those of foreign exchange through the official market and are often tied to foreign exchange trading operations. While in theory the sale of foreign exchange would involve the payments of counterpart funds in Kwanza, some clients obtain bank credit (at negative real interest rates) to pay for the already subsidised foreign exchange." Quoted in Hodges (2001, p. 118).

[15] On the oil cargoes and the Cabinda Trust, see Global Trade Review (2007). It is not clear if these extra-budgetary operations were legal at the time. Even after Angola promulgated Decree 30/95 in 1995 mandating that all oil revenues should be deposited in BNA accounts, these extra-budgetary practices continued.

the government's loss of its former military backers after the demise of the Soviet Union. Each oil-backed loan, typically for several hundred million dollars, was provided by a syndicate of international banks—often mainstream British, American, French, Swiss, and Dutch financial institutions.[16]

The very feature that made these arrangements attractive for bankers and President dos Santos—the fact that they were routed outside the Angolan financial system and instead co-managed by the "efficient" Sonangol—worsened the budgetary holes. The Finance Ministry, central bank and other ministries had no direct access to these flows—and little idea how the money was coming or going. The system helped President dos Santos to play divide-and-rule with different power centers. The IMF (2014, p. 8) refers to the Bermuda Triangle as "quasi-fiscal operations." Soares de Oliveira (2007, p. 607) calls it Angola's "parallel state."

A 1995 IMF report described the system's astonishing scale:

> About 40 percent of estimated expenditure up till September was carried out bypassing the Treasury, largely financed by petroleum revenues that were also outside the Treasury's purview.... Besides the so-called petroleum transactions, there was also a high level of expenditures which did not follow the established procedures... The mission estimates that the total expenditure outside the normal procedures for Treasury operations amounts to about 64 percent of total expenditure up to September.[17]

At the same time, the BNA was making payments without approval from the Finance Ministry, although in theory all oil revenues ought to have been deposited in the Treasury's single account at the BNA.

The missing billions were a public relations disaster for the Angolan government. Many observers assumed that all this money was stolen, but that is not quite accurate. The opacity, complexity, and fragmentation undoubtedly meant plenty ended in personal accounts. But a substantial chunk, perhaps even most of it, went to pay for the Angolan state's (presidency-directed) spending priorities, including wartime arms purchases, as in the "Angolagate" affair described below.

By the early 2000s, as oil prices fell towards their 1990 level, almost all of Sonangol's share in oil cargoes was earmarked for payments to oil-backed pre-financing arrangements. The government had to find new loans to stay afloat, like an addict seeking the next fix.

Under great pressure, the government (which was again at war) reached an agreement in 2000 with the IMF with a laundry list of reform promises, including a diagnostic study of the oil sector. This was a political compromise: it was not a full audit of all the squirrelly flows that were taking place, but a simpler comparison between how much oil revenue was generated and how much ended up

---

[16] See Economist Intelligence Unit (1999, p. 29); Economist Intelligence Unit (2002, pp. 32–33); and Economist Intelligence Unit (2003, p. 30).

[17] Quoted by Global Witness (1999, p. 16). See also Hodges (2001, p. 113).

being deposited in the BNA. KPMG won the $1.6 million contract and completed its first diagnostic report in 2002, followed by a series of quarterly reports.

Although the reports are poorly written and hard to untangle, they show the depth of inconsistencies in government accounts. For example, KPMG found a $2–$2.6 billion discrepancy between what the Finance Ministry said it received in oil revenues and what the BNA reported it received in 2000 alone.[18] While the Finance Ministry recorded inflows even before they had been received, the BNA recorded them only on arrival, so that paper transactions could not be reconciled. By January 2001 Sonangol had stopped paying into the BNA accounts, complaining that the BNA was delaying releasing the requisite sums in kwanzas, so that by the time it received the money, inflation had eaten into it. There were discrepancies in the figures for physical oil flows, too.

The IMF, in sharply critical staff reports in 2002 and 2003, estimated that Angola could not account for a total $4.2 billion from 1997 to 2002—equivalent to almost 10% of GDP. The unaccounted money was roughly the same size as Angola's total social spending for the period (Human Rights Watch 2004, p. 33).[19]

Angolagate

In the late 1990s, a massive financial scandal engulfed France after Eva Joly, an investigating magistrate in Paris, began probing the French state oil company Elf Aquitaine and steadily unearthed what turned into Europe's biggest corruption case since the Second World War. Elf's extensive operations in Africa, including in Angola, were used as a giant offshore slush fund outside the French budgetary system to channel covert financing to the main political parties in France, for off-the-books activities of the French intelligence services, and for channeling bribes around the world on behalf of major French corporations.[20] One tentacle of the Elf Affair was the "Angolagate" scandal.

When Angola returned to war in 1992, the MPLA government, under an international arms embargo, found little appetite in the international community to help. So, in some desperation, it turned to the French networks for help in securing weapons. Pierre Falcone, a French businessman involved in the arms trade, and Arkady Gaydamak, a Soviet-born financier, helped put together two arms

---

[18] The full title of what became known as the "Oil Diagnostic" study—which was in fact a series of reports—was "*Financial Diagnostic and Monitoring of the State Oil Revenues*," carried out by KPMG for the Ministry of Finance. The terms of reference for the diagnostic study stated: "The consultants [KPMG] shall *not* be expected or required to consider or investigate or conduct any form of enquiry into the conduct, practices, honesty, integrity or standards of, or nature or quality of work performed by, any person who has or may have had, any involvement in or connection with, directly or indirectly, the facts, matters, circumstances or events which shall be diagnosed, monitored, studied, assessed or considered by the consultants during the performance of these services." For a more detailed discussion of the "Oil Diagnostic," see Human Rights Watch (2004).

[19] Subsequent reconciliation exercises spurred by the IMF reduced these discrepancies over time.

[20] For a detailed account in English of the Elf affair, see Shaxson (2007a, Chapter 5).

deals—one for $47 million in 1993 and then a second for $563 million in 1994—through a Slovak armaments company. From 1993 to 1998, a total of $790 million in arms were purchased, with oil-backed loans arranged by the French bank Paribas (now BNP Paribas) and secured by future oil shipments by Sonangol.[21]

Kickbacks were paid to key Angolan, French and other players.[22] In October 2009, a Paris court found 36 people guilty of criminal activities in the affair, including Falcone, who was convicted of influence peddling, arms trafficking and misuse of corporate assets, and Gaydamak, who was convicted *in absentia* of arms trafficking, influence peddling and money laundering. Both men were sentenced to six years in jail.[23] A French appeals court subsequently reduced their terms, on the grounds that the sales did not constitute arms trafficking since they were conducted under an Angolan government mandate.[24] In November 2015 Gaydamak, who had hitherto been a fugitive from the remaining three-year jail term, handed himself in to French authorities in Paris (*Le Monde* 2015).

The Angola-Russia debt deal

Gaydamak and Falcone were also middlemen in a deal to restructure $5 billion in Angolan debts to Russia, in the course of which Angolan and foreign private individuals, in league with western commodity trading firms, banks, and of course tax havens, siphoned off a large share of the payments. I obtained a partial explanation regarding some of the flows in a 2005 interview with Gaydamak in Moscow, but a more detailed analysis subsequently appeared in a 2013 report published by two non-governmental organizations, UK-based Corruption Watch and Angola-based Associação Mãos Livres.[25]

At the end of the Cold War, the debts that Angola had incurred to the former Soviet Union accrued to Russia. President dos Santos turned to Gaydamak and Falcone to help negotiate an agreement to reschedule them. Under a deal in November 1996 Russia cut Angola's debts to $1.5 billion, writing off the rest, and Angola agreed to repay this amount in instalments, after a five-year grace period, between 2001 and 2016. Angola also agreed to pay $1.39 billion in interest accrued over the full 20-year period, bringing the total to $2.9 billion, but if Angola paid off the debts before the end of the grace period, the interest would be forgiven.[26]

---

[21] Global Witness (2002, p. 6). This report outlines the Angolagate scandal in greater detail.

[22] See *Keeping Foreign Corruption out of the United States: Four Case Histories,* US Senate Permanent Subcommittee on investigations, February 4, 2010, especially the section beginning on p. 247.

[23] See, for instance, Robert-Diard (2009), AFP (2009), Shirbon (2009) and France 24 (2009).

[24] Associated Press/Haaretz (2011) and BBC (2011).

[25] Associação Mãos Livres and Corruption Watch UK (2013). The details in this section are drawn principally from this report unless otherwise indicated.

[26] Interview with Gaydamak on September 16, 2005. "Everything was [to be] paid to the Russian federation before the end of the grace period," Gaydamak told me. "It was very important. If not, we should pay interest."

The parties agreed to a mechanism that was familiar to some Russian businesses: promissory notes that entitle the holder of the note to receive a given amount of money at a particular date. In January 1997 the BNA issued 31 notes to Russia, each with a face value of $48.4 million, for $1.5 billion in total. Every time Angola made an (oil-backed) debt repayment, Russia would redeem the appropriate number of notes to Angola along with a certificate of repayment.

Days after the November 1996 deal, Gaydamak and Falcone formed a shell company called Abalone Investments in the Isle of Man, a British tax haven. The following May, Russia granted Abalone an option to buy all the Angolan promissory notes at half their face value. That same month, Sonangol reached a separate deal with Abalone in which it agreed to buy all the notes and certificates by 2006 at their full $1.5 billion face value—implying a $750 million windfall profit for this Isle of Man shell company.[27] Why Russia offered these favorable terms to Abalone and not directly to the Angolans was never fully explained.[28] Gaydamak told me in 2005 that "I organized this affair for both sides from the beginning."

The UK affiliate of the commodities trading company, Glencore, received the Angolan oil cargoes and arranged for the funds to transfer to Abalone,[29] via Abalone's escrow account at Société de Banque Suisse (SBS, now the Swiss bank UBS).

Abalone then went further. According to Corruption Watch and Associação Mãos Livres, the agreements were modified in August 1999 so that Abalone could now pay Russia not in cash, but in high-interest Russian debt instruments (which Gaydamak told me he had been buying since 1997); at the time they were trading at 10–30% of face value in the Wild West Russian secondary debt markets. Russia, however, accepted them from Abalone at full face value, generating another round of big profits, this time at the Russian government's expense.

In December 2000, as the Angolagate investigations in Paris progressed, Falcone was arrested by French police, and the following month Gaydamak became a fugitive from an international arrest warrant issued by France.[30] In February 2001, Swiss authorities froze the promissory notes (Associação Mãos Livres/Corruption Watch UK 2013, p. 13).

[27] Associação Mãos Livres and Corruption Watch UK (2013) reported that although Abalone had the right to levy interest as well, in the end Angola was not forced to pay it.

[28] Gaydamak explained Russia's willingness to sell the notes to Abalone by saying that the debts of war-ravaged Angola were then worth just 5–15 cents on the dollar, and that the $750 million payment to Russia "in money equivalent" was a tremendously good deal for Russia. "It's considered probably the world's best rescheduling… everything was in accordance with the rules." This begs the question of why the Angolan government was willing to pay the full amount to Abalone.

[29] "From all appearances, Glencore seems closer to being an organiser for the Debt Deal than a mere retail financial services provider," concluded Associação Mãos Livres and Corruption Watch UK (2013, p. 28).

[30] See Associação Mãos Livres/Corruption Watch UK (2013, p. 49); Global Witness (2004, p. 40); and Human Rights Watch (2001).

Gaydamak persisted, however. He opened a new account at the Russian Commercial Bank in the offshore haven of Cyprus, which received a further $618 million from Sonangol between March and August 2001. The name on this account, Sberinvest, was almost identical to "Sberinvest Moscow," Russia's official banking agent for the deal—apparently fooling other parties into thinking that this private account was an official Russian one.[31] Payments then went from that account to various entities, including some beneficially owned by Gaydamak (Associação Mãos Livres and Corruption Watch UK 2013, pp. 50–56). In theory, the $618 million could have been enough to extinguish the remaining debts, but the Corruption Watch and Associação Mãos Livres report said that the Cyprus account paid Russia for only seven of the remaining 15 notes, leaving eight notes unpaid—though Gaydamak wrote to the Angolans in 2004 to tell them that the Russian debt had been paid in full (ibid., p. 53).

In the end, after a meeting in Moscow in 2005, Angola agreed to pay Russia an additional $387 million to retire the eight unredeemed notes. Gaydamak was supposed to repay part of this money, but it is unclear if he did so. As an odd postscript, Gaydamak then seems to have lost control of the money, because his financial administrators "did such a good job in hiding Gaydamak's links to the funds that he cannot now prove he is their 'actual' (beneficial) owner" (ibid., p. 62).

Associação Mãos Livres and Corruption Watch UK (2013, pp. 14, 55) estimated that had Angola paid the funds directly to Russia, the government would have saved at least $823 million (equivalent to more than 10% of Angolan GDP in 1996), while Russia could have received an extra $750 million.

Where did the money go? Citing investigations by the French and Swiss authorities, Corruption Watch and Associação Mãos Livres report that Abalone transferred large amounts from the funds it received to an array of recipients, including other shell companies belonging to Gaydamak ($138 million), Falcone ($125 million), Angolan President dos Santos ($36 million), Angolan ambassador Elísio de Figueiredo ($18 million), former Sonangol CEO Joaquim David ($13 million), and then Director-General of Sonangol UK, José Paiva ($4 million).[32]

It would be hard to find a better or more colorful example of a transnational plunder network.

---

[31] Associação Mãos Livres/Corruption Watch UK (2013, p. 13) cites "later evidence" suggesting that this name was chosen to fool the Angolans into paying the money straight into Gaydamak's private account. Gaydamak reportedly undertook this without the knowledge of Falcone, who later unsuccessfully sued in Israeli courts for cutting him out of the deal (ibid., pp. 14, 50; see also Roth 2008 and Roth 2011).

[32] Associação Mãos Livres and Corruption Watch UK (2013, pp. 12–18). See also Cabeche and Forrest (2013). For a list of banks, tax havens and companies involved in the payments, most of which were located in Switzerland, Cyprus, Luxembourg, Israel, Panama and Moscow, see Shaxson (2021, Annex E).

The Aguinaldo Jaime affair

An investigation conducted by the US Senate Permanent Subcommittee on Investigations, the findings of which were published in 2010, provides evidence that efforts to prevent state looting can prove effective. In 2002 BNA governor Aguinaldo Jaime ordered a transfer of $50 million from a Central Bank account at Citigroup in London to a private Bank of America account in California that had been opened in the name of a US corporation called MSA, Inc, a company officially set up to provide consulting and investment management services (US Senate Permanent Subcommittee on Investigations 2010, p. 269). Governor Jaime and a Togolese citizen, Mehenou Satou Amouzou, were co-signatories on the MSA account. Bank of America initially accepted the transfer, but then became suspicious and returned the funds to Citibank.

Two months later, Jaime instructed Citibank London to wire $50 million to HSBC Equator Bank in London and opened a new BNA account with himself as sole signatory at HSBC USA in New York. He then instructed HSBC to use the funds to buy $50 million in US Treasury Bills, and to transfer these to a personal securities account at Wells Fargo. The latter bank became suspicious, too, and returned the funds. Jaime tried again to transfer the securities to a personal account in another US bank. This attempt failed, too. After Jaime was replaced as BNA governor, the new governor ordered the funds returned to the BNA.

The US Senate report (ibid.) revealed an international network of intermediaries involved including a Florida company, a London-based broker "with alleged access to a secretive Swiss trading group," a purported principal in that group; and a California attorney who owned a Nevada company involved in a transfer. It also revealed that some banks seemed less vigilant than others:

> Bank of America and Wells Fargo personnel reacted quickly to possible signs of a suspicious transaction and reversed the $50 million transfer; Citibank reacted less quickly but eventually responded by ending its banking relationship, not only with the BNA, but with all government entities, including Sonangol.

> In contrast, HSBC personnel facilitated multiple wire transfers of the $50 million and the related Treasury bills in response to the instructions of a single BNA official, despite concerns about sending government assets to a private individual's account, until a compliance officer warned about a possible scam. HSBC has not only continued to provide banking services to the BNA in Angola and London but may also be providing the Angolan Central Bank with offshore accounts in the Bahamas.

(ibid., p. 299)

This fits a longstanding pattern of London and British banks tolerating greater levels of suspicious activity than their US counterparts, the result of an unwritten policy of turning a blind eye to foreign malfeasance in order to attract financial activity to the City of London.[33] Indeed, if taken together with its satellite tax havens in its Overseas Territories and Crown Dependencies, Britain and its City of London financial center could be called the world's most important center for offshore finance.[34]

The "Golden Decade"

While these financial flows swirled internationally, the Angolan army managed to isolate the UNITA rebel leadership in eastern Angola. It tracked Jonas Savimbi in Moxico province, heading for the relative safety of the Zambian border. In February 2002 an Angolan army unit caught up with him in a grassland firefight, killing him along with 21 followers. The Angolan civil war was finally over.

At the same time, a series of large deep-water oilfields was starting up. Angolan oil production more than doubled in the next six years, from around 900,000 bpd in 2002 to 1.9 million in 2008, a period during which world oil prices more than trebled. Both Angolan production and world prices remained at a high plateau until about 2014. During the 12-year period from 2002 to 2014, Angola's "golden decade," the country exported around $520 billion of oil, with the government receiving roughly half of that amount as state revenue. This postwar era was Angola's big chance for oil-fueled development. And Angola's leaders blew it.

A top-down development model

In a total population of roughly 30 million, the main domestic constituency of the Angolan regime was a few hundred families. The regime's secondary constituency was the urbanized middle class, numbering perhaps a million people. In distant third place, barely visible to top decision-makers, were the urban poor, and even behind them is the country's large agricultural population.

The national development model that prevailed in this period—widely accepted by the Angolan elites and most of the Angolan media—was one of authoritarian,

---

[33] See Shaxson (2018), Chapter 7. See also Corruption Watch (2019) and Thompson (2019).

[34] This can be measured in many ways. The Tax Justice Network's Financial Secrecy Index, a ranking of global "secrecy jurisdictions" (meaning, tax havens that provide financial secrecy laws for offshore money), states that "If the UK and its network of Overseas Territories and Crown Dependencies were treated as a single entity, this UK spider's web would rank first on the index," available at https://fsi.taxjustice.net/en/#:~:text=Introduction-,Introduction,financial%20flows%20or%20 capital%20flight (accessed on August 5, 2020).

state-driven, oil-financed modernization. It was symbolized by the gigantic shopping mall, the urban development on Luanda's seafront, the clearing of large and messy informal markets to make way for upper-class condominiums, and in the countryside the promotion of large-scale agro-industries roughly displacing many peasant farmers (Vines et al. 2005).

Oil fueled this elitist vision. Angola's leaders remained focused on the urban centers, above all Luanda, and while they rhetorically espoused regional and economic diversification and agricultural growth, in reality they all but scorned the "backward" agricultural hinterlands. The model turned resolutely outwards towards London, Paris, Lisbon, Miami, and New York, towards globalized finance with its sophisticated apparatus of special purpose vehicles, hedge funds, private equity firms, tax havens, and wealth management—all vehicles for capital flight.[35] Many showcase projects were driven less by the desire to provide public goods than by the possibilities for personal enrichment and the chance to stash the winnings offshore.

This shiny vision served as a legitimizing ideology for much of the large-scale capital flight Angola has suffered over the years.

Angola's post-war reconstruction phase also coincided with the Chinese government's pivot towards Africa, particularly mineral-rich countries like Angola. An "Angola model" of Chinese-led reconstruction and development emerged, based on a fairly straightforward resources-for-infrastructure swap (Corkin 2011) and consistent with the elitist, top-down Angolan development vision. Angola would pledge oil cargoes, and China would provide credit lines for construction projects, with 70% of the contracts going to Chinese corporations. Chinese state media reported in 2017 that China had cumulatively invested close to $50 billion in Angola (Xinhuanet 2017).

Meanwhile, as Angola's chaotic conditions of war gave way to oil-fueled peace after 2002, state finances gradually improved. Educated Angolans returned home to occupy positions in the Finance Ministry, central bank, and other state bodies, and technical assistance from the IMF and others strengthened record-keeping. As mentioned above, the IMF found a "large unexplained residual" in the government's fiscal accounts, totaling $31.4 billion for the years 2007–2010, equivalent to an astonishing 25% of Angolan GDP.[36] In 2015 the IMF reported that the discrepancies were mostly ironed out by incorporating Sonangol's activities into

---

[35] For history, see Shaxson (2012, Chapter 6).

[36] IMF (2011, p. 9, Box 2), and IMF (2014, p. 9). "Most of the difference between the oil revenue accrued to the government and the amount effectively deposited in the Treasury single account is explained by the amount retained by Sonangol to finance quasi-fiscal operations and the amount deposited in escrow accounts for servicing external credit lines," the IMF (2014, p. 10) observed. The $31.4 billion represented what the IMF called "a discrepancy between the revenue, expenditure, and external financing recorded by the Ministry of Finance and domestic financing to the government, based on central bank data."

the annual budget. Balanced against such improvements in accounting, however, dramatically higher oil revenues enhanced opportunities for capital flight.

Various avenues for possible capital flight need to be considered, to understand the discrepancies better.

Oil smuggling?

Smuggled oil could potentially result in capital flight on an enormous scale. In Nigeria's Niger Delta, for example, politically networked criminal groups have been able to tap oil flows without detection or interdiction (see Chapter 6 in this volume). Angola is different, however, because almost all its exports come from offshore platforms operated mostly by large foreign oil majors. The diversion of oil cargoes from these platforms would be difficult. The international oil companies could not be kept in the dark, and they would not be happy about it. Moreover, diversions quickly would have come to the president's attention. Dos Santos had a long track record of tolerating "controlled enrichment" in his patronage networks, but at the same time he was concerned to protect Sonangol's hard-earned reputation as a center of excellence, and he would have been unlikely to abide oil smuggling as a means of chaotic personal enrichment.[37]

Missing oil money

Although we can be fairly sure that the presidency (and the international oil companies) could ascertain exactly how much oil flowed from every Angolan oilfield, the same cannot be said for the Finance Ministry, the BNA, or other state bodies, in terms of the money flows where oil goes missing not physically, but financially.

Consider, for instance, contrasting estimates for Angolan oil production in 2008, one from the Petroleum Ministry and the other from the Finance Ministry: the former reported 675 million barrels, the latter reported 588 million.[38] The size of the discrepancy—87 million barrels (worth more than $600 million at the time), well over 10% of total production by either estimate—rules out timing of reporting of year-end shipments as the explanation.[39]

---

[37] A related possibility is mismeasurement—that is, oil companies shipping quantities of oil that exceed the volumes recorded for official purposes—but I have not seen indications that this happened in Angola, and again dos Santos would have likely taken a dim view of it. And once the volume of oil is known, the purchase price could be pinpointed fairly accurately based on international oil prices and shipment dates.

[38] Global Witness (2011, p. 17). International sources likewise report inconsistent data (ibid., p. 16).

[39] For another more recent discrepancy, where Finance Ministry records of detailed oil production do not match those published by BP, see Shaxson (2021, Annex G).

In the case of Angola, a lack of data rules out direct comparisons between the country's recorded exports and the imports recorded by its trading partners (see Chapter 2 in this volume). Any oil revenue that went unrecorded on the books of the BNA would therefore constitute unmeasured capital flight.

Signature bonuses

A signature bonus is an upfront payment by oil companies to the government upon signature of a license to explore a block of territory.[40] A 2002 report by the International Consortium of Investigative Journalists (ICIJ) tracked one such payment: a $13.7 million signature bonus from Marathon Oil Company paid into a Sonangol account in the Channel Island of Jersey in July 2000, and then transferred on the same day to another Sonangol account in an unknown location.[41] "Most or all of the money goes to offshore bank accounts and disappears somewhere," explained an accountant familiar with the diagnostic study being conducted at the time by KPMG, so that dollars were "bypassing the central bank" (quoted by Van Niekerk and Peterson 2002).

The bonuses grew larger during Angola's golden decade of oil-fueled peace.[42] A 2011 report by Global Witness and the Open Society Initiative for Southern Africa compared known payments by the oil companies to what was recorded as revenue in government budget data, and found wide discrepancies. In 2006, for instance, of more than $3 billion in known signature bonus payments, the government budget reported only $1 billion in revenue (Global Witness (2011, pp. 38–39).

On the signing of an exploration or production contract, Sonangol also receives one-off "social contributions," which are supposed to be earmarked for worthy projects. The implementation of these projects has long been controversial too (see, for example, Reuters 2016).

The main oil revenue flows

More important than upfront bonuses are the flows of revenue from producing oilfields. Each oil license or "Block" (which may contain several oilfields, clustered into development areas) is operated by a "Contractor Group" nearly

---

[40] There are other bonuses too: exploration bonuses, commercial discovery bonuses, first oil bonuses, contract renewal bonuses, and more.

[41] Van Niekerk and Peterson (2002). See also Global Witness (2004, p. 49).

[42] For examples and further discussion, see Shaxson (2021).

always involving international companies like BP, Exxon, Chevron or Total, sometimes with Sonangol as an equity partner in the group. Lesser-known Angolan or international companies sometimes are minority partners.[43]

Oil revenues flow in four main streams:

i) "Cost oil" goes to the contractor group to repay the costs of exploration, development and running the oilfield, plus an "uplift" factor. If Sonangol is an equity partner in the block, it receives its share.

ii) A share of "Profit oil" goes to the contractor group. When Sonangol is an equity partner, it again receives its share.

iii) The remainder of the "Profit oil" goes to Sonangol acting as concessionaire for the Angolan state.[44]

iv) Taxes are paid in dollars or kwanzas to the Finance Ministry's Single Treasury Account at the BNA.

In theory, bribes paid into offshore accounts or other inducements could be applied to shift the nominal share of profit oil in the favor of foreign partners. This has happened in some African countries, notably in the Elf Affair.[45] I found no evidence that the oil majors engaged in such activities systematically in Angola.[46]

The flows of physical oil to Sonangol (as equity partner and as concessionaire) are more likely candidates as sources of capital flight. An experienced businessman described the possibilities:

> Sonangol will have contracts selling in the international market. You will have middlemen who take a cut. If you are favored enough to be able to sell oil for Sonangol, you'll be paid by Sonangol and you will probably be paid by the other side. There will be Angolan trading companies that are nominally foreign-based but owned by Angolans: they will be trading. That's already offshore money. You take a cut before it arrives in Angola.[47]

Sonangol has international trading offices in London, Houston, Singapore, and China to market its share of crude oil. The trading offices are in constant touch with other oil traders and financial institutions offering swaps and oil-related financial derivatives. These open up possibilities for off-the-books flows that would be easy to keep out of BNA or Finance Ministry data (and therefore outside the scope of

---

[43] For details and examples, see Shaxson (2021, Table 5 and Annex B).

[44] Profit oil is divided between the contractor group and the Angolan state is on a sliding scale and depends on many factors including oil prices. An example is provided by the US Securities & Exchange Commission (undated).

[45] See, for instance, Shaxson (2007a, Chapter 6).

[46] Bribery could also take place to influence the *awards* of oil licenses. Anecdotally, I once heard of such an instance in Angola, but that was seen as an anomaly at the time.

[47] Interview with a European businessman.

capital flight measurements). An example would be secret price-hedging contracts where Sonangol pays the bill in the event of contract losses, while any gains from price movements could be reaped by private Angolan players as offshore flows from the hedging counterparty.

Investment flows in the oil sector

It has long been known that capital flight has been fueled in part by inflows of capital in the form of external borrowing.[48] Similarly, research has shown that a rise in *foreign investment* inflows into African countries is often accompanied by a rise in capital flight, a link that appears to be particularly strong in resource-rich countries, especially oil producers (Ndikumana and Sarr 2019). The main potential channel for capital flight originating from foreign direct investment (FDI) as well as from external borrowing is indirect: some of the resources provided to the Angolan government or private sector are then transferred abroad illicitly through the mechanisms described in this chapter.

Another possibility is round tripping whereby Angolans take capital offshore and then bring it back into Angola disguised as FDI because foreign capital may receive preferential treatment over domestic capital. Profits on such FDI could then be remitted overseas through official channels (and not measured as capital flight). In Angola's case, however, most FDI has come from western oil companies.

The black box of "cost oil"

The cost oil component in Angolan oil contracts, amounting to tens of billions of dollars in recent years, is extremely opaque to outsiders and possibly a most fruitful source of capital flight. The oil majors outsource many of the nuts and bolts of building and developing oilfields to independent firms that provide oil drilling rigs, offshore production and storage facilities, piping, catering, air transport, sea transport, security, insurance and other services. In the case of Angola, these often involve joint ventures between Sonangol and foreign companies.[49] While oil majors generally try to keep costs down (so as to maximize the profit oil), the outsourcing arrangements create ample possibilities for diversion of funds.

Take, for example, the case of Weatherford International, a Houston-based oil services company. In a complaint that resulted in a November 2013 plea agreement, the US Securities and Exchange Commission (SEC) charged the firm with violating the US Foreign Corrupt Practices Act (FCPA) by authorizing bribes and

---

[48] See, for example, Boyce (1992) and Ndikumana and Boyce (2003, 2011).
[49] See Shaxson (2021, Annex A) for a detailed account.

other improper services for foreign officials. The SEC stated that a Weatherford subsidiary retained a Swiss freight-forwarding and logistics services company to pay bribes to a Sonangol official, to secure renewal of a contract to provide services to oil operations off Cabinda. According to the complaint, Weatherford Services Ltd (WSL), a Bermuda-registered subsidiary of Weatherford, "produced sham work orders for consulting services that the Swiss Agent never performed, and the Swiss Agent, in turn, generated sham invoices for those same non-existent services" (US SEC 2013, p. 6).[50] The Swiss firm then passed the money, minus a commission, to the Angolan official in cash or wire transfer. The SEC put Weatherford's "profits from increased pricing" in the contract at $11.7 million (ibid.).

The same SEC complaint outlined a second bribery scheme by which Weatherford obtained control of "one hundred percent of the Angolan well screens market." (Well screens filter out sands that otherwise would damage oil wells.) To do so, a Weatherford subsidiary "entered into a joint venture in Angola with two local entities selected by the Sonangol officials," one controlled by the Sonangol officials themselves and the other by a relative of an Angolan government minister, neither of which contributed personnel, expertise, or capital to the ventures (ibid., pp. 6–7).

After pleading guilty, Weatherford agreed to pay $87.2 million in criminal penalties for these and other violations of the FCPA (US Department of Justice 2013). In announcing the agreement, the acting Assistant Attorney General of the Justice Department's criminal division commented, "This case demonstrates how loose controls and an anemic compliance environment can foster foreign bribery and fraud by a company's subsidiaries around the globe" (ibid.).

In another case, the US oil services giant Halliburton agreed in 2017 to pay $29.2 million to settle an SEC action charging the firm with violations of the FCPA. Under pressure from Sonangol to meet local content requirements, Halliburton had entered into an agreement with "a local Angolan company owned by a former Halliburton employee who was a friend and neighbor of the government official who would ultimately approve the award of the contracts" (US SEC 2017, p. 2). Halliburton then outsourced over $13 million of work to the firm but "did not receive any meaningful services" in return (ibid., p. 7).[51] Sonangol meanwhile awarded seven subcontracts to Halliburton from which the firm obtained "ill-gotten gains" amounting to $14 million (ibid., p. 9).

---

[50] See also United States of America v. Weatherford Services, International (2013, p. 29).

[51] In the end the Angolan firm received only $3.7 million as monthly payments were interrupted in April 2011 after allegations of impropriety began to surface.

Indigenous oil companies and their foreign partners

The "Angolanization" of the country's oil sector involved indigenous companies not only in oil services and downstream operations, but also as direct stakeholders in upstream oil licenses. Financing, deploying and managing oil rigs and other offshore oil exploration and production infrastructure requires more technical competence and capital than, say, providing catering or transport services to oil operators. Before the late 1990s President dos Santos had been somewhat reluctant to bring politically connected companies into upstream oil production, aware of adverse impact this could have on Sonangol's reputation for competence (and thus its access to large-scale external borrowing). A few Angolan companies have acquired the necessary expertise. For example, Somoil is regarded in oil industry circles as a relatively serious and competent player—even though its shareholders, according to media reports, include well-connected Angolan politicians and former Sonangol officials (Africa Energy Intelligence 2018). However, the patronage system raised its profile as the dos Santos era progressed, and a number of new players now populate the oil licenses as minority partners, with few obvious qualifications other than their political connections.

A first wave came in the late 1990s with two major awards in Angolan ultra-deep waters: a 20% stake for a company called Prodev in Block 32 operated by Elf; and stakes of 10% and 5% to companies called Falcon Oil (Panama) and Naphtha, respectively, in Block 33 operated by Exxon. These stakes were forced onto the oil majors. BP successfully avoided taking a "mystery partner" in its Block 31; oil sector sources told me at the time that BP had had to fight hard to resist using powerful local connections. Falcon was widely reported to be linked to the arms dealer Pierre Falcone and to António "Mosquito" Mbakassy, a local Angolan businessman; Naptha was described as being part of a "complex" web of ownership involving Israeli military interests; and Prodev also reportedly had military connections.[52] These valuable awards reflected Angola's dire military situation at the time, though it seems likely that members of the presidential circle made money, too. Since then, a number of other companies have appeared in the Angolan oil exploration and production licenses, including firms intertwined in corruption scandals in Portugal, Brazil, and the United States, and with politically well-placed Angolans.[53]

---

[52] These connections were widely reported at the time. See, for instance, Global Witness (1999, p. 13). A filing at Companies House UK for Falcon Oil Holding Angola S.A., available at https://beta.companieshouse.gov.uk/company/FC031019/filing-history (company registered October 11, 2012, file accessed on January 22, 2020) lists the company secretary as Mrs. Eduarda Mosquito-Mbakassy, under the authority of Mr. Antonio Mosquito.

[53] For details, see Shaxson (2021).

Sonangol and Its Foreign Partners

A deeper dive into Sonangol's universe of foreign partnerships illustrates the role of transnational networks in plundering Africa's wealth.

Sonangol joint ventures

Sonangol joint ventures (JVs) with foreign oil services firms took off after the massive deep-water oil discoveries of the 1990s brought about a rise in scale and complexity of extraction operations. Three main justifications were offered for the joint ventures: first, to profit from equity participations in oil services; second, to increase local content and Angolan expertise and training; and third, perhaps most importantly, to keep tabs on what foreign firms were up to. Like many oil-producing countries, Angola from the beginning has been suspicious that the international oil companies and international oil service companies have been profiting from inflated contracts in the cost base, transfer mispricing, and other financial deceptions that leave less revenue for the state.

On my visit to Luanda in 2017, Arnaldo Lago de Carvalho, an outspoken Angolan official involved in the oil services industry, explained the system bluntly:

> They invested in tankers, rigs: everything you can imagine. That allowed them to appoint employees of Sonangol as directors of most of these JVs. Then, you have [them] partnering with members of the top echelons of this country, not just Sonangol... these were vehicles to give money to these people.[54]

The same model was extended to other sectors of the Angolan economy unrelated to oil. To the extent that Sonangol provided its own capital and expertise to the joint ventures, they could be regarded as normal risk-taking business operations. But when politically well-connected individuals, with Sonangol's assistance, invested nothing and took a slice of the profits, the effect was pure rent-seeking. "The laudable desire to build a domestic business class led to the creation of essentially parasitical positions," remarked Ricardo Soares de Oliveira (2007, p. 608), benefiting "a veritable who's who of the *Futungo* [the presidency] and the upper ranks of the bureaucracy, the military, the party, and their families."

Details on the revenues flowing through Sonangol's JVs are not published. Some JVs provide snippets of information on bare-bones websites, but often it is impossible to find basic information on shareholdings or even the identities of partners. Will-o'-the-wisp subsidiaries located in tax havens appear on public and leaked databases, each of them raising new clouds of questions. A few case studies will illustrate the remarkable complexity of Sonangol's sprawling international

---

[54] Arnaldo de Carvalho, interviewed in Luanda, October 11, 2017.

structure, with its interlocking shareholdings and financial flows among offshore entities.

Puma Energy, Trafigura, and General Dino

Sonangol's (2016) accounts listed a 27.9% shareholding, valued at around US$600 million, in a firm called Puma Energy Holdings, in partnership with the Singapore-incorporated global commodities trading firm Trafigura, which holds 49.6%, and others.[55] This implies that Puma's total worth was about $2 billion. Puma operates midstream and downstream hydrocarbons facilities in 48 countries (Puma Energy 2015).[56] Puma has a duopoly with Sonangol itself for petrol stations in Angola, while according to the *Financial Times* Trafigura had a "near-monopoly" over the supply of diesel and gasoline into the country (Hume and Sheppard 2016).

Puma's board of governors, according to the 2017 prospectus, includes four officers in the Trafigura constellation and three officers linked to Angola (Puma Energy 2017, p. 139): Sarju Raikundalia, who had been put in charge of Sonangol's financial affairs by Isabel dos Santos (Verde 2016), and was dismissed in November 2017 when Isabel dos Santos was ousted as head of Sonangol; João dos Santos, a member of Sonangol's board of governors; and Leopoldino Fragoso do Nascimento, known to Angolans as "General Dino," one of the most influential people in president dos Santos' inner circle, who served as chief adviser to General Helder Vieira Días "Kopelipa," head of the presidency's feared *Casa Militar*.[57]

Puma's other main shareholder, with a 15.4% holding, is Cochan LLC, based in the Marshall Islands and owned by General Dino. Cochan's website describes it as "one of the main business groups in Angola," with a diversified investment portfolio, "established in 2009 by businessman Leopoldino Fragoso do Nascimento."[58] Cochan also reported that it had a 50-50 joint venture shareholding with Trafigura in an Angola-focused investment firm called DT Group that General Dino also founded.[59]

Tax havens that rank high on the Financial Secrecy Index feature heavily in these structures.[60] A 2011 annual financial statement for Cochan Singapore Pte Ltd described the firm as a "wholly owned subsidiary of Cochan Ltd., incorporated in

[55] For details on Puma's ownership structure, see Shaxson (2021, Table 6). Sonangol (2016, p. 157) valued its stake at Kz 101.4 billion (here converted at an exchange rate of Kz 166.72:$1).

[56] *Fuelling Success*: Corporate Brochure 2015, Puma Energy, p. 12, available at https://pumaenergy.com/media/488705/corporate-brochure-2015.pdf (accessed on December 2, 2020).

[57] *Maka Angola* described Dino and Kopelipa as part of a "Presidential triumvirate" whose third member was Manuel Vicente, the former head of Sonangol (de Marais 2018).

[58] See https://www.cochan.com/en/about-cochan (accessed on September 26, 2020).

[59] Trafigura (2016, p. 69). On DT Group, see https://www.dtsholding.com/en/about-us/our-structure/ (accessed on January 22, 2020).

[60] The Financial Secrecy Index can be accessed at https://fsi.taxjustice.net/Archive2015/Notes%20and%20Reports/FSI-Rankings-2015.pdf (accessed on July 21, 2021).

the Bahamas." It also reported that the Singapore entity had a 100% stake in the investment holding company Cochan Holdings LLC in the Marshall Islands, which in turn held the group's investment in Puma Energy Holdings LLC, also in the Marshall Islands.[61] The Offshore Leaks database lists multiple further interlocking entities connected to Cochan, DT Group and Puma, most of them located in the British Virgin Islands.[62]

After the 2014–2015 fall in world oil prices, Angola faced a severe shortage of foreign exchange. Describing the gravity of the situation in 2016, President dos Santos explained, "The government has not received revenues from Sonangol since the start of the year … since the revenues which are collected hardly cover the debts contracted by the state and by Sonangol itself."[63] The investigative website *Maka Angola* (2016) reported that under Isabel dos Santos' orders, the BNA was "transferring US$100 million each month to pay down an existing billion-dollar debt to one particular creditor, the DT Group."

Sonangol's Alice-in-Wonderland connections with China

Angola was a pioneer in China's global "oil-for-infrastructure" strategy, in which Chinese companies have built infrastructure in exchange for access to crude oil (and other minerals). This was similar to Angola's Bermuda Triangle model of extra-budgetary spending, in the sense that the financial flows mostly occurred offshore, bypassing the inefficiencies of the Angolan budgetary system but also creating great opacity—with the attendant potential for capital flight. A comparison can also be drawn with the Angola-Russia debt deal described above, in that private intermediaries have inserted themselves into lucrative choke points in the relationship between the two nations.

The relationship began in March 2004 with a $2 billion oil-backed loan from China's Exim bank, to finance a first set of Chinese-built infrastructure projects. The loan operated like a revolving credit facility, with Exim bank disbursing funds directly to Chinese contractors via an escrow account and Angola paying in oil.[64] By 2007, China had overtaken the United States as the largest destination for Angolan oil. Meanwhile, western oil-backed loans continued alongside the Chinese loans.[65]

---

[61] Ernst & Young (2011, pp. 12, 23). This prospectus is reproduced in Weiss (2014). For further details, see Shaxson (2021).

[62] For further details, see Shaxson (2021).

[63] Quoted in Expresso (2016).

[64] For a summary of the loan terms, see China-Africa Research Initiative, *China and Oil-Backed Loans*, Johns Hopkins University, October 17, 2011.

[65] Within months of the Chinese loan, Standard Chartered arranged a new $2.35 billion commercial loan for Angola, with Barclays, Calyon, Commerzbank, Deutsche Bank, KBC, Natexis, RBS and

The key intermediary between China and Angola has been the Queensway Group, a Hong Kong-based network of companies linked by complex and opaque cross-shareholdings, with interests in a number of African countries, run by the influential Chinese moneyman Sam Pa. Though not an official Chinese state body, it has close links to the Chinese government. "Pa and his associates have connections to powerful interests in Beijing, including Chinese intelligence and state-owned companies," the *Financial Times* reported in an in-depth series. "The Queensway network has played a pivotal role in advancing China's African quest" (Burgis et al. 2014).

Although he had long experience of operating in war-torn African environments, including Angola, Sam Pa's first major entry to the country came with the help of Helder Bataglia, a colorful and controversial Portuguese-Angolan businessman with interests in Angolan banking and diamonds, and other interests stretching from Venezuela to Iraq to Germany. Queensway introduced Bataglia to top Chinese officials, and Bataglia in turn introduced Queensway to Angolan officials, notably Sonangol's boss, Manuel Vicente, who travelled to China and Hong Kong many times in 2003 and 2004 and developed a close relationship with Queensway (ibid.).

In September 2004, the Queensway company Beiya International Development (BID) formed a 70–30% joint venture with Sonangol called China Sonangol International Holdings. China Sonangol, focusing both on acquiring upstream oil interests and securing oil-backed loans, became one of Queensway's two main operating arms in Angola. The other was the China International Fund (CIF), set up in 2003 to carry out infrastructure reconstruction in Angola (among other international projects, such as the construction of a new metro line in Moscow). CIF soon became a high-profile actor in Luanda. China Sonangol and CIF went on to set up over a dozen affiliates in Hong Kong and several more in Singapore. "CIF seems to have successfully positioned itself between the Chinese and the Angolan governments," according to a 2009 Chatham House report, "and controls access to Angolan resources" (Vines et al. 2009, p. 51). Beneath these top-level actors, the Chatham House researchers uncovered a complex maze of business operations.

China Sonangol acquired stakes in a number of Angolan oil licenses, starting with a stake in BP's prolific deep-water Block 18, obtained after Sam Pa reportedly persuaded Sonangol to grant it to a Cayman Islands-based joint venture called Sonangol Sinopec International (SSI) between Sinopec (the Chinese Petroleum and Chemical Corporation), Dayuan International Development (formerly Queensway's Beiya interests, renamed after a fraud scandal[66]), and China Sonangol.

Banco Espírito Santo participating in the loan consortium. It was, according to John Goodridge of Standard Chartered, "the largest oil-backed transaction in the entire history of the structured trade finance market" (Pallister 2005).

[66] See Mailey (2015, p. 24).

CIF worked in Angola with the Gabinete de Reconstrução Nacional, a body exclusively accountable to president dos Santos, again bypassing Finance Ministry controls. The Chatham House report describes an extensive web of influence, featuring "some illustrious personalities who are no strangers to doing business in Angola at the highest level," including Helder Bataglia, Arcady Gaydamak, Pierre Falcone, and Israeli diamond king Lev Leviev. "Through their connections the contracts kept coming, and CIF's position as the bridge to Angola became virtually unassailable" (Vines et al. 2009, p. 51).

By 2009, China had reportedly facilitated between $13.4 billion and $19.7 billion in loans to Angola. An estimated 50,000 Chinese nationals were working in the country, mostly as laborers on infrastructure projects, living in closed enclaves with little contact with Angolan society.

Relations began to sour fairly early, with accusations that Chinese firms were excluding Angolans, complaints of financial irregularities and non-performance, racism, and other problems. A French journalist visiting a Chinese construction site that was dismantled amid contractual disputes was told by a former watchman in 2007: "The Chinese spent months getting the camp together and bringing in brand-new bulldozers. Then instead of beginning to repair the line, they dismantled it all, ate their dogs and left" (Michel 2009). Since the 2014 fall in oil prices, relations have become lower-key, with non-payments and project delays adding to the difficulties.

While delivering some tangible public benefits to Angola, Sonangol's China connections also delivered handsome private profits to a network of opaque intermediaries. Because most of these financial flows have taken place offshore, flowing inside Chinese or private structures delivering projects of hard-to-measure value, standard estimates would struggle to capture the resulting capital flight. Presumably, the Chinese state suffered losses at the hands of these intermediaries too. The Queensway group became influential enough in each country to make it indispensable to relations with the other. It leveraged this position to obtain remarkable privileges—another example of the transnational plunder networks that operate across national frontiers.

Beyond Oil

Opportunities for elite enrichment in Angola have not been confined to the oil sector. Other avenues include the granting of large loans to well-connected individuals, often backstopped by the state (as illustrated below in the Espírito Santo affair); public contracts with the potential for large-scale diversion of funds; preferential access to foreign exchange in times of multiple exchange rates; and the granting (or sale below their true value) of stakes in valuable businesses. This section focuses on international non-oil trade, where smuggling and misinvoicing not only offer opportunities for enrichment but also serve as vehicles for capital flight.

Smuggling

Outright or "pure" smuggling is a crude, straightforward mechanism: the player clandestinely transports goods across borders, sells them, and stashes the money offshore. As noted above, it would be hard to smuggle oil out of Angola given the controls in place. This is not the case with other exports.

In interviews, Carlos Rosado, a prominent Angolan economist, and others pointed to significant timber smuggling, especially into Namibia, to Angola's south, and into Zambia, to Angola's east.[67] In 2018 an Angolan newspaper reported that the Luvo market, on Angola's northern border with the Democratic Republic of Congo (DRC), was receiving fifty 36-ton truckloads of Angolan cement *per day* for sale in the DRC (Filipe and Bernardo 2018). Given that Luanda is sometimes ranked as the world's most expensive city, it was rather anomalous, one banker told me acidly, that Angolan exporters could undercut Congolese firms on price.[68] They explained why this is possible:

> It is very cheap for these people to import. The reason is that these companies manage to buy at a subsidized exchange rate. They buy whatever they can: the ones who get the foreign exchange and have a strong lobby at the central bank. These guys don't sell in Angola, they smuggle it into Congo, and there they are paid in dollars. They get hard currency. They make tons of money.[69]

At a conservative price of $100/ton for cement, fifty 36-tonne trucks daily would be worth more than $60 million a year—and this is just for Luvo market, just for cement. Such anecdotal evidence suggests that overall totals for smuggled exports could be substantial.

Another mechanism of capital flight involves cash dollars carried in suitcases. An Angolan banker who had worked at the BNA told me that billions of dollars were sold by commercial banks and exchange bureaus to customers. The politically exposed persons, he explained, "don't go through the same channels in the airport that I do. They can easily take a briefcase with them."[70] In principle, this capital flight is measurable as a mismatch between inflows and outflows of foreign

---

[67] Interviewed October 9, 2017, in Luanda.
[68] Interview with a foreign banker in Luanda. On Luanda being the world's most expensive city, see, for instance, Vanham (2015).
[69] Interview with a foreign banker in Luanda.
[70] Interview with an Angolan banker.

exchange, since the dollars would flow in measurably through the banking system, and flow out unmeasurably in suitcases.

Export misinvoicing: The case of diamonds

Another channel for capital flight is export misinvoicing. In this case, the exports are recorded but not at their full value, by virtue of deliberate understatement of their quantity, price, or both—a phenomenon known as "technical" smuggling (as opposed to pure smuggling, where the goods simply are not reported at all). For example, a firm may export $10 million worth of coffee, but submit paperwork for only $7 million, remitting this amount to the BNA as required by law, while putting the remaining $3 million into a private overseas account undetected by the Angolan authorities. By reducing the firm's recorded profits, this may also cut its tax bill.

Diamonds have been a much bigger channel for export misinvoicing and smuggling. Officially, Angola's diamond exports were running at between $500 million and $1 billion per year in the late 1990s and early 2000s, according to IMF and official government reports. Additional production of unknown size was smuggled out from government-owned diamond mines. Large quantities also flowed from UNITA-held areas until the late 1990s, when government forces pushed them out of the diamond zones.[71]

Angola's diamond sales did not always flow neatly along military lines. Many were dug by small-scale, subsistence (also known as "artisanal") miners, often with no particular loyalty to either side. Their diamonds were purchased inside Angola and in neighboring countries. One of the main buyers inside Angola was a company called RDR, part-owned by the president's daughter, Isabel dos Santos. RDR was a predecessor to the state-controlled diamond marketing monopoly Ascorp, which started operations in 2000 with Isabel as a 25% shareholder through a Gibraltar-based firm, Trans Africa Investment Services (TAIS), that she controlled with her Russian mother, Tatiana. It is not clear exactly how she obtained these stakes, nor how much of her own capital she contributed to the ventures.[72]

In 1998, Global Witness published its report, *A Rough Trade*, on the links between Angola's diamond industry and the civil war. This kick-started a global campaign to halt the trade in "blood diamonds," helping to lead to the Kimberley Process, a program for diamond certification established by the United Nations in 2003.

[71] For data, see Shaxson (2021, Table 8). For an account of the routes and mechanisms of diamond flows from UNITA-controlled areas, see United Nations (2000).
[72] Ana Gomes, a Portuguese MEP (Member of the European Parliament) in 2016 created a document outlining dos Santos' history. It is available at https://www.anagomes.eu/PublicDocs/cec6bdfd-72b3-487a-8bb0-41462a0bc8b9.pdf (accessed on July 21, 2021). See also Freedberg et al. (2020).

Diamonds from war-ravaged Angola traded at a significant discount due to their dubious provenance. Schemes were devised to launder them by concealing their origin. A Belgian company called Omega allegedly bought diamonds at low cost and brought them to Luanda, where they obtained Kimberley certificates as originating from official mines.[73] The diamonds were then sent to Dubai, where they were mixed with Congolese diamonds and given new Kimberley certificates as being "of mixed origin," along with new invoices marking up their value to the full market price. At one time around $100 million worth of Angolan diamonds reportedly flowed this way each month, with payments routed through "a daisy chain of briefcase companies registered in tax havens" including Luxembourg, the British Virgin Islands, and Cyprus (Sharife and Grobler 2013).

An estimate as to the scale of Angolan diamond smuggling and misinvoicing can be made for recent years. The UN Comtrade database covers Angolan diamond exports since 2007, permitting mirror data comparisons with imports recorded by trading partners. These reveal substantial discrepancies: over the 2007–2018 period, Angola's recorded diamond exports amounted to $13.1 billion, while the imports recorded by its trading partners came to $18.2 billion—a discrepancy of more than $5 billion.[74] This suggests that measures of capital flight that do not include adjustments for trade misinvoicing are likely to underestimate its true magnitude.

In many other countries, the overall magnitude of trade misinvoicing can be estimated by comparing the country's recorded exports (or imports) to its trading partners' recorded imports (or exports). But in the case of Angola this is generally not possible, due to inadequate reporting by the government; in its absence, sources such as the IMF's *Direction of Trade Statistics* simply derive Angola's data from what is reported by its trading partners (see Chapter 2 in this volume).

Imports and capital flight

The import sector offers an even larger channel for capital flight. Angola imported around $205 billion worth of goods and services during the golden decade of 2002–2014, according to BNA data, and a further $83 billion in the period 2015–2020.

One avenue involves inflated contracts for public procurement. An experienced businessman explained:

All contracts need to have a local partner, who could be 30 percent or whatever of the contracts, and who would be expected to do very little for that contract. It

---

[73] Tulip Diamonds FZE v Minister for Justice and Constitutional Development and Others, South African Constitutional Court, June 13, 2013, available at http://www.saflii.org/za/cases/ZACC/2013/19.pdf (accessed on March 22, 2021).
[74] In 2018 dollars. For details, see Shaxson (2021, Table 10).

will be an obvious leakage to politically connected companies … That leakage will pay for all the bribes needed to pay to the ministers and so on to get that contract paid.[75]

The 30% figure was not plucked out of thin air—it is, multiple interviewees confirmed, not unusual. The same businessman then described a recent contract worth hundreds of millions of dollars that was awarded directly to a very well-connected Angolan:

> The first money is paid by the Angolan government to a foreign contractor. Part of that down payment is, in theory, payable to the local partner. But the local partner is appearing as a foreign company. What [the person] asked for immediately in this case was for that money to be paid to an offshore account.

When, as is typically the case, the padded public procurement contracts involve imported goods and services, the actual cost of the imports is often overstated in trade documents.

But import over-invoicing is not confined to public procurement: it is a widespread mechanism for illicit capital flight around the world. Every knowledgeable interviewee in Angola whom I asked about the practice knew exactly what it meant and agreed that this is a standard way to export dollars secretly. Say, for example, that a company imports $7 million worth of goods and submits paperwork to the BNA saying the machinery cost $10 million. The BNA provides $10 million in hard currency to the company in return for kwanza at the official (often subsidized) exchange rate, and the company then remits $7 million to its supplier and sends the remaining $3 million to a private offshore account.

In more extreme cases, money leaves Angola to purchase imports that never happen. Interviewees told me extraordinary stories in which hundreds of millions have been paid to foreign firms, where the supposed foreign supplier had no record of receiving any orders for equipment. In other cases, some equipment was imported and then left to rot because the point of the transaction was not to obtain the equipment but to get dollars out.

Services are often even easier to manipulate than goods, because their value can be harder to pinpoint. "It's been a classic method in Angola," explained a government official. "You pay for fictitious consultancy services to a company registered abroad to get the money out of the country."[76] Or if not fictitious, the services can be overpriced as a way to get ahead of the queue for dollars from the Central Bank in times of scarcity, again with the difference tucked into a private bank account.

---

[75] Interview with a European businessman.
[76] Interview with an Angolan government official.

There are also incentives for under-invoicing of imports. For example, if tariffs on imported goods are 10% (which is typical in Angola), an importer bringing in $10 million worth of goods is supposed to pay $1 million to the government. If the importer submits an invoice stating that the goods are worth only $5 million, they only pay half that amount (and if they smuggle them into the country without declaring the imports at all, they pay zero). In aggregate, the incentives to over-invoice imports for purposes of capital flight and to under-invoice them for purposes of tariff evasion pull in opposite directions. Where mirror data comparisons with trading partners are possible, these can reveal only their net impact, thereby understating the scale of both capital flight and smuggling.[77]

The exchange rate merry-go-round re-emerges

In the early years of the golden decade, dollars were relatively plentiful and exchange rate differentials narrowed, at times reaching parity and free convertibility. When this occurred, one avenue of private enrichment closed off (though with plentiful oil dollars, fabulous sources were available elsewhere). But when the oil price crashed in 2014, the government again rationed dollars, and at the time of my visit in 2017 the official dollar rate mark-up over the parallel rate was around 300%.

The exchange-rate subsidies generally end up not in the hands of consumers through cheaper prices, but in the hands of the wealthy businesspeople who dominate the import trade (and use import misinvoicing and other tricks to channel their profits into capital flight). Arnaldo Lago de Carvalho, a veteran Angolan CEO who is active in the import sector (though mostly in the oil industry), told me:

> The prices in supermarkets, they are completely irrational, compared to markets in South Africa. Three, four times more. All this needs to be studied. Imports: this was always the way for money to fly out. The prices for some medicines are ten times the price in a pharmacy in Lisbon. Beef, milk, juice, eggs, half the eggs are imported, everything.

He pointed to senior Angolans who ran large companies and supermarket chains that import consumer goods as being the principal beneficiaries of the exchange-rate discrepancies.[78]

[77] Bilateral import misinvoicing estimates for recent years, based on comparisons between BNA data on imports and international data on exports to Angola, show that the net impact varies in sign as well as magnitude across trading partners (Shaxson 2021, Table 11).

[78] For an example of a breakdown of a month's allocation of foreign exchange by the BNA, see Shaxson (2021, Annex D).

Blowback in Portugal

Lisbon has long been the favorite foreign playground for Angolan elites, just as wealthy Nigerians look to London (or New York), or wealthy Ivoirians look to Paris. In the later stages of Angola's 2002–2014 golden decade, when oil prices were high and the Portuguese economy itself was stagnating, the scale of Angolan influence grew to the point that some in Portugal fretted about "reverse colonialism." Angolans acquired substantial holdings in Portuguese banking, energy and media companies, alongside large real estate holdings, wineries, and sports teams (Costa et al. 2014; Ames 2015).

After the oil price crash and spurred by media reports expressing alarm at Angolan interventions in Portugal, Portuguese judges began prosecuting corruption cases against senior Angolans. In February 2017 Portuguese prosecutors charged Angolan vice president and former Sonangol CEO Manuel Vicente with bribing a magistrate to suspend a 2012 inquiry into the origin of funds for his purchase of an apartment in Portugal.[79] Most dramatically, in March 2020 a Portuguese judge ordered the seizure of Isabel dos Santos' assets in Portugal, following an Angolan request for help recovering an alleged $1.1 billion extracted from the Angolan state.[80]

The Banco Espírito Santo affair

In mid-2014 European stock markets began falling amid rumors that the 140-year-old Banco Espírito Santo, one of Portugal's biggest banks, was in trouble. Founded by the aristocratic Espírito Santo family, the bank was controlled by a holding company in Luxembourg, Espírito Santo Financial Group, with a convoluted structure of shareholdings and cross-shareholdings, many held in offshore jurisdictions. The group had diamond mining and commercial interests in Angola via its Escom group (founded and part-owned by Helder Bataglia, who was mentioned in the China-Sonangol section above).

In 2001 Banco Espírito Santo became the first foreign bank to incorporate an Angolan subsidiary, Banco Espírito Santo Angola (BESA). Two years later BESA sold a 19% stake to a company called GENI Novas Tecnologías S.A., controlled by

---

[79] Reuters (2017). A Portuguese court subsequently ruled that Vicente should be tried in Angola. In September 2020 Angolan prosecutors seized some of his assets and put him in "preventative custody." See Angop (Agência Angola Press), "Businessman Carlos Sao Vincente in Preventive Detention," September 22, 2020, available at http://www.angop.ao/angola/en_us/noticias/politica/2020/8/39/Businessman-Carlos-Sao-Vicente-preventive-detention,d607055b-b04a-44ec-83a6-1137df76cdd5.html (accessed on July 21, 2021). See also Reuters (2018a). For "bribing a magistrate" see Cabral (2017). For the court of appeal decision, see Batalha (2018).

[80] Widely reported. For example, see Dalby (2020) and Demony and Waldersee (2020).

Isabel dos Santos, and in 2009 it sold a further 24% stake to Portmill Investimen-
tos e Telecomunicações, a company controlled by the "presidential triumvirate" of
General "Kopelipa," General Dino, and Manuel Vicente.[81]

Subsequent audits revealed that between 2009 and 2013 BESA doled out billions of dollars in unsecured loans to people believed to be members of the MPLA
elite, and by 2013 it had granted credit worth well over twice the value of customer deposits.[82] KPMG, the bank's auditor, did not raise red flags until after the
problems became public (it was subsequently fined by Portugal's Central Bank).[83]
But worries soon began to emerge. A January 2013 internal report by BPI, a rival Portuguese Bank, reckoned that the Espírito Santo Group had been effectively
insolvent since 2011.[84]

In December 2012, BES CEO Ricardo Salgado met with president dos Santos and announced a $500 million capital increase to fund an expansion of bank
branches across Angola (raising the number from 40 to 71, in addition to a "private and affluent banking" office and five "corporate banking" offices). At the
same time, in a remarkable move the Angolan government agreed to guarantee
70% of BESA's loan portfolio. There was, as an interviewee in Lisbon described it,
a "channel of liquidity" between the BES parent and its Angolan subsidiary.[85]

As investor worries grew about BES, the Angolan subsidiary became a focus
of concern. The Portuguese newspaper *Expresso* reported in June 2014 that BESA
"did not know" the identities of the recipients of some $5.7 billion in loans, or
about four-fifths of its entire debt portfolio.[86] In August that year, prompted by
concerns of the European Central Bank, and conscious that a dramatic fall in the
oil price would not only turn many of BESA's politically-networked credits sour,
but also would make it harder for dos Santos to stand by the Angolan guarantee
for those loans, the Portuguese central bank (BdP), stepped in to bail out the BES

[81] Shareholdings drawn from BES annual reports. Amilcar Pires, a former administrator of BES,
identified Kopelipa and Dino as shareholders of Portmill, in declarations to a Portuguese commission of enquiry, December 11, 2014: "Comissão de Inquérito Parlamentar à Gestão do BES e do
Grupo Espírito Santo, ao Processo que Conduziu à Aplicação da Medida de Resolução e às suas Con-
sequências, nomeadamente quanto aos Desenvolvimentos e Opções relativos ao GES, ao BES e ao
Novo Banco," December 11, 2014, pp. 8, 10, 11, available at https://www.pcp.pt/comissao-de-inquerito-
gestao-do-bes-do-grupo-espirito-santo (accessed on July 31, 2020). At the time of writing the Angolan
government was starting to seize their assets: see, e.g., Mendes (2020).
[82] See Comissão Parlamentar de Inquérito à Gestão do Bes e do Ges, Assembleia da República (Portugal's Parliament), Relatório Final, April 28, 2015, Tabela 3.8 p. 83 and p. 86. See also "Entities linked
to BES managers got loans from Angola branch—audit," *Reuters*, March 17, 2015. In an interview,
a private sector investigator in Lisbon stated that "there is a list of all the people who received all the
loans, but this list never appeared," adding that he believed the funds went to members of the "Angolan
regime."
[83] Ibid. See also "BES: Statement by Carlos Costa on KPMG's appeal to BdP fines was postponed,"
Jornal Económico, September 22, 2020.
[84] See the Portuguese parliamentary Commission's report, pp. 81–92, especially p. 90, and Asalto ao
Castelo, Episodio 1, Sic Noticias, March 1, 2017, at about 24.30.
[85] Interview with a private sector investigator in Lisbon.
[86] Expresso (2014) and Observador (2014).

parent company and split it into two entities: a sustainable operating entity and a "bad bank" containing the problem assets.

Subsequent investigations revealed further complications, including an interesting tale involving the see-no-evil tax haven of Dubai. According to an in-depth investigation by Portugal's SIC Notícias television station, in 2007 the Espírito Santo Group incorporated a subsidiary, ES Bankers (Dubai), in Dubai.[87] Leaked correspondence between the BdP and the Dubai Financial Services Authority revealed that this entity served as a secretive offshore staging point for Angolan money, and that these and other funds, including money from small depositors in Portugal, were being used to recapitalize other entities in the badly damaged Espírito Santo group.[88]

SIC Notícias reported that $563 million flowed from the BNA to ES Bankers (Dubai) in 2010. This was then forwarded to an Espírito Santo entity in London, partly to buy the ES Group's debt instruments. Another $750 million of Angolan money was found in the Dubai entity in 2011, 61% of which was in the accounts of just four Angolan "politically exposed persons," including $284 million reportedly held by Kopelipa. This money was then routed overseas to buy shares of the Espírito Santo parent company, and into "fiduciary deposits" at ES Group in Panama.[89] "Between Luanda and Dubai an air bridge was created where millions of euros of money of doubtful origin circulated," the SIC Notícias investigation concluded, "as if the BES affiliate in Dubai had transformed itself into a giant mega-laundry for the Angolan regime."[90] Another subterfuge in the effort to shore up the group's capital, according to SIC Notícias, involved exotic financial instruments, marketed as high-interest "saving" products, to hoover up deposits from unsuspecting Portuguese investors, many of whom lost their savings in the debacle.[91]

The Espírito Santo Group had once been a solid "establishment" bank in Portugal, but in the end, it had turned into the core of a transnational financial network that amassed riches for a few insiders while harming the state finances of both Angola and Portugal. When BES collapsed in 2014, it turned out that the hole in the bank's last financial accounts, 5.3 billion Euros, was roughly the same size as the $5.7 billion guarantee provided by president dos Santos to the group in 2013. This

---

[87] The SIC Notícias investigation is available at https://sicnoticias.pt/programas/assalto-ao-castelo.

[88] See the three-part SIC Notícias investigation, "Assalto ao Castelo," by reporter Pedro Coelho, March 2017. It quotes a Bank of Portugal document as saying: "It seems clear that ES Bankers Dubai was used as a conduit entity for Angolan funds to finance the Espírito Santo group, linked to the activities of Banco Espírito Santo in Angola."

[89] Ibid., and interview with anonymous source in Lisbon. See also "Bank Scandals hit MPLA Hard," *Africa Confidential*, March 3, 2017.

[90] See Pedro Coelho, "Assalto ao Castelo – Episódio 1," first of three-part investigative series for Portugal's *SIC Notícias* television, aired on March 2017.

[91] From the SIC Notícias report. See also Comissão Parlamentar de Inquérito à Gestão do Bes e Do Ges, Assembleia da República (Portugal's Parliament), Relatório Final, April 28, 2015, p. 73.

illustrates the fact that illicit financial flows out of Africa not only harm Africans but also inflict damaging "blowback" into the (mostly western) countries on the receiving end.

Isabel dos Santos and the Luanda Leaks

A central player in the Angola-Portugal nexus is Isabel dos Santos, the daughter of President José Eduardo dos Santos and reputedly Africa's richest woman.[92] She has portrayed herself as a smart and successful dealmaker, who started out selling eggs at the age of six (Guardian 2020).[93] Her Instagram and Facebook accounts give the impression of a dynamic and glamorous entrepreneur, a woman blazing a trail in a man's world from Luanda to Lisbon and beyond. Others with less charitable views have seen her as having used her unassailable political position (until her father re-linquished power in September 2017) to obtain strangleholds on vital chokepoints in Angola's position in the global economy and exploit them for personal gain.

Isabel began to enter the Angolan public consciousness in 1997, at the age of 24, when she became a partner in Miami Beach, one of Luanda's best-known beach-front restaurants, reportedly with a minimal investment and helping its owner who was encountering difficulties with the health inspectors and tax authorities (Dolan 2013). I first became aware of her vaulting aspirations in 1999, when I reported on her diamond interests for the insider newsletter *Africa Confidential* (Shaxson 1999). Subsequent media articles record that by that time she had already set up her first offshore company in the British tax haven of Gibraltar, in partnership with her mother Tatiana, as a vehicle for her stakes in Angolan diamonds.[94] Later she became a substantial shareholder in Ascorp, the official Angolan state diamond-buying monopoly, and began to steadily acquire stakes in banking, trucking, telecommunications, energy, retail, construction, media, and other sectors of the economy.

---

[92] Costa et al. (2014, p. 38) estimated that of Isabel's roughly $3 billion fortune at the time of their writing, roughly half was in the form of shares of Portuguese companies. Forbes estimated her wealth at US$1.8 billion in June 2020 (down from $3.7 billion in 2014, before the oil price crash and Covid-19) based on assets they could track, but they admitted it could be higher. This would make her Africa's 13th richest individual, and its richest woman. Given that she received an estimated $1.25 billion in dividends alone from her stake in Unitel while a shareholder, however, it may be that her net worth is significantly higher. See below and also Dolan (2013).

[93] See Guardian Staff, "Isabel dos Santos responds to Luanda Leaks investigation," *The Guardian*, January 23, 2020. https://www.theguardian.com/world/2020/jan/19/isabel-dos-santos-issues-response-luanda-leaks-investigation (accessed on July 21, 2021).

[94] The fact of her involvement in Angolan diamonds is widely reported. On TAIS, see Marques (2012). See also ICIJ (2020). The ICIJ also provides a spreadsheet of Isabel's companies, which says TAIS was founded on March 27, 1997. The spreadsheet was available on February 20, 2020, at https://docs.google.com/spreadsheets/d/1qZ3vBDZpXhb9ssmGQ72EV03eSruQvp3XWgZc9xEllo0/edit#gid=0 (accessed on July 21, 2021).

Over the years, investigations by Rafael Marques de Morais, a prominent Angolan journalist and anticorruption campaigner, who has been jailed for exposing the private enrichment of senior government figures,[95] and more recently in the "Luanda Leaks" by the International Consortium of Investigative Journalists (ICIJ), have revealed a rabbit's warren of over 400 companies amassed by Isabel and her husband, Sindika Dokolo.[96]

Isabel's most high-profile asset in Angola was her stake in the highly profitable telecommunications company Unitel. The firm was set up in 2001 to compete with the state firm Movicel. I interviewed a manager at a new Unitel office in Huambo province in the early 2000s—at a time when poverty was so severe that market traders were selling single bundles of five or ten matches wrapped in thread because people could not afford a whole matchbox—and being astonished at the thousands of dollars he told me were flooding into this office every day. The ICIJ reported that Unitel served as a "cash machine," paying out more than $5 billion in dividends to shareholders from 2006 to 2015 (Freedberg et al. 2020, p. 7). For much of this period, Unitel had four shareholders with 25% each: MSTelecom, a subsidiary of Sonangol; PT Ventures, owned by the Brazilian telecommunications firm Oi; Geni, owned by General Leopoldino do Nascimento "Dino"; and Vidatel, controlled by Isabel dos Santos.[97] If the ICIJ calculation is correct, this would mean that roughly $2.5 billion was paid out to companies controlled by two of the most important figures in the dos Santos constellation: Isabel dos Santos and General Dino.

Isabel's appointment as head of Sonangol in the dying months of the dos Santos presidency was touted as bringing political clout and a fresh Business School perspective to the company. But in a September 2017 interview, an official at an international oil company was scathing about her role:

Isabel was going around in June saying "we want cash, which means accelerate production." The IOCs (international oil companies) were pushing back, saying "you will trash the oilfields." Production is already heading downwards.[98]

---

[95] Marques was the dos Santos regime's most prominent domestic critic when I lived in Luanda in the 1990s, and remarkably he kept up the pressure for decades, most recently through his website makaangola.org which has carried a steady stream of detailed investigations into figures close to the dos Santos regime (and indeed to some associated with the subsequent Lourenço regime).

[96] See also Villalobos (2015) and Zierer et al. (2017).

[97] This shareholding has been widely reported. See, for example, "Sonangol holds 50% of Unitel's capital," Angola Press (Angop) January 20, 2020, reporting Sonangol's acquisition of the 25% stake held by Brazil's Oi. It was reported in December 2017 that Unitel had stopped paying dividends to shareholders, ostensibly because of the Angolan currency crisis that prevented kwanzas (received for phone services from an estimated 11 million Angolan phone users) being exchanged for dollars, but also, perhaps more importantly, because of the change of government which had meant that the BNA was no longer prioritizing Unitel in the "queue" to be able to exchange Kwanzas for hard currency. See, for instance, ECO News (2017).

[98] Interview with a western oil industry official.

This would be consistent with a *fin de régime* attempt by the dos Santos family network to maximize revenues ahead of President dos Santos' imminent departure, whatever the cost to future state revenues.

An experienced oil sector veteran in Luanda added:

> Isabel doesn't know anything about oil, and she doesn't know anything about management.... If you want to reform Sonangol, you need both a strategy and good guys inside. Instead she has gone out to Boston Consulting Group and created a very bad atmosphere. They parachuted in young Portuguese juniors, marginalizing more experienced Angolans, good guys.[99]

The *New York Times* reported that when Boston Consulting and other international firms, including McKinsey and PricewaterhouseCoopers (PwC), signed on to help restructure Sonangol, they agreed to be paid not directly by the Angolan government but instead through a Maltese company called Wise Intelligence Solutions, which acted as project manager for the Sonangol restructuring—and happened to be owned by Isabel and her husband.[100] In May 2017 Wise was replaced by a company in Dubai owned by a friend of Isabel's—and the project fees soared. Just hours after she was fired from Sonangol by the new administration in November 2017, $38 million reportedly flowed to the Dubai shell company.[101]

The role played by these and the other management consulting and accounting firms mentioned in the Luanda Leaks—including all the Big Four accounting firms, PwC, KPMG, Deloitte, and EY—has several common features.

First, consulting and accounting firms played an outsized role in Isabel's business affairs. When international banks hear about Isabel, the *New York Times* quoted the head of corporate finance for a Portuguese firm that managed many of her companies, "they run like the Devil from the cross." Being far less regulated than banks, the *Times* reported, consulting firms "readily embraced her business."[102]

Second, while these firms are often viewed as technocratic advisors to inexperienced companies and governments, it is more accurate to describe them as technocratic advisors to elites. In the words of Oxford professor Ricardo Soares de Oliveira, "They are there as all-purpose providers of whatever these elites are trying to do."[103]

---

[99] The official was José de Oliveira, interviewed October 11, 2017, in Luanda.

[100] Forsythe et al. (2020).

[101] Ibid. The *New York Times* story quoted Carlos Saturnino, who became Sonangol's new head, as saying that dos Santos in total had approved $135 million in consulting fees, with most routed through the Dubai shell company. Dos Santos herself was quoted as saying that these were legitimate fees, charged at "the standard rate" for Boston Consulting, McKinsey, PwC, and other western firms. See also Reuters (2018b).

[102] Ibid. See also Hallman et al. (2020).

[103] Forsythe et al. (2020).

Third, their provision of technocratic expertise ironically may have sapped rather than increased Angola's own technical capacity. As Soares de Oliveira has observed:

> The government's incapacity to achieve its ambitions single-handedly and a desire for overnight results lead it to splurge on all the consultants and subcontractors that oil money can buy. The resulting rampant "culture of consultancy" means that even where there is the illusion of an Angolan role, the actual tasks are being performed by KPMG, Ernst & Young, McKinsey, Deloitte and lesser international providers of myriad services handsomely paid by the Angolans…. Worryingly, the Angolan side of these arrangements seldom seems interested in "concrete, technical learning" or transfer of knowledge… For their part, foreigners are in no hurry to making themselves redundant.
>
> (Soares de Oliveira 2015, p. 76)

One corporate executive added that this culture means "big business and endless business" for him and his competitors (ibid.).

Fourth, the international consulting and accounting firms not only provide technical services but also act as "the interface with international players," Soares de Oliveira explains. "That last part is crucial: they are a turntable to the outside world."[104] This returns us to the concept of market power rooted in the ability to sit astride choke points in the economy, leveraging knowledge and political connections to generate profits.

The activities of Isabel dos Santos exemplify the large grey areas that exist when trying to distinguish between illicit and licit financial flows. For example, the Unitel dividends paid to her and General Dino would not be captured in the usual capital flight measures, assuming that they either were recorded in both Angolan and Portuguese data as normal flows or followed circuitous offshore routes that these would never have touched the Angolan payment systems. Whether or not there was an illicit element to these payments, many would regard this money as capital lost to Angola.

The Bankers

The core business model of international private bankers, including private equity firms, hedge funds and other asset managers, is to attract what is known in the industry as "OPM"—Other People's Money—so as to be able to extract fees for investing and managing it. The more OPM they obtain, the more in fees they

---

[104] Telephone interview with Soares de Oliveira, January 24, 2020.

make. One important way to attract OPM is by credibly promising attractive investment opportunities and high returns for the outside investors. Another is to offer financial secrecy in tax havens or elsewhere.

OPM often flows out of countries like Angola into countries like the United States or Britain via "blocker" corporations in financial secrecy jurisdictions such as the Cayman Islands and Jersey whose role is to strip out identifying features, allowing the capital to enter western economies anonymously and enabling the investors to hide the sources of their funds.[105]

Interviewees said Angolans were often rather "unsophisticated" in this respect, and not necessarily motivated by the prospect of high returns. As a European businessman put it:

> Angolans are incredibly conservative when it comes to their money overseas. I hear the money that goes into Swiss bank accounts sits in low-interest bearing accounts, the lowest form of return.... They are making money in their own countries, not looking for this money that they are bringing overseas to necessarily make money.[106]

This isn't just an Angolan phenomenon. A Citibank official in Mexico City made the same point to financial flows expert James Henry: "The money my clients put offshore is for safe keeping... When they want 200 percent returns, they keep the money here."[107]

Angola's sovereign wealth fund

Bankers also manage assets that belong, at least in principle, to governments. Angola's Sovereign Wealth Fund (SWF) was set up in 2011 with an initial $5 billion grant from the government. It was chaired by José Filomeno dos Santos, the son of the president. During the dos Santos era, its website said it invested in real estate, treasury bills, equities, derivatives and other financial instruments, mostly via private equity funds.[108]

The SWF's main asset manager was Quantum Global, an outfit set up in 2007 and run by Jean-Claude Bastos de Morais, a personal friend of José Filomeno dos

---

[105] For discussion, see Shaxson (2002) and Henry (2003).

[106] Interview with a European businessman.

[107] James Henry's interview with "Mexican Citibanker" in July 1988, quoted in Tax Justice Network (2012, p. 30).

[108] Accessed in November 2018. Subsequently, following a re-vamping of the SWF under President Lourenço, the website has been completely changed.

Santos, and whom Quatum's website described as "a Swiss-African citizen fasci-
nated by the dream of unleashing and developing economic power in Africa."[109]
Quantum received funds from private individuals as well as from the Angolan
state. A banker in Luanda told me: "Quantum was put there to channel funds out
from Angola into Switzerland."[110]

According to its website, Quantum's two main subsidiaries are a portfolio investment management and advisory firm based in Zug, Switzerland, and a private
equity firm based in Mauritius (a tax haven popular with African investors).[111] It
also described a joint venture with a global property firm and listed real estate investments in expensive parts of London (Savile Row in Mayfair), New York (Fifth
Avenue), Paris (Tour Blanche, La Défense) and Munich (the Atrium). According
to a BBC report, Bastos de Morais had been convicted in Switzerland for "qualified
cases of misappropriation" (Meisel and Grossman 2017).[112]

Spokespersons for Quantum and the SWF told the ICIJ that the firm was selected as investment manager because of its "exemplary performance" on previous
mandates with Angolan authorities, and that the friendship between Bastos and
José Filomeno had nothing to do with Quantum's selection (Fitzgibbon 2017).

The Angolan banking system

The Angolan banking system has been of central importance in Angola's elite-
driven model of national development since the end of the war. Until the early
1990s, Angolan banking was largely state-owned. Portuguese banks slowly began
to establish a presence starting in 1993. This was followed by the rise of Angolan
private banks, which began in 1997 with the creation of the Banco Africano de In-
vestimentos (BAI, still Angola's biggest private bank, with Sonangol as its largest
shareholder). These private banks were part-owned by powerful figures closely
connected to the MPLA and President dos Santos.[113] "Everyone of consequence
has a stake but the former president's children are particularly well represented,"
observed Ferreira and Soares de Oliveira (2019, p. 58). Isabel dos Santos' holdings,
discussed above, are the prime example.

[109] See "DIFF welcomes Quantum Global to sponsor the prestigious Muhr awards competition," http://quantumglobalgroup.com/article/diff-welcomes-quantum-global-sponsor-prestigious-
muhr-awards-competition/, December 4, 2017, accessed on February 21, 2020.
[110] Interview with a foreign banker in Luanda.
[111] From quatumglobalgroup.com, various pages, accessed on February 20, 2020. The website describes several other Quantum subsidiaries: Quantum Global Real Estate in Zug, Quantum Global
Private Wealth Ltd. In Lugano, Switzerland; Quantum Global Capital Advisers Ltd. In Baar, Switzerland; Quantum Global Alternative Investments, Ltd., QG Investments Africa Management Ltd. in
Mauritius, Quantum Global Hotel Fund. See also Sharife (2016).
[112] See also Brönnimann (2017).
[113] For instance, ion May 2017 Danilo, the youngest son of Ana Paula dos Santos and President dos
Santos, got a banking license for his 25th birthday.

The Angolan banking sector has provided two main avenues for enrichment: first, by making their shareholders rich, and second, by enabling other members of the Angolan elite to obtain loans on advantageous terms and by helping them to transfer their riches overseas.

The Angolan banks have made large profits not from lending to enterprises but instead largely from hoovering up deposits and paying relatively low rates of interest on them, then investing money with the state on highly favorable terms.[114] What is more, most bank services and lending that do serve the real economy go primarily to large corporations, often with links to the oil sector. In 2015 agriculture, the mainstay of most Angolan livelihoods outside the urban centers, accounted for only five percent of overall bank credit to the economy (Deloitte 2016, p. 63)—and nearly all of that was granted to large agro-industrial concerns. A senior BNA figure remarked in 2009, "about 85 percent of Angolan credit goes to two hundred or so clients" (quoted by Ferreira and Soares de Oliveira 2019, p. 62).

Loans provided to powerful people are often guaranteed by the government, and some are never repaid. Sometimes, this is a case of big bets going bad. The viability of loans for commercial real estate projects during the "golden decade," for example, depended on oil prices staying high. After prices crashed in 2014, construction stopped, hotels stood empty, and the loans (especially those denominated in dollars) were not repaid.[115] Others may have borrowed with no intention of ever building anything, let alone repaying. Many borrowers, a banker in Luanda told me in September 2017, "do not even in their wildest dreams think about returning the money." He explained their self-justifications: "They are doing a service for the country ... they are providing jobs, industry, diversification, sacrificing themselves by building these projects. Obviously, with government money."[116]

International wealth management

During the early years of the golden decade, it was not hard for members of the Angolan elite to find foreign collaborators who would help them hide their winnings overseas. "It used to be that there were Swiss bankers, wealth bankers, private bankers: a lot travelling in and out of Angola and marketing for business," a European businessman in Luanda told me in 2017. "Ten years ago, Angola was awash with them."[117]

---

[114] A simple average of the top eight private banks' holdings of securities was 18% higher than their portfolio of credits, which is usually the largest portion of a bank's portfolio. Author's calculations based on Deloitte (2016, p. 82).

[115] In 2015 the IMF estimated that 30% of Angolan domestic banks' loans were dollar-denominated IMF (2015, p. 35).

[116] Interview with a foreign banker in Luanda.

[117] Interview with a European businessman.

Things became somewhat more difficult, however, following the tightening up of compliance rules at western banks in the wake of the global financial crisis and amid high-profile campaigns to tackle money laundering and capital flight. Angola's reputation led most international banking institutions active in the country to terminate correspondent banking relationships by 2015. The last one providing US dollar clearing services was Deutsche Bank, which left in November 2016. Since that time, international banking relationships have been largely restricted to Portuguese and South African banks handling transactions in Euros for large clients like Sonangol. The loss of access the international payments system precipitated some efforts to reform Angola's banking system towards international best practices (from an exceptionally low base). However, much of the resulting change has been called "mock compliance," whereby international standards are introduced onto the books but not seriously implemented and enforced (Engebretsen and Soares de Oliveira 2020).

Demand for services to get hard currency transferred overseas remained as strong as ever. Capital flight is not just a question of corrupt officials sending looted money to offshore havens that passively receive it: it involves an industry of enablers—global banks, family offices, law and accounting firms, wealth management offices—descending on countries, rich and poor, to recruit wealthy clients. The big money-center banks with household names—banks like HSBC, Citibank, Standard Chartered, Barclays, and Deutsche Bank—the European businessman explained, are "so process-driven now and so compliance-driven that I'd be very surprised if they are assisting in this." As a result, today "you are automatically dealing with smaller banks" (ibid.).

What happens once the money is safely out of Angola is another matter. The businessman described a Swiss banker he knew who still comes to Angola to find individuals and companies to open accounts in Switzerland. "How they get the money there is their problem," he explained. "He is creating an environment to receive money" (ibid.).

Since the United States began cracking down on Swiss private banking and the European Union started adding to the pressure, Switzerland has been significantly more open and transparent in its dealings with western countries. But, again quoting the businessman, although tax avoidance and secrecy no longer work for clients in western countries, "they totally work for Africa still." One way of recruiting new clients is via "cocktail bankers," wealthy or connected people in the country who act as referral agents and collect a fee:

It's extremely low profile. You're not going to know this is happening. There's maybe one guy and his boss, they fly in, have meetings, it's deliberate and has to be very opaque. It has to be. This is not a showy business, it's the exact opposite.

(ibid.)

Compliance rules for offshore payments have been tightened up, too. Whereas previously payments to Angolan sleeping partners were fairly easy to make, now it is getting harder both because the multinational companies themselves are much stricter and because the banks that process the transactions are asking more questions. But the European businessman explained that it's still "pretty easy" to find a way around the rules:

> If you're an Angolan businesswoman, say, you need to set up a company somewhere offshore with zero tax. It is super easy, incredibly easy—there's a whole industry that helps you set up a company, which doesn't cost much. You just need to know the beneficial owner, and I imagine in a lot of cases people lie.

> Setting up a bank account is less easy, but still it is on the scale of pretty easy.... Often the person who's helped you set up the company will introduce you to banks. You will have to go through a process and be serious about it and be consistent in the truths and the lies that you tell.

> (ibid.)

In the case of politically exposed persons, a trusted surrogate needs to appear to the bank as the "beneficial owner" of the account. These practices again highlight the complicity of the international banking system in facilitating capital flight.

Tax havens

A favorite tax haven for wealthy Angolans is Dubai. Indeed, based on my long-standing work as a tax haven researcher, I would describe it as arguably the least regulated and most crime-friendly of the world's major tax havens.[118] In 2016, at a time when tax havens and their advisers were busy trying to find ways around the Common Reporting Standard (CRS), a global transparency scheme launched by the OECD, a Zurich-based tax adviser told me, "In Dubai it is more like 'What is this CRS thing? How do you spell it?'"[119]

Other Angolan favorites have included Malta (whose main marketing angle is its membership of the European Union, allowing it to move capital freely within the Eurozone); Singapore (for trade in Asia in particular); Panama (especially for shell companies and trusts); Mauritius (more often for corporate vehicles); the British

---

[118] Shaxson (2012). For a colorful treatment, see also Glenny (2008) who describes Dubai's role as providing a platform for several global mafia organizations with almost no questions asked.
[119] Interview with a South African financial adviser based in Zurich.

Virgin Islands (for shell companies, not bank accounts); and Madeira (a minor tax haven that has the advantage of being Portuguese speaking).[120]

Portugal itself is not widely regarded as a tax haven, but it is in the game of selling passports to wealthy people, enabling them to escape international reporting requirements. And as the Banco Espírito Santo episode shows, at times the Portuguese regulators have been exceptionally lax in policing their own laws. Portuguese banks have been especially receptive to Angolan money: as a businessman put it, "you'll have a whole lot of people who will be willing to help you without you having to go through [an] English-speaking bank."[121] Moreover, because many Angolans have Portuguese passports, their bank accounts in Portugal are registered as belonging to Portuguese non-residents and therefore tax exempt.

The Luanda Leaks revelations of January 2020 provided an interesting snapshot of the use of tax havens. Isabel dos Santos and her husband Sindika Dokolo were shown to own more than 400 companies. Fewer than one quarter of them were Angolan, while nearly one third were in Portugal, and another quarter were registered in recognized tax havens.[122]

While tax havens have helped many powerful people loot Angola and stash their winnings offshore, there also have been more legitimate reasons for using tax havens or at least sending money overseas. These include worries about the safety of Angolan banks, fear of devaluation, and fear of not being able to get the money out in future. For local companies that need access to hard currency, offshore accounts also provide a way to receive and hold foreign exchange for later use.

Conclusions

From the end of the civil war in 2002 until the oil price crash of 2014, Angola exported some $530 billion dollars' worth of oil. The country also took on roughly $48 billion in foreign debts, for a total inflow of nearly $580 billion, or about $27,000 per inhabitant. Most Angolans saw few benefits from this "golden decade." Now, as its oil starts to run out, Angola faces a major transition.

One reason for Angola's failure to grasp the opportunity for development during this period is that a big chunk of the money disappeared into private

---

[120] Most of my interviewees highlighted Dubai as a prime location for Angolan-owned assets. The one who consented to be named in this respect was Ana Gomes, a vocal Member of the European Parliament (and 2021 presidential candidate in Portugal) whom I interviewed on June 26, 2017. She and others also identified Malta as a key Angolan-favored tax haven for holding assets. All highlighted Portugal, however, as the most important location of many Angolan assets. This pattern was subsequently supported in greater detail by revelations in the Luanda Leaks scandal.

[121] Interview with a European businessman.

[122] For a list, see Shaxson (2021, Table 12). "Tax haven" is a flexible term; here I count jurisdictions that have high secrecy scores in the Financial Secrecy Index, or which feature highly on the Corporate Tax Haven Index. Both indices are produced by the Tax Justice Network.

hands overseas. This chapter's investigation of this phenomenon leads to several conclusions.

Capital flight is part of a bigger phenomenon of lost capital

The usual methods for measuring capital flight cannot capture all of Angola's lost capital. There are three main reasons for gaps in the data.

First, a significant portion of capital flight is often captured by analyzing trade misinvoicing, based on mirror data of trading partners. In Angola's case, however, this often cannot be measured because Angola itself does not provide the necessary data.

Second, capital flight is usually measured as unrecorded outflows. As this chapter has repeatedly shown, Angolan capital losses also include flows that may have been duly authorized by the Presidency or Central Bank or Finance Ministry, and yet originate in wealth obtained through means that range from the unfair or abusive to the illegal. A banker interviewed in Luanda summarized this grey area with more than a touch of sarcasm: "There is not an issue of legality here. This is a conflict-of-interest-free country."[123]

Third, some transactions take place entirely offshore—for example, with a bribe paid and received in Dubai—so that the financial flows bypass the Central Bank coming as well as going. As an experienced businessman put it, "the big money is in getting it before it hits Angola."[124]

Choke points and market power

Personal enrichment in Angola has often relied on the leveraging of market power and political influence. A few hundred well-placed families have taken advantage of key choke points in the Angolan economy, where they are able to extract wealth as it passes through while using their influence to maximize throughput. The exercise of monopolistic market power by the state and private actors, sometimes legally and sometimes not, looms large in the origins of much capital flight. Analyses of economies like Angola's can usefully incorporate insights from the fast-growing antitrust movement in the United States and elsewhere.[125]

---

[123] Interview with a foreign banker in Luanda.

[124] Interview with a European businessman.

[125] See, for example, the work of the Open Markets Institute, which has put together a coherent and potent analysis of the nature and dangers of the monopolistic power along with a wide range of solutions.

The enablers

Much attention has rightly been paid to the role of international banks in encouraging and facilitating capital flight.[126] However, because banks play a central role in any economy, and given the systemic risks an unstable banking system imposes, historically they have been subject to stronger regulation than in many other economic sectors. This remained the case even after an era of financial deregulation. And since the 2008 global financial crisis there has been a tightening of global and national standards for due diligence and the prevention of money laundering.

There is another range of actors who are subject to far less regulation, however, and who have been arguably just as important as the banks in enabling capital flight and other illicit activities with little prospect of being sanctioned. These include the global consulting and accounting firms, along with law firms, hedge funds, and private equity firms. Since they generally have not been perceived as posing the same scale of systemic risks to western economies, they have been subjected to far less scrutiny. Imposing bank-like legal obligations on this broader range of firms would be an important step forward in the fight against illicit financial flows.

Transnational networks of plunder

Transfers of Angolan capital into private overseas accounts and financial structures are being carried out by what can be characterized as transnational networks of plunder. These networks comprise Angolan elites operating in partnership with (mostly western) bankers, accountants, law firms, intermediaries, and at times private firms—and, of course, the global infrastructure of offshore tax havens. The transnational networks are not mere passive handlers of capital flight that would have occurred anyway: they solicit, encourage, and amplify its scale.

Each network, though loosely defined and not a formally constituted body, is more than the sum of its parts. In any analysis of capital flight and its remedies, the transnational network of plunder should be considered as a relevant unit of analysis. In the case of Angola, perhaps the most interesting and unique player has been the state oil company Sonangol, which was nurtured since independence as an island of competence and capability carved out from the surrounding milieu of political, economic, and military chaos. The firm became an extraordinarily useful tool in the service of the Angolan elite, and a fascinating transnational network in its own right. This chapter also describes several more nefarious networks.

Similar transnational networks are active in looting rich country economies, too, through legal and illegal practices of tax avoidance and evasion and through the broader processes of "financialization" in which wealth is extracted unfairly,

---

[126] For a good investigation, see Henry (2003).

and sometimes illegally, from poorer sections of those societies, passing into the hands of a small, globalized elite. Living in the same offshore world, Angolan and western elites in many respects often have more in common with each other than with their own poorer compatriots. Today the old Westphalian system of sovereign nation-states is breaking down, observe foreign policy analysts David Adler and Ben Judah (2019), "displaced by a new set of transnational networks often dominated by non-state actors," creating a new global context in which "the boundaries between foreign and domestic have blurred." International legal cooperation and greater transparency in global finance will be essential to check the power of these transnational networks.

Blowback

Capital flight from Angola and other low-income countries damages not only the source countries but also countries on the receiving end of illicit financial flows. "Too much finance" harms the host economies in multiple ways.[127] Countries receiving large inflows can suffer a "finance curse" whose impacts are similar in some respects to those of the resource curse that afflicts Angola. Potential ill effects include a finance-sector variant of the "Dutch disease" (whereby the financial inflows lead to currency appreciation, hollowing out the tradable goods sector by making industries less competitive); economic volatility associated with movements of hot money; and a "brain drain" into the high-paid financial firms managing the inflows. One of the most important aspects of the finance curse, however, is only now starting to gain attention: the criminalization of western elites and institutions through the corrosive effects of dirty money from overseas. The Elf Affair in France provided dramatic early warning of this threat, with similar phenomena now becoming apparent in other western countries including the United States, Britain, and Portugal.

These contagion effects of capital flight again suggest that majorities of citizens across the world, from Angola to Europe and North America, share something in common. If widely understood, blowback can boost the political resolve in western countries to tackle cross-border illicit financial flows and the institutional infrastructure that enables them. In contrast, if policy makers and voters in the receiving nations, despite the distaste they may feel for the effects on countries like Angola simultaneously perceive a benefit for their own economies, the resulting ambivalence is a recipe for inaction. The finance curse analysis transforms these calculations to "this hurts them, and it hurts us too." This opens the way to building powerful transnational anti-looter alliances, where the focus expands beyond fostering development in low-income countries—important though that would

---

[127] See, for example, Shaxson (2018), Baker et al. (2018), and Cecchetti and Kharroubi (2015).

be—towards re-engineering the global economy in the interests of the majority of the world's people, in rich and poor countries alike.

The search for solutions

In thinking about what needs to be done, it helps to start from the "triangle of power" that exists in an oil-dominated economy. At one vertex sit the state and the country's ruling classes. At another sit the people. At the third sits the international oil industry. Prior to the 1970s, in countries like Angola the oil companies sat securely at the apex of this system. With the advent of OPEC, states and their rulers began to assert their power, and in Angola's case they managed to turn the triangle so that they were at the top, or at least on a par with the oil companies—with the people still firmly at the bottom.

Can this triangle be turned once again, so that the people rise up to the top?

Efforts by international agencies to foster political and economic reforms in Angola have had disappointing results. This is for three main reasons. First, oil wealth has insulated the Angolan leadership from pressures for reform. Second, the long history of disastrous and self-interested western meddling in Angola has generated widespread mistrust, not just among the country's leaders. Third, the logic of Angola's oil-fueled patronage system has acquired a tremendous momentum of its own.

There is another key avenue, however, by which the international community can help to improve governance and development in Angola: reform of the international financial system, including the infrastructure of offshore tax havens and other institutions that host and facilitate transnational networks of plunder. This will require not only dedicated efforts by policy makers and concerted international actions, but also, underpinning these, broad-based public understanding of the need for reform and demand for it in the interests of the majority of people throughout the world.

A second powerful way to achieve more inclusive economic development and more responsive governance in Angola would be to distribute much or all of the country's oil revenues directly to its population on an equal per-person basis.[128] While this would be devastating for current power structures and, at least in the short run, for government revenue, it would transform Angola's power dynamics, bringing political as well as economic benefits. Governments would have to negotiate with the citizens to raise tax revenues, empowering the public to demand accountability and better public services. The result would almost certainly be greater prosperity for the vast majority of Angolans.

---

[128] For more on this idea, see Shaxson (2007b); Shaxson (2008); and Shaxson and Sandbu (2009).

References

Adler, D., and Judah, B. 2019. Traditional 'foreign policy' no longer exists. Democrats are the last to know. *The Guardian*, December 2.

AFP (Agence France Press). 2009. Angolagate: prison ferme pour Falcone, Gaydamak, Pasqua et Marchiani, *Libération*, October 27, available at https://www.liberation.fr/france/2009/10/27/angolagate-prison-ferme-pour-falcone-gaydamak-pasqua-et-marchiani_590313 (accessed on December 8, 2020).

Africa Confidential. 1999. Vol. 40, No. 10, May 14.

Africa Energy Intelligence. 2018. Switch in top role for the most pro-MPLA of oil firms, Somoil. May 22.

Ames, P. 2015. Portugal is becoming an Angolan financial colony. *Politico*. April 28.

Associação Mãos Livres and Corruption Watch UK. 2013. *Deception in high places: The Corrupt Angola-Russia debt deal*, available at https://shadowworldinvestigations.org/wp-content/uploads/2019/09/54261c_8eed8c6d8b39460e8c7dbcb6ee67 6c4b.pdf (accessed on November 25, 2020).

Associated Press/Haaretz. 2011. French Court Clears Gaydamak of Most 'Angola-gate' Charges. May 1.

Baker, A., Epstein, G., and Montecino, J. 2018. The UK's Finance Curse? Costs and Processes. *Sheffield Political Economy Research Institute*.

Batalha, J. 2018. Risk of impunity increases with outcome of Portuguese-Angolan corruption trial. Transparency International, available at https://www.transparency.org/en/news/risk-of-impunity-increases-with-outcome-of-portuguese-angolan-corruption-tr# (accessed on July 21, 2021).

BBC. 2011. France ex-minister Pasqua acquitted over Angola arms. April 29.

Boyce, J.K. 1992. The revolving door: External debt and capital flight. *World Development*, 20(3), 335–349.

Brönnimann, C. 2017. Wie ein Schweizer von Angolas Milliarden profitiert. *Tages-Anzeiger*. November 5, available at https://interaktiv.tagesanzeiger.ch/2017/paradise-papers/angola-bastos/?openincontroller (accessed on July 21, 2021).

Burgis, T., Sevastopulo, D., and O'Murchu, C. 2014. China in Africa: How Sam Pa became the middleman. *Financial Times*. August 8.

Cabeche, C., and Forrest, D. 2013. Swiss release 'Angolagate' fugitive. *Mail & Guardian*, December 12, available at https://mg.co.za/article/2013-12-12-swiss-release-angolagate-fugitive/ (accessed on July 30, 2020).

Cabral, T. 2017. Portuguese prosecutors charge Angolan VP with corruption. Yahoo News. 16 February, available at https://news.yahoo.com/portuguese-prosecutors-charge-angolan-vp-corruption-180449400.html (accessed on July 21, 2021).

Cecchetti, S., and Kharroubi, E. 2015. Why does financial sector growth crowd out real economic growth? *BIS Working Papers*, No. 490.

Collier, P., and Goderis, B. 2012. Commodity prices and growth: An empirical investigation. *European Economic Review*, 56(6), 1241–1260.

Corkin, L. 2011. Uneasy allies: China's evolving relations with Angola. *Journal of Contemporary African Studies*, 29(2), 169-180.

Corruption Watch. 2019. *Corporate Crime Gap: How the UK Lags the US in Policing Corporate Financial Crime*, March.

Costa, J., Lopes, J.T., and Louçã, F. 2014. *Os Donos Angolanos de Portugal*. Lisbon: Bertrand Editora.

Cotterill, J. 2020. Angola sharpens fight to recover stolen cash as debt pressure mounts. *Financial Times*, November 11.

Dalby, D. 2020. Portuguese 'super judge' orders total seizure of dos Santos assets. ICIJ, available at https://www.icij.org/investigations/luanda-leaks/portuguese-super-judge-orders-total-seizure-of-dos-santos-assets/ (accessed on July 21, 2021).

de Marais, R. 2018. Angola's Path to Justice: Prosecuting the Guilty and Recovering the Stolen Billions. *Maka Angola*. 23 October, available at https://www.makaangola.org/2018/10/angolas-path-to-justice-prosecuting-the-guilty-and-recovering-the-stolen-billions/ (accessed on December 4, 2019).

Deloitte. 2016. Banking Review 2016, available at https://www2.deloitte.com/ao/pt/pages/financial-services/topics/banca-em-analise-2016/banking-review-2016.html (accessed on July 21, 2021).

Demony, C., and Waldersee, V. 2020. Angola may ask Portugal to seize dos Santos' assets, says prosecutor. Reuters.

Di John, J. 2007. Oil abundance and violent political conflict: A critical assessment. *Journal of Development Studies*, 43(6), 961–986.

Dolan, K.A. 2013. Daddy's Girl: How an African "Princess" Banked $3 Billion in a Country Living on $2 A Day. *Forbes*, September 2.

ECO News. 2017. Isabel dos Santos justifies the lack of Unitel dividends with the currency crisis in Angola, available at https://econews.pt/2017/12/13/isabel-dos-santos-justifies-the-lack-of-unitel-dividends-with-the-currency-crisis-in-angola/ (accessed on July 21, 2021).

Economist Intelligence Unit. 1999. Angola Country Report. Q3.

Economist Intelligence Unit. 2002. Angola Country Report. February.

Economist Intelligence Unit. 2003. Angola Country Report. May.

Engebretsen, R., and Soares de Oliveira, R. 2020. "For the English to see—The politics of mock compliance." In Emily Jones (Ed.), *The Political Economy of Bank Regulation in Developing Countries: Risk and Reputation*. Oxford: Oxford University Press, pp. 283-304.

Ernst & Young. 2011. Cochan Singapore Pte. Ltd. and its Subsidiary, Annual Financial Statements, December 2011, available at https://www.scribd.com/document/206840701/120531-Cochan-Singapore-Pte-Ltd-Annual-Report-2011 (accessed on July 21, 2021).

Expresso. 2014. Generais angolanos pressionam Sobrinho a contar para onde foi o dinheiro no BESA, available at https://expresso.pt/dossies/diario/generais-angolanos-pressionam-sobrinho-a-contar-para-onde-foi-o-dinheiro-no-besa=f903132 (accessed on July 21, 2021).

Expresso. 2016. José Eduardo dos Santos exige ao BNA solução para falta de divisas. *Lusa News Agency*, reported by Portugal's Expresso newspaper on July 1, 2016, available at https://expresso.pt/internacional/2016-07-01-Jose-Eduardo-dos-Santos-exige-ao-BNA-solucao-para-falta-de-divisas (accessed on July 21, 2021).

Ferreira, M., and Soares de Oliveira, R. 2019. The political economy of banking in Angola. *African Affairs*, 118(470), 49-74, January.

Filipe, D., and Bernardo, S. 2018. De bens alimentares e panos do Congo a diamantes e armas, tudo se compra e vende na fronteira Luvo/RDC. *Novo Jornal*. January 4.

Fitzgibbon, W. 2017. Rise of tax haven Mauritius comes at the expense of rest of Africa. *Irish Times*, November 7, available at https://www.irishtimes.com/business/rise-of-tax-haven-mauritius-comes-at-the-expense-of-rest-of-africa-1.3282982 and at https://www.icij.org/investigations/paradise-papers/tax-haven-mauritius-africa/ (both accessed on July 21, 2021).

Forsythe, M., Gurney, K., Alecci, S., and Hallman, B. 2020. How U.S. Firms Helped Africa's Richest Woman Exploit Her Country's Wealth. *New York Times*. January 19, available at https://www.nytimes.com/2020/01/19/world/africa/isabel-dos-santos-angola.html (accessed on July 21, 2021).

France 24. 2009. Jail terms for 'Angolagate' power players. October 27.

Freedberg, S., Alecci, S., Fitzgibbon, W., Dalby, D., and Reuter, D. 2020. *How Africa's richest woman exploited family ties, shell companies and inside deals to build an empire.* ICIJ. January 19.

Ghazvinian, J. 2007. *Untapped: The Scramble for Africa's Oil*, Houghton Mifflin Harcourt, cited in Ovadia, J. 2016. *The Petro-Developmental State in Africa: Making Oil Work in Angola, Nigeria and the Gulf of Guinea.* London: Hurst.

Glenny, M. 2008. *McMafia: A Journey Through the Global Criminal Underworld.* New York: Knopf.

Global Trade Review. 2007. Best Deals of 2006—Sonangol Sinopec International (SSI), Angola, March.

Global Witness. 1998. *A Rough Trade: The Role of Companies and Governments in the Angolan Conflict*, Global Witness, London. available at https://cdn2.globalwitness.org/archive/files/pdfs/a_rough_trade.pdf (accessed on August 30, 2020).

Global Witness. 1999. *A Crude Awakening: The Role of the Oil and Banking Industries in Angola's Civil War and the Plunder of State Assets*, available at https://cdn.globalwitness.org/archive/files/pdfs/a%20crude%20awakening.pdf (accessed on August 3, 2020).

Global Witness. 2002. *All the President's Men: The Devastating Story of oil and banking in Angola's privatised war*, available at https://cdn.globalwitness.org/archive/files/import/all_the_presidents_men.pdf (accessed on December 6, 2019).

Global Witness. 2004. *Time for Transparency: coming clean on oil, mining and gas revenues*, London, March.

Global Witness. 2011. Oil Revenues in Angola, Much More Information but Not Enough Transparency. December, available at https://cdn2.globalwitness.org/archive/files/library/v15_live_angola_report_0.pdf (accessed on December 30, 2020).

The Guardian. 2020. Isabel dos Santos responds to Luanda Leaks investigation. January 23, available at https://www.theguardian.com/world/2020/jan/19/isabel-dos-santos-issues-response-luanda-leaks-investigation (accessed on July 21, 2021).

Hallman, B., Gurney, K., Alecci, S., and de Haldevang, M. 2020. Western advisers helped an autocrat's daughter amass and shield a fortune. ICIJ. January 20.

Henry, J. 2003. *The Blood Bankers: Tales from the Underground Economy.* New York: Four Walls Eight Windows.

Hodges, T. 2001. *Angola from Afro-Stalinism to Petro-Diamond Capitalism.* Bloomington, IN: Indiana University Press.

Hodges, T. 2003. *Angola: Anatomy of an Oil State.* Bloomington, IN: Indiana University Press.

Hodges, T. 2004. *Angola: Anatomy of an Oil State.* Lysaker, Norway: Fridtjof Nansen Institute.

Human Rights Watch. 2001. *The Oil Diagnostic in Angola: An Update.* March, available at https://www.hrw.org/legacy/backgrounder/africa/angola/index-04.htm (accessed on November 25, 2020).

Human Rights Watch. 2004. *Angola: Some Transparency, No Accountability: The Use of Oil Revenue in Angola and Its Impact on Human Rights*. New York: Human Rights Watch.

Hume, N. and Sheppard, D. 2016. Angola overhaul tests ties with Trafigura. *Financial Times*, September 23.

ICIJ. 2020. Luanda Leaks: Key Findings. January 20.

IMF. 1997. Angola—Recent Economic Developments. November 17.

IMF. 2011. Angola—Fifth Review Under the Stand-By Arrangement, Request for Waiver of Applicability of Performance Criteria, and Request for Modification of Performance Criteria. Country Report No. 11/346, December.

IMF. 2014. Angola: Second Post-Program Monitoring. Country Report No. 14/81, March, available at https://www.imf.org/external/pubs/ft/scr/2014/cr1481.pdf (accessed on August 4, 2020).

IMF. 2015. Angola: Selected Issues and Statistical Appendix. November 3.

IMF. 2017. Angola: Staff Report for the 2016 Article IV Consultation. February 6.

Mailey, J.R. 2015. *The Anatomy of the Resource Curse: Predatory Investment in Africa's Extractive Industries*. Africa Center for Strategic Studies, May.

Maka Angola. 2016. Sonangol paga US 100 milhões mensais a trio do PR. August 30, available at https://www.makaangola.org/2016/08/sonangol-paga-us-100-milhoes-mensais-a-trio-do-pr/ (accessed on July 21, 2021).

Marques, R. 2012. Isabel dos Santos: Honour and Lies. *Maka Angola*. February 24.

Meisel, A. and Grossman, D. 2017. Paradise Papers: Tycoon made $41m from 'people's fund'. *BBC News*. November 7, available at https://www.bbc.com/news/world-africa-41906123 (accessed on November 26, 2020).

Mendes, C. 2020. Angola seizes assets of allies of former president Dos Santos. Bloomberg, available at https://www.bloomberg.com/news/articles/2020-10-14/angola-seizes-assets-of-allies-of-former-president-dos-santos (accessed on July 21, 2021).

Michel, S. 2009. When China met Africa. *Foreign Policy*. October 7.

Le Monde. 2015. Angolagate: Arcadi Gaydamak se rend à la justice, November 24, available at https://www.lemonde.fr/police-justice/article/2015/11/24/angolagate-arcadi-gaydamak-se-rend-a-la-justice_4816421_1653578.html (accessed on December 8, 2020).

Natural Resources Governance Institute. 2015. The Resource Curse The Political and Economic Challenges of Natural Resource Wealth. March, available at https://resourcegovernance.org/sites/default/files/nrgi_Resource-Curse.pdf (accessed on August 17, 2019).

Ndikumana, L., and Boyce, J.K. 2003. Public debts and public assets: Explaining capital flight from sub-Saharan African countries. *World Development*, 31(1), 107–130.

Ndikumana, L., and Boyce, J.K. 2011. New Estimates of Capital Flight from Sub-Saharan African Countries: Linkages with External Borrowing and Policy Options, *International Review of Applied Economics*, 25(2) 149–170.

Ndikumana, L., and Sarr, M. 2019. Capital flight, foreign direct investment and natural resources in Africa. Resources Policy, 63 (October).

Observador. 2014. BES Angola não sabe a quem emprestou 5,7 mil milhões de dólares, available at https://observador.pt/2014/06/07/bes-angola-nao-sabe-quem-emprestou-57-mil-milhoes-de-dolares/ (accessed on July 21, 2021).

Ovadia, J. 2016. *The Petro-Developmental State in Africa: Making Oil Work in Angola, Nigeria and the Gulf of Guinea*. London: Hurst.

Pallister, D. 2005. Alarm bells sound over massive loans bankrolling oil-rich, graft-tainted Angola. *The Guardian*. June 1.

Puma Energy. 2015. Corporate Brochure, available at https://pumaenergy.com/media/488705/corporate-brochure-2015.pdf (accessed on July 21, 2021).

Puma Energy. 2017. Offering Memorandum, Puma International Financing S.A., $600,000,000. 5.125% senior notes due 2024. Obtained from the Luxembourg Stock exchange, available at https://www.bourse.lu/issuer-notices/PumaInternFinan/70873 (accessed on July 21, 2021).

Reuters. 2016. UPDATE 1-Statoil says briefed Norwegian police on Angola payments. December 19, available at https://www.reuters.com/article/statoil-angola-idUSL8N15Y2EB (accessed on July 3, 2020).

Reuters. 2017. Powerful Angolan VP charged with corruption in Portugal.

Reuters. 2018a. Portugal lets Angola try ex-VP in graft case, hopes to improve ties. May 10.

Reuters. 2018b. UPDATE 1-Angola's Isabel dos Santos misses summons from prosecutors, available at https://www.reuters.com/article/angola-politics/update-1-angolas-isabel-dos-santos-misses-summons-from-prosecutors-idUSL5N1UR73H (accessed on July 21, 2021).

Robert-Diard, P. 2009. Angolagate: Prison ferme pour les principaux prévenues. *Le Monde*. October 28, available at https://www.lemonde.fr/societe/article/2009/10/28/angolagate-prison-ferme-pour-les-principaux-prevenus_1259726_3224.htm (accessed on November 23, 2020).

Roth, N. 2008. Suit claims Gaydamak defrauded Angolans of $365 million. *Haaretz*, December 4, available at https://www.haaretz.com/1.4968043 (accessed on November 25, 2020).

Roth, N. 2011. Gaydamak beats civil suit over Angola debt deal. *Haaretz*, October 25, available at https://www.haaretz.com/1.5203686 (accessed on November 25, 2020).

Sachs, J., and Warner, A. 1999. The Big Rush, Natural Resource Booms and Growth. *Journal of Development Economics* 59(1), 43–76.

Sharife, K. 2016. Leaks reveal extensive siphoning of $5bn Angola sovereign wealth fund. ICIJ, available at https://panamapapers.investigativecenters.org/angola/ (accessed on July 21, 2021).

Sharife, K., and Grobler, J. 2013. Kimberley's Illicit Process. *World Policy Journal*, 34(4), 65–77.

Shaxson, N. 1999. Stolen Stones. *Africa Confidential*. October 8, available at https://www.africa-confidential.com/article-preview/id/1332/Stolen_stones (accessed on January 20, 2020).

Shaxson, N. 2002. Where the Money Lives. *Vanity Fair*. August.

Shaxson, N. 2007a. *Poisoned Wells: The Dirty Politics of African Oil*. London: St. Martin's Griffin.

Shaxson, N. 2007b. Oil, corruption and the resource curse. *International Affairs*, 83(6), 1123–1140.

Shaxson, N. 2008. Oil for the People: a Solution to the 'Resource Curse'. Association for Accountancy and Business Affairs, July.

Shaxson, N. 2012. *Treasure Islands: Tax Havens and the Men Who Stole the World*. London: Vintage Books.

Shaxson, N. 2018. *The Finance Curse: How Global Finance is Making Us All Poorer*. London: Bodley Head.

Shaxson, N. 2021. Oil and Capital Flight: The Case of Angola. Amherst, MA: Political Economy Research Institute, Working Paper 534.

Shaxson, N., and Sandbu, M. 2009. Give the People their Resource Wealth. *Financial Times*, June 4.

Shirbon, E. 2009. French power brokers convicted over arms to Angola. *Reuters*, October 27.

Smiley, X. 1983. Inside Angola. *New York Review of Books*, February 17.

Soares de Oliveira, R. 2007. Business success, Angola-style: postcolonial politics and the rise and rise of Sonangol. *Journal of Modern African Studies*, 45(3), 595–619.

Soares de Oliveira, R. 2015. *Magnificent and Beggar Land: Angola since the civil war*. London: Hurst.

Sonangol. 2016. 'Management report and consolidated accounts,' available at https://www.sonangol.co.ao/English/AboutSonangolEP/AccountsAndReport/Documents/Relatorio_Contas_e_Gestao_Sonangol_2016_en.pdf (accessed on November 11, 2020).

Sonangol. 2017. Management Report and Consolidated Accounts, 2016.

Subcommittee on Africa. 1974. *The Complex of United States-Portuguese Relations: Before and After the Coup. Hearings Before the Subcommittee on Africa, Committee on Foreign Affairs, House of Representatives, Ninety-third Congress, Second Session*. Washington, DC: US Government Printing Office.

Tax Justice Network. 2012. *The Price of Offshore Revisited*. July.

Thompson, B. 2019. UK's poor record on corporate crime comes under attack. *Financial Times*, March 5, available at https://www.ft.com/content/52101b3e-3f51-11e9-b896-fe36ec32aece (accessed on July 29, 2020).

Trafigura. 2016. Annual report 2016, available at https://www.ise.ie/debt_documents/Trafigura%20Group%20Pte.%20Ltd.%20Annual%20Report%202016_6f2756e2-aba1-45c4-b520-3a57cb34f3fc.pdf (accessed on July 21, 2021).

United Nations. 2000. Final Report of the UN Panel of Experts on Violations of Security Council Sanctions Against UNITA, known as the 'Fowler Report'. March.

United Nations. 2018. Level & Trends in Child Mortality. Estimates developed by the UN Inter-agency Group for Child Mortality Estimation.

United States of America vs Weatherford Services, International. 2013. United States District Court, Southern District of Texas, Houston Division. Plea Agreement. Criminal No. 13 CR 734, November 26, available at http://fcpa.stanford.edu/fcpac/documents/3000/002144.pdf (accessed on December 31, 2020).

US Department of Justice. 2013. Three Subsidiaries of Weatherford International Limited Agree to Plead Guilty to FCPA and Export Control Violations, November 26.

US Securities and Exchange Commission. 2017. In the Matter of Halliburton Company and Jeannot Lorenz, Respondents. Order Instituting Cease-and-Desist Proceedings, July 27, available at https://www.sec.gov/litigation/admin/2017/34-81222.pdf (accessed on January 2, 2021.

US Securities & Exchange Commission 2013. Complaint: U.S. Securities and Exchange Commission, plaintiff v. Weatherford International LTD., Defendant, United States District Court for the Southern District of Texas, Houston Division, available at https://www.sec.gov/litigation/complaints/2013/comp-pr2013-252.pdf.

US Securities & Exchange Commission. Undated. Production Sharing Contract between Sociedade nacional de Combustíveis de Angola, Empresa Pública – (Sonangol, E.P.) and CIE Angola Block 20 Ltd., Sonangol Pesquisa e Produção, S.A., BP Exploration Angola (Kwanza Benguela) Limited, China Sonangol international Holding Limited, in the Area of Block 20/11. Article 12.

US Senate, Permanent Subcommittee on Investigations. 2010. Keeping Foreign Corruption Out of the United States: Four Case Histories, 4 February, available at https://www.hsgac.senate.gov/imo/media/doc/FOREIGNCORRUPTIONREPORT FINAL710. Accessed 4 December 2019.

Van Niekerk, P. and Peterson, L. 2002. *Greasing the Skids of Corruption*, ICIJ.org, November 2, available at https://www.icij.org/investigations/makingkilling/
greasing-skids-corruption/ (accessed on August 24, 2020).

Vanham, P. 2015. Why is Angola's capital the most expensive city in the world? *World Economic Forum*. June 15.

Verde, R. 2016. Sarju Raikundalia: ilegalidade do governo no Sonangol. *Maka Angola*, October 29, available at https://www.makaangola.org/2016/10/sarju-raikundalia-ilegalidade-no-governo-da-sonangol/ (accessed on July 21, 2021).

Villalobos, L. 2015. Isabel dos Santos formaliza compra da Efacec Power Solutions. *Público*. October 23, available at https://www.publico.pt/2015/10/23/economia/noticia/isabel-dos-santos-formaliza-compra-da-efacec-power-solutions–1712165 (accessed on July 21, 2021).

Vines, A., Shaxson, N., Rimli, L., and Heymans, C. 2005. Angola: Drivers of Change—Position Paper 1: Economic Change and Reform. London: Chatham House, April, available at https://gsdrc.org/topic-guides/political-economy-analysis/examples/drivers-of-change-country-studies/ (accessed on December 20, 2019).

Vines, A., Wong, L., Weimer, M., and Campos, I. 2009. *Thirst for African Oil: Asian National Oil Companies in Nigeria and Angola*. Chatham House. August.

Weiss, M. 2014. The 750 Million Dollar Man. *Foreign Policy*. February 13, available at https://foreignpolicy.com/2014/02/13/the-750-million-dollar-man/ (accessed on July 21, 2021).

Xinhuanet. 2017. Chinese firm contracted to build massive hydropower plant in Angola. August 5.

Zierer, M., Kühne, S., Dangelmayer, P., and Kerler, W. 2017. *Das System Madeira*, available at http://web.br.de/madeira/artikel/ (accessed on July 21, 2021).

4

Côte d'Ivoire

Bitter Chocolate

Jean Merckaert

Introduction

In the period from 1970 to 2018, cumulative capital flight from Côte d'Ivoire has been estimated at US$55.4 billion (in 2018 dollars) (Ndikumana and Boyce, Chapter 2 in this volume). Among African countries, the country ranks among the top ten in the sheer magnitude of capital flight, and relative to GDP, Ivorian capital flight is roughly 50% above the continental average (Ndikumana and Boyce 2021).

Capital flight from Côte d'Ivoire peaked in the 1980s at about $2.6 billion per year and continued through the 1990s. It trailed off after the turn of the century, reflecting among other things the drying up of foreign lending following the outbreak of civil war in 2002, followed by the revival of investment opportunities after the war in 2010. Accordingly, this chapter devotes particular attention to the circumstances that fostered capital flight in the earlier decades. But a number of the same features remain in place today, implying that large-scale capital flight could re-emerge as a serious drain on the country's development resources in future years.

The roots of Côte d'Ivoire's contemporary political economy lie in the period of French colonial rule, which formally ended with independence in 1960. Colonization was a project of subjugation and exploitation for the benefit of the metropolitan countries. Cacao, the tree crop from whose beans cocoa and chocolate are produced, arrived in West Africa from Latin America, and today Côte d'Ivoire is the world's top producer.[1]

Félix Houphouët-Boigny, a trade union leader who became the first president of Côte d'Ivoire in 1960, held that position until his death in 1993. He was the most

---

[1] "Cocoa" is cacao that has been roasted at high temperatures. For simplicity, hereafter it is used to refer to both.

Jean Merckaert, *Côte d'Ivoire*. In: *On the Trail of Capital Flight from Africa*.
Edited by Léonce Ndikumana and James K. Boyce, Oxford University Press.
© Jean Merckaert (2022). DOI: 10.1093/oso/9780198852728.003.0004

prominent figure of Ivorian emancipation, the "father of independence," but he had also served as a *député* in French governments in the late 1950s, and he chose a policy of continuity rather than a sharp break with the former colonial power.

Côte d'Ivoire's currency, until today the West African CFA franc, was tied by a fixed exchange rate to the French franc and then to the Euro, and it was guaranteed by the French treasury.[2] This arrangement has greatly benefited French companies, which have enjoyed fixed parity and free movement of capital. It also benefits Ivorian civil servants and other employees in the formal sector, securing their purchasing power to buy imported goods and to send their children to France for studies (Cogneau et al. 2018).

Côte d'Ivoire was long considered a model of economic development and political stability, the "showcase of West Africa" (Losch 1999, p. 9). The 1960s and 1970s were characterized by strong growth: GDP rose fivefold in 20 years, spurred by growth in the cocoa and forestry sectors (Berthélemy and Bourguignon 1996). While coups proliferated in neighboring countries, Félix Houphouët-Boigny's political rule seemed utterly firm.

But appearances proved to be deceptive. The country's high dependence on cocoa rendered the country economically and socially vulnerable. By the 1980s, Côte d'Ivoire was collapsing under an unsustainable debt burden, and cocoa producer incomes plummeted. For a time, perhaps, it had been the "country of hospitality" proclaimed in its national anthem, the country for hundreds of thousands of cocoa and coffee workers who came from the north of the country and from neighboring Burkina Faso and Mali. (See the map showing major cocoa areas in Figure 4.1). But when economic problems arose, these outsiders became scapegoats.

The country's political elite maintains its dominance by skillfully parceling out incomes among different groups of supporters. This arrangement, known to political scientists as "clientelism," is not a strong cement with which to unite a nation. Nor does it encourage robust, transparent, and impartial institutions. It ran into its limits in the 1980s as the money ran out (Cogneau and Mesplé-Somps 2002, 2003). As in other African countries, the creditors imposed painful and ultimately unsuccessful structural adjustment programs. Côte d'Ivoire went "from a developing country to a poor one" (Losch 1999, p. 14). When Alassane Ouattara, the former director of the IMF's African department, was appointed as prime minister in 1990, it seemed to many observers as though the international financial institutions had put Côte d'Ivoire under their own supervision.

Institutionally, a multi-party system also began to develop. Houphouët-Boigny had come to power under a system with a single party, the Parti Démocratique de la Côte d'Ivoire (PDCI), and did not break with this model until the end of his rule, under pressure from the democratic movement stirring across Africa. In the

---

[2] At the end of 2020, the CFA franc is about to be renamed "eco." The fixed exchange rate to the Euro remains, but France will play a lower role in the governance of the new currency.

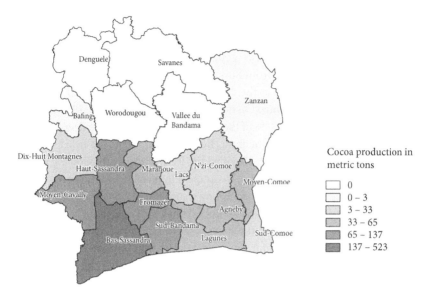

Fig. 4.1 Map of major cacao areas

Note: CGFCC and BCC were dismantled in the late 2012. The cocoa sector is now managed by state-owned Conseil Café-Cacao (Coffee and Cocoa Council). Its website does not have data on cocoa production by region.
Source: Comité de Gestion de la Filière Café-Cacao (CGFCC) and Bourse Café-Cacao (BCC), 2008-09.

years since, three main political forces have shaped the Ivorian party system. Henri Konan Bédié took over the leadership of the PDCI after Houphouët-Boigny's death. Laurent Gbagbo, an exiled history professor, had launched the Front Patriotique Ivoirien (FPI) in 1982. The liberal Rassemblement des Républicains (RDR), founded in 1994, was led by Alassane Ouattara.

Regardless of which party holds power, the rules of the game established under Houphouët-Boigny remain much the same. Michailof (2005, pp. 393–403) noted that "controlling political power enabled control of revenues, and this ensured that power would be perpetuated." The best way to get rich in Côte d'Ivoire was to acquire political power—although it would be an exaggeration to say this was the only way.

Upon the death of Félix Houphouët-Boigny in 1993, Bédié, who had been the speaker of the national assembly, took power. He continued the economic liberalization policies demanded by creditors. The French government proceeded to devalue the CFA in 1994—a step it had promised not to take during Houphouët-Boigny's lifetime—sharply increasing the prices of imported goods (Noble 1994; Cogneau and Gérald 1998). In politics, Bédié introduced the toxic notion of *ivoirité*—Ivorian national identity—into public debate. Although he presented this as a way to unify the country, in fact it served to stigmatize those from the north and thwart political opponents.

Modifying the electoral law, Bédié introduced a requirement that candidates be born in Côte d'Ivoire. That alone would not have been enough to disqualify his main rival, Ouattara, so he also required that both of a candidate's parents be Ivorian. (Ouattara's father was from Burkina Faso.) Ouattara rallied those from the north to support him, as well as the country's Muslims who made up 35% of the population.[3] Gbagbo's FPI joined Ouattara's RDR in boycotting the 1995 elections, and Bédié was "elected" with 96% of the vote. The country became deeply divided.

Building on his political momentum, Bédié put *ivoirité* at the heart of his reforms to the country's land code. He jailed the RDR leadership following protests in 1999, although Ouattara managed to escape. Financial scandals during his rule may have been the final straw in prompting a surge of discontent in the military, and on Christmas Eve of 1999, General Robert Gueï announced on television that the military had taken control of the state.

While Bédié waited in vain for France to restore him to power, Ivorians celebrated in the streets. Their joy was short-lived. Initially, Gueï declared that he had no interest in power, but soon he changed his mind. Ouattara's RDR and Bédié's PDCI boycotted the October 2000 presidential election. But to Gueï's surprise, his opponent, Gbagbo, won the vote. Unwilling to admit defeat, he ordered his troops to fire on the crowds, but popular pressure forced him to cede power. The new president's declared ambition was to enable Ivorians as a whole, rather than just a few privileged groups, to increase their wealth.

As soon as Gbagbo became head of state, armed supporters of Ouattara took to the streets to demand new elections. The protests ended in clashes with Gbagbo's FPI supporters. Sympathizers of Ouattara's RDR then were violently repressed by the gendarmerie and Gbagbo's followers.

In September 2002, an attempted coup took place, with part of the army led by Sergeant Ibrahim Coulibaly rising up against Gbagbo. It did not topple the president, but the coup achieved military success in the northern half of the country which fell under control of the rebel Forces Nouvelles (FN).[4] France gradually became an arbiter in the ongoing conflict. It ratified the de facto partition of the country, as French soldiers were deployed along a supposedly secure buffer zone. France sought to "multilaterize" its engagement first by enlisting support from ECOWAS (Economic Community of West African States) troops and then from UN peacekeepers under a Security Council mandate (Cogneau et al. 2016).[5]

In January 2003, France sought to have the warring parties agree to form a national unity government, but Gbagbo refused to implement fully the resulting Marcoussis Agreements. South African president Thabo Mbeki also tried to bring about national reconciliation. The resulting Pretoria Agreement of 2005 allowed

---

[3] The remainder of the population consisted of Christians (41%), traditional religions (17%), and without religion (17%), according to the Demographic and Health Survey of 1994.

[4] For accounts of the crisis, see Banégas (2003) and Dozon (2011).

[5] For an account of the UN engagement, see Novosseloff (2018).

Ouattara to stand in the next presidential election, but Gbagbo played for time, and the election was delayed repeatedly until 2010. The interim 2007 Ouagadougou Agreement divided power, with the position of prime minister going to the head of the Forces Nouvelles, Guillaume Soro.

A striking feature of the eight-year conflict was the brutality that quickly emerged on both sides, claiming large numbers of civilian victims. Some of Gbagbo's supporters in the south went on veritable murder sprees. In the north, rival "comzones" (zone commanders) competed violently to control and exploit the local population. In the midst of this violence, unsurprisingly, rural poverty intensified (Cogneau et al. 2016).

Gbagbo came first in the initial round of the 2010 election with 38% of the vote, ahead of both Ouattara (32%) and Bédié (25%). The latter was eliminated, and called on his supporters to back Ouattara. The results of the second round remain controversial to this day. At the beginning of December, Côte d'Ivoire found itself with two self-proclaimed presidents, but most of the international community regarded Ouattara as the winner. On April 11, 2011, the French Army intervened. Gbagbo was detained and extradited to the Hague in November 2011 to stand trial at the International Criminal Court.[6]

Following Ouattara's ascension, Côte d'Ivoire enjoyed robust support from the international community, and the economy—at least, as measured by GDP—boomed. In the World Bank's view, impressive growth and controlled inflation made Côte d'Ivoire a "remarkable economic success" and a promising country for investment.[7] This enthusiasm echoed earlier praise for the "Ivorian miracle" in the 1960s and 1970s. History suggests prudence, however, particularly as the country's social indicators remain abysmal: life expectancy is only 53 years, and 46% of the population subsists below the poverty line.[8]

Ouattara did not meet with unanimous approval within Côte d'Ivoire itself. *Le Monde* summarized the situation in 2018. On the one hand, "his election put an end to the sense of marginalization felt by part of Côte d'Ivoire, and [he] has reestablished order and state sovereignty across the whole of the country, launching several large-scale infrastructure projects." But on the other, "he has not been able to convert the 9% annual GDP growth into an improvement in quality of life for the majority of Ivorians, corruption remains widespread, [and the] work of reconciliation is mostly unfinished" (Bozonnet 2018).

In 2020 Ouattara initially declined to run for a third presidential term, which is not allowed by the Ivorian Constitution. He changed his mind, however, when his

---

[6] Gbagbo was acquitted on January 15, 2019 and initially freed under the condition that he remain in a foreign country (Belgium), pending resolution an appeal lodged by the prosecution. See Richard (2019). He returned to Côte d'Ivoire in June 2021.

[7] The assessment is given on the World Bank's website, available at http://www.worldbank.org/en/country/cotedivoire/overview (accessed on December 20, 2018).

[8] World Bank data for 2015. See also Cogneau et al. (2017).

chosen successor, Amadou Gon Coulibaly, suddenly died in July. In a highly con-troversial election, the 78-year-old Ouattara was "reelected" with ostensibly 94% of the votes, in October, and in response to the ensuing protests his government cracked down on opponents.[9]

Who Profits from Cocoa?

Every year, the world consumes more than four million tons of cocoa. This works out to almost half a kilogram per person—fourfold more than 40 years ago. Europeans and North Americans are the biggest consumers, but other markets are growing quickly (BASIC 2016). Côte d'Ivoire is the world's top producer—the only African country that can claim this title in any agricultural commodity—with about 40% of global production (Figure 4.2).

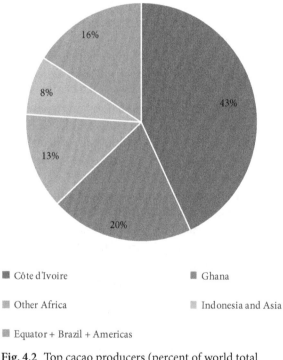

- ■ Côte d'Ivoire ■ Ghana
- ■ Other Africa ■ Indonesia and Asia
- ■ Equator + Brazil + Americas

Fig. 4.2 Top cacao producers (percent of world total production)

Source: International Cocoa Organization (CCO), https://www.icco.org/statistics/.

[9] See, for example, BBC News (2020) and UN News (2020).

Cocoa cultivation in the country began under French rule in the early twentieth century. Today, French chocolate producers still source 70% of their cocoa from Côte d'Ivoire. With a turnover of more than $5 billion in 2015, the cocoa sector is crucial for the economy. "Brown gold" accounts for 15%–20% of GDP and 32% of exports, employs between 600,000 and 900,000 growers, and supports roughly six million people—almost a quarter of the population.[10]

The commodity chain

The commodity chain that runs from the raw cocoa bean to the finished chocolate bar resembles a funnel. The hundreds of thousands of growers are extremely decentralized, while the global cocoa trade and processing industries are highly centralized.

Ivorian cocoa growers cultivate farms with an average size of three to five hectares.[11] After the harvest, the farmers ferment and dry the beans, which are then collected and transported in jute sacks to the port. There, authorized buyers and traders act as intermediaries in negotiating the price.[12] This part of the cocoa chain remains much as it was before independence. More change has occurred at the neck of the funnel.

Through the 1980s, some of Côte d'Ivoire's beans went to big brands like Suchard, Nestlé, Cadbury, and Lindt & Sprüngli, that had integrated systems from grinding the beans to packaging finished chocolate. The rest went to independent grinders, *couverturiers* (who produce high-quality industrial "couverture" chocolate), and artisanal chocolatiers.

In the 1990s, increasing product standardization coupled with the liberalization of financial markets attracted the commodity giants Cargill and ADM. The sector became more concentrated, notably with the merger of the French group Cocoa Barry and the Belgian group Callebaut to create Barry Callebaut. Four international firms today control the processing of 90% of Ivorian cocoa (BASIC 2016, pp. 43–44).[13]

---

[10] The figure of 600,000 growers is from the Conseil du Café-Cacao, the public authority in Côte d'Ivoire which regulates, stabilizes, and develops the coffee and cocoa sector. The figure of 900,000 is from is the International Cocoa Organization (ICCO). See also Schweisguth (2015).

[11] This figure is cited by Wessel and Quist-Wessel (2015), who add, however, that no reliable statistics are available.

[12] For a list of buyers and exporters approved by the Conseil du Café-Cacao, see http://www.conseilcafecacao.ci/ (accessed on July 21, 2021).

[13] See also SEO Amsterdam Economics (2016, p. 23).

What growers receive

Meanwhile, the majority of Ivorian cocoa farmers live well below the poverty line (Fountain and Hütz-Adams 2018, p. 45). Fairtrade International estimates that to meet their basic needs, their incomes would need to triple (Rusman et al. 2018). Households in rural areas often lack access to roads, electricity, drinking water, medical services, and education (BASIC 2016, p. 32).

Like many commodities, the price of cocoa is susceptible to wide fluctuations. A system to stabilize the price received by Ivorian growers was in place prior to the liberalization of the sector in 1991. During a price slump in the mid-1980s, the government-backed CAISTAB guaranteed producers up to twice the world price. The anticipated rebound in the global market did not happen, and in 1989 pressure from the Bretton Woods institutions, whose structural adjustment plans were in full swing, forced Côte d'Ivoire to slash the price paid to producers by 50%.

CAISTAB itself was finally eliminated in 1999, leaving small producers to bear the full brunt of global price fluctuations (Cogneau and Jedwab 2012). New reforms, initiated in 2011, sought to ensure that at least 60% of the value of cocoa as defined by its world price went to growers.[14] But their low incomes are first and foremost a result of low world prices.

Cocoa has brought a large influx of workers from the north of the country into the south, as well as from neighboring Mali and Burkina Faso. Land pressures became a major source of tension, the political instrumentalization of which helped to spark the conflict in the 2000s.

Cocoa is not only the heart of the Ivorian economy, but also a key source of state revenue. Taxes are levied on exporters, rather than directly on producers. The main levy is the longstanding *droit unique de sortie* (single exit duty, or DUS). There have also been levies for the sector's regulatory bodies, for supporting cooperatives, and so on. These drive a wedge between the export price and the price received by growers. In the 2016–2017 season, for example, the farm-gate price was 1,100 CFA francs per kilogram, while the export price was about 1,800 CFA francs. Of the difference, about 300 CFA francs went for the costs of transport to the port and drying, packaging, and storage, while almost 400 CFA francs went for taxes.

The Ivorian growers at the beginning of the cocoa value chain receive a small fraction of the final product value, with processors, manufacturers and distributors taking the lion's share, as shown in Figure 4.3 (Barrientos 2016). At the Paris Agricultural Show in March 2018, Ivorian Minister of Agriculture Sangafowa Coulibaly expressed unhappiness at the current state of affairs, stating that the chocolate

---

[14] For the last 50 years Ivorian producers have been receiving between one-third and almost the entire value at which cocoa beans are marketed for export. See figure 23, BASIC (2016, p. 30) reproduced Bonjean and Brun (2016).

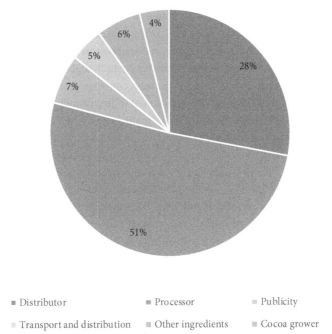

- Distributor
- Processor
- Publicity
- Transport and distribution
- Other ingredients
- Cocoa grower

Fig. 4.3 Breakdown of the price of a milk chocolate bar sold in Europe

Source: Barrientos, S. (2011) "Beyond Fairtrade: Why are Chocolate Companies Pursuing Sustainability in Cocoa Sourcing?" in Barrientos, S., M. Squicciarini, M. and J. Swinnen (eds.). *The Economics of Chocolate*. Oxford: Oxford University Press, 2015, Chapter 12.

industry generates $100 billion each year, but that producing countries only get 6% of this, and farmers themselves barely 2% (Etwareea 2018).[15]

Scaling the value chain

In these circumstances, cocoa-producing countries understandably would like to attract a greater share of processing activity. Having put an attractive tax regime in place in 2012, Côte d'Ivoire has won a significant portion of the processing market, supplanting the Netherlands as the global leader (ICCO 2016). As Côte d'Ivoire moves into processing, Abidjan's status as the world cocoa capital is reflected in the 2017 decision of the International Cocoa Organization (ICCO) to transfer its headquarters there from London (d'Abbundo 2015).

[15] See also *AfricaFocus Bulletin*, August 15, 2018.

With support from the African Development Bank, Côte d'Ivoire and neighboring Ghana are also developing cocoa bean storage facilities to better control supply to the global market in the event of overproduction (Etwareea 2018). The idea of a cocoa cartel is on the rise. The two countries—which together account for more than 60% of world production—set a minimum common price for the 2020–2021 cocoa season (Deveaux 2019). In the opinion of industry analysts, however, a "cocoa OPEC" will only become reality if the main producing countries' marketing systems are brought closer together (Fages 2018b; see also Jacque 2018).

To capture a larger share of the value chain that lies between the cocoa bean and the chocolate bar, producing countries will need to pay closer attention to the share devoted to so-called intangible factors—R&D, patents, branding, and publicity—that can account for as much as 30–50% of the final price (BASIC 2016, p. 32). Intangible assets confer special advantages to companies with multiple international locations, among which revenues can be shifted to minimize taxation. It is perfectly legal to pay a subsidiary for use of a trademark or a patent, even when the subsidiary is based in a tax haven. But whether it is legal to create fictitious subsidiaries or inflate their remuneration in order to avoid taxes is less clear. French MEP Eva Joly, a former magistrate who investigated the famous financial scandal known as the Elf affair, has described tax havens as a modern form of colonization.[16]

Documenting the extent of such maneuvers in the cocoa market would require access to a company's internal accounts—a closely guarded secret. But the annual reports of the leading firms leave little doubt that the main players know where to locate subsidiaries so as to maximize tax benefits. Intangible activities and holdings—group headquarters, intellectual property, trading, financial management, and other services—are often located in territories with favorable tax regimes, such as Belgium, Delaware, Luxembourg, Malta, Mauritius, the Netherlands, Panama, Singapore, and Switzerland (Merckaert 2020).

Statistical Peculiarities of the Cocoa Trade

What happens to cocoa when it leaves the Ivorian ports of Abidjan and San Pedro? Over the 2000–2018 period, the Netherlands, the United States, Germany, France and Belgium together have imported 65% of Ivorian cocoa. But a close examination of statistics on the cocoa trade reported by UN Comtrade, the UN statistics agency, raises two interesting puzzles.[17] The first is that Germany and several other trading partners appear to import more cocoa from Côte d'Ivoire than the latter

---

[16] See "La colonisation moderne c'est les paradis fiscaux—Eva Joly," available at https://www.dailymotion.com/video/xgvdym (accessed on December 20, 2018).

[17] These questions were initially raised by an UNCTAD study, "Trade misinvoicing in Primary Commodities in Developing Countries," July 2016.

reports exporting to them. The discrepancies are substantial: over the 16-year period from 2000 to 2018, Côte d'Ivoire reported that it sent a total of around $4.5 billion (in 2018 dollars) of cocoa to Germany, whereas Germany reported around $9.1 billion in imports of Ivorian cocoa. Deducting the cost of shipping, the discrepancy between the official German and Ivorian figures is about $4.5 billion (see Table 2.3 in Chapter 2). The picture is similar in several other countries, including France, the United States, and Belgium, although the differences are smaller.

The second curiosity is the mirror image of the first. It centers on the Netherlands, the world's largest cocoa importer, and to a lesser extent Estonia. In the same period, Côte d'Ivoire reported that it exported a total of $19.6 billion (excluding shipping costs) to the Netherlands, while the latter recorded only $17.7 billion of imports (including shipping costs). Adjusting for costs of freight and insurance, the discrepancy is almost $3.2 billion.

Summing across its nine major trading partners, Côte d'Ivoire's reported cocoa exports were roughly $4 billion less than the corresponding imports reported by the partner countries. This is equivalent to about 7% of the declared value of the country's exports to them. The transshipment of cocoa from the Netherlands to other countries may help to explain the contrasting patterns shown in the table, but the net discrepancy suggests an overall pattern of export under-invoicing.

Export under-invoicing as a conduit of capital flight

Export under-invoicing—the deliberate misrepresentation of the value of export shipments by understating their quantity, price, or both—can occur for several reasons. One is to evade any taxes levied on exports. A second is to conceal foreign exchange earnings from the government, so that they can be parked abroad or used to finance undeclared imports. These motives can be mutually reinforcing.

Like most developing countries, Côte d'Ivoire requires its exporters to surrender foreign exchange earnings at the central bank in return for local currency. Some exporters may prefer to conceal some earnings abroad as a way to evade controls on foreign exchange outflows. Exporters may decide to remit concealed earnings for exchange on the parallel ("black") market, when its exchange rate is more advantageous than the official one. But when unreported earnings remain overseas, export under-invoicing is a conduit for capital flight.

For much of its history, Côte d'Ivoire has had fairly stringent controls of capital outflows as well as an official exchange rate that is less favorable for exporters than the parallel market rate.[18] It is quite plausible, therefore, that export

---

[18] The Chinn-Ito index of capital account openness places it among the quarter of the world's countries with the most restrictive policies. See Ito and Chinn (2006).

under-invoicing for purposes of capital flight helps to explain the curious discrepancies in the country's cocoa trade statistics.

Data reliability

Other defects in the available data may exacerbate the anomalies.[19] The fact that export values are reported fob, while most import values are reported cif, means that one must adjust for insurance and shipping costs to compare exports and imports. The calculations reported in Table 2.3 use an estimated cif factor by product and partner obtained from the OECD's International Transport and Insurance Costs (ITIC) database.[20] These are estimates, not the actual costs of shipping. While this approach introduces a degree of uncertainty, it cannot explain the striking difference in the sign of the discrepancies for the Netherlands and France.

Errors may occur in the recording of export quantities. A 2004 audit found that "cases of differences between the real and theoretical weight" were commonplace, "a result of the weakness of upstream quality controls" (IDC 2004). Year-to-year discrepancies may occur, for example when cocoa is exported at the end of one year and reaches its destination the next. Again, such errors would not explain cross-country differences, and timing discrepancies would average out over the years.

So, two puzzles remain to be solved. Why is the Netherlands different from other major importers? And why, despite the Dutch anomaly, did reported worldwide imports of Ivorian cocoa systematically exceed Côte d'Ivoire's reported exports?

The Dutch exception

Some industry professionals maintain that deliberately falsifying trade documents would entail an unacceptable risk for large companies, especially as technical advances have made it easier for governments to identify such manipulation.[21] And large companies often enlist legal and tax advisers to help them remain within the letter, if not the spirit, of the law.

One possible explanation for the Dutch discrepancy is that the Netherlands is registered as the destination country, whereas it often is really a country of transit. The Dutch data may not record shipments that are in transit to processing facilities elsewhere. UN trade statisticians report that Ivorian customs officials rarely

---

[19] The following paragraph draws heavily on an interview with the French economist Denis Cogneau, August 11, 2016.

[20] Data from https://stats.oecd.org/viewhtml.aspx?datasetcode=CIF_FOB_ITIC&lang=en (accessed on July 21, 2021).

[21] According to the trader quoted in Van de Klundert (2016).

know the final destination of the containers, but only the first port at which they will arrive.[22] Another possibility is misrecording by Ivorian officials. Ferry Lapré of Statistics Netherlands (CBS) says that "Amsterdam might be marked as the destination when the ship's final stop is actually Antwerp."[23] In that case, the cargo would never be seen by Dutch customs.

Another possibility, that has been documented for other goods, is that the official data confuse trading, in the sense of the buying and selling of commodities, with actual trade in the sense of movement of the commodities. "Contracts for the sale and purchase of commodities are concluded in Switzerland, where the goods are sold and the ships are chartered," a study of Swiss trading reports. "But the commodities never cross the Swiss border, except for gold. And so these flows never appear in customs statistics" (Déclaration de Berne 2011).

Jack Steijn, the manager of a Dutch logistics company and a member of the European Warehouse Keepers Federation, offers another possible key to the mystery. Steijn served as president of the international technical committee in charge of developing an ISO standard intended to ensure the traceability of sustainable cocoa. Steijn explains that European customs allow imported goods to be stored in bonded warehouses.[24] In 2014 and 2015, Amsterdam and Rotterdam together held around 40% of European stocks (ICCO Expert Group 2016). Although physically on European soil, these goods are technically considered to be outside the EU until they are moved to a final destination in the EU. The owner of the beans can resell them without the beans leaving the warehouse. Meanwhile, the Ivorian authorities will have recorded the cocoa as an export. If ultimately it is transferred outside the EU, the goods will never have been declared as entering the EU at all, and the importer may not know where the cocoa originated.

This may also explain the statistical quirk in Estonia's case. Like the Netherlands, the country reports importing less Ivorian cocoa than Côte d'Ivoire claims to export to it. The port of Tallinn specializes in managing and storing imports of raw materials, including cocoa. For the most part, these beans are in transit to Russia, Ukraine, Belarus, and elsewhere.

Trading and storage companies are aware of the volumes of goods in transit, their origins, and their destinations. Are these data shared with government agencies? The author asked Statistics Netherlands, and the answer was simple: No. The Netherlands does not "have complete information about warehoused goods, or exports from these warehouses."[25]

If we are ever to find a full explanation for the inconsistencies in trade statistics, companies in the sector will have to provide transparent data on the whole

[22] Interviews carried out during a UN Comtrade conference at Geneva in late September 2017 by Matthias Cortin, from the Bureau d'Analyse Sociétale pour une Information Citoyenne.
[23] Interview, May 1, 2018.
[24] Interview with Jack Steijn, of the European Warehouse Keepers Federation, August 11, 2016.
[25] Interview with Ferry Lapré of Statistics Netherlands (CBS), May 1, 2018.

supply chain. Today outside observers have no way to compare trading and warehouse management companies' internal transactions with customs declarations. As researcher Christophe Alliot explains, "in trade matters, the only information available about companies takes the form of very general charts, making it impossible to find out the values, countries, products, or import and export departments involved."[26] Edward George, a British analyst at Ecobank, explains, "Trading companies have this data, but it's very sensitive and will probably never be communicated to the media."[27] If the governments whose territory acts as a hub for the global cocoa trade do not have access to these data, it might be time for them to get it—and to update the figures communicated to UN Comtrade.

Fiscal motives?

Why is cocoa stored in the Netherlands rather than another country with adequate port facilities? There may be a fiscal motive: a company could have its Dutch subsidiary settle the bill from its Ivorian subsidiary, and then rebill the cocoa at a higher price to German, Belgian, or French subsidiaries or others that ultimately process the beans. The profit then would be recorded by the Dutch subsidiary—in a country known for its fiscal leniency.

As the Federation of Cocoa Commerce acknowledges, much of the cocoa trade occurs between subsidiaries of the same firm. To book profit for the Dutch subsidiary, it may not even be necessary to manipulate transfer prices (transaction prices within the same company); the firm can simply time the date of the transactions carefully to take advantage of variations in global prices.

It would not be surprising if multinational firms were exploiting cross-country differences to minimize their liabilities; indeed, it would be surprising if they were not. To this end, multinational firms often create holding companies domiciled in the Netherlands. This is not done out of love for Gouda cheese and tulips.

Such tax minimization maneuvers do not always go uncontested. In a 2019 Letter to Stockholders, ADM reports that its Dutch subsidiary, ADM Europe B.V., "received a tax assessment from the Netherlands tax authority challenging the transfer pricing aspects of a 2009 business reorganization," and that as of December 31, 2018, this assessment was $93 million in tax plus $31 million in interest. "The Company has appealed the assessment," the letter continued, and "plans to vigorously defend its position," but cautions that "the judicial appeal may take an extended period of time and could result in additional financial impacts of up to the entire amount" (ADM 2019, p. 91).

---

[26] Interview, August 16, 2016.
[27] Quoted by Van de Klundert (2016).

Cocoa smuggling

German researcher Friedel Hütz-Adams, an expert on the Ivorian cocoa sector, maintains that cocoa was smuggled out of Côte d'Ivoire on a massive scale during the conflict years.[28] Comtrade data for neighboring Ghana show exceptional export levels during those years. Similarly, more than 100,000 tons of cacao ostensibly were imported from Togo by its trading partners in the 2007/2008 season, even though Togo's own production was less than 10,000 tons (UN Group of Experts 2009, p. 57).

Earnings from smuggled cocoa are not reported to Ivorian authorities, and this could be another conduit for capital flight (or for financing smuggled imports). But this does not help to explain the shortfall in Côte d'Ivoire's recorded cocoa exports when compared with the imports recorded by its trading partners, since the smuggled cocoa would be recorded by importers as coming from the neighboring countries. Laurent Pipitone, the former statistical director of the ICCO, does not believe that Ghana would export bags of cocoa marked "Côte d'Ivoire." There is no reason to suppose that customs officers—who are not specialists who might be able to recognize where the cocoa originated—would record shipments from Ghana or Togo as Ivorian cocoa (United Nations Group of Experts 2009, p. 57).

Export recording

The most likely explanation for the gap between the official data on cocoa exports and the total imports recorded by trading partners probably lies in Côte d'Ivoire itself, in the recording of exports when the goods set out. Exporters have a clear financial interest in bypassing accurate customs recording so as to evade the DUS export duty, which until recently was set at 44% of the declared value of the goods.[29] And, as noted above, even in the absence of taxes on exports, they may prefer to understate the quantity or price of exports in order to evade controls on the exchange rate and outflows of capital.

Criticisms of Ivorian customs are not new. In May 1986, a French customs mission noted that "out of a sample of sixty declarations, seventeen were false, [which] suggests a continuous, well-established tendency towards fraud in both imports and exports" (Péan 1988, p. 200). In the wake of this finding, Lamine Diabaté, Houphouët-Boigny's Minister of Economy, published an official report which found that "under- and over-invoicing alone have cost Côte d'Ivoire between 50 and 90 billion CFA francs from year to year."[30] This was equivalent to 1.6–2.9%

---

[28] Interview with Hütz-Adams, August 10, 2016.
[29] The DUS is currently 9.6–11% for processed cocoa and 14.6% for cocoa beans (World Trade Organization 2017, p. 221).
[30] Author's calculation, based on World Bank GDP data, and on the University of Sherbrooke's exchange rate data.

of GDP. Today there are measures in place to minimize malfeasance. An exporter described them:

> There are checks at every stage. Authorized by the Conseil Café-Cacao (CCC), concessionaires set themselves up for six months or a year at the entrance to each exporter's factory, checking the quality of the product that the processor or the cooperative brings in by truck. They are authorized to reject any product whose quality they think is too poor, or to adjust prices and impose discounts on these products. Their word is final. Inside the factory, where the beans are dried and conditioned, another CCC agent checks the weighbridge. Another concessionaire like Bureau Veritas or SGS is selected to check the quality of the product leaving the factory, and is subject in turn to random checks by the CCC.[31]

There then follows a series of administrative procedures, including registration and payment of taxes, until the ship finally departs. On paper, the system appears to leave little room for fraud with respect to reporting of export quantities. But it is harder to ensure accurate recording of prices, leaving room for export under-invoicing.

The statistical curiosities in the Ivorian cocoa trade are many and vast. Some inconsistencies are likely the result of deliberate misrecording of exports. But ware-housing merchandise in transit also may be important, and there could be fiscal motivations in this, too. Just as a recent audit highlighted the shortcomings in regulation of the Ivorian cocoa sector (Fages 2018a), a careful audit of Ivorian customs and freight forwarders' activities could shed further light on defects in the recording of the country's cocoa exports.

"I Love Gold"

In March 1990, IMF managing director Michel Camdessus expressed regret that aid to Africa "serves simply to fuel capital flight and the purchase of apartments in the most elegant parts of Europe" (Koudou 1990, p. 429). This was undoubtedly an exaggeration, but it raises an interesting question: where does capital flight from African countries go?

In an effort to find out, the author examined the real estate holdings of Ivorians in France, using data on rental value from the French housing ministry.[32] Estimating the average value of a property in France to be equivalent to 20 years of rent, the holdings of Côte d'Ivoire residents are around $200 million.[33] Many of

---

[31] Interview, December 29, 2017.

[32] This is reported in the FILOCOM database. The author is grateful to economist Denis Cogneau, who suggested this approach, for obtaining and sharing data on non-resident real estate holdings from the French Ministry of Housing.

[33] The owners could include some French citizens, since the data refer to country of residence, not nationality.

the properties in question are modest in size: 60% of the value is represented by properties of less than 75 square meters (800 square feet).

We also examined the total holdings of Ivorian residents in banks of the 44 countries, including the world's main financial centers, that report to the Bank for International Settlements (BIS).[34] These data show substantial flows of Ivorian capital to western banks in the late 1980s, with recorded deposits reaching about $2 billion (in 2015 dollars) by the end of that decade.[35] Most capital flight is likely to escape this measure. Deposits for which the nationality of the beneficial owner was not disclosed are not included, nor are deposits held in bank secrecy jurisdictions, nor all assets apart from bank deposits.

The 1980s saw a global wave of economic liberalization policies championed by the IMF. In Côte d'Ivoire, the decade also marked the closing years of the reign of the "Old Man," Félix Houphouët-Boigny, who had served as president since 1960. Houphouët-Boigny's personal fortune provides a window on the world of Ivorian capital flight. It is impossible to give a precise estimate of its size. Some put it at "between €50 and 100 million," but that is surely an understatement (Soudan 2009). Others have estimated it at €7 billion (Baker 2015, p. 52), €6–9 billion,[36] or even €15 billion (Bouquet 2008, p. 213). Guéniat (2016) speaks cautiously of "more than a billion."

Houphouët-Boigny never hid his love for money. In 1983, he claimed to have the largest fortune in the country. "People are amazed that I love gold," he said. "It's because I was born in it" (Nantet 1999). Even before his rise to the presidency, he already had wealth abroad: "I wasn't yet president of Côte d'Ivoire when I bought Jean Gabin's house [in France]. I wasn't the president when I bought an apartment in the 11th [arrondisement of Paris] for my son!" (Péan 1988, p. 176).

His wealth included investments in pineapples, coffee, avocados, and poultry farming:

It is the fruit of my labor. I have 4 billion [CFA francs] of turnover from pineapples.... I had gotten up to 3,000 tons of pineapple a month, a third of national production.... Before, we received very little, maybe a hundred million, but those hundred million are worth billions today. And I transferred all that money to bank accounts in Switzerland, which gave lots of interest. For one bank in Abidjan, my money makes up a quarter of its holdings .... There is even a bank that manages my profits on avocados—I believe I'm the main producer in Côte d'Ivoire. Another bank manages the modest profits from my chicken farm. But those billions—because all of this is in the billions—are all in the country.[37]

---

[34] The author is again grateful to Denis Cogneau for assistance in accessing and interpreting these data.

[35] See Merckaert (2020). For further discussion of the BIS data, see Cogneau and Rouanet (2015).

[36] Journal du Dimanche (1990), which estimates his fortune at 40–60 billion French francs, is quoted in Koudou (1990).

[37] Speech by Houphouët-Boigny, Fraternité Matin, April 29, 1983.

As early as 1952, his UBS account in Geneva held more than 150 million Swiss francs.[38] Part of his fortune was in a sense owned collectively: "Nothing I built in Yamoussoukro [the country's 'alternative capital'] belongs to me. The hotels belong to the Party, and so to the state; the Maison du Parti, the Houphouët-Boigny Foundation, etc., are all state-owned buildings" (Péan 1988, p. 178). This was no small part of his legacy, for Yamoussoukro—the village where he grew up—became the stage for some of his grandest follies. In 1983, he made it Côte d'Ivoire's administrative capital and had a number of sumptuous buildings constructed, including the town hall, an engineering school, an international airport, and a basilica that was to be bigger than Saint Peter's in Rome.[39] He claimed to have personally spent €115 million on the basilica, which was constructed by the French company Bouygues at a reported cost of €250 million.[40]

The origins of Houphouët-Boigny's pre-independence wealth are disputed. Some authors claim that it came initially from the planters' union which he led, and from gold from the Dabou region which was brought to him by supporters of the Rassemblement Démocratique Africain (RDA) to support the emancipation struggle (Traoré 2014, pp. 201, 213–214). But his fortune flourished once he became president. Developing a "peanut roaster philosophy"—the peanut roaster must taste a few to check the quantity of salt—he set up a system of constant levies on the country's resources, especially cocoa.[41]

His empire grew to include around 30 properties in Paris, including a castle and 33-hectare estate in Bombon acquired in 1985, a Louis XIV *gentilhommière* in Soisy-sur-École, a mansion on the Rue de la Chaise in the 7th arrondissement, and the famous Hôtel Masseran, an eighteenth-century jewel also known as the Hôtel de Beaumont. Also in the stylish 7th arrondissement were three apartments on Avenue Bosquet, another on Rue de Grenelle, others on Rue de la Comète and the Passage Jean Nicot, and other handsome properties on the Rue Saint-Simon, the Boulevard des Invalides, and—if his daughter Hélène is to be believed—the Rue Duroc.[42] The Old Man also had an apartment in the 11th arrondissement, and no fewer than 17 villas in Marne-la-Coquette in the western suburbs of Paris (Collombat 2015a).

His real estate holdings also included apartments in London and New York, a property in the Bahamas, another in Italy in Castel Gondolfo, and others in

---

[38] This is according to Maître Baduel, who was Marie-Thérèse Houphouët-Boigny's lawyer until the early 2017. Interview, December 28, 2017.

[39] The basilica of Notre-Dame de la Paix in Yamoussoukro is 8,000m², with a dome inspired by St. Peter's.

[40] Some estimates put the basilica's cost as high as $600 million: see Langer and Brown (2008, p. 47).

[41] "You shouldn't stop a peanut roaster from checking how much salt there is." In Côte d'Ivoire this metaphor is applied to the normalization of corruption. Traoré (2014, p. 14).

[42] All these properties are named in the well-respected *La Lettre du Continent*. See La Lettre du Continent (2004). The precise addresses, including that of the Rue Duroc property, are given by Hélène Houphouët-Boigny in a post on her blog, http://succession-mr-f.houphouet-boigny.over-blog.net/article-11257253.html (accessed on December 27, 2018).

Morocco, Senegal, and Côte d'Ivoire itself, including 18 luxuriously furnished villas in Yamoussoukro (Madelin 1993). In Switzerland, he owned a house in Chêne-Bourg, as well as several real estate companies whose holdings included two homes near Geneva, one in Collonges-sous-Salève in Haute-Savoie (France), and the other on "Billionaires' Hill" in Cologny (Switzerland).[43]

Apart from real estate, Houphouët-Boigny had foreign bank accounts in France, Luxembourg, and especially Switzerland, with UBS, SIB, and Merrill Lynch,[44] and a substantial stock portfolio that included holdings in the coffee and cocoa firm Intercafco (Dulin and Merckaert 2009). According to bank records consulted by the author, in the mid-1980s the Old Man's UBS account alone was tapped to spend more than $10 million at the jewelers and watchmakers Piaget and Harry Winston over a four-year period.

Houphouët-Boigny himself was amused by recriminations about his Swiss assets, asking "What serious man doesn't have some of his fortune in Switzerland?" (Madelin 1993, p. 314). This comment may not have seemed amusing to the striking Ivorian teachers whom he was addressing, who were suffering at the time from deep cuts in social spending by a state bled dry by disappearing public funds.

Today, more than a quarter century after his death, a battle for control of the fortune he left behind still rages among his heirs. But apart from some of the properties in Paris, little was ever recouped by the Ivorian government (Merckaert 2020).

CAISTAB: A Channel for Wealth Extraction

Prior to its closure in 1999, CAISTAB, the government's Fund for the Stabilization and Support of Agricultural Products, had become a centerpiece of "corrupt and patrimonial practices," in the words of a study by Global Witness, an international NGO based in London. "By regularly asking for and receiving money from the cocoa trade via CAISTAB without being made to account for it, the president, Félix Houphouët-Boigny, effectively encouraged those handing him the money to help themselves to a share" (Global Witness 2007, p. 46).

CAISTAB was founded in 1962 to "oversee the entire process of buying and selling coffee and cocoa in order to stabilize and improve the incomes of those working in the sector."[45] Its main job was to guarantee a minimum price for producers in case prices fell, using a reserve fund supported by tax levies on exports. But the fund was not used solely for producers. In 1966, 40% of the fund's

---

[43] According, at least, to the blog post by Hélène Houphouët-Boigny cited above.
[44] According to Baduel, the existence of this last account is based on transfers flagged by UBS to the courts in Geneva. Interview, December 28, 2017.
[45] Study on the cocoa sector in the West African Economic and Monetary Union by BCEAO, June 2014, p. 11.

expenditures were used to finance the state budget, a share that rose above 60% when cocoa prices peaked in the 1970s (Losch 1999).

Nor was CAISTAB characterized by transparency. Between 1978 and 1985, according to a report by a major French bank, there was a discrepancy of 830 billion CFA francs between actual receipts and official receipts—equivalent to $2–3 billion (Péan 1988, pp. 172–174).[46] Its expenses included infrastructure projects unrelated to cocoa: in Houphouët-Boigny's home village of Yamoussoukro, these included "an international airport, a golf course, splendid technical and civil engineering schools, luxury hotels, Olympic swimming pools, stadiums, the Maison du Parti complex, the grandiose Houphouët-Boigny Foundation, an international hospital, and a sumptuous guest residence whose profusion of marble and gold sometimes unsettled its tenants" (Péan 1988, p. 182). With so much of its money diverted to other uses, the fund had difficulty maintaining stable grower incomes when cocoa prices slid in the 1980s.

Political quota-holders

CAISTAB's other role, allocating approvals and export quotas, made it a focal point for the pursuit of wealth by the president and his family, among others. Amidst controversies over the omnipresent role of foreign exporters, the young Ivorian state decided to encourage the creation of locally owned public or mixed companies (Losch 1999, p. 385).

The idea came from a young deputy minister of economy and finance, Konan Bédié, who at the same time actively promoted development of a quota system for cocoa exports that came into existence in 1969. Officially, the quotas were meant to encourage new Ivorian entrepreneurs to take their place alongside established European firms. CAISTAB allocated export quotas to companies it had approved, so that it not only set prices but also determined which companies could export and in what quantities (ibid., p. 388). Each year roughly 30 exporters were approved, rising to an average of 45 in the 1980s. The economist Bruno Losch divided them into three types: "autonomous exporters (possessing all the necessary technical facilities), dependent exporters (with no equipment, limited to contractual transactions), and fictitious exporters (or *quotataires politiques*, political quota-holders) who give up their rights to other exporters in return for money" (Losch 1997, p. 215).

The president personally oversaw the list of approved companies every year (Losch 1999, p. 389). Each was given a percentage of the total volume of cocoa to be exported. The political quota-holders resold their quotas to actual exporters. SIFCA, an Ivorian industrial group founded in 1964, ended up selling one-quarter

---

[46] 830 billion CFA francs was equal to 16.6 billion French francs. One dollar was worth 4–5 French francs at the start of the period, and 10 French francs towards the end.

of the country's cocoa in the 1980s, supplementing its own quota of less than 5% with those of political quota-holders and other companies under its control (ibid., pp. 400–401).

The happy *élus*

Who benefited from the cocoa quotas? While it is "extremely difficult to collect data on the sixty or so companies created during the quota period,"[47] Losch has sketched a typology of the *élus*, the chosen ones: the political class, children of the "companions of Liberation," and individuals personally close to Houphouët-Boigny. Some of the beneficiaries are still shaping Côte d'Ivoire's political and economic life today (ibid., pp. 390–1).

One example is Georges Ouégnin, who as director of state protocol from 1960 to 2001 was among those closest to Houphouët-Boigny. He was rewarded in 1973 with a quota for his company, SAIE, which amounted to roughly 2% of national production between 1978 and 1990.[48] "Monsieur Georges," who remained in office under Bédié, and was a key figure in Franco-African networks, and godfather to a son of Jacques Foccart, de Gaulle's "Monsieur Africa" and Jacques Chirac's adviser on African affairs. He later set up a lobbying firm, and returned to politics in 2011 to work for Ouattara.[49]

Houphouët-Boigny also rewarded some of his earliest friends. The Gon Coulibaly family—descendants of the patriarch who sheltered young Félix during colonial repression—enjoyed a quota of nearly 2% in the 1970s and 1980s, through their company, Comivoire (later bought by the French firm Bolloré) and its purchase of a 35% stake in a large exporter, DAF-CI.[50] Despite changes in government, the family has never left the spheres of political and economic power. Amadou Gon Coulibaly served as Gbagbo's minister of agriculture, became secretary general of the presidency under Ouattara, and in 2017 was appointed prime minister. In March 2020, he was chosen by Ouattara to stand for president in October's election after Ouattara himself had decided not to seek another term. But Gon Coulibaly's sudden death in July eventually convinced Ouattara to run for re-election as a "civic duty" (RFI 2020).

Another example is Marcel Amon Tanoh, the son of an "old friend of Houphouët-Boigny's" (Gombeaud et al. 1990, p. 57). He was also the husband of Houphouët-Boigny's daughter Hélène until their divorce in 1992. In the late 1980s he received a quota of 1% of national production through the company SIEPAM.[51]

---

[47] In total, 86 received quotas in the period. See Losch (1999), volume 2, appendix G.

[48] Losch (1999), volume 2, appendix G-8. Losch estimated that a 1% quota generated an average net profit of 25 million CFA francs per year in the mid-1980s.

[49] Interview with a French businessman in Côte d'Ivoire.

[50] Over this period, COMIVOIRE was granted quotas fifteen different times. See Losch (1999) volume 2, appendices G-7 and H-10.

[51] See Losch (1999) volume 2, appendix G-5.

He went on to become Ouattara's cabinet director in 1999 and a minister under Gbagbo from 2002 to 2010.[52] He later became Ouattara's foreign minister, stepping down in March 2020.[53]

Although magnanimous with old friends and their children, Houphouët-Boigny did not neglect his own interests. A colossal quota was reserved for himself. In 1987, no less than 100,000 tons of cocoa—one-sixth of Ivorian production at the time—went to the president via Intercafco. The customs fees on this cocoa were not paid to the Treasury as usual, but instead into Intercafco's special account, a sovereign privilege that meant that the president could undercut his competitors (Gombeaud et al. 1990, p. 34).

A tangle of interests

The favors dispensed by the president also included seats on the boards of foreign firms (Losch 2003). The main exporters from the colonial period were rapidly losing ground to new cocoa importing companies based in Le Havre (France), Switzerland, and the Netherlands (Losch 1999, p. 78). They were also threatened by the development of local firms established by expatriates, including JAG (founded by Jean Abile-Gal) and SIFCA (founded by Henri Tardivat) which gradually acquired dominant positions. To consolidate its relationship with the authorities, JAG granted Houphouët-Boigny 26% of its shares.[54] Unicafé, created by SIFCA in the late 1970s, granted his children Guillaume and Marie Houphouët-Boigny 6.25% of its capital each (ibid., pp. 394–5). And Intercafco, the president's company, acquired significant shares in other cocoa-exporting companies.

Henri Konan Bédié, who had developed these systems to promote Ivorian entrepreneurship, was one of the best at navigating this tangle of capital. He was a major shareholder of Comafrique, the first company created under the new mixed capital regime in 1966, which specialized in importing vehicles and later went into exporting coffee and cocoa. Other key shareholders were Pierre Billon, the father of Jean-Louis Billon who served as minister of commerce from 2012 to 2017, and Philippe Yacé, a member of another prominent Ivorian family, who was president of the National Assembly at the time.[55] When the quota system was set up in 1969, the approved exporters in the first growing season included Comafrique along with other Ivorian companies created expressly for the occasion. Over time, Comafrique acquired shares in other cocoa exporters, including SIFCA. Bédié also held a substantial stake (8%) in JAG.

---

[52] See http://www.gouv.ci/doc/photos/CV-AMON-TANOH_Marcel.pdf (accessed on December 20, 2018).

[53] See http://www.gouv.ci/_legouvernement.php?recordID=15 (accessed on December 20, 2018).

[54] Losch (1999, p. 384). See also Losch (1999), volume 2, appendix H-5.

[55] The Yacé family made its fortune especially in rubber, and is now also heavily invested in livestock.

The system goes off the rails

The breach opened by CAISTAB in the late 1960s whetted a lot of appetites, and others wanted to rush in. In 1975 a new director was appointed who wielded less power to oppose the president. The breach became a gaping hole that those in power could use to increase their own wealth. Cocoa money evaporated, although the high world prices temporarily gave an illusion of a functional system.

New "fictional companies" kept appearing and obtaining quotas. The 1980s saw "the system go off the rails for good" (Losch 1999, p. 430). Power became ever more personalized around Houphouët-Boigny, who granted favors to his many courtiers to maintain the balance of power among them. In 1986, Losch reported, "31% of Ivorian politicians officially held shares in 33% of the country's 750 companies. [They acted as] these companies' intermediaries, brokers, and even protectors, both in dealing with the state and with the banking system, securing them aid, advantages, dispensations, and other arrangements."[56]

CAISTAB's activities and accounts became more and more opaque (ibid., pp. 433–435). The fund was supposed to accumulate a surplus during the good times, so it could support the sector when the going was tough. What firms paid into the fund, or received from it, depended on their export contracts. There was a great temptation to falsify the value of these contracts to pay less than the fund was owed or receive more. One form of fraud involved manipulating dates, volumes, and values to exploit price fluctuations between the moment the Fund issued a contract and the time the sale was carried out, sometimes with the complicity of CAISTAB insiders (ibid., pp. 434–435). When prices fell, the coffers were soon empty, and crisis was close at hand.

A losing battle

The late 1980s saw a losing struggle against falling prices on the world market that turned into a rout. Houphouët-Boigny suspended external debt repayments in May 1987. CAISTAB suspended cocoa sales in July, aiming to increase prices. In his public pronouncements, Houphouët-Boigny attacked speculators and un-equal terms of exchange, reverting to themes of his trade union days in the 1940s. "The Old Man's final battle," ran a November 1988 headline in the weekly *Jeune Afrique*.[57]

The situation became nightmarish for growers, who sold their beans at half price, sometimes for promissory notes instead of cash that were later described as "scribbled pieces of paper with no real value" (Bouquet 2008). In effect, wrote

---

[56] See Losch (1999 p. 379); and Losch (1999), volume 2, appendix H-1.
[57] Jeune Afrique (1988).

Radio France International correspondents Jean-Louis Gombeaud and Corinne Moutout and Stephen Smith, at the time a reporter for *Libération* (now a professor at Duke University), in their 1990 book *La Guerre du Cacao,* "the 1988–89 season was mostly financed by a forced loan from the farmers, who were never reimbursed (Gombeaud et al. 1990, pp. 127–128)."

By 1989 the Ivorian government was in a corner, and the IMF forced it to halve the prices paid to growers. Houphouët-Boigny lamented that "cocoa has made us all sick" (ibid., p. 216). The country was sick, too, as its dependence on cocoa revenues came to haunt it. The poverty rate soared from 10% in 1985 to 36.8% in 1995 (Cogneau and Mesplé-Somps 2002, p. 73).

In 1990, with protests in the streets and under constant pressure from his creditors, Houphouët-Boigny was forced to make concessions. He created the post of prime minister, which he entrusted to Alassane Ouattara—a manager picked to reassure Washington—and he opened the country to a multiparty system. The liberalization of the cocoa sector began that year, too, although CAISTAB would hold on until 1999.

In 1998, the Ivorian government announced the sale of one million tons of cocoa at 904 CFA/kg—a price that was undervalued by about 100 CFA/kg, according to the Bretton Woods institutions, meaning that 100 billion CFA francs (about €150 million) apparently disappeared (Verschave 2000, p. 269). The Bretton Woods institutions were not reassured by the explanations offered by the Ivorian authorities, and they commissioned an audit from Arthur Andersen in 1999 that found a gap of 80 billion CFA francs (about €120 million) between CAISTAB's declared and actual revenues (Campbell 2000, pp. 143–4).

With CAISTAB shut down for good in the same year, some observers hoped that the Ivorian cocoa trade would become less vulnerable to wealth extraction: "Real and fake quotas, privileges, fraud, and the crudest misdealings involving cocoa and coffee exports," Losch (1999, p. 528) predicted, "will be eliminated by the newly liberalized environment." In the end, however, the change brought little benefit to growers or ordinary Ivoirians. In the new exporting landscape, Ivorian firms along with the historically dominant French operators lost ground, as the giants of the global cocoa industry—Barry Callebaut, Cargill, and ADM—acquired their assets. A few years later, Losch (2003, pp. 52–53) would conclude: "Today, the three biggest cacao processors in the world are well established in Côte d'Ivoire and control its exports."

Fruits of Power

In 1992 the fortune of Henri Konan Bédié, Houphouët-Boigny's future successor, already was estimated at $400 million (Madelin 1993, p. 310). When he ascended to the highest office in the land, it grew further. Mamadou Koulibaly, who became budget minister in the following government, described Bédié's presidency as a "kleptocracy" comparable to those of Mobutu in Zaire and Suharto in Indonesia (Contamin and Losch 2000). As deputy minister and then minister for the economy and finance, Bédié had shown a great appetite for business, investing in construction and public works, portfolio management and real estate, import-export, metallurgy, cocoa milling, and agricultural equipment imports. He placed friends on the boards of directors of companies in each of these sectors (Baulin 2000, p. 94).

In 1977, Houphouët-Boigny set out to "put an end to a system of corruption and deceit infecting the entire state".[58] The sugar complex affair may have been the straw that broke the camel's back. In his book L'Argent Noir (Black Money), French investigative journalist Pierre Péan reports that Bédié was among those involved in overbilling agro-industrial sugar production complexes to the tune of 35 billion CFA francs (about €100 million) (Péan 1988, pp. 187–189). Jacques Baulin, a former advisor to Houphouët-Boigny, described Bédié as "by far the most compromised minister in the sugar complex affair" (Baulin 2000, p. 113). Bédié claimed that the affair was simply a pretext for the president to oust him.[59]

Bédié's banishment to the political wilderness did not last long. In 1983 he returned as head of the National Assembly. When Houphouët-Boigny died in December 1993, he became the nation's second president—a position he held for six years, until his overthrow in December 1999. Koulibaly, who became budget minister in the transitional government, offered a frank assessment of the era:

> Whatever we gained after the devaluation [of the CFA franc in January 1994] was wasted in embezzlement and theft, and that hurt public finances. It involved more than 500 billion CFA francs (€760 million).... A local mafia was systematically established, one whose job was to appropriate state property.
>
> (Contamin and Losch 2000)

At the time of his overthrow, Bédié was in his native village near Daoukro. In addition to an extravagant palace in Daoukro, built at a cost of 100 billion CFA (€150 million) according to the Ivorian press,[60] Bédié's property holdings included a luxury apartment in the fashionable 16th arrondissement of Paris (Hofnung 2011, p. 49). In the presidential residence in Abidjan he left behind 6 billion CFA francs (more than €9 million) in bundles of banknotes (Ficatier 2000).

The former president denied owning Swiss bank accounts, but after his fall from power the Federal Office of Justice announced that it had frozen his accounts in Switzerland in response to a formal request for mutual legal assistance

---

[58] Houdin (2015, pp. 32ff). See also Koudou (1990. p. 430).
[59] Bédié (1999, pp. 99–104); Mel (2010, pp. 312–315).
[60] Fraternité Matin, April 30, 2000, cited by Bouquet (2008, p. 206).

from the Ivorian judiciary (Le Monde 2000). Five to seven million Swiss francs were blocked in nine banks. Bédié was charged with "misappropriation of public funds" by the Ivorian attorney general (Libération 2000). The French newspaper *L'Express* reported that he was suspected of having embezzled $24.8 million in European health aid.[61] The Ivorian authorities issued an international arrest warrant for Bédié, who then was living in France, but the French government chose not to comply.[62]

Bédié, sometimes described as the "number one opponent" of Alassane Ouattara, remains an important figure on the Ivorian political chessboard. In February 2019 he hosted former Ouattara ally Guillame Soro at his residence near Daoukro at a poolside dinner "surrounded by peacocks," and the next day they toured "his vast plantations of cocoa and rubber."[63] At 86, he ran again for president in 2020 and headed up a "council of transition" formed with opponents after Ouattara was declared the winner of the October election.

When Brown Gold Turns Red

Cocoa played a central role in the violence that tore Côte d'Ivoire apart in the opening decade of this century. The conflict pitted the new government headed by Laurent Gbagbo against rebels based in the country's north headed by Alassane Ouattara. On both sides, the economy was harnessed for the war effort. Although cocoa cultivation is concentrated in the south, which remained under government control, it also provided a major source of income in the rebel-held area. As money was drained from the cocoa sector to fund the war, some in positions of power—though not, it seems, Gbagbo himself—took the opportunity to enrich themselves on the side.

Fortunately, this turbulent period in Côte d'Ivoire's history is fairly well documented: in the investigative work of the Franco-Canadian journalist Guy-André Kieffer, who disappeared in Abidjan in 2004 while investigating corruption and money laundering;[64] in audits commissioned by creditors and the government; and in reports issued by the UN Group of Experts and the NGO Global Witness, among others. Together these provide a picture of how the cocoa economy worked in the war years.

---

[61] The case is well documented in Dupuis and Pontaut (2000).
[62] Dulin and Merckaert (2009, p. 102); Fabre (2000).
[63] La Lettre du Continent (2019b).
[64] On Kieffer's disappearance, see Carroll (2004).

Taxing the cocoa sector

About 90% of Ivorian trade passes through the port of Abidjan, which accounts for the overwhelming majority of the country's customs income. The port was therefore a hub for financing the regime. In November 2000, Gbagbo appointed a loyal follower, Marcel Gossio, to run the Autonomous Port. Gossio quickly took on another role: he became the grand financier of Gbagbo's party, the FPI, and of the Jeunes Patriotes, the pro-Gbagbo militia (Hugeux 2009).

Ivorian cocoa production continued to grow. Between 2002 and 2007, exports increased by 39%—bringing an additional $1.1 billion into the country's economy (UN Group of Experts 2009, p. 52). The government accessed this windfall through heavy taxation. The DUS exit duty rose from 120 CFAF/kg in 2000 to 220 CFAF/kg in 2003. Together with registration fees and payments to regulatory bodies, this brought in revenues of about $500 million per year to government coffers.[65]

The uses of the money were far from transparent. In 2005, Finance Minister Paul Antoine Bohoun Bouabré compelled cocoa exporters to pay at least $20 million of the DUS in advance. How these funds were used is unknown (Global Witness 2007, p. 22). Nor did the UN experts who revealed this mystery get any official answer about how tax revenues for 2006–2007 were used (UN Group of Experts 2009, p. 54).

The Gbagbo government set up a complex scheme to regulate the cocoa sector. No fewer than five new institutions were created—in addition to the existing Fonds de Prudence and Sacherie Brousse—to make up for the loss of CAISTAB: the Autorité de Régulation du Café et du Cacao (ARCC), the Bourse du Café et du Cacao (BCC), the Fonds de Régulation et de Contrôle du Café et Cacao (FRCC), the Fonds de Développement et de Promotion des Activités des Producteurs de Café et de Cacao (FDPCC), and the Fonds de Garantie des Coopératives Café et Cacao (FGCC).[66] Power in these organizations was held mainly by nominal representatives of the cacao growers—who were designated by the Ministry of Agriculture—in the Association Nationale des Producteurs de Café-Cacao de Côte d'Ivoire (ANAPROCI). State officials, the banks, and large international firms were represented, too, but they were in the minority "and simply had to resign themselves to accommodating any wrongdoing, and what they perhaps viewed as local custom" (Bayart and Hibou 2003, p. 54).

Audits pointed out how odd this system was, especially as "these structures behave autonomously, almost independently of any supervisory bodies, [even

---

[65] UN Group of Experts (2009, p. 53). See also Global Witness (2007, p. 22).
[66] See Global Witness (2007, p. 60), where the status, role, and sources of financing for each of these is explained.

though they] exist only because the state wants them to."[67] The organizations "have no accounts or budget" (Bayart and Hibou 2003, p. 55). As one indication of the scale of mismanagement, an audit commissioned by the European Union found that the combined budgets of the ARCC, BCC, and FRCC were three times that of the old CAISTAB (Amiri and Gourdon 2006, p. 135).

Each of these organizations owed their existence to the regime and contributed to the war effort. For example, the FDPCC, an entity ostensibly meant to finance development in the cocoa sector, wrote the president a series of checks totaling 10 billion CFA francs (about $20 million) when war broke out in October 2002 (Global Witness 2007, p. 24). In October 2005, an Ivorian newspaper reported that it was also providing vehicles to national security forces (ibid., p. 25). Audit missions noted that between 2000 and 2008 the Fund paid 33 billion CFA francs (more than $60 million) for services that could not be documented (Ministère de l'économie et des finances 2010, p. 3). Similarly, a financial audit conducted for the EU found that the FRCC "lent" billions of CFA francs to the government as part of the war effort (Global Witness 2007, p. 27).

The individuals at the helm of these institutions were well rewarded. The NGO Global Witness reported that Henri Amouzou, the FDPCC president who personally presented Gbagbo with checks on television and chaired the cocoa producers organization ANAPROCI, bought luxury cars including a Hummer H2 and a Porsche Cayenne (ibid., p. 52). The $341,000 monthly salary and benefits of the BCC president, Global Witness reported, amounted to almost twice the official salary of President Gbagbo himself (ibid.).

Meanwhile Ivorian growers were suffocated. The government and its affiliated organizations were siphoning more than 300 CFA francs per kilogram, widening the gap between world market prices and what growers received. The farm-gate price paid to growers often amounted to less than half the world market price (ibid., p. 18). In 2005 the UN estimated that illegal sales of Ivorian beans via Ghana were equivalent to more than 10% of Côte d'Ivoire's total production (ibid., p. 45).

After the war, the weekly news magazine *Jeune Afrique* reported an ex-post assessment of the scale of missing funds: "The audits of the coffee and cocoa sector carried out by KPMG and SEC Diarra, at the request of the Bretton Woods institutions, show the disappearance of some 370 billion CFA francs between 2002 and 2008" (Duhem 2013). In total, this is equivalent to about $740 million.

At the urging of the international community, Gbagbo launched a clean-up effort in 2008. About 20 "cocoa barons" were arrested and detained.[68] The

---

[67] See Investissement Développement Conseil (IDC) (2004, pp. 29–30), quoted by Amiri and Gourdon (2006, p. 33).

[68] In 2013, after Gbagbo himself had been overthrown, fourteen defendants were sentenced to twenty years in prison. See Duhem (2013). The court also ordered the seizure of their personal property and real estate. See *Abidjan.net* (2013).

organizations they ran were closed one after another. Farewell, then, to the FDPCC, the FRCC, the ARCC, and the BCC. But the regime showed great institutional creativity, and new organizations—the Fonds Interprofessionnel pour la Recherche et le Conseil Agricoles, the Fonds d'Investissement, and the Comité de Gestion de la Filière Café-Cacao—quickly filled the void.

The extent of levies imposed by the regulatory bodies fell, but transparency was still lacking. In 2009 the UN Group of Experts concluded that "the Government of Côte d'Ivoire has replaced a para-fiscal scheme, which proved highly inefficient and corrupt, with an equally opaque system.... [T]here remains the potential for the unaccountable use of funds, funds that could, conceivably, be used to purchase arms and related materiel" (UN Group of Experts 2009, p. 54). In its 2011 report, the UN Group of Experts estimated that unrecorded cocoa revenues from 2007 to 2011 amounted to nearly $400 million.[69]

After being ostracized by the international community following the November 2010 electoral crisis, the Gbagbo regime resorted to desperate measures to obtain money to pay the security forces, foreign mercenaries, and civil servants. According to the UN Group of Experts, these included the "unregulated appropriation of private funds" from offices of the nation's biggest banks, and from the BCEAO (Banque Centrale des États de l'Afrique de l'Ouest, the Central Bank of West African States), from which it took $400 million (UN Group of Experts 2011c, pp. 38–39).

It will never be possible to expose fully the extent of the misappropriations, the UN Group of Experts explained, because "the former Government of President Gbagbo destroyed, at almost every ministerial agency, multiple records that may have assisted the Group in determining the nature of the diversion of public funds and their use in violation of the arms embargo" (UN Group of Experts 2011a, p. 9). Moreover, they added, "many of the suspicious transactions were reportedly made through verbal agreements in order to avoid possible retracing" (ibid.).

The Forces Nouvelles in the north

In the north, home to about one-tenth of the country's cacao production, the Force Nouvelles (FN) rebels also taxed the trade. They moved block shipments to the southern ports of Abidjan and San Pedro, diverting about 60% of northern cocoa production to other markets (Global Witness 2007, pp. 31–35 and 41–43). Much

---

[69] Author's calculation based on data from UN Group of Experts (2011c, pp. 32, 35). The same report estimated that more than $1 billion in oil revenues went missing.

of it went through to Burkina Faso en route to the port of Lomé in Togo (ibid., pp. 39–43).[70]

In March 2004, the Forces Nouvelles set up a "Centrale" to collect taxes in the territory under their control—including, of course, taxes on cocoa. The nominal tax rate on beans was lower than the government's, but on top of this came bribes, escort taxes, the cost of passes, and taxes in the transit countries. Global Witness estimates that the Forces Nouvelles obtained an average of around 15 billion CFA francs ($30 million) annually from this parallel cocoa trade between 2004 and 2007—a figure similar to that reached by the UN experts (Global Witness 2007, pp. 33–35).[71] Trucks could be taxed multiple times before leaving the country, and the UN experts observed that not all the money found its way to La Centrale, the Forces Nouvelles treasury (UN Group of Experts 2009, p. 47).

The UN Group of Experts estimated the revenues collected in 2009–2010 by FN commanders Ouattara Issiaka (known as "Wattao") and Losseni Fofana (known as "Loss") at more than $5 million each (UN Group of Experts 2011b, p. 37). This came not only from cocoa but also from trade in gold and diamonds. A 2013 documentary for French television later showed Wattao at his residence in the elegant Abidjan district of Cocody, where his associates brandished weapons, along with his Ferrari and Maserati, a €40,000 watch, a solid gold gun said to be taken from Gbagbo's residence, and his expansive seafront villa. Wattao told the reporters that his fortune came from his import business in luxury cars (Langlade and Hondelatte 2013). The truth may never be fully revealed, as Wattao died in January 2020.

Many of the trucks carrying cocoa from the rebel zone went to Bobo Dioulasso, the second largest city in Burkina Faso, where packing plants were set up. The main one was established by means of an investment by a French company based in Saint-Denis routed through a Luxembourg holding company. Global Witness reported in 2007 that Adama Bictogo, a businessman and the national secretary of Ouattara's RDR, was "effectively running the factory" with a turnover estimated at around $100 million per year.[72]

Global Witness also reported that two French companies were transporting conflict cocoa from Burkina Faso to the Togolese port of Lomé. By comparing the volume of cocoa produced in Togo and leaving the port, the UN Group of Experts inferred that smuggled Ivorian cocoa grew from about 16,000 tons in 2003–2004 to 96,000 tons in 2007–2008 (UN Group of Experts 2009, p. 57). The buyers included Dutch, Polish, and French companies (Global Witness 2007, p. 43). "In its meetings with company representatives," the UN experts stated, "the Group has made clear the risk that revenues from cocoa sales might fund the acquisition of arms

[70] See also UN Group of Experts (2009, pp. 55–56).
[71] Global Witness (2007, pp. 33–35). The UN Group of Experts (2011b, p. 38) reported annual incomings of between $22 and $38 million between 2007 and 2010.
[72] Global Witness (2007, p. 40). See also Jeune Afrique (2016); Jeune Afrique (2017a).

and related materiel" (UN Group of Experts 2009, p. 58). This warning apparently did little to deter the trade.

The Luxembourg Money Trail

The word "ministry" comes from the Latin *ministerium*, meaning "service." For some government ministers, it is a small step from serving others to serving oneself. Consider the case of Paul Antoine Bohoun Bouabré, a key figure the Gbagbo years who served as finance minister from January 2001 to December 2005, and then as planning minister from 2005 to 2010. Pursued by the Ivorian authorities after the regime's downfall, Bouabré took many of his secrets to his grave when he died in Israel in 2012 at the age of 54. But some traces of his financial activities have been found.

Due diligence?

As early as October 2002, Bouabré was quietly organizing the transfer of funds from the FRCC to the Ivorian state to help finance the war against the rebels (Global Witness 2007, p. 27). He appears to have been an enthusiast of secretive finance for more personal reasons, too. According to French journalist Benoît Collombat, records for two bank accounts in Luxembourg "anonymously reached the desk of judge Ramaël," the French magistrate investigating the 2004 disappearance of journalist Guy-André Kieffer.[73] Both accounts were held at Dexia Luxembourg, the Luxembourg unit of the Franco-Belgian bank Dexia.

A review of these records indicates that one well-stocked euro account had a balance of €5.3 million at the end of June 2008. This account, which held €7.3 million a few months earlier, was assigned to Paul Antoine Bohoun Bouabré by name. The second was a US dollar account linked to it, with $19 million, whose owner was not specified by name on the statements (Collombat 2015b, p. 32). "Asked about these documents," Collombat reported, "Dexia Luxembourg replied on September 5, 2008, that the accounts were not registered 'on its books,' and suggested looking to Belgium" (ibid.).

Following this trail, the present author contacted Belfius (formerly Dexia Belgium), which stated that Bouabré had never been its client and explained that Dexia Luxembourg (now BIL) is a separate entity. When contacted, BIL's denial

---

[73] Collombat (2015b, p. 32). The present author gained access to these account statements for October 2007 to June 2008. These were missing a three-month period during which more than €3 million was spent.

was less categorical: "BIL is not authorized to provide such information about a person, whether a customer of our bank or not."[74]

The six months of bank statements examined by the present author reveal a number of regular contributors to the accounts. These include 13 transfers received from different entities of the multinational company Audit Control and Expertise (ACE).[75] In 2003, acting on behalf of the Ivorian state, the Chamber of Commerce and Industry had granted ACE a monopoly on weighing and quality control in the cocoa and coffee sector at the port of Abidjan, moves subsequently described in a 2006 EU-financed audit as "unlawful" and as "acts that can be considered favoritism" (Amiri and Gourdon 2006, p. 122). Compared to its predecessors, SGS and Cornelder, "the cost of controls went from 147 CFAF/ton to 2,000 CFAF/ton"—a 13-fold increase (ibid., p. 123).[76]

The records indicate that each month ACE transferred an average of nearly €240,000 to the Luxembourg accounts. Did ACE's founder, André Soumah, who served as managing director from 1996 to 2008 (and as chairman of the board prior to his death in 2016) also want to express his personal gratitude to the minister?[77] The bank statements show that on October 12, 2007, according to the Dexia statements, Soumah—who was the former husband of Félix Houphouët-Boigny's daughter Florence[78]—wrote Bouabré a personal check for more than €42,000.

Other companies also transferred money regularly to the accounts. A commodities brokerage on the Chicago Mercantile Exchange paid almost every month, with an average transfer of €100,000. Several individuals also are recorded as making transfers to the accounts. Kouassi Oussou, director general of the ministry of economy and finance, is listed as having made three transfers averaging €80,000 each. According to the statements, Bouabré's account also received large transfers from accounts at other banks whose owners are not identified, including a check for €650,000 from a private bank in Switzerland.

At the time, banks were moving away from physical currency, but Dexia Luxembourg had no problem handling cash. On nine occasions in the space of

---

[74] Communication with the author, September 28, 2018.

[75] The entities included ACE Private Holdings, ACE Global Travel Tours, ACE Ltd Geneva, and ACE SA Senegal.

[76] ACE lost its monopoly position as the Gbagbo decade ended but regained it in 2012: see La Lettre du Continent (2011).

[77] "Executive Profile: André Soumah," bloomberg.com, available at https://www.bloomberg.com/research/stocks/private/person.asp?personId=67098053&privcapId=46510764&previous CapId=46510764&previousTitle=ACE%20-%20Audit%20Control%20and%20Expertise%20SA, accessed on June 20, 2019. André Soumah died in Geneva on August 9, 2016.

[78] See municipality of Gland (Switzerland), "Préavis municipal n°31 relatif à l'octroi de la bourgeoisie de Gland en faveur de Félicia Marie-Aude Soumah," August 17, 2007, available at http://www.gland.ch/fileadmin/documents/pdf/Preavis_ancienne_leg/Preavis-municipal-no-31-relatif-a-loctroi-de-la-bourgeoisie-de-Gland.pdf, accessed on November 5, 2019.

the six months, one or more unidentified persons stood at the counter and deposited a total of €435,000 in cash into Bouabré's account. The transactions also record a withdrawal of €600,000 in small denomination bills in November 2007.

EU directives require banks receiving deposits of more than €10,000, whose origin cannot be explained, to file a suspicious transaction report to the national anti-money laundering unit.[79] This requirement is particularly important in the case of politically exposed persons (known as PEPs): ministers, members of parliament, magistrates, and so on. Did Dexia Luxembourg exercise due diligence? When asked, the bank (now BIL) declined to comment.

Those receiving payments from the account included Bouabré himself, to whom the records show transfers totaling €935,000. A real estate company located near Saint Tropez (on the French Riviera), is recorded as receiving nearly €430,000 over the period. A travel agency is recorded as having received €122,000 in three transfers. After Gbagbo's downfall, Bouabré was blacklisted by the Ouattara government, which froze his accounts—or at least the ones they could identify (Adams 2012).

The Nembelessini affair

One name that is listed among the contributors to Bouabré's Luxembourg bank account is Victor Jérôme Nembelessini-Silué, who according to the records made three transfers of €47,500 each in the six-month period. There are two very different versions of his story. One owes much to the writings of the abducted journalist Guy-André Kieffer, who described him as a close friend of Bouabré and dubbed Nembelessini "a little Mozart of finance in Côte d'Ivoire" who had done "his apprenticeship in the secret funding networks of Angola and South Africa."[80] The other is the version given by Nembelessini himself. In a lengthy interview with the present author, he denied having a close relationship with Bouabré and claimed to be a victim of fake news.[81]

Victor Nembelessini studied economics at the University of Abidjan at the same time as Bouabré, but says that at the time he only knew him by face. Why, then, did Bouabré, when he became finance minister in January 2001, first hire him as an advisor and then appoint him to head the Caisse Autonome d'Amortization (CAA), the state bank that handled Ivorian public debt? "With HSBC-Equator Bank, I had

---

[79] Each of the member states had to adopt the third anti-money laundering directive before December 15, 2007. This directive increased the requirements for non-financial professions, and for any transaction involving politically exposed persons. Earlier EU directives already contained due diligence provisions, including Know Your Customer (KYC) rules.

[80] Kieffer (2004). This unpublished note is quoted in Kieffer (2015). See also Global Witness (2007).

[81] The interview, held on December 11, 2018, at the author's office at Secours Catholique-Caritas France, in Paris, lasted almost four hours.

restructured debts and encouraged Côte d'Ivoire to buy back its debt on the secondary market, which was a brilliant success," Nembelessini explained. "Bouabré was so impressed he asked me to become the chief of his ministerial cabinet, which I refused because I was a private sector man. I eventually accepted to become his special advisor, a position I held gracefully for six months."[82]

When Nembelessini became its director in 2001, the CAA (which later became the Banque Nationale d'Investissement) had come to look so much like a presidential slush fund that international financial circles refused to touch it. "The World Bank wanted the liquidation of the CAA," Nembelessini acknowledges, and it suspended its lending to Côte d'Ivoire until privatization took place or an external partner was brought in to participate in managing it.

In 2003, the BNI entered into a partnership with a company called Lev Mendel.[83] They formed a joint subsidiary, Lev-Ci, with Nembelessini as its chairman.[84] A fellow board member, according to Global Witness, was Israeli arms dealer Moshe Rothschild, who had brokered the purchase of two Mi-8V helicopters for the Ivorian army (Global Witness 2007, p. 30). Paris-based *Jeune Afrique,* the most widely read pan-African news magazine, would later name Rothschild as one of the main players in arms sales to the Gbagbo regime (Perez 2010).

According to Kieffer's account, Nembelessini initially conceived this partnership as a response to the World Bank's concerns (Kieffer 2004; see also Global Witness 2007, p. 30). But its true goal, Kieffer believed, was to siphon funding from creditors that was meant for public works into the hidden financing networks of Ivorian politics (Kieffer 2004). Kieffer had no time to prove his suspicions: he was abducted from an Abidjan parking lot in April 2004, never to be seen again.

According to Kieffer, Lev-Ci supported a near-bankrupt company called Gold 2000, whose shareholders included the infrastructure minister, the mayor of Le Plateau (the central business district of Abidjan), and Nembelessini's own offshore investment fund (Kieffer 2004). Gold 2000 had been awarded a 4.4 billion CFA francs (about $6.2 million) contract to refurbish San Pedro's roads and port, 80% of which was financed by the World Bank. The firm could only account for 400 million CFA francs of expenses and had "absorbed" the rest of the money, according to Kieffer. Global Witness reports that the BNI had provided an overdraft of 5.5 billion CFA francs to the firm (Global Witness 2007, p. 32). It also was entrusted with dredging the port of San Pedro for 12 billion CFA francs (Kieffer 2004).

---

[82] Interview with the author, December 11, 2018.

[83] Lev Mendel later became Lev Group, both being trading names of HTM Beheer BV, a company registered in 1990 in the Netherlands. HTM Beheer BV's unique shareholder was Euro Trade Services NV, a company based in Curaçao, a secrecy jurisdiction in the Dutch Antilles. See Global Witness (2007) pp. 30–33.

[84] Global Witness (2007) pp. 30, 32. As of this writing, Nembelessini is in litigation with BNI.See http://www.ohada.org/index.php/fr/ohada-au-quotidien/role-des-audiences-publiques-de-la-cour-cc ja/2599-affaire-victor-jerome-nembelessini-silue-contre-banque-nationale-d-investissement-bni (accessed on January 9, 2019).

Nembelessini had trouble keeping calm when hearing this account. "How would Lev have reassured donors about the problems of the BNI?" he asked. "Yes the BNI had problems, but we developed structured financing, by recovering some of the coffee and cocoa deposits that were at the BCEAO. This allowed us to finance SMEs (small and medium enterprises) and help the cooperatives, and that was the strength of the BNI."

Why did Lev Mendel become a partner? "The BNI financed SMEs in all sectors in Côte d'Ivoire, because there had been a disengagement of French banks. The Ministry of Infrastructure asked us to help a company named Gold 2000 that had an important contract from the World Bank, but did not have the necessary funding. When a partner came to me and said 'We have heavy equipment—tractors, shovels—that we can get you cheaper,' I thought this would be useful to Ivorian SMEs in a time of crisis. That was Lev Mendel."

Nembelessini does not deny having had troubles with Lev-Ci and Gold 2000. A 2006 audit by PricewaterhouseCoopers supported accusations that Lev-Ci misappropriated funds to the tune of 7 billion CFA francs ($13 million). But Nembelessini contends that he was the one chasing corruption: "When the managers are not in good faith, it falls on you, and that's what happened. We provided equipment to Gold 2000, but that was not enough. We realized that the guy from Gold 2000 had committed embezzlement. I also dismissed the managing director of Lev-Ci who had begun to make personal enrichment and I lodged a complaint against him, which brought me a lot of trouble."

Nembelessini questions Kieffer's sincerity: at the time, the journalist was an employee of Commodities Corporate Consulting, a company meant to support the government in reforming the cocoa sector. Nembelessini was outraged by the contract awarded to them (3 billion CFA francs, about €4.5 million) even though the company was not yet incorporated, and he had persuaded Bouabré to stop advance payment. In his view, this was the origin of a grudge held by Kieffer against him. Nembelessini was so upset by what he considered "fake news" against him that he thought of taking the matter to court: "I am gonna sue you until your last shirt," he told Kieffer. But he was advised by a lawyer not to do so.[85]

A question that remains is why would Nembelessini have transferred funds into Bouabré's Luxembourg account—the bank statements showed three deposits by check in November 2007 and May and June 2008. When asked about this, he appeared quite surprised: "I did not manage any account in Luxembourg. I don't even know Dexia. Who could have put my name? Where would I have found all this money? I don't have coffee or cocoa, I don't take levies. I don't know how my name could show up there. You would do me a great service if you help me understand."

---

[85] Interview of Victor Nembelessini with the author, December 11, 2018.

Nembelessini also expressed bitterness against Bouabré, whom he characterized as having been a valuable politician until the September 2002 *coup d'état*, when the bosses of his party accused him of playing into the hands of the World Bank and blamed him for not having cleared enough funds to arm the country. "Henceforth he became like a carpet, he couldn't say no. From then on, we could not agree any more. We stopped talking to each other."[86]

Is Nembelessini a good actor? He seemed sincere. If so, either bank documents are a fake, or he was the victim of some deceptive manipulation. The latter is not impossible given Bouabré's ability to seek to discredit opponents. After Gbagbo's downfall, Nembelessini says, he initially feared for his life but was protected by the German embassy.[87] Ouattara subsequently appointed him as administrator of Côte d'Ivoire for Afreximbank, the African Export-Import Bank (Abidjan.net 2011).

In the Shadow of the Speculators

The growing role of powerful international firms in the Ivorian cocoa trade that began in the late 1980s was accompanied by growing financialization of the sector. "Paper cocoa moves ten times faster than physical cocoa," remarks former Gbagbo adviser Bernard Houdin.[88] This may be an understatement. Youssouf Carius, an Ivorian investment fund director, says that "a cocoa bean sold physically out of the port of Abidjan may represent as many as sixty transactions on the international markets" (Bensimon 2017).

The trend was rooted, first and foremost, in the financing requirements for purchases of cocoa (as well as other commodities like coffee and rubber). The Ivorian banking sector was still weak in the 1980s, having long been "controlled by subsidiaries of the major French banks (BNP-Paribas, Société Générale, Crédit Lyonnais), who limited themselves to small-scale customer services" (Losch 2000, p. 12).

Financialization also met a need on the part of cocoa traders to hedge against risk, in a context where the bulk of the harvest is sold as futures. There is no single spot price for immediate delivery of cocoa, as there is for oil or gas. Instead, prices are fixed for a given quantity and date of delivery and can be renegotiated. The contracts may include possible price increases or reductions when they mature, depending on how the price has changed in the interim. Along with associated insurance derivatives, these futures transactions became objects of intense speculation. New players appeared in the cocoa market who were uninterested in the

---

[86] Interview with the author, December 11, 2018.

[87] Interview with the author, December 11, 2018.

[88] Interview, December 5, 2017. According to SEO Amsterdam Economics, the remark is accurate: "The trading turnover on cocoa futures markets is about ten times higher than actual world production." See SEO Amsterdam Economics (2016, p. 31).

"real" side of the trade, that is, in beans or processed cocoa itself. "About 30% of cocoa transactions were made by investment funds," according to Carius, "not by professionals working in the sector" (Bensimon 2017). Reflecting a broader trend in world agricultural commodity markets, cocoa speculation increased four-fold between 1986 and 2005 and has continued to grow (Ohemeng et al. 2016). Financialization has been accompanied by a tendency to greater product stan-dardization, but this does not necessarily guarantee quality—to the irritation of chocolate makers, who sometimes complain of deliveries of beans "that an animal wouldn't touch!"[89]

Banks and pension funds played the leading role in the cocoa futures market at the turn of the millennium (Roche 2001). Their involvement shrank somewhat, however, when new regulations were introduced in the wake of the 2008 financial crisis. There are now limits on the number of contracts they can hold. Most im-portantly, the Volcker Rule banned proprietary trading (trades with the firm's own money) in the United States, although the Trump administration subsequently made the rule more flexible (Bloch 2019) and the European Commission decided against a total ban on the practice.

As banks pulled back from commodity markets, this opened space for trading companies, many of which have set up shop in Switzerland (like Bunge, Cargill, Louis Dreyfus, and ADM's agricultural concerns) or Singapore (like Noble and Olam). These commodities giants can continue trading on their own account—this makes up roughly 80% of their electronic exchanges—while at the same time acting as asset managers for other investors (Damgé 2012).

For Ivorian cocoa producers, financialization had two notable effects. The first was greater price instability. When Ivorian cocoa lost 30% of its value on world markets between March and October 2016, speculation was widely regarded as the main cause. According to Gaël Giraud, then chief economist at the Agence Française de Développement (AFD), "commodity prices were no longer dictated by actual supply and demand, but by speculative capital movements" (Vergnaud 2017).

The basic problem, according to Giraud, arises from a simple fact: "The spec-ulators in their Manhattan offices never take delivery of a single cocoa bean. The underlying physical product doesn't interest them at all—lucrative deals are the only thing they care about" (Vergnaud 2017). Proposals have been made to require speculators to take delivery themselves of at least part of their con-tracts. But the World Trade Organization, which is responsible for rules regarding trading in commodities themselves, has no authority over financial transactions involving them. It is the financial hubs that would have to regulate these, and

---

[89] Interview with the former director of the chocolate firm Beussant, based in the north of France, July 21, 2017.

they are reluctant to constrain activities that might simply be relocated to a competitor.

The second important effect of financialization has been to siphon money from the cocoa sector to financial speculators, who unlike exporters and industrial firms contribute no value to the final product itself.[90] In commodity markets where a small number of players buy a large percentage of the product, speculators can take positions that are substantial enough to move prices up or down (Damgé 2013). For speculators, political instability can create profitable opportunities. After the outbreak of Côte d'Ivoire's civil war, the authoritative London-based fortnightly newsletter *Africa Confidential* described its dramatic impact on the cocoa market:

> The cocoa price recovered last year as Côte d'Ivoire, the world's biggest producer, was plunged into chaos. A supply deficit pushed prices to their highest levels for 15 years by mid-2002, even before the 19 September army mutiny. London trading house Armajaro, founded by former Phibro boss Anthony Ward, made a killing by stockpiling five per cent of world production from the 2001–2002 season. Then as the Ivorian conflict deepened, a conspiracy theory circulated claiming Armajaro had funded the rebellion to boost the cocoa price and raise cash to cover its partner AIG Fund's losses from the destruction of the World Trade Center on 11 September 2001.[91]

This story is recounted in greater detail by Guy-André Kieffer, the journalist who disappeared in 2004.[92] According to Kieffer, Armajaro acquired about 5% of the global cocoa supply in late 2001, at a time when the price of cocoa was oscillating between £750 and £900 per ton.[93] After the rebel offensive was launched in September 2002, Ivorian cacao bean exports plummeted and the world price rose to more than £1,400 per ton. According to Kieffer, the firm's profit came to over $500 million (Kieffer undated, p. 165).[94] An article by senior *Le Monde* journalist Alain Faujas put it lower at a mere £40 million (Faujas 2010).[95]

---

[90] Interview with Christophe Alliot, December 23, 2017.
[91] Africa Confidential (2003). Ward himself categorically denies any involvement in the rebellion (communication with the author, September 25, 2018). See also Gazzane (2013), who reported that Ward is "suspected of fueling local rebellions to serve his cause," and that Ward denied this claim: "He presents himself as a simple financier, who thanks to his personal fortune and his sense of timing, manages to make rain and good weather on the cocoa market."
[92] Kieffer (undated). This document was published on various websites after Kieffer's disappearance: see, for example, Ivoirebusiness.net (2017); Atelier des Medias (2012). See also Frindethie (2016, pp. 116–117).
[93] Cowell (2002); Kieffer (undated, pp. 161–162).
[94] Kieffer (undated, p. 165).
[95] When contacted by the present author, Anthony Ward refused to comment on the profitability of these trades (communication with the author, September 25, 2018).

This alleged episode earned Armajaro's founder, Anthony Ward, the nickname "Chocolate Finger" in the British press.[96] He made the news again when he bought up to 6% of the world cocoa supply in July 2010, shortly before the electoral crisis in Côte d'Ivoire (Merckaert 2020). In May 2011 Côte d'Ivoire's new first lady, Dominique Folloroux-Ouattara, invited Ward to sit at the table of honor during her husband Alassane Ouattara's gala inauguration dinner (Pigeaud 2015, p. 214). From his prison cell in The Hague, former president Laurent Gbagbo remarked bitterly that "in the last few years, if you wanted to find out whether a coup was on the horizon in Côte d'Ivoire, all you had to do was watch the price of cocoa!" (Gbagbo and Mattei 2014).

Long Live Clientelism

When Alassane Ouattara became president of Côte d'Ivoire in 2010 with the backing of France after a controversial election, he made reform of the country's cocoa sector a top priority. In January 2012 he set up the Conseil Café-Cacao (CCC), in an effort to cushion the vulnerability of growers to the price fluctuations on the world market to which they had been exposed since the dismantling of CAISTAB.

Based on expectations regarding the upcoming harvest and world prices, the CCC sets a farm-gate price that is about 60% of the export price. It holds daily auctions of rights to export, and 80% of the future harvest is sold in this way (Tano 2012, pp. 153–154). The system has advantages over the previous laissez-faire policy, but it also has pitfalls: potential cronyism in how exporters are selected, and the risk of inaccurate forecasts of the harvest and prices by the CCC.[97]

After world cocoa prices tumbled in 2016, speculative exporters who had bought 400,000 tons of cocoa in advance, wagering that prices would go up, defaulted on their payments and canceled purchase orders equivalent to about 15% of the country's annual production. Côte d'Ivoire wound up with large stocks of unsold cocoa on its hands. Prices slid a further 10% in early 2017 (Girard 2017). The farm-gate price, which was supposed to guarantee the income of growers, was not paid in early 2017. The CCC was slow to tap its 140 billion CFA francs (€210 million) reserve fund, leading SYNAP-CI, a union for nearly 100,000 cocoa producers, to voice suspicion that the money had been stolen (Bouessel 2017). This episode left the CCC bruised and wary, and it cut the guaranteed price from 1,100

---

[96] See, for example, Fletcher (2003), where the nickname is explained as follows. "Although the scheme was compared to James Bond villain Goldfinger's plan to stockpile gold, Ward always denied claims that he was trying to 'corner' the market."

[97] Economists are divided on the benefits of state regulation, and there is some evidence that cacao growers typically receive a higher share of the world price in countries with less regulated sectors, such as Cameroon and Indonesia. See SEO Amsterdam Economics (2015), especially p. 49.

CFA francs per kilogram to 750 CFA francs for the 2017–2018 season. At the new price, most Ivorian growers were earning less than $1.20 per day.[98]

Cocoa smuggling reportedly declined by 80% (UN Group of Experts 2013, p. 12). But a parallel system persisted in the country's north, a legacy of the de facto partition during the civil war. Between 2012 and 2015, an estimated 120,000 tons of cocoa were smuggled out annually (UN Group of Experts 2016, p. 34). The smugglers know the terrain well, and have developed their own producer cooperatives as well as working with existing producer groups.[99] Smuggling to Ghana increased in 2017 when the CCC passed on the drop in world prices to the farm gate, while its Ghanaian counterpart, Cocobod, kept its own producer price constant, stoking fears that in the following year one-fifth of all Ivorian production could exit the country to the port of Accra.[100] The Ivorian and Ghanaian authorities agreed in 2018 to consult each other before setting farm-gate prices, with the aim of reducing the disparity between the two sides of the border (Fages 2018b).

International institutions looked favorably upon Ouattara, a former IMF official, and welcomed improvements in the Ivorian business environment. Many Ivorians also welcomed the prospect of a new president "who was already rich, and so wouldn't steal public money and would lead the country in an honest, upright, disinterested way" (Traoré 2014, p. 436).[101] In the Mo Ibrahim Foundation's annual governance rankings, Côte d'Ivoire made the greatest progress from 2010 to 2016 among all African countries in security, transparency, and the rule of law (Michel 2016). But the government's handling of the cocoa sector has remained controversial, and many in the business community complain about the ruling family's grip on the national economy.

An audit of the cocoa sector conducted by the international accounting firm KPMG was delivered to the Ivorian ministry of agriculture in March 2018. Its conclusions were harsh: due to state support for overproduction and the resale of export contracts that had fallen into default, the CCC had incurred losses of nearly 185 billion CFA francs (€280 million) for the 2016–2017 season.[102] International institutions pressed the government to publish the results, and an abbreviated version of the audit was posted online.[103] It does not discuss the fate of the 326 billion CFA francs (about €500 million) in cocoa levies that were collected by the state

---

[98] In 2014–2015, despite somewhat higher prices (850 CFA francs per kilogram), almost 55% of Ivorian growers lived on less than 757 CFA francs (US $1.20) per day. See Banque Mondiale (2019, p. 31).

[99] Interview with BASIC's Marion Feige-Muller and Christophe Alliot, June 7, 2016.

[100] See Jeune Afrique (2017b); Agence Ecofin (2017).

[101] Ouattara's personal wealth may owe more to his wife, Dominique, who reportedly was the mistress of Felix Houphouët-Boigny and inherited assets from him, than to Ouattara's prior career as an IMF official and governor of the BCEAO [Central Bank of West African States]. See Bernard (2011) and Merckaert (2020).

[102] See Afrique sur 7 (2018); La Lettre du Continent (2018a).

[103] See http://www.conseilcafecacao.ci/index.php?option=com_k2&view=item&id=853&Itemid=18 (accessed on August 22, 2019).

during the last few cocoa seasons, an issue raised in the original report.[104] The auditors concluded that favoritism continues to plague the sector, citing "dysfunctional application of the rules for managing commercial operations," "export authorizations which were not always justified," "exporters being awarded volumes out of line with their financial capacities," and "conflicts of interest" (KPMG 2018, pp. 8, 124, 132).

A new firm called Africa Sourcing, founded by Loïc Folloroux, the son of the first lady, emerged as a significant player in Ivorian cocoa exports. Folloroux previously worked at the commodity trading firm Armajaro. In 2012, he and another former employee bought its Ivorian subsidiary, Armajaro Négoce (Fick 2015). Renamed Africa Sourcing, the firm exported 41,000 tons in the 2015–2016 season. Though not on a par with Cargill, which exported 181,000 tons of beans that season, Africa Sourcing was not small fry (La Lettre du Continent 2016b). The firm received a boost the following season when the CCC granted tax exemptions on 200,000 tons of cocoa, at a cost to the public exchequer of roughly 11 billion CFA francs (€17 million). Africa Sourcing was a prime beneficiary of this largesse, receiving an exemption for 60,000 tons. Other well-connected exporters who benefited at the treasury's expense included the brother of the interior minister (La Lettre du Continent 2016a).

In the cocoa sector, as elsewhere in the Ivorian economy, reliance on relationships with those in power for the accumulation of personal wealth remains deeply entrenched. The clientelist system extends across diverse sectors, from the all-important cocoa trade to other agricultural, industrial, and commercial sectors (Merckaert 2020). Associated with this are numerous shortcomings in state finances: deficiencies in external oversight, opaque budget implementation, and complex procurement procedures in which contracts are often awarded directly without competitive bidding (World Bank 2015). The clientelist system has endured throughout the decades since independence, from the years of Houphouët-Boigny through those of Bédié, Gbagbo, and Ouattara. Whatever its cost to the nation, select members of the Ivorian elite have benefited handsomely, as have their foreign friends and partners, a transnational coterie whose power no doubt helps to explain its persistence.

Conclusions

The magic of international trade not only allows cacao beans grown in West Africa to be transformed into chocolate bars for consumers in Europe, North America, and Asia. It also allows fortunes to be accumulated from a crop that is grown by people who make less than $2 per day. In the classification scheme of the World Bank, Côte d'Ivoire ranks as a lower-middle income country with a per capita

---

[104] La Lettre du Continent (2018b); and La Lettre du Continent (2019a).

income of about $1,700—less than $5 per person per day—in 2018. Like many averages, this conceals wide disparities: the richest 1% of households receive a larger share of the national income (17%) than the poorest half combined (13.5%).[105]

As the single most important sector in the economy, cocoa is deeply implicated in the patterns of wealth and poverty in Côte d'Ivoire. The country is the world's top cocoa producer, accounting for 40% of global supply. Yet the World Bank reports that the country receives only 5–7% of the profit generated globally by cocoa, noting that "profit is essentially concentrated in the processing and distribution phases" and that as a result the sector "has not contributed much to the country's wealth" (World Bank 2019).

While the latter statement is certainly accurate for the majority of the country's people, it does not apply to all Ivorians. For well-situated members of the elite, cocoa has been a source of great wealth. Control over the sector has been a key source of political power, and a major prize for the winners of political contests. Although their share of the global profits is modest compared to those of foreign processors and distributors—and, more recently, financial speculators—it is enormous relative to the incomes of the average Ivorian cocoa producer, many of whom eke out a living below the poverty line (ibid.).[106]

Indeed, in many respects the gap between Ivorians at the top and bottom tiers of the cocoa wealth pyramid are starker than the differences between the Ivorian elite and their foreign counterparts in the trade. The majority of Ivorians, who form the pyramid's base, do the hard work of planting and tending the cocoa trees, harvesting the beans, and carrying them to collection points for sale. Those at the top extract wealth they themselves did little or nothing to create. Patron-client ties, by which those on top compete for the political allegiance of followers by bestowing favors and concessions, lubricate the system and help to bind it together.[107]

The modes by which wealth is siphoned from the cocoa sector are various and ingenious, as shown in this chapter. They include monopolization in the purchasing of cocoa from growers (strictly speaking, this is called monopsonization); the misinvoicing of trade documents in order to evade taxes and exchange controls and covertly park money abroad; outright smuggling, especially during the civil war; and profits from speculation in the world market. In some cases, a certain amount of value is added in the course of these activities—in packing, transport, freight, and insurance, as well as cocoa processing. But much of the profit harvested along the commodity chain can be attributed to market power interwoven with political power.

---

[105] Data from the World Inequality Database: https://wid.world/country/cote-divoire/. These shares refer to 2014, the most recent year for which this information was available as of this writing. See also Cogneau et al. (2017).

[106] For discussion of poverty trends in Côte d'Ivoire, see also Cogneau et al. (2017).

[107] Political scientists use the term "competitive clientelism" to describe such a system. See, for example, Abdulai and Hickey (2016).

At the top of the pyramid, we find a network of close relationships between the Ivorian elite and international firms and financial institutions. Foreign firms participate in everything from the cocoa trade to the country's construction industry, while banks, accountancy firms, and lawyers, both foreign and national, lubricate and handle the movement of money. In this context, it is little surprise to find that the wealth extracted in Côte d'Ivoire is held transnationally, too, with a particular penchant for high-end real estate markets such as Paris and the Côte d'Azur, and bank secrecy jurisdictions such as Luxembourg and Geneva. Capital flight can be understood as one aspect of this larger business model.

Acknowledgments

I wish to express my deepest gratitude to Matthieu Gonzalez, who was a tireless and passionate research assistant throughout this work. I am also indebted to the many academics, officials, businessmen, journalists, activists and politicians who assisted this research by responding to queries. Though not all are cited by name, sometimes at their request, they collectively helped to shed light on the issues investigated here.

References

Abdulai, A., and Hickey, S. 2016. The politics of development under competitive clientelism, *African Affairs*, 115(458), 44–72.

Abidjan.net. 2011. Afreximbank: Nembelessini, nouvel administrateur pour la Côte d'Ivoire, August 2, available at http://news.abidjan.net/h/406445.html (accessed on July 21, 2021).

Abidjan.net. 2013. Café-cacao: les avocats de la défense dénoncent 'un procès politique' après la condamnation de leurs clients à 20 ans de prison, November 6, available at http://news.abidjan.net/h/479571.html (accessed on January 14, 2019).

Adams, T. 2012. Obsèques de Bohoun Bouabré. Sa famille refuse des millions de Ouattara: Voici la raison, *Ivoirebusiness.net*, March 28, available at https://www.ivoirebusiness.net/articles/obsèques-de-bohoun-bouabré-sa-famille-refuse-des-millions-de-ouattara-voici-la-raison (accessed on September 30, 2019).

ADM. 2019. Letter to Stockholders Proxy Statement, available at https://assets.adm.com/Investors/Shareholder-Reports/2018/ADM-Annual-Report-Letter-to-Stockholders-2019-Proxy-Statement-and-2018-Form-10-K-final-.pdf.PDF (accessed on July 21, 2021).

Africa Confidential. 2003. Rebel forces, market forces, *Africa Confidential*, 44(3), February 7, 1–8.

Afrique sur 7. 2018. Côte d'Ivoire: Audit KPMG, les fossoyeurs de la filière cacao (enfin) arrêtés?, April 28, available at https://www.afrique-sur7.fr/392322-audit-kpmg-fossoyeurs-cacao-arretes (accessed on January 28, 2019).

Agence Ecofin. 2017. La Côte d'Ivoire pourrait perdre 400,000 tonnes de cacao en 2017/2018 en raison de la contrebande, September 1.

Amiri, S. and Gourdon, A. 2006. Étude diagnostic des organisations et des procédures de la filière café-cacao de Côte d'Ivoire. *Rapport du cabinet Ghelber et Gourdon*, for the Ivorian government (a report financed by the European Union), May.

Atelier des Medias. 2012. Voici l'article qui a coûté la vie a Kieffer, available at http://atelier.rfi.fr/forum/topics/voici-l-article-qui-a-coute-la-vie-a-kieffer-les-soutiens-de (accessed on July 21, 2021).

Baker, R. 2015. *Capitalism's Achilles Heel*. Hoboken: John Wiley & Sons.

Banégas, R. 2003. La Côte d'Ivoire en guerre: les enjeux d'une crise régionale, *Questions Internationales*, No. 3.

Banque Mondiale. 2019. Situation Economique en Côte d'Ivoire: Au pays du cacao—comment transformer la Côte d'Ivoire.

Barrientos, S. 2016. Beyond Fair Trade. In M. Squicciarini and J. Swinnen (Eds.), *The Economics of Chocolate*. Oxford: Oxford University Press, 213-227.

BASIC (Bureau for the Appraisal of Social Impacts for Citizen Information) and Plate-Forme pour le Commerce Équitable. 2016. The Dark Side of Chocolate: An Analysis of the Conventional, Sustainable and Fair Trade Cocoa Chains. Paris, May.

Baulin, J. 2000. *La succession d'Houphouët-Boigny*. Paris: Karthala.

Bayart, J.F., and Hibou, B. 2003. Libéralisation économique et crise politique en Côte d'Ivoire. Entretien avec Bruno Losch, *Critique internationale*, n°19, April.

BBC News. 2020. Ivory Coast Election: Alassane Ouattara wins amid boycott. November 3, available at https://www.bbc.com/news/world-africa-54778200 (accessed on July 21, 2021).

Bédié, H.K. 1999. *Les Chemins de ma vie: Entretiens avec Eric Laurent*. Paris: Plon.

Bensimon, C. 2017. Côte d'Ivoire: 'ce qui fait chuter les cours du cacao, c'est la spéculation,' *Le Monde*, April 6.

Bernard, P. 2011. Dominique Ouattara, une 'première dame' d'influence," *Le Monde*, May 20.

Berthélemy, J.C., and Bourguignon, F. 1996. *Growth and Crisis in Côte d'Ivoire*. Washington, DC: World Bank.

Bloch, R. 2019. Banques: les États-Unis recalibrent la « règle Volcker », *Les Échos*, 9 October.

Bonjean, C., and Brun, J.F. 2016. Concentration and price transmission in the cocoa-chocolate chain. In M. Squicciarini and J. Swinnen (Eds.), *The Economics of Chocolate*. Oxford: Oxford University Press, 339-362.

Bouessel, C. 2017. Comment la Côte d'Ivoire se retrouve avec 400,000 tonnes de cacao invendues sur les bras, *Le Monde*, February 16.

Bouquet, C. 2008. *Géopolitique de la Côte d'Ivoire*. Paris: Armand Colin.

Bozonnet, C. 2018. La présidentielle ivoirienne de 2020 est dans toutes les têtes, *Le Monde*, 12 April.

Campbell, B. 2000. Réinvention du politique en Côte d'Ivoire et responsabilité des bailleurs de fonds multilatéraux. *Politique Africain 2000/2* (No. 78), 142–156.

Carroll, R. 2004. Missing reporter stirs trouble on three continents, *The Guardian*, June 6.

Cogneau, D., Czajka, L., and Houngbedji, K. 2017. The triumphant elephant's return? Growth and income inequality in Côte d'Ivoire (1988–2015), *Afrique Contemporaine*, 263–264(3–4), 221–225.

Cogneau, D., Dupraz, Y., and Mesplé-Somps, S. 2018. Fiscal Capacity and Dualism in Colonial States: The French Empire 1830-1962. Working Paper No. 2018–27, Paris School of Economics, available at https://hal.archives-ouvertes.fr/halshs-01818700v3 (accessed on July 21, 2021).

Cogneau, D., and Gérald, C. 1998. Les effets à moyen terme de la dévaluation des francs CFA: une comparaison Cameroun - Côte-d'Ivoire, *Revue d'économie du développement*, 6(3–4), 125–147.

Cogneau, D., Houngbedji, K., and Mesplé-Somps, S. 2016. The fall of the elephant: Two decades of poverty increase in Côte d'Ivoire (1988–2008). In C. Arndt, A. McKay, and F. Tarp (Eds.), *Growth and Poverty in Sub-Saharan Africa*. Oxford: Oxford University Press.

Cogneau, D., and Jedwab, R. 2012. commodity price shocks and child outcomes: The 1990 cocoa crisis in Côte d'Ivoire, *Economic Development and Cultural Change*, 60(3), 507–534.

Cogneau, D., and Mesplé-Somps, S. 2002. L'économie ivoirienne, la fin du mirage? DIAL (Développement et insertion internationale) Working Paper DT/2002/18, available at http://www.dial.ird.fr/media/ird-sites-d-unites-de-recherche/dial/documents/publications/doc_travail/2002/2002-18 (accessed on June 2, 2020).

Cogneau, D., and Mesplé-Somps, S. 2003. Les illusions perdues de l'économie ivoirienne et la crise politique, *Afrique Contemporaine*, 206(2),87–104.

Cogneau, D., and Rouanet, L. 2015. Capital exit from developing countries, Paris School of Economics, January.

Collombat, B. 2015a. Les milliards envolés de Félix Houphouët-Boigny, France Inter, December 4.

Collombat, B. 2015b. Préface: Une affaire d'État franco-ivoirienne, in Bernard Kieffer, *Le frère perdu: L'affaire Guy-André Kieffer, enquête sur un crime d'État au cœur de la Françafrique*. Paris: La Découverte.

Contamin, B., and Losch, B. 2000. Côte d'Ivoire: Entretien avec Mamadou Koulibaly, ministre du Budget du gouvernement de transition, *Politique africaine*, 77, 129–142.

Cowell, A. 2002. War Inflates Cocoa Prices But Leaves Africans Poor, *New York Times*, October 31.

d'Abbundo, A. 2015. Abidjan devient la capitale mondiale du cacao, *La Croix*, 1 October.

Damgé, M. 2012. Les négociants prennent la main sur le marché des matières premières, *Le Monde*, April 6.

Damgé, M. 2013. Les profits des négociants de matières premières dépassent ceux des banques, *Le Monde*, April 16.

Déclaration de Berne. 2011. *Swiss Trading SA, La Suisse, le négoce et la malédiction des matières premières*. Lausanne: Éditions d'En Bas.

Deveaux, J. 2019. Ghana et Côte d'Ivoire jettent les bases d'une "Opep" du cacao, France Télévisions, June 13, available at https://www.francetvinfo.fr/monde/afrique/economie-africaine/ghana-et-cote-divoire-jettent-les-bases-dune-opep-du-cacao_3488055.html (accessed on February 29, 2020).

Dozon, J.P. 2011. *Les clefs de la crise ivoirienne*. Paris: Karthala.

Duhem, V. 2013. Côte d'Ivoire: 20 ans de prison pour 14 anciens barons de la filière café-cacao, *Jeune Afrique*, 6 November, available at http://www.jeuneafrique.com/167460/politique/c-te-d-ivoire-20-ans-de-prison-pour-14-anciens-barons-de-la-fili-re-caf-cacao/ (accessed on January 14, 2019).

Dulin, A., and Merckaert, J. 2009. Biens mal acquis: À qui profite le crime?, CCFD-Terre solidaire.

Dupuis, J., and Pontaut, J.M. 2000. Main basse sur l'aide européenne, *L'Express*, April 6, available at https://www.lexpress.fr/actualite/monde/afrique/main-basse-sur-l-aide-europeenne_493143.html (accessed on July 21, 2021).

Etwareea, R. 2018. L'Afrique exige une part décente du gâteau au chocolat, *Le Temps*, April 22.

Fabre, T. 2000. Nigéria: le trésor du clan Abacha est dans nos coffres, *L'Expansion*, July 6.

Fages, C. 2018a. Cacao en Côte d'Ivoire: une gestion 'approximative' selon KPMG, RFI, April 30.

Fages, C. 2018b. L'Afrique peut-elle former un cartel du cacao? RFI, October 2.

Faujas, A. 2010. Le financier 'Chocolate Finger' tente d'assécher le marché mondial du cacao, *Le Monde*, July 21, available at https://www.lemonde.fr /economie/article/2010/07/21/le-financier-chocolate-finger-tente-d-assecher-le-marche-mondial-du-cacao_1390560_3234.html (accessed on January 28, 2019).

Ficatier, J. 2000. Le coup d'Etat fait appel au culte des ancêtres, *La Croix*, January 14.

Fick, M. 2015. Ivory Coast president's stepson defends cocoa export role, *Financial Times*, July 16.

Fletcher, R. 2003. 'Chocolate finger' makes a £10 million bean as stockpiling gamble pays off, *The Telegraph*, July 13.

Fountain, A., and Hütz-Adams, F. 2018. *Cocoa barometer 2018*, available at http:// www.cocoabarometer.org/Cocoa_Barometer/Download_files/2018%20Cocoa%20 Barometer.pdf (accessed on July 21, 2021).

Frindethie, K. 2016. *From Lumumba to Gbagbo: Africa in the Eddy of the Euro-american Quest for Exceptionalism.* Jefferson, NC: McFarland.

Gazzane, H. 2013. 'Chocolate Finger' laisse tomber le cacao, *Le Figaro*, 14 November.

Gbagbo, L., and Mattei, F. 2014. *Pour la vérité et la justice.* Paris: Éditions du Moment. Quoted in Mathieu Olivier. 2014. "Côte d'Ivoire: les extraits du livre-choc de Laurent Gbagbo," *Jeune Afrique*, June 26.

Girard, L. 2017. Le cacao broie du noir, *Le Monde*, March 18.

Global Witness. 2007. *Hot Chocolate: How Cocoa Fuelled the Conflict in Côte d'Ivoire*, June.

Gombeaud, J.L., Moutout, C., and Smith, S. 1990. *La Guerre du Cacao: Histoire secrète d'un embargo.* Paris: Calmann Levy.

Guéniat, M. 2016. Un château, héritage d'Houphouët-Boigny, sème la zizanie dans un village français, *Le Monde*, December 30.

Hofnung, T. 2011. *La Crise Ivoirienne.* Paris: La Découverte.

Houdin, B. 2015. *Les Ouattara: une imposture ivoirienne.* Paris: Éditions du Moment.

Hugeux, V. 2009. La guerre des ports africains, *L'Express*, January 31.

ICCO. 2016. Quarterly Bulletin of Cocoa Statistics 42, number 1, cocoa year 2015/16.

ICCO Expert Group on Stocks. 2016. Report on the Annual ICCO Survey of Cocoa Bean Stocks, January 22.

Investissement Développement Conseil (IDC). 2004. Audit des flux financiers de la filière café-cacao de Côte d'Ivoire, September, quoted in: Sid Amiri and Alain Gourdon. 2006. Étude diagnostic des organisations et des procédures de la filière café-cacao de Côte d'Ivoire, *Rapport du cabinet Ghelber et Gourdon*, May.

Ito, H., and Chinn, M. 2006. What Matters for Financial Development? Capital Controls, Institutions, and Interactions, *Journal of Development Economics*, 81(1), 163–192.

Ivoirebusiness.net. 2017. Financement de la rebellion des Forces nouvelles: Voici l'article de Guy-André Kieffer qui a signé son arrêt de mort!, available at https://www.ivoirebusiness.net/articles/financement-de-la-rebellion-des-forces-nouvelles-voici-larticle-de-guy-andr%C3%A9-kieffer-qui (accessed on May 21, 2020).

Jacque, M. 2018. Afrique de l'Ouest: les premiers pas d'une Opep du cacao, *Les Échos*, 4 October.

Jeune Afrique. 1988. n°1453, November 9.

Jeune Afrique. 2016. Affaire Bictogo-Soeximex: la guerre du cacao, December 21.

Jeune Afrique. 2017a. Affaire Soeximex-Bictogo: droit de réponse d'Adama Bictogo, January 16.

Jeune Afrique. 2017b. Le Ghana maintient son prix du cacao, alimentant les craintes de contrebande depuis la Côte d'Ivoire, October 13.

Journal du Dimanche. 1990. Afrique: les comptes très spéciaux des dirigeants contestés, March 11.

Kieffer, B. 2015. *Le frère perdu: L'affaire Guy-André Kieffer, enquête sur un crime d'État au cœur de la Françafrique*. Paris: La Découverte.

Kieffer, G.A. 2004. Le montage CAA-Lev Mendel Group.

Kieffer, G.A. undated. Origine d'un des financements des mutins.

Koudou, K. 1990. Pratiques éducatives et développement moral (Ph.D. dissertation, Université de Toulouse-Le Mirail, November), volume 1.

KPMG. 2018. Audit du système de commercialisation du cacao. Ministère de l'Agriculture et du Dévelopment Rural (MINADER). March 12.

Langer, A., and Brown, G. 2008. Cultural status inequalities: An important dimension of group mobilization. In F. Stewart (Ed.), *Horizontal Inequalities and Conflict: Understanding Group Violence in Multiethnic Societies*. Basingstoke: Palgrave Macmillan, 41-53.

Langlade, L., and Hondelatte, C. 2013. Passeport pour le crime: Abidjan, documentary by CAPA, broadcast September 27 on *13ème Rue*, https://www.youtube.com/watch?v=rqD-2Itye3c (accessed on July 21, 2021).

Le Monde. 2000. Un mandat d'arrêt international lancé contre l'ex-président ivorien Bédié, June 8.

La Lettre du Continent. 2004. Les comptes secrets d'Houphouët, No. 455, September 30.

La Lettre du Continent. 2011. *ACE reprend des couleurs à Abidjan, No. 624*, December 1.

La Lettre du Continent. 2016a. "Cadeau en chocolat pour les proches du Palais!", No. 730, May 25.

La Lettre du Continent. 2016b. Cargill domine le négoce de cacao, *No.* 735, August 24.

La Lettre du Continent. 2018a. Le rapport explosive qui met à nu la filière du cacao, No. 775, April 25.

La Lettre du Continent. 2018b. Les comptes alambiqués du gouvernement sur le cacao, *No.* 785, October 3.

La Lettre du Continent. 2019a. Cacao: la transparence du secteur bloquée à la primature, No. 795, February 27.

La Lettre du Continent. 2019b. Guillame Soro dans l'intimité de Bédié. No. 795, February 27.

Libération. 2000. Henri Konan Bédié poursuivi par la justice Ivoirienne, June 7.

Losch, B. 1997. A la recherche du chaînon manquant. In B. Contamin and H. Memel-Fotê (Eds.), *Le modèle ivoirien en question*. Paris: Karthala, 205–230.

Losch, B. 1999. Le complexe café cacao de la Côte d'Ivoire, une relecture de la trajectoire ivoirienne" (PhD dissertation, Montpellier 1 University).

Losch, B. 2000. Coup de cacao en Côte d'Ivoire. *Critique internationale*, n°9, October.

Losch, B. 2003. Libéralisation économique et crise politique en Côte d'Ivoire, *Critique Internationale* 19 (April).

Madelin, P. 1993. *L'or des dictatures*. Paris: Fayard.

Mel, F.G. 2010. *Félix Houphouët-Boigny, La fin et la suite*. Abidjan: Cerap, and Paris: Karthala.

Merckaert, J. 2020. Bitter Chocolate: Wealth Extraction in Côte d'Ivoire. Amherst, MA: Political Economy Research Institute, Working Paper 517, July.

Michailof, S. 2005. Côte d'Ivoire 2005: bienvenue sur le Titanic, *Commentaire* 110 (Summer 2005), 393–403.

Michel, S. 2016. Les progrès de la Côte d'Ivoire et six autres leçons du classement africain de Mo Ibrahim, *Le Monde*, October 5.

Ministère de l'économie et des finances. 2010. Synthèse des audits du FDPCC et de l'ARCC, Republic of Côte d'Ivoire, February.

Nantet, B. 1999. "Félix Houphouët-Boigny," in *Encyclopédie Universalis*. Available at https://www.universalis.fr/encyclopedie/felix-houphouet-boigny/ (accessed on July 21, 2021).

Ndikumana, L., and Boyce, J. 2021. Capital Flight from Africa, 1970–2018: New Estimates with Updated Trade Misinvoicing Methodology. Amherst, MA: Political Economy Research Institute, May.

Noble, K. 1994. French Devaluation of African Currency Brings Wide Unrest, *New York Times*, February 23.

Novosseloff, A. 2018. The Many Lives of a Peacekeeping Missions: The UN Operation in Côte-d'Ivoire, New York: International Peace Institute, June, available at https://www.ipinst.org/wp-content/uploads/2018/06/1806 Many-Lives-of-a-Peacekeeping-Mission.pdf (accessed on July 21, 2021).

Ohemeng, W., Sjo, B., and Danquah, M. 2016. Market efficiency and price discovery in cocoa markets. *Journal of African Business*, 17(2), 209–224.

Péan, P. 1988. *L'argent noir*. Paris: Fayard.

Perez, M. 2010. Security business, *Jeune Afrique*, April 5.

Pigeaud, F. 2015. *France Côte d'Ivoire, une histoire tronquée*. La Roque-d'Anthéron: Vents d'Ailleurs.

RFI (Radio France International). 2020. Présidentielle ivoirienne: Alassane Ouattara revient sur sa décision et se porte candidat, August 6, available at https://www.rfi.fr/fr/afrique/20200806-pr%C3%A9sidentielle-ivoirienne-alassane-Ouattara-roevient-d%C3%A9cision-et-porte-candidat (accessed on July 21, 2021).

Richard, F. 2019. Côte-d'Ivoire: Laurent Gbagbo libéré, ses partisans galvanisés, *Libération*, 1 February, available at https://www.liberation.fr/planete/2019/02/01/cote-d-ivoire-laurent-gbagbo-libere-ses-partisans-galvanises1706913 (accessed on July 21, 2021).

Roche, M. 2001. Heurs et malheurs des négociants internationaux de matières premières, *Le Monde*, February 8.

Rusman, A., Toorop, R., De Boer, J., and De Groot Ruiz, A. 2018. Cocoa Farmer Income: The household income of cocoa farmers in Côte d'Ivoire and strategies for improvement, True Price/Fairtrade Report, available at http://www.fairtrade.net/fileadmin/user_upload/content/2009/resources/2018-04_Report_Fairtrade_Cocoa_Farmer_Income.pdf (accessed on July 21, 2021).

Schweisguth, M. 2015. Evaluating the Effects of Certification on Smallholders' Net Incomes, with a Focus on Cacao Farmers in Cooperatives in Côte d'Ivoire. Masters thesis in International Agricultural Development, University of California Davis.

SEO Amsterdam Economics. 2016. Market Concentration and Price Training in the Global Cocoa Value Chain, Report commissioned by the Dutch Ministry of Foreign Affairs, November 15.

Soudan, F. 2009. Où est passé le trésor d'Houphouët? *Jeune Afrique*, January 21.

Tano, A. 2012. Crise cacaoyère et stratégies des producteurs de la sous-préfecture de Meadji au sud-ouest ivoirien. PhD dissertation, Toulouse le Mirail—Toulouse II University.

Traoré, Y. 2014. Problématique de la Gouvernance politique en Afrique: Sociogenèse et enjeux de la crise de l'État-nation en Côte d'Ivoire. Ph.D. dissertation, Paris 2 University.

UN Group of Experts. 2009. Letter dated October 9, 2009 from the Chair of the Security Council Committee established pursuant to resolution 1572 (2004) concerning Côte d'Ivoire addressed to the President of the Security Council. UN Security Council Report S/2009/521.

UN Group of Experts. 2011a. Letter dated October 17, 2011 from the Chair of the Security Council Committee established pursuant to resolution 1572 (2004) concerning Côte d'Ivoire addressed to the President of the Security Council. UN Security Council, Report S/2011/642.

UN Group of Experts. 2011b. Report S/2011/271.

UN Group of Experts. 2011c. Letter dated April 20, 2011 from the Chair of the Security Council Committee established pursuant to resolution 1572 (2004) concerning Côte d'Ivoire addressed to the President of the Security Council. UN Security Council, Report S/2011/272.

UN Group of Experts. 2013. Letter dated October 14, 2013 from the Chair of the Security Council Committee established pursuant to resolution 1572 (2004) concerning Côte d'Ivoire addressed to the President of the Security Council. UN Security Council, Report S/2013/605.

UN Group of Experts. 2016. Letter dated March 15, 2016 from the Chair of the Security Council Committee established pursuant to resolution 1572 (2004) concerning Côte d'Ivoire addressed to the President of the Security Council. UN Security Council, Report S/2016/254.

UN News. 2020. Côte d'Ivoire: 'Tone down the hateful rhetoric', find peaceful solutions – UN rights chief. November 9, available at https://news.un.org/en/story/2020/11/1077252 (accessed on July 21, 2021).

Van de Klundert, M. 2016. VN rapport over megafraude grondstoffen blijft vragen oproepen, Follow the Money, available at https://www.ftm.nl/artikelen/verontwaardigde-reacties-vn-rapport-grondstoffraude (accessed on December 20, 2018).

Vergnaud, C. 2017. Journée mondiale du cacao et du chocolat: quand la spéculation appauvrit les petits producteurs, *Franceinfo* (Radio France), October 1, available at https://www.francetvinfo.fr/economie/emploi/metiers/agriculture/journee-mondi-ale-du-cacao-et-du-chocolat-quand-la-speculation-appauvrit-les-petits-producteurs_2394980.html (accessed on June 2, 2019).

Verschave, F.X. 2000. *Noir Silence: Qui arrêtera la Françafrique?* Paris: Les Arènes.

Wessel, M., and Quist-Wessel, P.M.F. 2015. Cocoa Production in West Africa: A review and analysis of recent developments. *NJAS—Wageningen Journal of Life Sciences*, 74, 1–7.

World Bank. 2015. La Force de l'Éléphant: Pour que sa croissance génère plus d'emplois de qualité, December, available at http://documents.worldbank.org/curated/en/

437971468194941284/pdf/102021-v2-FRENCH-WP-PUBLIC-Box394824B.pdf (accessed on December 2, 2019).

World Bank. 2019. Côte d'Ivoire Economic Outlook: Why the Time Has Come to Produce Cocoa in a Fully Inclusive and Responsible Manner, July 11. Online at https://www.worldbank.org/en/country/cotedivoire/publication/cote-divoire-economic-outlook-why-the-time-has-come-to-produce-cocoa-in-a-responsible-manner.print (accessed on February 20, 2020).

World Trade Organization. 2017. Trade Policy Review: Members of the West African Economic and Monetary Union (WAEMU). Annex 3, Côte d'Ivoire Secretariat report, available at https://www.wto.org/english/tratop_e/tpr_e/tp462_e.htm (accessed on October 23, 2020).

5

South Africa

Capital Flight, State Capture, and Inequality

Adam Aboobaker, Karmen Naidoo, and Léonce Ndikumana

Introduction

The second largest and most industrialized economy on the continent, South Africa is a middle-income country with vast natural resources, a developed financial system, a modern infrastructure network, and a vibrant service sector, all of which are a cause of envy for other countries in the continent. It has managed a peaceful transition from the oppressive apartheid regime, establishing a modern pluralistic democracy, which is still elusive in many other African countries. At the same time, however, the country is confronted by daunting economic, social, and institutional challenges that compromise not only the wellbeing of the majority of the population but also the country's political stability. South Africa has the unfortunate reputation of being "the most unequal country in the world" (Pomerantz 2019).

Wealth and income are concentrated in the hands of a few, the middle class is thin and financially insecure, and the majority of the population lives below or close to the poverty line. This is partly an enduring legacy of the institutionalized racial inequalities of the apartheid regime which have shown strong resilience to economic reforms undertaken in the post-1994 period under the African National Congress (ANC) governments. Quality education continues to be inaccessible for a large fraction of the population, and higher education remains elitist and costly, out of reach for the youth from under-privileged communities.

South Africa faces steady hemorrhage of wealth in the form of capital flight and other illicit financial flows, a phenomenon that has accelerated over the past three decades. This period was marked by aggressive liberalization of the national economy and rapid integration into the global economy. The threat of capital flight has always been on the minds of South African policy makers, especially during the apartheid regime in the context of international economic embargo and heightened political instability, when strict capital controls were seen as a means of keeping private capital in the country. In the post-apartheid era, the

Adam Aboobaker, Karmen Naidoo, and Léonce Ndikumana, *South Africa*. In: *On the Trail of Capital Flight from Africa*. Edited by Léonce Ndikumana and James K. Boyce, Oxford University Press.
© Adam Aboobaker, Karmen Naidoo, and Léonce Ndikumana (2022). DOI: 10.1093/oso/9780198852728.003.0005

policy stance turned toward liberalization with the aim of attracting capital inflows and incentivizing domestic investment. The evidence presented in this chapter suggests, however, that this new policy stance has been ineffective or worse. Rather than abating, capital flight in fact has accelerated during the era of political and economic liberalization. Meanwhile, special measures to address the problem, such as tax amnesties, have not yielded the expected results.

Capital flight from South Africa is a major development concern for several reasons. First, by diminishing domestic savings and eroding the tax base, capital flight deprives the country of resources needed to finance capital accumulation to support long-term economic growth, including public investments in infrastructure and services that are required to meet development needs. Second, from a policy perspective, evidence of capital flight serves as an indictment against the policy and regulatory framework, in that it demonstrates the failure to incentivize domestic investment and reign in illicit capital outflows. Third, capital flight is symptomatic of endemic institutional corrosion that facilitates illicit acquisition of wealth, illicit cross-border transfers of foreign exchange, and the concealment of private assets in offshore havens out of sight of the national authorities. In this respect, capital flight is closely connected to the phenomenon of state capture emerging from collusion between the political elite and domestic and foreign private-sector interests.

This chapter examines the mechanisms, actors, enablers, and institutional environment that facilitate capital flight from South Africa and the resulting accumulation of offshore wealth. The chapter views capital flight as an institutional and development problem which, if not tackled appropriately, carries risks to South Africa's growth prospects and also its political stability in the near future.

The chapter is organized as follows. The next section presents the magnitude, trends and channels of capital flight since the 1970s, measured using the methodology described in detail in Ndikumana and Boyce (2019). We then discuss the policy regimes regarding capital flows under apartheid, after which we examine the post-apartheid reforms, including tax amnesties, and their implications for capital flight and taxation of offshore wealth. Next we focus on the mining sector, discussing how it has been the scene of financial scandal, corporate tax evasion, and capital flight through export misinvoicing. This sets the stage for a discussion of state capture. We then review the consequences of capital flight for development, stressing the urgency of the problem, and conclude with a summary and policy recommendations.

Capital Flight and Hidden Offshore Wealth

Capital flight is a subject of both great interest and great controversy in South Africa, as it constitutes a drain on national resources in a country that remains stuck in a low-growth equilibrium and faces daunting social and economic problems including high unemployment, multidimensional poverty, and deep inequality.[1] Capital flight is seen as one of the causes of these highly visible problems and as a serious handicap to strategies to address them.

The literature on capital flight exhibits substantial controversy, meanwhile, for two main reasons. One is that because capital flight is difficult to measure with precision, and estimates are subject to contestation by government officials, independent analysts and, of course, those who have something to hide, including politically exposed persons. The second reason is the tendency in the literature and the media to conflate capital flight with other closely related but distinct phenomena, such as other types of illicit financial flows, money laundering, grand corruption, and transfer pricing. Ndikumana and Boyce (2019) discuss the distinctions among these.

The statistics presented in this section refer specifically to capital flight, measured as unrecorded cross-border flows.[2] The data show that capital flight has become a major problem in South Africa, accelerating from the end of the apartheid era, even as the government embarked on a process of liberalization of its policy regime and integration into the global economy. The baseline measure of capital flight is the balance of payments (BoP) residual, calculated as the discrepancy between recorded sources of foreign exchange inflows and recorded uses of foreign exchange. The sources of foreign exchange include export earnings (recorded in the current account) and external borrowing and private capital inflows (recorded in the capital account). The uses include payments for imports (in the current account) and recorded capital outflows, including debt amortization (in the capital account). In principle, changes in the stock of official reserves should correspond to the difference between inflows and outflows, yielding the "balance" in the BoP. In practice, there is often a residual, particularly when the BoP statistics on external borrowing are replaced with more complete data from other official sources.[3] In South Africa, as in most developing countries, the residual often indicates that recorded inflows exceeded recorded outflows. The "missing money"—systematic discrepancies between sources and uses of foreign exchange—is taken as a measure of capital flight.

[1] From 1994 to 2018, per capita GDP grew by an average of 1.09% per annum. During the seven years leading to global financial crisis (from 2000 to 2007), it grew at 2.5% annually. However, during 2011–2018, per capita grew by a meager average of 0.16% per annum. These rates are calculated compound annual changes in GDP per capita at constant 2010 prices from the SARB.
[2] A detailed description of the methodology of the estimation of capital flight, the data, and its channels is presented in Ndikumana and Boyce (2019). Other estimates of capital flight from South Africa can be found in earlier studies, including those of Ashman et al. (2011), Fedderke and Liu (2002), Mohamed and Finnoff (2005), Ndikumana et al. (2015), Nicolaou-Manias and Wu (2016), Rustomjee (1991), Smit and Mocke (1991), and Wood and Moll (1994).
[3] The debt flow data recorded in the balance of payments often understate the extent of foreign borrowing. Hence, these are replaced with the more accurate data provided by the World Banks' International Debt Statistics (IDS), a successor of Global Development Finance (GDF), itself successor of the World Debt Tables (WDT).

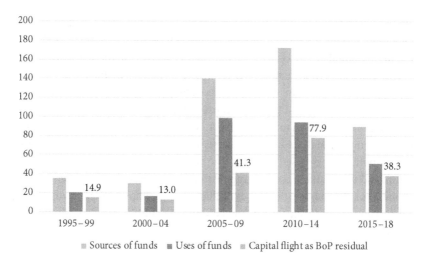

Fig. 5.1 Capital flight from South Africa: 5-year totals (billion, constant 2018 dollars)

Source: Authors' computations.

In the case of South Africa, capital flight thus measured has increased dramatically since 1995, alongside a rapid increase in foreign exchange inflows, mostly through external borrowing and portfolio inflows (Figure 5.1). Capital flight rose from $14.9 billion (in 2018 dollars) in the five-year period 1995–1999 to $77.9 billion in 2010–2014. Over the 1995–2018 period as a whole, South Africa's cumulative capital flight by the simple residual measure amounted to $185.5 billion.

Trade misinvoicing

One important channel of capital flight is through misinvoicing of imports and exports. The extent of trade misinvoicing can be estimated by comparing South Africa's recorded imports and exports with the data recorded by its trading partners (with adjustments for the costs of freight and insurance).[4] Due to the lack of suitable data for earlier years, the estimates presented here cover only the period starting from 1998, from which time South African imports and exports are recorded in the IMF's electronic Direction of Trade Statistics database.

Over the 1998–2018 period, total net trade misinvoicing amounted to $135.5 billion. This is the result of $51.7 billion in net import under-invoicing (resulting in the use of foreign exchange to pay for unrecorded imports) and $185.2 billion in

---

[4] The methodology for estimating trade misinvoicing is described in detail in Ndikumana and Boyce (2019). Also see Ndikumana and Boyce (2010) and Ndikumana et al. (2015).

net export under-invoicing (resulting in unrecorded receipts of foreign exchange). Adding this to the unadjusted BoP residual yields total capital flight of $329.5 billion during the 1998–2018 period.

Underlying the aggregate figures is misinvoicing in specific products and specific bilateral trade routes. The analysis of South Africa's top export products presented in Ndikumana and Boyce (2019) generally shows substantial under-invoicing in exports of primary commodities (see also Chapter 2 of this volume).[5] In particular, precious metals appear to be especially prone to export misinvoicing. In the case of silver, the results show very large discrepancies in trade with India, with export under-invoicing amounting to $82 million over the period 2000–2018. In the case of platinum, exports to China were underinvoiced by as much as $21.5 billion, out of a total of $24.2 billion of imports from South Africa.

In the case of gold, the analysis is focused on the non-monetary gold category, which is reported in Comtrade, the trade database of the United Nations. Non-monetary gold is gold that is not held as reserve assets (this is referred to as monetary gold) by national authorities (central banks). The comparison reveals large discrepancies between the value of gold exports declared by South Africa and the value of gold imports reported by its trading partners.

For example, while India recorded $49 billion in gold imports from South Africa over the 2000–2018 period, the latter's data show only $200 million in gold exports to the former (Table 5.1). The United Kingdom (UK) reported a total of $32.5 billion in gold imports from South Africa, while the latter recorded only $300 million in gold exports to the UK. China's trade records show gold imports of $38.4 billion from South Africa, while the latter's data show virtually no gold exports to China.

It is not clear what is behind the large differences in gold trade statistics given that both trading partners should, in principle, use the same classification codes to report imports and exports. One possibility is confusion arising from transit trade, whereby gold that is recorded as imported from South Africa on the partner's side transited through another country that was recorded in South Africa's books as the final destination. Another possibility is that some of the gold imported from South Africa is actually not South African but rather was produced in another country and sold to South Africa, and that when the South African trader sells the gold it is not recorded as South African exports, while the trading partners record it as imports from South Africa.

These explanations would be inconsistent with the international conventions governing the compilation and reporting of trade statistics. First, if South African gold is sold to, say, an Indian buyer but it transits in another country, India should be marked as the destination in South Africa's records. Second, gold that transits in South Africa should not be recorded as South African by the importers and

Table 5.1 Non-monetary gold exports in South Africa, 2000–2018 (billion, constant 2018 dollars)

Partner	SA exports	Partner imports	Share in SA exports (%)	Share in world imports (%)
China	0.0	38.4	0.0	18.1
Hong Kong	2.7	30.7	4.5	14.5
India	0.2	49.0	0.4	23.1
Italy	0.03	18.1	0.1	8.5
Switzerland	0.4	8.1	0.7	3.8
Thailand	0.0	5.9	0.0	2.8
Turkey	0.05	12.0	0.1	5.7
United Arab Emirates	0.1	5.8	0.1	2.7
United Kingdom	0.3	32.5	0.5	15.3
Total major partners	3.7	200.6	6.2	94.5
Rest of the world*	56.4	11.7	93.8	5.5
World (all partners)	**60.1**	**212.3**	**100.0**	100.0

* Rest of the world includes non-major partners and other areas "not elsewhere specified (n.e.s)" in South Africa's export statistics. Unlike in Table 2.5 (Chapter 2), in this table, total exports and imports cover all years including those where data for either South Africa or its partners are missing.
Source: Authors' computations using data from Comtrade.

should be recorded in South Africa's data as "goods in transit." Therefore, if the trading firms and government statistical services on both sides of the transaction follow the UN reporting conventions, their figures should be mutually consistent.

South Africa's trade statistics exhibit a further mystery: the majority of recorded gold exports is reported as going to unspecified destinations (labelled as "other areas not elsewhere specified"). Over the 2000–2018 period, exports to these areas accounted for $55.6 billion out of the $60.1 billion reported by South Africa. The amount so recorded is not nearly enough, however, to account for the total magnitude of the discrepancies between South Africa's recorded exports and the gold imports recorded by its trading partners.

Another problematic feature of the South African data is that starting from 2011, the Department of Trade and Industry has merged its reporting of non-monetary gold and monetary gold. However, this practice cannot explain the discrepancies in which South Africa's numbers are lower. If anything, the conflation of the two categories would produce the opposite results: if South Africa combines the two, while its trading partners continue to treat them separately, then South Africa's total gold export figures should be larger, not smaller, than the non-monetary gold imports recorded by its partners.

Table 5.2 External debt burden indicators in South Africa, 1994–2018

	1994	2005	2010	2018
External debt stock ($ billion) of which:	21.7	42.3	108.3	173.0
General government ($ billion)	7.8	9.9	32.6	63.7
Private nonguaranteed ($ billion)	5.2	9.4	47.6	62.1
Public and publicly guaranteed ($ billion)	7.8	18.3	36.2	71.6
Short term debt ($ billion)	7.7	14.3	21.7	36.8
Use of IMF credit ($ billion)	0.9	0.3	2.7	2.5
External debt stocks (% of GNI)	15.8	16.7	29.5	48.5
Total debt service (% of exports)	9.4	6.6	5.6	24.7
Interest payments on external debt (% of exports)	2.9	2.7	2.5	6.0

Source: World Bank, International Debt Statistics.

We have submitted requests to South African government agencies for clarification of the reasons for the discrepancies in gold trade statistics. At the time of writing, we have not received replies to our queries.

External debt and capital flight

The post-apartheid era has been characterized by both an explosion of capital flight and the rapid growth of external debt. In 1994, South Africa's external debt stock stood at $21.7 billion, equivalent to 15.8% of gross national income (World Bank's *International Debt Statistics* database). It rose to $42.3 billion in 2005 (16.7% of GNI), after which it accelerated, reaching $108.3 billion in (29.5% of GNI) in 2010 and $173 billion (48.5% of GNI) in 2018. The increase was driven by both public debt and private non-guaranteed debt (see Table 5.2).

Rising external borrowing translated, with a lag, into rising debt-service obligations. By 2018, the ratio of debt service to exports had grown to 24.7%, up from 6.6% in 2005. Interest payments alone became equivalent to 6% of the country's export earnings.[6] In 2018, the country recorded the largest negative net transfer

---

[6] A noteworthy feature of South Africa's external debt burden has been a steady increase in the share of rand-denominated debt, which rose from 20% in 1989 to 50% in 2019 (SARB data). This may mitigate to some extent the foreign exchange constraint for the country's capacity to service its debt.

on external debt in its history, as debt service payments exceeded new borrowing by $7.4 billion.

These numbers raise serious concerns about the sustainability of external borrowing as a means of financing growth in South Africa. To reduce its reliance on external borrowing and minimize the resulting drag on the economy, the South African government will need to expand its domestic resource mobilization capacity. This would also help in preserving policy space and government accountability. But doing so will require coming to grips with the issue of capital flight.

Accumulation of offshore wealth

While capital flight is a cost to South Africa's domestic economy, it is a benefit to the owners of the associated assets and for their enablers. Some of the funds that are illicitly transferred out of the country are used for consumption expenditures by their owners. But since much capital flight is originated by economic and political elites, a substantial portion of the funds is likely to be saved and invested in offshore financial instruments and real estate. These assets accumulate value over time thanks to investment income and capital gains. The resulting accumulation of offshore wealth is difficult to estimate, given that different assets have different rates of return and the composition of the portfolio is unknown. Using a methodology based on reasonable assumptions about the fraction that is saved and rates of return, James Henry (2016) estimated the stock of offshore wealth owned by South Africans at about $146 billion in 2010.[7]

Ndikumana and Boyce (2019) estimate the opportunity cost of cumulative capital flight by calculating its stock, assuming that all the money was saved and earned a modest rate of return equal to that on the 3-month U.S. Treasury bill. Using this approach, the stock of capital flight from South Africa amounted to $303 billion at the end of 2018. To put this in perspective, in that year South Africa's total stock of external debt was $173 billion. In this sense, South Africa was a "net creditor" to the rest of the world.

The cumulative stock of capital flight thus measured is equivalent to 34% of the total private wealth held by South African residents at home and abroad, which was estimated at $875 billion for 2017 by the Credit Suisse Research Institute (Credit Suisse 2019). As it happens, this percentage is close to the various estimates of the share of private wealth held abroad by Africans in general: Zucman (2013,

---

[7] See the *Global Haven Industry* website, available at http://globalhavenindustry.com/africa-countries (accessed on July 22, 2021).

p. 53)[8] puts this at 30%, while Collier et al. (2001) earlier put it at 40%. All three studies find the ratio for Africa to be the highest of any region in the world. In other words, African private wealth holders exhibit a *negative home bias* relative to their counterparts elsewhere, being more inclined to prefer foreign assets over domestic assets.

The estimates of offshore wealth accumulated from capital flight are consistent with both the stock of private wealth in South Africa and its skewed distribution in favor of the rich and ultra-rich. South Africa has the highest amount of private wealth among African countries, according to AfrAsia Bank (2019), at $649 billion in 2018, accounting for almost 30% of the entire continent's total (Table 5.3). Credit Suisse (2019) put the stock of private wealth in South Africa somewhat higher at $787 billion in 2018, equivalent to about 20% of its estimate of the continent's total. The *Africa Wealth Report* (AfrAsia Bank, 2019) data show that private wealth has been rising faster than national income in South Africa: in per capita terms over the 2000–2019 period, it increased by 169% compared to 109% for GDP. The faster increase in private wealth is both a cause and effect of the country's widening economic inequality.

Table 5.3 Private wealth and number of High Net Worth Individuals, 2018

Country	Stock of private wealth (2018)		Growth of private wealth (2008–2018)	Number of HNWIs[*]	Number of billionaires
	Total ($ billion)	Per capita ($)			
South Africa	649	11,450	13%	39,200	5
Egypt	303	3,100	−10%	16,700	6
Nigeria	225	1,170	−4%	9,900	4
Morocco	114	3,170	5%	4,600	3
Kenya	93	1,870	64%	8,600	–
Angola	69	2310	25%	3,100	1
Côte d'Ivoire	43	1780	37%	2,500	0
Total Africa[**]	2,200	6571		140,000	23
South Africa's share	29.5%			28.0%	21.7%

[*] HNWIs = High Net Worth Individuals (possessing $1 million or more in liquid assets).
[**] Of the $2.2 trillion of private wealth, $920 billion is held by HNWIs.
Source: AfrAsia Bank, *Africa Wealth Report* 2019, available at https://www.afrasiabank.com/en/about/newsroom/africa-wealth-report-2019.

[8] Also see Zucman (2013b).

Exchange Controls and Capital Flight

The 1960s–1970s: The consolidation of exchange controls

Capital flight has been a long-standing matter of concern for policymakers in South Africa. This was especially so during the apartheid era, in the context of political instability fueling fears of elites moving their wealth abroad. The international sanctions imposed on the apartheid regime created legal blockages as well as financial disincentives for foreign capital inflows. This meant that the government had to utilize policies at its disposal to "trap" residents' capital domestically. Exchange controls and regulation of capital flows became important tools for government macroeconomic and financial policy.

The use of exchange controls in South Africa dates at least from 1939, when the country was a member of the British Sterling Area.[9] At that time, the United Kingdom asked member countries to impose restrictions on capital flows outside of the Sterling Area, while facilitating free movement of capital from the UK within the area (Stals 1998). In South Africa, exchange controls were tightened in 1961 in response to large outflows of capital following political unrest in the aftermath of the Sharpeville massacre of March 21, 1960 and the country's withdrawal from the British Commonwealth.

The 1961 Exchange Control Regulations Act required explicit authorization by the Treasury to "take or send out of the Republic any bank notes, gold, securities or foreign currency, or transfer any securities from the Republic elsewhere" (South African National Treasury 1961). It prohibited repatriation of the proceeds of sale of South African securities and profits from investment in the country by non-residents. It further required that any sale of foreign currency or any foreign asset by residents must be declared to the Treasury within 30 days.

Thereafter, exchange controls were extended over time in response to worsening domestic political conditions and external political and economic pressure, including trade and investment sanctions against the apartheid regime. Exchange rate management was implemented through a parallel exchange rate system known as the "blocked rand," which evolved via the "securities rand" into the "financial rand." Blocked rand accounts were held by non-residents at commercial banks and could be used to deposit the proceeds of sales of South African government securities, to purchase shares on the Johannesburg Stock Exchange (JSE), and to purchase government, municipal, and public utilities bonds. The proceeds of these transactions could be repatriated only after they had been held for five years (Farrell and Todani 2004).

In 1976, the "securities rand" was introduced as part of efforts to attract foreign investment and increase incentives for transactions on the JSE. This instrument

---

[9] It can be argued that it began even earlier; see Scott and Pettersson (2019).

allowed transfers among non-residents as well as currency trading through bro-kers on the JSE. Three years later, the "financial rand" replaced the securities rand, upon the recommendation of the De Kock Commission's Interim Report. The Commission's view was that the country should embark on a gradual process of re-laxing exchange controls and moving towards a market-determined exchange rate regime. This was expected to alleviate market distortions, increase net returns to investments, and ultimately attract higher short-term as well as long-term foreign investments into the country, while curbing capital flight.

The 1980s: The crisis—things fall apart

Early moves towards liberalization were pursued throughout the 1980s, but pol-icy reforms during that decade were overshadowed by political and economic problems that plunged the economy into a deeper crisis. In 1983, the government abolished the dual exchange rate and moved towards phasing out all exchange con-trols on non-residents. However, the efficacy of these reforms was compromised by the effects of political unrest. Foreign exchange markets and capital flows be-came highly volatile. The situation was aggravated by debt distress, precipitated by the refusal of American banks to roll over the country's short-term debt. The South African government found no other option but to impose repayment restrictions on foreign debt as it was running out of hard currency. This move exacerbated pressure on the rand, causing a substantial depreciation of the currency.

In 1989, liberalization momentum picked up with the appointment of Chris Stals as Governor of the South African Reserve Bank (SARB). The exchange rate became the anchor of monetary policy, and the latter would become the central instrument of the liberalization reforms from the 1990s until today.

1960s–1980s: Lessons learnt

Did the exchange controls of the 1960s–1980s work? Most importantly, did they halt or reduce capital flight? The effectiveness of exchange controls was un-dermined by the structural economic and political problems that made them necessary in the first place. The controls proved incapable of alleviating the ef-fects of the deep political instability that engulfed the country and the devastating effects of international economic embargo against the apartheid regime.

It is possible that exchange controls may not only fail to curb capital flight but instead exacerbate it. In particular, poorly enforced capital controls may induce capital flight through trade misinvoicing. When trade-exposed firms find it dif-ficult or costly to access foreign exchange, they may attempt to circumvent the controls by under-invoicing exports (to retain foreign exchange abroad and avoid having to surrender it to the Central Bank at the official rate), and by over-invoicing imports (to obtain foreign exchange from the Central Bank at the official rate). Several studies have linked exchange controls to capital flight through trade misinvoicing in South Africa in the 1970s and 1980s. Estimates of the amounts range from \$12.4 billion by Smit and Mocke (1991) to \$20 billion by Kahn (1991) and \$55 billion by Rustomjee (1991).[10]

The failures of the exchange controls are further revealed by an examination of the financing gaps that held back the country's growth potential. The country confronted structural saving-investment gaps and fiscal deficits that compromised capital accumulation and long-term growth. These gaps deepened in the 1970s in the context of global shocks (oil prices) and political upheaval, especially following the Soweto uprising. The adverse effects of political and macroeconomic instability in the 1980s ushered in a secular downward trend in domestic saving and capital accumulation that continues to the present (Figure 5.2). This trend has been a major reason for the country's inability to sustain high growth rates in the post-apartheid era. While a pick-up of investment and saving

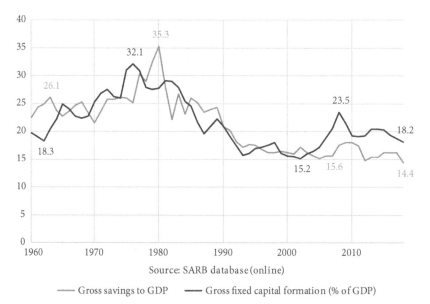

Source: SARB database (online)

—— Gross savings to GDP   —— Gross fixed capital formation (% of GDP)

Fig. 5.2 Domestic saving and investment, 1960–2018 (% of GDP)
Source: SARB database.

---

[10] Wood and Moll (1994) discuss limitations of these estimates of trade misinvoicing including statistical and methodological issues. Due to lack of suitable mirror trade data, we were not able to produce our own estimates of trade misinvoicing during this period.

sustained the growth acceleration from 2000 to 2007, the subsequent downturn in saving and investment coincides with growth deceleration. Anemic growth has turned into a contraction of per capita income in recent years.[11] Boosting domestic capital accumulation and saving must be a central part of any strategy to boost growth—combating capital flight must be part of this strategy.

It is clear that the control regime failed to boost domestic investment and saving. Did exchange controls have an impact on foreign capital flows? During the 1970s, South Africa managed to attract modest foreign capital, mainly in the form of foreign direct investment (FDI). But throughout the 1980s, the country experienced net outflows in most years. In cumulative terms, during the decade of the 1970s, the country attracted a total FDI of $5.1 billion (in 2018 prices) but saw an exit of $2.6 billion, yielding net FDI inflows of $2.5 billion. In contrast, during the 1980s, the country experienced cumulative net outflows of $4.7 billion, as only half a billion came into the country compared to $5.1 billion that exited.[12]

In sum, the foreign exchange and capital controls pursued by successive governments in the apartheid era failed to stem capital outflows and foster domestic investment. The measures were implemented at a time when the country was confronted by deep structural and political problems, at home and internationally, that these policies did not and could not address. The political instability arising from domestic resistance and the apartheid regime's international isolation produced high levels of uncertainty that discouraged investment and created market instability. The policies failed because they merely addressed symptoms while ignoring the underlying disease.

Liberalization and Capital Flight in the Post-Apartheid Era

Gradual liberalization

The transition to democracy in 1994 carried high expectations of "liberation dividends" in terms of employment, access to education and other social services, and the elevation of living standards in general for the historically disadvantaged population—women and people of color. The primary challenge faced by the ANC government was to mobilize sufficient resources to respond to these expectations by financing its ambitious growth and redistribution agenda. The post-apartheid government inherited a culture of deep public distrust of the state

---

[11] Real per capita GDP declined from R56,549 in 2014 to R55,595 in 2018, shrinking every year except in 2017 when it virtually stagnated (growing at 0.028%). These figures are from the SARB database.

[12] The data are from UNCTADstat, available at https://unctadstat.unctad.org/wds/ReportFolders/reportFolders.aspx (accessed on July 22, 2021).

that disincentivized tax compliance. At the same time, the uncertainty of the post-liberation environment was a potential motive for smuggling capital out of the country. To address these challenges, a number of economic and tax reforms were implemented.

The post-apartheid government embarked on a series of market-oriented policy frameworks starting with the 1996 Growth, Employment, and Redistribution (GEAR) program, which among other things liberalized financial controls, slashed tariffs, and privatized "non-essential" state enterprises.[13] This was followed by the Accelerated and Shared Growth Initiative for South Africa (ASGISA) under President Thabo Mbeki in 2005, the New Growth Path (NGP) under President Jacob Zuma in 2010, and the National Development Plan (NDP) in 2013.[14] Alongside these development plans, the government initiated specific measures intended to entice the repatriation of private wealth held offshore, in the form of tax and capital flight amnesties. The expectation was that these reforms would boost confidence in the economy and put the country on a path to rising economic prosperity.

The liberalization strategy was driven by three main factors in the domestic economy and the global context. First, the dominant school of economic thought in the 1990s held the view that exchange controls, like any other government interventions in the economy, were counter-productive in that they created distortions and impeded the proper functioning of price mechanisms. South African policymakers were sympathetic to this view, which has helped to sustain the liberalization movement even to this day.

Second, the decade of the 1990s was characterized by a concerted push by the Bretton Woods Institutions (BWIs) for full market liberalization. Given its relatively low external debt at the beginning of the decade, South Africa was less vulnerable than many other developing countries to this pressure from the BWIs. But for the purpose of building relationships with international institutions, there was high appetite for liberalization in domestic policy circles.

The third factor was the removal of economic and political sanctions against the country following the downfall of the apartheid regime, which shifted the policy focus towards integration into the global economy. It was expected that once wealth holders overcame initial fears about possible instability and the risk of their capital being "trapped in the country" or nationalized in a regime run by the previously disenfranchised Black majority, South Africa's economic environment would become increasingly attractive to domestic as well as foreign investors.

---

[13] For accounts of GEAR and related policies, see Weeks (1999), Taylor (2001), Streak (2004), and Marais (2011).

[14] See "South Africa's Key economic policies changes (1994–2013)," retrieved from: South African Story Online, available at https://www.sahistory.org.za/article/south-africas-key-economic-policies-changes-1994-2013.

This reasoning was questionable, however, given the considerable interest in *internationalization* among major South African firms. Ashman et al. (2011, p. 13) have argued that since 1994, "major South African corporations have primarily pursued a strategy of corporate globalization in the form of the increasing internationalization and financialization of their operations." An example was Gencor's spin-off of its non-precious metals mining assets and the creation of Billiton, which went on to merge with the Australian mining firm BHP (Chabane et al. 2003, p. 12). The mining giant Anglo-American focused its gold interests in AngloGold, sold South African Breweries, pared its financial services interests to FirstRand, and together with Billiton bought out the minority shareholders in its chrome company, Samancor.[15] The relaxation of the regime of capital controls facilitated the internationalization process. The allowance of dual listing of major South African firms on the JSE *and* the London Stock Exchange (LSE), for instance, made possible significant volumes of legal capital outflows that had been restricted under the previous regime. It is not surprising that the liberalization of exchange controls enjoyed support from firms interested in pursuing internationalized business strategies.

Arguments made against the liberalization of exchange controls stressed their role in protecting the economy against financial instability, including instability originating from external factors.[16] The 1998 Asian financial crisis bolstered support for a more cautionary stance on liberalization. Apprehension regarding possible pent-up demand for capital outflows following the long period of strict exchange controls added to concerns.

The main debate, however, was not whether to liberalize or not, but about the appropriate speed of liberalization. The gradualist approach of a phased-out dismantling of exchange controls, supported by the SARB, won out over supporters of a more immediate "big bang" approach to lifting exchange controls. In 1993, several relaxations of the control regime were introduced, including the removal of exchange controls on capital account transactions. In March 1995, the two-tiered exchange rate ("financial rand") system was terminated. This meant that non-residents were allowed to bring capital to South Africa for any purpose and repatriate the principal and capital gains without restrictions. Resident corporations also were allowed—up to specified limits—to invest and raise capital abroad. In June 1995, further reforms were introduced to allow resident institutional investors to diversify some of their assets into foreign currency-denominated investments. In June 1997, private individuals were allowed to make investments abroad up to specified limits.

---

[15] Samancor recently has been accused in court proceedings of having extracted as much as $500 million from 2005 to 2010 via practices such as transfer pricing and the pocketing of secret management and "facilitation" fees. See van Rensburg (2019).

[16] See, among others, McKenzie and Pons-Vignon (2012) and Stals (1998). For a review of the evolution of views on capital controls, see Klein et al. (2012).

As a result, by mid-1998, the Reserve Bank Governor confidently declared that "South Africa has reached a stage where there are no effective exchange controls anymore on current account transactions and on the movement of funds of non-residents… On balance, South Africa has now removed more than seventy percent of all exchange controls of the past" (Stals 1998, p. 3). Today the policy regime in South Africa is considered relatively open and liberalized, not only from a historical perspective but also compared to many other countries.[17]

Tax amnesties

To address issues of tax compliance, the government set up the Commission of Inquiry into Certain Aspects of the Tax Structure of South Africa, known as the Katz Commission after its chairman, Professor Michael Katz (see Steenkamp 1996). One recommendation of the Katz Commission was the use of tax amnesty to boost revenue and enhance compliance.

The first tax amnesty was issued in 1995 with the aim of providing taxpayers in default with a one-off time-bound window of opportunity to voluntarily declare and pay previously evaded taxes in exchange for exoneration of financial penalties and criminal prosecution. In addition to boosting tax revenue by incentivizing compliance, it was hoped that the amnesty would reduce the incentives for capital flight, insofar as it is driven in part by fear of penalties for tax evasion.

The second tax amnesty was introduced as the Exchange Control Amnesty and Amendment of Tax Laws Bill, passed in 2003 (South African National Treasury 2003a). The major innovation in the 2003 tax amnesty was that it covered wealth held offshore, enabling qualifying applicants to pay an "amnesty levy" of 5% of the fair market value (assessed as of February 2003) of foreign assets disclosed and repatriated to South Africa, and 10% of the market value of assets disclosed but kept offshore.

From the government's perspective, the 2003 tax amnesty was motivated by four main factors. First, in its assessment South Africa offered opportunities for higher returns than investment abroad, given its relatively high interest rates and strong GDP growth. Second, enhanced international cooperation in tax compliance was increasing the probability of detection of tax fraud, which would encourage past evaders to take advantage of the amnesty. Third, enhanced international cooperation in surveillance of capital flows, alongside bilateral tax treaties, was expected to help curb illicit capital outflows and thereby further encourage demand for domestic assets (South African National Treasury 2003b). Finally, the government's economic reform objectives also included new, complementary laws and

---

[17] For current details on the currency and exchange control regime, see SARB (2019).

institutions to combat tax evasion and illicit financial flows, such as the Financial Intelligence Act. For these reasons it was hoped that, going forward, the new policy environment would make it harder to evade taxes and less attractive to smuggle capital from the country and conceal it abroad.

In 2006, the government introduced the Small Business Tax Amnesty (South African National Treasury 2006), initially to address problems in the taxi industry; it subsequently was broadened to all small businesses with annual revenues not exceeding R10 million. The main objective was to facilitate the formalization of small enterprises, so as to bring them into the tax net by alleviating concerns related to past non-compliance and any resulting tax liabilities, penalties and interest (SARS 2006).

In further efforts to enhance tax compliance and encourage taxpayers to regularize their tax affairs with the South African Revenue Service (SARS) without the fear of large penalties or prosecution, the government enacted a Voluntary Disclosure Program (VDP) in 2010. A Special Voluntary Disclosure Program (SVDP) was enacted from October 2016 to August 2017 that again offered a one-time window of opportunity for South African residents to regularize the status of their foreign assets vis-à-vis the Exchange Control Regulations of 1961 (as amended).[18]

The SVDP excluded residents under current or pending investigation for contraventions of regulations, as well as assets that were obtained from illegal activities. To that effect, under the SVDP disclosures had to include "confirmation of the sources of all unauthorized foreign assets, details of the manner in which such assets were transferred and retained abroad as well as proof of the market value of the unauthorized assets as of February 28, 2016" (SARB 2016, p. 10). Application for SVDP carried a fee, a price in exchange for the pecuniary and legal benefits that would accrue from a successful application.[19]

Did liberalization help to attract capital inflows?

Among liberalization proponents it was expected that removing controls on foreign exchange would result in a net inflow of capital into the country, despite also facilitating capital outflows, both recorded and illicit. The key empirical question is which effect dominated—increased inflows or increased outflows—in post-apartheid South Africa.

---

[18] The VDP remains an ongoing program while the SVDP was a one-off program. For more details on the SVDP, see SARS, "Special Voluntary Disclosure Programme (SVDP)," available at https://www.sars.gov.za/legal-counsel/voluntary-disclosure-programme-vdp/special-voluntary-disclosure-programme/.

[19] See Ndikumana et al. (2020) for a description of the benefits from the tax dimension (enforced by SARS) and the exchange control dimension (enforced by the SARB) of the program.

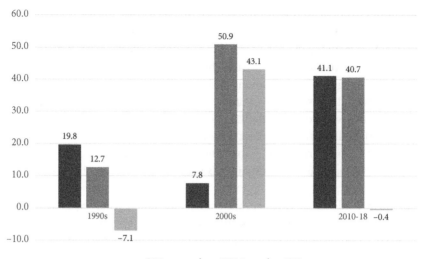

Fig. 5.3 Foreign direct investment: cumulative inward, outward, and net inflows by decade (billion, constant 2018 dollars)
Source: UNCTAD database.

As discussed earlier, the 1980s witnessed net capital outflows despite the government's attempts to use exchange and capital controls to prevent them. In terms of FDI, the data suggest that the country did not perform better in the 1990s. On a net basis, the decade saw an outflow of $7 billion, with about $20 billion of outward investment compared to $13 billion of inward investment (in 2018 US dollars). However, in the first decade of the new century, South Africa received massive inward investment to the tune of $51 billion, coupled with only modest outward investment ($8 billion), yielding a net inflow of $43 billion. These gains have not been sustained, however, in the following decade, when inward and outward flows virtually neutralized each other at about $41 billion in each direction (Figure 5.3).

South Africa has had greater success in attracting other types of foreign capital, portfolio flows in particular. Net portfolio investment inflows reached $45 billion in the 1990s, eased to $34 billion in the 2000s, and then skyrocketed to $109 billion from 2010 to 2018. The country also attracted other types of private investments to the tune of $24 billion over 2000–2009 and $42 billion during 2010–2018.[20]

Overall, the liberalization period has been associated with improved levels of foreign exchange reserves. In contrast, the crisis-plagued decade of the 1980s had been marked by a depletion of foreign exchange reserves serious enough to jeopardize the country's ability to import. The stock of reserves declined to barely one

---

[20] "Other investments" reported in the balance of payments refer to equity and debt flows (assets and liabilities) that are not recorded under foreign direct investment, portfolio investment, or financial derivatives and employee stock options in the financial account of the balance of payments. See IMF (2009).

month of import cover at the end of the decade, according to SARB data. The country's reserves initially remained low in the transition period, but they began a steady increase from mid-1996. In this respect, liberalization can claim some success.

Finally, it was expected that liberalization of exchange controls would incentivize equity investment into the national stock market. The rationale was that easing restrictions would encourage non-residents to bring funds into the country, purchase domestic assets and repatriate the gains from their investments, thus giving an edge to the JSE relative to foreign stock markets, including the LSE. While the JSE did attract net resources during the years following the establishment of democracy, as well as in the years before the 2008 global crisis, in other years, the gains were either minimal or there were net outflows. Starting in 2015, the stock market has seen a substantial drain of resources from the country, posting negative net purchases each year.[21] In this respect, the benefits of liberalization appear to have been, at best, mixed.

Has liberalization helped to curb capital flight?

Contrary to expectations regarding the anticipated benefits of financial liberalization in South Africa, the period of dismantlement of exchange controls has been characterized by a remarkable increase in capital flight. Between 1990 and 1999, recorded foreign exchange inflows exceeded the recorded uses of these resources to the tune of $27.8 billion. This corresponds to the simple BoP residual measure of capital flight. In addition, $4.9 billion left the country through net trade misinvoicing, leading to a cumulative total capital flight of $32.7 billion during the decade. Matters only got worse in the subsequent decades, with cumulative capital flight totaling $152.1 billion over 2000–2009 and $147.2 billion over 2010–2018.[22] The evidence that trade misinvoicing persisted and even increased despite exchange rate liberalization suggests that the motives behind it have not been simply to avoid surrendering foreign exchange earnings at a below-market official rate.

The positive gloss on capital outflows, or at least officially recorded outflows, is that South African wealth owners have been able to take advantage of greater economic openness to diversify their portfolios. But any resulting gains arguably pale in relation to the secular decline of domestic capital accumulation and its adverse impact on economic growth.

One plausible motive for the unrecorded capital outflows is tax evasion by private wealth holders and traders, as well as profit shifting by South African firms and multinational corporations operating in the country. South Africa is the top

[21] See Ndikumana et al. (2020) for details.
[22] Details can be found in Ndikumana and Boyce (2019).

source of intra-African foreign direct investment, with its firms dominating major sectors such as services (telecom and banking) and retail trade (grocery stores). To the extent that these foreign investments are duly recorded at both the source and destination, and that the appropriate taxes are paid on the profits they generate, they can be considered normal and desirable correlates of economic prosperity, regional integration, and globalization. Problems arise, however, when these outflows are not duly recorded upon exit, and when the money is channeled to offshore jurisdictions with opaque financial and tax regimes, where the proceeds of the investments are hidden to evade taxation.

Trade misinvoicing, a major channel of capital flight, is poorly addressed by reforms of exchange controls and openness of the capital account regime. While rigid restrictions on access to foreign exchange and outward investment create incentives for export and import misinvoicing, it does not necessarily follow that liberalizing exchange controls will eliminate these practices. There are additional motives for trade misinvoicing other than access to foreign exchange. Again, these motives include tax evasion and tax avoidance. By understating the proceeds of their exports or overstating cost of imports, firms are able to understate their profits and reduce tax liabilities. Such tax minimization strategies are especially pronounced among multinational corporations, where a large share of trade takes place between units of the same global entity.

The problem is exacerbated by the opacity in global trade perpetuated by "trading hubs" such as Switzerland, the Netherlands, Hong Kong, and Dubai. "Free ports play an important role in anonymizing international trade analogous to that of anonymizers in the world of virtual currencies," observes Ayogu (Chapter 6 in this volume). "They make the task of trade data reconciliation more difficult, while increasing opportunities for trade-related capital flight." For example, the United Arab Emirates (UAE) has emerged as the primary destination, or transit point, for precious metals from Africa such as gold and diamonds. The analysis of mirror trade data on these precious metals reveals very large discrepancies between the (lower) values declared by the exporting countries and the (much higher) values reported in the UAE's own trade statistics, suggesting systematic export under-invoicing of mineral exports by African countries. A study by Reuters showed that, based on importers' statistics, the UAE was the top importer of gold from Africa in 2016 with $15.1 billion worth, surpassing China ($8.5 billion) which earlier had been the leader, followed by Switzerland ($7.5 billion) (McNeill and Shabalala 2019). Interestingly, Reuters' investigators were told by industrial mining firms in Africa, including AngloGold Ashanti, that they did not send gold to the UAE. This further illustrates the lack of consistency in the reporting of gold trade.

The limited capacity to track, monitor, and record trade flows along the entire transaction chain from the source (exporter) to the ultimate destination (final importer) poses a challenge in efforts to curb capital flight through misinvoicing.

The South African customs services have made efforts to modernize their electronic platform to improve the tracking of international trade. But in reality, the SARS can effectively verify only a small fraction of total imports and exports. A government official interviewed by the authors reported that the SARS is able to inspect only about three percent of all the containers moving through the country's ports.[23] This leaves ample opportunity for manipulation of export and import quantities and values for the sake of minimizing fiscal liabilities and moving money abroad.

It is sometimes argued that persistent capital outflows are due to a shortage of skilled labor in the country, forcing investors to set up shop abroad.[24] This assertion was voiced by two senior government officials who were interviewed by the authors.[25] There is limited empirical evidence to support this argument. In any case, even if a shortage of skills were an issue, this would matter for legitimate capital outflows that leave the country for the sake of portfolio diversification and rate-of-return maximization. In the case of the unrecorded outflows that comprise capital flight, the owners of the funds are likely to be more interested in safe keeping and concealment of their wealth rather than chasing higher profit rates abroad. The liberalization of international financial and trade transactions can do little to discourage such outflows; indeed, it may make them easier. Nor can policies aimed merely at increasing the quality of labor skills or raising the domestic rate of return to investment.

Did tax amnesties pay off?

A number of questions can be raised as to the results of the various amnesties adopted over the years. Answers to these questions may help in assessing the merit of such initiatives and exploring remedial strategies going forward. Three key questions are considered here.

1. *Did the taxpayers take up the opportunities to regularize tax arrears and contraventions of exchange controls?*

While there is inadequate data to provide a thorough assessment of the effectiveness of the tax amnesties, the available data indicate only modest revenue returns from the two VDPs. In a 2018 speech at the SARS, the Minister of Finance reported that the ongoing VDP had yielded R10.8 billion since 2012 (South African National Treasury 2018b). SARS reports that the VDP collected an additional R3.2

---

[23] Interview on November 25, 2019 (anonymity requested).
[24] See, among others, (Lewis, 2001, 2002). Gelb and Black (2004) find no robust empirical evidence for the view that the shortage of skilled labor is a binding constraint to foreign investment.
[25] Interviews on November 25 and 26, 2019 (anonymity requested).

billion in tax revenue for the 2018–2019 financial year (SARS 2019). This would bring the cumulative additional revenue collected under the program over seven years to R14 billion (US $1 billion), equivalent to roughly 0.5% of total personal income tax collections over the period.[26]

On October 10, 2017, less than two months after the close of the window for SVDP applications, it was announced that approximately 2,000 taxpayers had taken advantage of the program (Tuffias Sandberg 2017). In March 2018, SARS reported R2.7 billion in revenue receipts out of a total of R3.3 billion in settlements from approved applications (ibid.). The R3.3 billion in approved settlements represented 0.7% of total personal income tax collected in 2017/18.[27] The pool of applicants included 759 high net worth individuals (individuals with liquid assets over $1 million). According to the SARS, some of the agreements were prompted by revelations contained in the "Panama Papers."[28]

2. Did the amnesties help curb capital flight?

It is even more difficult to assess the impact of tax amnesties on capital flight and private wealth held offshore. The post-1994 era was marked by an acceleration of capital flight, as discussed above, as well as substantial licit capital outflows in the form of outward FDI and portfolio investment. Amnesties for transgression of exchange control regulations do not appear to have reduced the appetite for unauthorized foreign assets. South Africans still hold substantial wealth offshore. Some of these assets undoubtedly were not only transferred abroad illegally, but also acquired illegally in the first place, and then concealed abroad in contravention of tax laws and exchange control regulations.

High Net Worth Individuals (HNWIs) are notorious for low tax compliance. The SARS rather gently points this out in its 2017/18 *Annual Performance Plan*: "A significant number of HNWIs do not timeously pay the correct amount of taxes due to non-declaration of income sources, overstating expenses and splitting of income through trusts" (SARS 2018, p. 12). The extent to which amnesties induce repatriation of private wealth held abroad by HNWIs remains an open question.

---

[26] Cumulative personal income tax from 2011/2012 to 2018/2019 amounted to R2957.58 billion. Amounts in rand are converted in US dollars using the average R/$ exchange rate for 2018 and 2019.

[27] SARS online data, https://www.sars.gov.za/about/sas-tax-and-customs-system/tax-statistics/.

[28] SARS, media release, "SARS reaches R3.3-billion mark in SVDP," Pretoria, 08 March 2018 (https://www.sars.gov.za/media-release/8-march-2018-sars-reaches-r33-billion-mark-in-svdp/). In 2019, the SARS updated the amount collected under the SVDP to R3.6 billion in 2017–2018 and a further R817 million in 2018–2019, resulting in a total of R4.4 billion in additional tax revenue from the program (SARS, 2019). The SARS media releases suggest that the value of foreign assets disclosed under the SVDP amounted to about R35 billion (equivalent to $2.4 billion at the 2019 R/$ exchange rate) (SARS, 2019, p. 65).

3. *Did the amnesties improve tax compliance?*

It is also difficult to evaluate the impact of the amnesties on tax compliance. One argument against amnesties is that they can create perverse incentives, inducing some taxpayers to default on their taxes or send their wealth abroad in anticipation of future amnesties, which typically have low repayment levies. If so, there is a risk that amnesties may decrease compliance over time.

Several structural and institutional factors have undermined the effectiveness of tax amnesties in South Africa. The first is limited capacity of the SARS and the SARB to detect and investigate transgressions of tax laws and exchange control regulations, which has been exacerbated by politically induced instability in leadership, especially at the SARS. The resulting public perception of poor governance also discourages tax compliance. The 2017/2018 *Annual Performance Plan* of the SARS identified "unfavorable public perception of poor state delivery and corruption" as one of the major constraints to improved tax performance (SARS 2018, p. 12). The effectiveness of instruments such as tax amnesties hinges on the quality of governance throughout the state system, and especially on a leadership committed to setting and enforcing high standards of honesty and transparency and demonstrating this commitment by example. Unfortunately, this has not been the rule in recent years in South Africa, with former President Jacob Zuma having been accused of tax evasion and embroiled in a web of corruption that includes several state actors and private sector companies, on which we elaborate in the next section.

A second obstacle to tax compliance is the large size of the nation's illicit economy. The SARS 2017/18 *Annual Performance Plan* cites the example of the illicit trade in cigarettes and tobacco (p. 11). Similarly, tax performance is undermined by smuggling and fraud in international trade, a major channel of transgressions of exchange control regulations and illicit capital outflows to secrecy jurisdictions (SARS 2018, p. 13).

A third factor constraining tax compliance in South Africa is the large number of multinational corporations operating in key sectors, such as mining. As the SARS has observed, these firms are often adept at avoiding taxes and skirting exchange controls: "SARS has detected an evolution from businesses, especially multinational enterprises, whereby they utilize domestic and international loopholes to evade tax and impermissibly avoid tax, take advantage of cross-border structuring and transfer pricing manipulations" (SARS 2018, p. 12).

The fundamental question of whether and if so, how much, the government and the economy at large have benefited from the tax and exchange control amnesties declared over the past 25 years remains open. But an important concern is the public's unease with measures that are seen as inevitably benefiting large corporations and high net worth individuals who amassed wealth abroad, often illegally. Amnesty for tax evasion and transgressions of exchange controls is ultimately amnesty for capital flight, too. In a country facing serious challenges of systemic and grand corruption, there is a real risk that tax and exchange control amnesties are seen as just another way of exonerating the sins of the economically and politically influential corporations and individuals while depriving the state of valuable resources that could be used to improve living standards.

It is clear that the economic liberalization efforts undertaken over the years in South Africa have not resolved the problem of capital flight. Stemming capital flight will instead require deeper structural economic and institutional reforms aimed at encouraging and enforcing transparency in financial transactions and cross-border trade.

The Mining Industry, Tax Evasion, and Capital Flight

The mining sector plays a key role in the South African economy (US Department of Interior 2019). It has also been a scene of financial scandals, struggles between capitalists and workers that have turned deadly (a prominent example being the Marikana massacre in 2012), mismanagement of state-owned enterprises, corporate tax evasion, capital flight through export misinvoicing, and regulatory capture by corporate interests.

As in other resource-rich countries, the mining sector in South Africa is vulnerable to capital flight through misinvoicing as well as profit shifting for tax avoidance through aggressive transfer pricing (Antin 2013, Ashman et al. 2011). As discussed above, there is evidence of substantial trade misinvoicing in the sector, with large and systematic discrepancies between the (smaller) value of exports declared by South Africa and the (larger) value of imports reported by the country's trading partners (Ndikumana and Boyce 2019).

A glimpse of the mechanisms by which capital flight may occur was provided in an October 2019 complaint filed by the Association of Mineworkers and Construction Union (AMCU) in the Johannesburg High Court against Samancor Chrome, the world's second largest chrome producer. The complaint alleged that the company had illicitly transferred funds offshore through transfer pricing, secret management and facilitation fees, and secret asset sell-offs (Hosken 2019). Citing an affidavit from Miodrag Kon, a former Samancor director who turned whistleblower, the AMCU alleged that the company had siphoned funds at the expense of minority shareholders to benefit the directors of a company called Kermas Limited, registered in the British Virgin Islands (Faku 2019).[29] AMCU president Joseph Mathunjwa explained that the diversions came to the union's attention

---

[29] A Samancor spokesperson responded that the allegations were "malicious and opportunistic" (Faku 2019).

when it noticed "suspiciously low returns" on the workers' employee share owner-ship plan (Malope 2019). In one instance cited in the affidavit and complaint, when a Samancor subsidiary was sold in 2007 to the Chinese state-owned conglomerate Sinosteel for $225 million, "Kermas received $125 million from Sinosteel directly" via a transfer into a London bank account.[30]

Similarly, Lonmin Plc, a London-based platinum producer, has been alleged to have engaged in profit shifting to the detriment of mineworkers and minority shareholders.[31] The Marikana Commission of Inquiry—an official body appointed by South African President Jacob Zuma to investigate the massacre of 44 striking workers at a Lonmin mine in 2012—reported that over the 2007–2011 period, when Lonmin claimed that its platinum mining operations in South Africa could not afford to meet housing obligations to workers that were budgeted at R665 million (about $85 million), the firm "paid more than R1.3 billion in 'marketing commission' payments" to its management services branch "and/or its Bermu-dan registered subsidiary."[32] In an analysis of the firm's accounts, economist Dick Forslund concluded that "terminating the Bermuda profit shifting arrangement" and cutting back on management fees to "a reasonable amount" would have en-abled Lonmin to meet the wage demands that were one of the main issues in the August 2012 strike (Forslund 2015a, p. 9). Forslund argues that aggressive trans-fer pricing by multinational mining firms enables not only tax avoidance, but also "wage avoidance" and "dividend avoidance in relation to investors holding shares in subsidiaries," as profits are "effectively moved from the stakeholder table" in South Africa.[33] Such practices help to explain why the benefits of mineral re-source extraction in South Africa often accrue disproportionately to their majority and foreign shareholders at the expense of mineworkers, minority and domestic shareholders, and the domestic economy as a whole.

State Capture and Enablers: The Gupta Case

Capital flight from South Africa is a symptom of deep structural and governance problems that enable private appropriation of public resources and undermine the efficacy of government regulations and mechanisms to enforce transparency in

---

[30] Miodrag Kon, Supporting Affidavit submitted to the High Court of South Africa (Gauteng Di-vision, Johannesburg) in the Matter Between Association of Mineworkers and Construction Union, Applicant, and Samancor Chrome Limited, First Respondent, p. 27, available at https://cdn.24.co.za/files/Cms/General/d/9427/ef3cd3230b9a40c9962b3ca1286e1467.pdf (accessed on June 8, 2020). See also van Rensburg (2019).

[31] Lonmin Plc is a British holding company (at 80%) with two South African operating subsidiaries, Western Platinum Limited and Eastern Platinum Limited (Forslund, 2015a).

[32] Marikana Commission of Inquiry (2015), p. 538. See also Forslund, 2015a, 2015b) and Bond (2019).

[33] Forslund (2015a, pp. 10, 35.)

trade and financial transactions. This syndrome often entails collusion between individuals inside the government and actors in the private sector.

In recent years, South Africa has been rocked by accounts of corruption and capital flight that have embroiled a former president, other prominent members of the political elite, the private sector, and international financial networks.[34] To illustrate, this section recaps a scandal that has been the focus of a special investigation by the South African government's Office of the Public Protector as well as extensive reporting by teams of investigative journalists.

The story centers on the Gupta family, in particular the three brothers, Ajay, Atul and Rajesh (a.k.a. Tony).[35] Immigrating from India to South Africa in 1993, the family's business interests in South Africa began in the computer equipment and IT sector, and eventually expanded into other parts of the economy from mining and energy to mass media. Oakbay Investments became their core parent company. Oakbay's holdings included Tegeta Exploration & Resources, a mining company in which Oakbay was the leading shareholder with a 29.05% ownership stake (Office of the Public Protector South Africa 2016, p. 112). The second largest shareholder of Tegeta was Mabengela Investment (28.53%), which in turn was owned by President Zuma's son Duduzane Zuma (45%), Rajesh Gupta (25%) and others (Office of the Public Protector South Africa 2016, p. 112). Tegeta's third biggest shareholder (21.5%) was the firm Elgasolve, whose sole director was Salim Essa, a close associate of the Guptas (ibid.).

In October 2016 the South African government's Office of the Public Protector released a comprehensive report, *State of Capture*, examining the alleged links between former President Zuma, state-owned enterprises, and Gupta family (Office of the Public Protector South Africa 2016). Ongoing investigations and legal processes are led by the Judicial Commission of Inquiry into Allegations of State Capture (also known as the Zondo Commission), established in 2018 by President Cyril Ramaphosa.[36] In July 2018 Duduzane Zuma was charged by the National Prosecuting Authority (NPA) with corruption for his alleged involvement in an attempt by one of the Gupta brothers in 2015 to bribe Mcebisi Jonas—the Deputy Minister of Finance at the time—and Duduzane Zuma has since testified before the State Capture Commission (Cotterill 2018a; Office of the Public Protector South Africa 2016). The charges against him were "provisionally" withdrawn in January 2019 pending further evidence (Reuters 2019).

---

[34] This section relies heavily on the Office of the Public Protector's report titled *State of Capture*, released in October 2016, and on reporting from the #GuptaLeaks, a collaborate investigation into state capture by the amaBhungane Centre for Investigative Journalism, *Daily Maverick*, *News24*, and the Organised Crime and Corruption Reporting Project (OCCRP).

[35] For a more detailed discussion on the Gupta family's history in South Africa, see Ndikumana et al. (2020).

[36] Hearings and other activities of the Commission are available on its website, https://sastatecapture.org.za/.

Opaque deals

The Guptas invested heavily in the mining sector, including coal mining, and had extensive dealings with the public energy companies, especially Eskom (the Electricity Supply Commission), which generates more than 90% of the country's power. Their dealings in the mining and energy sector have been under scrutiny for alleged corruption through opaque deals.

The role of the Gupta family's political connections in facilitating the growth of their business interests is illustrated by their purchase of Optimum Coal Mine (OCM) from the international mining giant Glencore. This mine is of strategic interest since it supplies Eskom's ten-unit Hendrina power station. In July 2015 OCM's parent entity, Optimum Coal Holdings (OCH), then owned by Glencore, filed to be placed under business rescue, a legal process that suspends payments to creditors during restructuring supervised by a court-appointed official (Office of the Public Protector South Africa 2016, p. 268).[37] The move came after Eskom's chief executive at the time, Brian Molefe, and the Eskom chair refused to renegotiate the price of a long-term supply contract with Glencore, putting financial pressure on the firm.[38] Also in July 2015, Eskom demanded that Optimum pay a R2.17 billion penalty for allegedly having supplied substandard coal (ibid., p. 251).

That same month, Glencore received a letter from KPMG Services (Pty) Ltd conveying an offer from a client who wished to "remain anonymous" to purchase OCM or its parent entity for R2 billion. The anonymous client turned out to be the Gupta company Oakbay, lead shareholder of the mining company Tegeta (ibid., pp. 247, 251).

Eskom CEO Brian Molefe had close ties to the Guptas, and Ajay Gupta called him "a very good friend" (ibid., p. 86). Records show numerous phone calls between the two at the time when the disputes between Eskom and Glencore were ongoing (ibid., pp. 122–123).[39] Eskom executives reportedly pressed Mining Minister Ngoako Ramatlhodi to suspend Glencore's mining license (Sole and Comrie 2017). The firm's license was temporarily suspended, but Ramatlhodi pushed back and quickly managed to reinstate it (ibid.). In September 2015, President Zuma fired Ramatlhodi and replaced him with Mosebenzi Zwane, a politician reportedly connected with the Guptas through the Estina dairy project scandal, described below (ibid.).

---

[37] See also Sole and Comrie (2017).
[38] Ibid., p. 145. See also Bezuidenhout (2019).
[39] See also Sole and Comrie (2017).

In December 2015, President Zuma fired Finance Minister Nhlanhla Nene, replacing him with little-known Des van Rooyen.[40] In terms of institutional capacity, the Treasury historically has been one of the strongest pillars of South Africa's state, exercising an important oversight role. The unexpected appointment of a new Finance Minister with little experience met with strong pushback from financial markets, local business leaders, and some within the ruling party. A few days later, the well-respected Pravin Gordhan, a previous Finance Minister, was reinstated to restore stability. Gordhan arrived too late to intervene in the OCM case, however: shortly before he took office, it was announced that Tegeta had purchased the firm.[41]

The purchase arrangements were facilitated by Bank of Baroda, an Indian state-owned bank with multinational operations (ibid., pp. 272–273). The bank offered a letter of support for the Guptas' attempt to buy OCM after other banks in South Africa had cut ties with the Guptas (Onishi and Gebrekidan 2018).[42]

The events surrounding the purchase of OCM have raised questions as to the motives of Eskom executives. OCM had a long-term "fixed-price" contract with Eskom for coal that by 2013 had started to become unaffordable for the mine. Was Eskom's refusal to sign a new price agreement with Glencore to supply coal "at cost" intended to force OCM into financial distress and reduce its potential sale price? "Glencore appears to have been severely prejudiced by Eskom's actions in refusing to sign a new agreement with them for the supply of coal," concluded the Office of the Public Protector South Africa (2016, p. 352). "It appears," the report continued, "that the conduct of Eskom was solely to the benefit of Tegeta" (ibid.).

"Further evidence of the apparent prejudice caused by Eskom," the Office of the Public Protector (2016, p. 341) observed, "is that once the sale agreement was signed in December 2015, Tegeta appears to have easily managed to secure lucrative contracts to supply coal to the Arnot power station with coal from OCM." Eskom awarded Tegeta multiple coal supply agreements (CSAs) (ibid., p. 20).

After an extensive financial analysis, the Office of the Public Protector concluded that a CSA prepayment to Tegeta in the amount of R659 million, ostensibly to service the Arnot contract, "appears to have been used by Tegeta solely to fund the purchase of OCH [Optimum Coal Holdings]" (ibid., p. 20). The prepayment

---

[40] Office of the Public Protector South Africa (2016), p. 87; Sole and Comrie (2017). At the beginning of his second term in office in May 2014, Zuma had already unexpectedly dismissed the country's well-respected Minister of Finance, Pravin Gordhan, replacing him with Nhlanhla Nene who was deputy Finance Minister at the time.

[41] The timeline of events leading up to the purchase is recounted in November 2017 testimony by one of the two business rescue practitioners appointed for OCM and OCH before the Parliamentary Committee on Public Enterprises: "Corporate governance in Eskom—How Optimum coal mine was purchased," Parliamentary Monitoring Group, 1 November 2017, available at https://pmg.org.za/committee-meeting/25367/ (accessed on June 12, 2020). See also Sole and Comrie (2017).

[42] See also Sethi and Gopakumar (2018).

"possibly amounts to fruitless and wasteful expenditure," in the opinion of the Office of the Public Protector, "as it appears that the prepayment was not used to meet production requirements at OCM" (ibid., p. 20). The decision "appears to have been in contravention" of the Public Finance Management Act (PFMA), which states that the Board of a state-owned enterprise has the obligation to "prevent fruitless and wasteful expenditure" (ibid., p. 20). Moreover, "it appears highly improbable that some, if not all, of the Eskom Board who approved the payment had no knowledge of the true nature of the payment" (ibid.).[43]

The network of enablers

The corruption that has facilitated state capture, capital flight, and money laundering in South Africa is intermediated by a transnational network of enablers with deep connections in the public and private sectors in South Africa and complex linkages across the world. The enablers include banks, accounting firms, clearing houses, law firms, and management consulting firms.

The bankers

Foremost among the banking institutions that have been implicated in state capture in South Africa is Bank of Baroda (BoB). In February 2018, after 21 years of operating in the country, the bank notified the SARB that it would close down its operations (Mehta 2018). The announcement came in the midst of a SARB probe into alleged breaches of banking regulations, many of which involved transactions related to the Gupta family and its companies. BoB asserted that its decision to exit South Africa was part of a "strategic plan for rationalization of overseas branches" (Bhardwaj 2018). In 2019, after its withdrawal, BoB was fined a modest R400,000 (about $25,000) for what the South African Reserve Bank termed "deficiencies relating to compliance with the FIC [Financial Intelligence Center] Act" and "weaknesses in controls to prevent potential money laundering and terrorist financing" (Omarjee 2019).[44]

Over time, "the Guptas gradually came to account for a disproportionate share of BoB's South Africa business," report journalists investigating what came to be known as the GuptaLeaks scandal, "to the point that it posed a risk to the bank" (Sethi and Gopakumar 2018). A Bank of Baroda executive suggested, speaking off the record, that the Guptas accounted for 40% of the Bank's loans in the country

---

[43] An Oakbay spokesperson stated that "speculation that ESKOM's prepayment for the Arnot contract had facilitated the funding of the purchase of Optimum was unfounded" (Office of the Public Protector, 2016, p. 272).

[44] The decision came after the bank successfully appealed a R11 million fine (Omarjee 2019).

(ibid.). The Office of the Public Protector South Africa (2016, pp. 273–274) described the Bank of Baroda's conduct as "highly suspicious," and maintained that the frequency and amounts deposited "should have attracted attention and an investigation… due to money laundering risks based on the Financial Intelligence Centre's (FIC's) guidance note concerning the reporting of suspicious and unusual financial transactions."

Data collected from the bank show that in the ten years between 2007 and 2017, about R4.5 billion (approximately US $530 million) was transferred among Gupta-related companies, with many of the transactions labelled as inter-company loans (Table 5.4). On some days, it is reported, Bank of Baroda employees filed up to half a dozen suspicious activity reports (SARs) related to Gupta transactions, but bank management intervened to void them so that most were not reported to the South African FIC (Sharife and Joseph 2018). The *New York Times* reports that an investigation by the South African Reserve Bank found that "Baroda's internal systems had flagged about 4,000 suspicious transactions in the Guptas' accounts," but that employees "dismissed nearly all of the alerts 'without adequate reasons being provided,' according to a confidential report by PwC, the international auditing firm, that was reviewed by the Times" (Onishi and Gebrekidan 2018).

Bank of Baroda was not the only major bank touched by the scandals. *Business Day* reported that Nedbank, one of South Africa's "Big Four" domestic banks, had a "correspondent banking relationship" with Bank of Baroda, clearing transactions for the latter through control accounts at the SARB (Gous 2018). *The Enablers*, a joint report submitted to the Zondo Commission on State Capture in February 2020 by researchers from the non-governmental organizations Open Secrets and Shadow World Investigations, states that Standard Bank, another member of the Big Four, was used by the Guptas to launder funds looted from the Free State government in the Estina dairy scandal, reporting that "in a large number of cases, deposits made into Standard Bank accounts were immediately transferred onto external beneficiaries" (Marchant et al. 2020, pp. 102–103). The transactions reportedly included the transfer of $8.3 million offshore into a Standard Chartered account of a Dubai-registered company (Marchant et al. 2020, pp. 102–103). When asked whether it had filed any suspicious activity reports in connection with these transactions, Standard Bank replied that it could not disclose confidential information relating to its clients and assured the investigators that it had "complied with its regulatory responsibilities" (Marchant et al. 2020, pp. 102–103).

The accountants

The Estina dairy scandal, involving the Gupta network and the Free State provincial government, illustrates the enabling role of international accounting firms. Between 2013 and 2016, journalists reported a web of alleged linkages between

Table 5.4 Sample list of transactions labelled as "inter-company loans" at Bank of Baroda, 2007–2017

Entity transferring funds	Number of transfers	Total value of transfers (ZAR)	Entity receiving funds
Koornfontein Mines	9	159,000,000	Tegeta Exploration and Resources
Oakbay Investments	35	708,100,000	Tegeta Exploration and Resources
Oakbay Investments	2	30,200,000	Idwala Coal
Oakbay Investments	3	13,500,0000	Infinity Media
Oakbay Investments	25	576,321,190	Islandsite Invest- ments180
Oakbay Investments		5,500,000	Shiva Uranium
Oakbay Investments	2	14,200,000	TNA Media
Oakbay Investments	26	380,200,000	Westdawn Investments
Confident Concepts	5	174,400,000	Islandsite Investments 180
Infinity Media	4	26,500,000	Oakbay Investments
Islandsite Investments 180	30	655,788,000	Oakbay Investments
Islandsite Investments 180	10	88,819,190	Confident Concepts
Islandsite Investments 180	8	105,300,000	Sahara Computers
Tegeta Exploration and Resources	26	303,900,000	Koornfontein Mines
Tegeta Exploration and Resources	26	579,150,000	Oakbay Investments
Tegeta Exploration and Resources	11	260,000,000	Optimum Coal Mine
Tegeta Exploration and Resources	1	24,000,000	Westdawn Investments
Trillian Management Consulting	1	160,246,000	Centaur Mining
Westdawn Investments	4	142,000,000	Oakbay Investments
Optimum Coal Mine	1	13,500,000	Koornfontein Mines
Optimum Coal Mine	1	25,000,000	Tegeta Resources

Source: Sharife and Joseph (2018).

Gupta enterprises and the provincial government (amaBhungane and Scorpio 2017b).[45] The province's Premier, Ace Magashule (later Secretary General of the African National Congress), had described the Estina dairy project near the town of Vrede as a "state-of-the-art certified facility" that would process 100,000 liters of milk per day (amaBhungane 2013b). The Free State department of agriculture, then under the leadership of Mosebenzi Zwane,[46] "promised Estina R114 million a year for three years to set up a farming operation and dairy, whose supposed purpose was to empower locals and boost provincial agriculture" (amaBhungane and Scorpio 2017b). Between 2013 and 2016, a total of R220 million was transferred from the department of agriculture to Estina, but according to investigative journalists most of this money was captured by the Gupta network (African News Agency 2019, Pather 2018). In 2018, the *Mail & Guardian* reported that there is "little evidence to suggest Estina ever processed a drop of milk"; meanwhile, R30 million (roughly $3 million) in state funds for the dairy project, routed through a company called Linkway, was used to pay for the lavish wedding of a Gupta family member, and a further R144 million was transferred to a Gupta-linked company based in Dubai (Pather 2018).

The global accounting firm KPMG had audited Linkway. In early 2019, KPMG partner Jacques Wessels was removed from South Africa's register of auditors for having engaged in what the Independent Regulatory Board for Auditors termed an "egregious form of dishonesty" in his work for the Gupta family in 2014 (Marriage 2019). The regulatory board concluded that Wessels had shifted R6.9 million of Linkway's wedding-related hotel and accommodation expenses from the firm's operating expenses to its cost of sales, and had treated this as an "unspecified tax deductible" amount even after having been advised by a KPMG colleague that the tax deduction was impermissible (Marriage 2019).[47]

The consulting firms

As reported by the *New York Times* and the South African media, in late 2015 McKinsey & Company, the global management consulting firm, entered into a contract with Eskom to draw up a reorganization plan to address the numerous problems the utility had faced in recent years (Bogdanich and Forsythe 2018).[48] This contract, which was awarded without competitive bidding, would become McKinsey's "biggest contract ever in Africa, with a potential value of $700 million" (ibid.). Under the terms of the contract, the firm would be paid for its work only if its advice generated results, but with no cap on what the final bill would be—a departure from the standard fee-for-service arrangement mandated by the

[45] Also see amaBhungane (2013a) and amaBhungane and Scorpio (2017a).
[46] Mosebenzi Zwane would go on to become the country's Mineral Resources Minister.
[47] See other examples on the KPMG involvement in Ndikumana et al. (2020).
[48] See also Marchant et al. (2020).

South African government, from which Eskom failed to receive a waiver, despite assuring McKinsey that it had done so (ibid.).

In its work for Eskom, McKinsey sub-contracted a partner called Trillian Management Consulting in order to comply with the Black Economic Empowerment (BEE) requirements for public procurement, despite the fact that Trillian refused to divulge its ownership (Bogdanich and Forsythe 2018).[49] Trillian's majority owner turned out to be Salim Essa, whose associations with the Guptas included part ownership of Tegeta, the firm that had purchased OCM in the same year (ibid.).

As the South African news media uncovered ever more evidence of the Gupta family's involvement, Eskom—not McKinsey—prematurely terminated the contract, the *New York Times* reported in 2018. "The abbreviated tab for barely eight months of work: nearly $100 million, with close to 40 percent going to Trillian" (Bogdanich and Forsythe 2018).[50] A "bitter irony," the *New York Times* reporters noted, was that "while McKinsey's pay was supposed to be based entirely on its results, it is far from clear that the flailing power company is much better off than it was before" (ibid.).

A forensic investigation commissioned by the National Treasury concluded that Eskom officials contravened the Public Finance Management Act by: (i) failing to curb "irregular and wasteful expenditure of R1.6 billion"; (ii) registering Trillian as an Eskom vendor, even though Trillian itself did not have a contract with Eskom; and (iii) failing to seek permission from National Treasury for the risk-based contract (South African National Treasury 2018, p. 241). The National Prosecuting Authority alleged that McKinsey had been instrumental in "creating a veil of legitimacy to what was otherwise a nonexistent, unlawful arrangement" (Bogdanich and Forsythe 2018). In December 2017 the Pretoria High Court decided to freeze the fees received by McKinsey and Trillian for advising Eskom (ibid.).[51]

A 2018 report by the South African Parliament's Portfolio Committee on Public Enterprises concluded that "McKinsey's potential use of Trillian, a Gupta-linked company, to extract rents from Eskom may constitute criminal conduct" (Portfolio Committee on Public Enterprises 2018, p. 49).[52] McKinsey elected to repay over one billion rand to Eskom, including interest on the amount received by the firm, while indicating that "the fee repayment was a consequence of Eskom's

---

[49] See also Marchant et al. (2020).

[50] The Portfolio Committee on Public Enterprises of the South African Parliament states that Eskom paid McKinsey and Trillian together around R1.6 billion (equivalent to about $110 million) for "work that substantially deviated from standard procurement processes and was never approved by the National Treasury" (Portfolio Committee on Public Enterprises, 2018, p. 35). Other published reports have stated that McKinsey earned about R1 billion from its work for Eskom (Marriage and Cotterill 2018).

[51] See also Winning (2018). In a statement, McKinsey said "We are returning this money not because we have done anything wrong but because Eskom has told us they did not follow the appropriate process" (Cotterill 2018b).

[52] See also Cameron (2017) and Marchant et al. (2020).

non-compliance with the relevant procurement laws and was not an admission of liability by McKinsey" (South African National Treasury 2018a, p. 232).

In June 2019, in a Gauteng High Court case between Eskom and respondents McKinsey and Trillian, the court ordered Trillian to repay a further R595 million, plus interest, to Eskom (South African Gauteng Division High Court 2016, p. 51). In October 2019, the US Treasury Department's Office of Foreign Assets Control sanctioned the three Gupta brothers and Salim Essa, describing them as "members of a significant corruption network in South Africa that leveraged overpayments on government contracts, bribery, and other corrupt acts to fund political contributions and influence government actions" (US Treasury 2019), adding "We will continue to exclude from the US financial system those who profit from corruption."

A schematic depiction of the Gupta-related network sketched above is presented in Figure 5.4. A full anatomy of the complex network that has facilitated capital

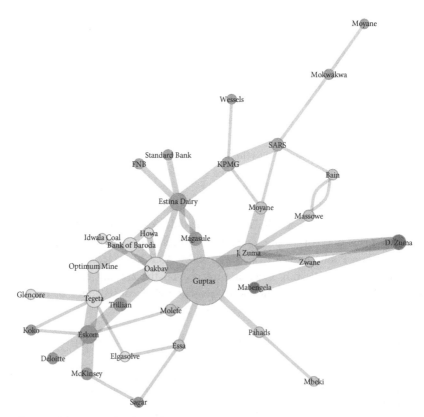

Fig. 5.4 The network of enablers

Source: Based on information from the sources cited in the text. The authors thank Professor Kevin Young of the University of Massachusetts Amherst who designed this chart.

flight, money laundering, tax evasion, and state capture in South Africa would require a book-length narrative in itself. Some of the links among the takers and enablers are formal, others informal; some are open, others hidden. Further untangling this and similar webs is a critical task in efforts to devise effective strategies to combat capital flight and its adverse consequences in South Africa.

Capital Flight as Anti-Development

The cover of the May 13, 2019 issue of *Time* magazine featured an eye-catching aerial photograph that provided a stark visual representation of inequality in South Africa (Pomerantz 2019). On one side of the photo is the upscale Johannesburg neighborhood of Primrose, and on the other, separated by a high wall, is the informal settlement of Makause. The contrast is striking, but in South Africa it is by no means unique.

A 2018 report titled *Overcoming Poverty and Inequality in South Africa*, by the World Bank, the UNDP, Statistics South Africa, and the government's Department of Planning, Monitoring and Evaluation, portrays South Africa as one of the most unequal country in the world, based on conventional measures of inequality (World Bank et al. 2018). Income inequality as measured by the Gini coefficient is not only far higher in South Africa than the world average, but also even higher today than it was under apartheid. In 2015 the richest 1% of South Africans received 19% of national income, almost double their share at the end of the apartheid era (World Inequality Database).

High inequality explains why, in spite of the country's status as an upper middle-income economy, South Africa has very high levels of poverty, especially in rural areas where it is estimated that roughly two-thirds of the population lives below the poverty line. Nationwide the country has registered some improvement, with the overall poverty headcount declining from 51% in 2006 to 40% in 2015 (World Bank et al. 2018). The reduction in poverty in recent years is partly due to an expansion in government redistribution and family support programs, including social grants, which have helped recipients to better afford basic needs such as food, shelter, and health services. The beneficiaries of these programs remain highly vulnerable to falling back into poverty, however, since they are one grant check away from deprivation. Clearly, more needs to be done to address the scourge of poverty. Tackling capital flight has an important role to play in this effort.

Capital flight worsens inequality in multiple ways. The smuggling of capital out of the country and the concealment of wealth offshore enables the wealth holders to evade taxation, further widening their income and asset advantages relative to the rest of the population. Meanwhile the wealth accumulated abroad is shielded from the negative effects of exchange rate depreciation and volatility. Because the wealth that is hidden offshore and income generated by it are not counted in official statistics, the existing measures of inequality in South Africa substantially underestimate the true levels of disparities. More accurate measures would further entrench the country's unenviable reputation as one of the most unequal countries in the world.

At the same time, capital flight reduces the government's capacity to implement redistributive fiscal policy by shrinking the tax base. Empirical analyses generally indicate that fiscal policy in South Africa has been highly redistributive, combining a relatively progressive taxation system and targeted government spending on social services (see, among others, Inchauste et al. 2015, Leibbrandt et al. 2010, and van der Berg 2009). Inchauste et al. (2015, p. 29) find that targeted fiscal policy leads to reduction in the Gini coefficient for income (after taxes and social expenditures) from 0.77 to 0.60 and reduces extreme poverty (defined as an income of $1.25 PPP per day or less) from 34% to 16.5%. Indeed, the available evidence indicates that redistributive efforts of fiscal policy are relatively higher in South Africa than in comparable middle-income countries (Inchauste et al. 2015, Lustig 2016). Without these progressive fiscal strategies, Inchauste et al. (2015, p. 2) estimate that two-fifths of the population would have witnessed declining incomes during the first 10 years of the democratic era.

Yet despite these efforts, South Africa's poverty rate remains high. This suggests a need for raising the rate of growth, which in turn requires scaling up domestic investment. This includes public investment, especially investment in infrastructure, which can help to boost private investment by reducing the costs of production and raising profitability (Ndikumana 2008). Instead, public investment has declined since the 1970s. From an average of 10% of GDP in the 1970s, it dropped to 7% in the following decade, 3.6% in the 1990s, and it has been around 3% since the turn of the century.[53] By draining the government's spending capacity, as well as reducing the availability of private savings, capital flight undermines the ability to raise both investment and growth (Ndikumana 2014, Fofack and Ndikumana 2010). It has been estimated that if all the capital that fled South Africa had been invested domestically at the average historical rates of return, the country would have been able to reach and even exceed the Millennium Development Goals target of halving poverty by 2015 (Nkurunziza 2015). The negative effects of slow growth on poverty reduction exacerbated the negative effects of high inequality.

Capital flight from a country with high poverty and inequality poses a serious threat to political stability and constitutes an impediment to inclusive economic development. For South Africa's non-white majority, the end of the apartheid regime was expected to bring dividends in the form of both political emancipation and improved economic well-being. Persistent inequality alienates the majority

---

[53] South African Reserve Bank's online statistical database.

who remain bypassed by prosperity in a land that boasts of being the most developed country on the continent. Economic inequity and political oppression galvanized the struggle against the apartheid regime. Going forward, inequality may stimulate fresh demands for social change that the government may not be able to contain. Taking inequality seriously means implementing policies and programs that address the concerns of ordinary citizens, instead of focusing on redistributing wealth among those who are already in higher strata of society as has often occurred under BEE initiatives. To finance such efforts, the government will need to mobilize adequate resources, and one of the ways to do so is to curb the country's financial hemorrhage through capital flight.

Conclusion

South Africa faces a range of daunting development challenges, with stubborn multidimensional poverty and high unemployment. Its government is confronted with chronic financing deficits that make it difficult to finance much-needed public infrastructure and social services such as education, health, and housing. These challenges are exacerbated by capital flight, which depletes funds for domestic investment and erodes the tax base.

We estimate that South Africa lost over $329 billion from capital flight from 1970 to 2018. A key channel for this was trade misinvoicing, which in net terms contributed to $135.5 billion in capital flight over the 1998–2018 period alone. Export under-invoicing appears to be especially rampant in the case of mineral resources, such as gold, silver, platinum, and diamonds.

An important step in combating capital flight is therefore to tackle trade-based outflows by implementing rigorous, symmetrical, and transparent reporting of trade statistics, starting with big-ticket items, including mineral exports. At the very least, it would constitute a significant improvement simply to ensure reliability and consistency across data published by various government agencies, and between these agencies and the international institutions that publish trade data. International cooperation will be crucial to ensure symmetrical reporting in South Africa's own data and that of its trading partners. A key step in achieving this would be to systematically apply international conventions on reporting of trade statistics to which South Africa already is a signatory.

Since the apartheid era, successive South African governments have tried to implement policies to tackle the problem of capital flight and encourage domestic investment. The analysis presented in this chapter suggests that these policies have not achieved much success in reining in capital flight or enticing repatriation of offshore wealth. The rigid capital controls established under the apartheid era proved ineffective, mainly because they were implemented at a time when the country was facing deep political instability and an international economic embargo. Since the turn to market liberalization, starting in the 1990s, the results have not been significantly better. Indeed, capital flight accelerated at the same time that the government ramped up market-based reforms. The efficacy of direct measures, including amnesties, that were adopted by the government to entice offshore wealth repatriation and increase tax compliance, remains uncertain.

In designing policies to curb capital flight and induce wealth repatriation, it is important to distinguish between legitimately acquired wealth and legal capital outflows on the one hand, and illegally acquired wealth and illicit outflows on the other. Reforms that raise the domestic rate of returns to investment and reduce market uncertainty may affect the former, but they are not likely to affect decisions regarding wealth that was illicitly acquired, transferred, and hidden offshore. In such cases, the asset holders are less interested in high rates of returns to investment than they are in the protection against legal prosecution provided by secrecy jurisdictions. To address this type of capital flight, what is needed instead are effective strategies to strengthen domestic legal systems and international cooperation, increase financial transparency, and enhance the automatic exchange of information on cross-border financial flows and international trade.

A key challenge facing South Africa in its quest to combat capital flight and the associated problems of tax evasion, profit shifting, and money laundering is the erosion of public confidence in state institutions that has been associated with the phenomenon of state capture. Recent reports and ongoing public investigations have uncovered a deeply troubling pattern of corrosive collusion between state actors and a network of enablers who have orchestrated the plunder of state resources to accumulate private wealth. These networks include powerful and politically well-connected individuals and families, domestic and foreign banks, auditing firms, consulting firms and others with close connections to the government and the private sector in South Africa and around the world. The case of the Gupta family enterprises illustrates the role of these networks in state capture and money laundering. Lamentably, and however astounding this may seem, it is likely that the Gupta scandal is only the tip of the iceberg, exposing much deeper problems faced by state institutions in South Africa today. This environment is fertile ground for capital flight and other illicit financial flows.

The severe adverse effects of capital flight and offshore wealth accumulation on economic development, institutional quality, and governance call for decisive action to prevent even more devastating consequences in terms of political and social instability. In sum, the problem of capital flight needs to be confronted and tackled urgently.

References

AfrAsia Bank. 2019. *Africa Wealth Report 2019*. Port Louis, Mauritius: AfrAsia Bank.

African News Agency. 2019. State capture commission turns to Estina dairy farm project. *Polity*, July 22, Available at https://www.polity.org.za/print-version/state-capture-commission-turns-to-estina-dairy-farm-project-2019-07-22 (accessed on June 22, 2020).

amaBhungane. 2013a. Gupta dairy project milks Free State coffers. *Mail & Guardian*, June 7, Available at https://mg.co.za/article/2013-06-07-gupta-dairy-project-milks-free-state-coffers/ (accessed on April 27, 2020).

amaBhungane. 2013b. Guptas' farm cash cows in Free State. *Mail & Guardian*, May 31, Available at https://mg.co.za/article/2013-05-31-00-guptas-farm-cash-cows-in-free-state/ (accessed on April 27, 2020).

amaBhungane and Scorpio. 2017a. GuptaLeaks: The Dubai Laundromat—How KPMG saw no evil at the Sun City wedding. *Daily Maverik*, June 30, Available at https://amabhungane.org/stories/guptaleaks-the-dubai-laundromat-how-kpmg-saw-no-evil-at-the-sun-city-wedding/ (accessed on October 18, 2019).

amaBhungane and Scorpio. 2017b. GuptaLeaks: The Dubai Laundromat—How millions milked from Free State government paid for Sun City wedding, June 30, available at https://amabhungane.org/stories/guptaleaks-the-dubai-laundromat-how-kpmg-saw-no-evil-at-the-sun-city-wedding/ (accessed on October 18, 2019).

Antin, D. 2013. The South African Mining Sector: An Industry at a Crossroads. Johannesburg: Hans Siedel Foundation—Economy Report South Africa (December).

Ashman, S., Fine, B., and Newman, S. 2011. Amnesty International? The nature, scale and impact of capital flight from South Africa. *Journal of Southern African Studies*, 37(01), 7–25.

Bezuidenhout, J. 2019. How State Capture business was conducted—former Optimun Coal CEO tells all. *BizNews*, February 28, available at https://www.biznews.com/leadership/2019/02/28/business-time-state-capture-glencore-optimum-coa (accessed on June 12, 2020).

Bhardwaj, T. 2018. Bank of Baroda to Shut Down its Operations in South Africa by March-end. *News 18*, February 12, available at https://www.news18.com/news/business/bank-of-baroda-to-shut-down-its-operations-in-south-africa-by-march-end-1658781.html (accessed on March 29, 2020).

Bogdanich, W., and Forsythe, M. 2018. How McKinsey Lost Its Way in South Africa. *New York Times*, June 26, available at https://www.nytimes.com/2018/06/26/world/africa/mckinsey-south-africa-eskom.html (accessed on March 10, 2020).

Bond, P. 2019. Lonmin's murder, by money. *Pambazuka News*, May 31, available at https://www.pambazuka.org/economics/lonmin%E2%80%99s-murder-money (accessed on March 28, 2020).

Cameron, J. 2017. JoiningTheDots: Meet McKinsey Gupta mole Vikas Sagar. *BizNews*, July 14, available at https://www.biznews.com/sa-investing/2017/07/14/vikas-sagar-mckinsey (accessed on April 9, 2020).

Chabane, N., Machaka, J., Molaba, N., Roberts, S., and Taka, M. 2003. 10 year review: Industrial structure and competition policy. Johannesburg: School of Economic and Business Sciences, University of the Witwatersrand, June.

Collier, P., Hoeffler, A., and Pattillo, C. 2001. Flight capital as a portfolio choice. *World Bank Economic Review*, 15, 55–80.

Cotterill, J. 2018a. Jacob Zuma's son charged with corruption in Gupta family probe. *Financial Times*, July 9, available at https://www.ft.com/content/83b5c11e-8365-11e8-a29d-73e3d454535d (accessed on November 13, 2019).

Cotterill, J. 2018b. McKinsey ordered to forfeit South African contract fees. *Financial Times*, January 15, available at https://www.ft.com/content/a0af77d8-fa17-11e7-a492-2c9be7f3120a (accessed on June 20, 2020).

Credit Suisse. 2019. *Global Wealth Report 2019*. Switzerland (online): Credit Suisse Research Institute.

Faku, D. 2019. Amcu ropes in human rights lawyer Richard Spoor in Samancor battle. *Independent Online*, 10 October, available at https://www.iol.co.za/business-report/companies/amcu-ropes-in-human-rights-lawyer-richard-spoor-in-samancor-battle-34489727 (accessed on May 22, 2020).

Farrell, G.N., and Todani, K.R. 2004. Capital flows, exchange control regulations and exchange rate policy: The South African experience Pretoria: Bond Exchange of South Africa, Background paper prepared for OECD seminar "How to reduce debt costs in Southern Africa?," 25 and 26 March 2004.

Fedderke, J., and Liu, W. 2002. Modelling the determinants of capital flows and capital flight: with an application to South African data from 1960 to 1995. *Economic Modelling*, 19(3), 419–444.

Fofack, H., and Ndikumana, L. 2010. Capital flight repatriation: Investigation of its potential gains for Sub-Saharan African countries. *African Development Review*, 22(1), 4–22.

Forslund, D. 2015a. The Bermuda Connection: Profit shifting, inequality and unaffordability at Lonmin 1999–2012. Cape Town: Alternative Information & Development Centre.

Forslund, D. 2015b. Briefing on the report The Bermuda connection: Profit shifting, inequality and unaffordability at Lonmin 1999–2012. *Review of African Political Economy*, 42(146), 657–665.

Gelb, S., and Black, A. 2004. Foreign Direct Investment in South Africa. In S. Estrin and M.E. Klaus (Eds.), *Investment Strategies in Emerging Markets* (pp. 117–212). New York: Edward Elgar Publishing.

Gous, N. 2018. Nedbank says no more to Bank of Baroda. *Business Day*, February 28, available at https://www.businesslive.co.za/bd/companies/financial-services/2018-02-28-nedbank-says-no-more-to-bank-of-baroda/ (accessed on February 25, 2020).

Henry, J.S. 2016. The Price of Offshore—Data by Region. The Global Haven Industry: http://globalhavenindustry.com/price-of-offshore-menu (accessed on July 21, 2021).

Hosken, G. 2019. Amcu mounts R7.5bn claim after accusing SA's chrome mining giant of corruption. *Sowetan Live*, October 2, available at https://www.sowetanlive.co.za/news/south-africa/2019-10-02-amcu-guns-for-sa-chrome-mining-giant-in-r75bn-claim/ (accessed on February 24, 2020).

IMF. 2009. *Balance of Payments and International Investment Position Manual*—Sixth Edition (BPM6). Washington, DC: IMF.

Inchauste, G., Lustig†, N., Maboshe, M., Purfield, C., and Woolard, I. 2015. The distributional impact of fiscal policy in South Africa Washington, DC: World Bank Policy Research Working Paper 7194, February.

Kahn, B. 1991. Capital Flight and Exchange Controls in South Africa. Research Paper No. 4. Centre for the Study of the South African Economy and International Finance, London School of Economics.

Klein, M.W., Forbes, K.J., and Werning, I. 2012. Capital Controls: Gates versus Walls [with Comments and Discussion]. *Brookings Papers on Economic Activity*, Fall, 317–367.

Leibbrandt, M., Woolard, I., Finn, A., and Argent, J. 2010. Trends in South African Income Distribution and Poverty Since the Fall of Apartheid. OECD Social, Employment and Migration Working Papers, 11.

Lewis, J.D. 2001. Reform and Opportunity: The Changing Role and Patterns of Trade in South Africa and SADC. Africa Region Working Paper Series, 14 (March).

Lewis, J.D. 2002. Promoting growth and employment in South Africa. *South African Journal of Economics*, 70(4), 727–776.

Lustig, N. 2016. Inequality and fiscal redistribution in middle income countries: Brazil, Chile, Colombia, Indonesia, Mexico, Peru and South Africa. *Journal of Globalization and Development*, 7(1), 17–60.

McKenzie, R., and Pons-Vignon, N. 2012. Volatile Capital Flows and a Route to Financial Crisis in South Africa, MPRA Paper No. 40119.

McNeill, R., and Shabalala, Z. 2019. New Gold Rush: Gold worth billions smuggled out of Africa. *A Reuters Exclusive*. Reuters, April 24, available at https://www.reuters.com/investigates/special-report/gold-africa-smuggling/ (accessed on March 21, 2020).

Malope, L. 2019. Amcu targets Samancor's 'missing billions'. *City Press*, October 14, available at https://city-press.news24.com/Business/amcu-targets-samancors-missing-billions-20191014 (accessed on April 16, 2020).

Marais, H. 2011. *South Africa Pushed to the Limit: The Political Economy of Change*. London: Zed Books.

Marchant, M., Mosiana, M., Holden, P., and van Vuuren, H. 2020. *The Enablers: The Bankers, Accountants and Lawyers that Cashed in on State Capture*. Cape Town: Open Secrets and Shadow World Investigations.

Marikana Commission of Inquiry. 2015. *Report on Matter of National and International Concern Arising Out of the Tragic Incidents at the Lonmin Mine in Marikana, in the North-West Province*. Pretoria: Office of the PResident, GG 38978, GeN 699 (10 July).

Marriage, M. 2019. Former KPMG partner struck off South Africa register over Gupta audits. *Financial Times*, 28 March, available at https://www.ft.com/content/2591c996-5157-11e9-9c76-bf4a0ce37d49 (accessed on February 20, 2020).

Marriage, M., and Coterrill, J. 2018. McKinsey unclear how to repay South Africa scandal fees. *Financial Times*, 4 March, available at https://www.ft.com/content/8e310198-1c91-11e8-aaca-4574d7dabfb6 (accessed on February 20, 2020).

Mehta, S. 2018. Bank of Baroda to shut down South Africa operation. *Economic Times*, 13 February, available at https://economictimes.indiatimes.com/markets/stocks/news/bank-of-baroda-to-shut-down-s-africa-operation/articleshow/62896851.cms?from=mdr (accessed on March 29, 2020).

Mohamed, S., and Finnoff, K. 2005. Capital Flight from South Africa, 1980–2000. In G. Epstein (Ed.), *Capital Flight and Capital Controls in Developing Countries* (pp. 85–115). New York: Edward Elgar.

Ndikumana, L. 2008. Can macroeconomic policy stimulate private investment in South Africa? New insights from aggregate and manufacturing sector-level evidence. *Journal of International Development*, 20(7), 869–887.

Ndikumana, L. 2014. Fuite des capitaux et paradis fiscaux: impact sur l'investissement et la croissance en Afrique. *Revue d'économie du développement*, 22(2), 113–141.

Ndikumana, L., and Boyce, J.K. 2010. Measurement of capital flight: Methodology and results for Sub-Saharan African countries. *African Development Review*, 22(4), 471–481.

Ndikumana, L., and Boyce, J.K. 2019. Magnitudes and Mechanisms of Capital Flight from Angola, Côte d'Ivoire and South Africa. Amherst, MA: Political Economy Research Institute, Working Paper 500.

Ndikumana, L., Boyce, J.K., and Ndiaye, A.S. 2015. Capital flight from Africa: Measurement and drivers. In S.I. Ajayi and L. Ndikumana (Eds.), *Capital Flight from Africa: Causes, Effects and Policy Issues* (pp. 15–54). Oxford: Oxford University Press.

Ndikumana, L., Naidoo, K., and Aboobaker, A. 2020. Capital flight from South Africa: A case study. Amherst, MA: Political Economy Institute, Working Paper 516.

Nicolaou-Manias, K., and Wu, Y. 2016. Illicit financial flows: Estimating trade mispricing and trade-based money laundering for five African countries. Global Economic Governance Africa (GEGAfrica), Discussion Paper 2016-17.

Nkurunziza, J.D. 2015. Capital flight and poverty reduction in Africa. In S.I. Ajayi and L. Ndikumana (Eds.), *Capital Flight from Africa: Causes, Effects and Policy Issues* (pp. 81–110). Oxford: Oxford University Press.

Office of the Public Protector South Africa. 2016. *State Capture*. Report No. 6 of 2016/2017.

Omarjee, L. 2019. Bank of Baroda SA fined R400 000 by Reserve Bank regulator. *Fin24*, 6 August, available at https://www.fin24.com/Companies/Financial-Services/bank-of-baroda-sa-fined-r400-000-by-reserve-bank-regulator-20190806 (accessed on March 28, 2020).

Onishi, N., and Gebrekidan, S. 2018. In Gupta Brothers' Rise and Fall, the Tale of a Sullied A.N.C. *The New York Times*, December 22, available at https://www.nytimes.com/2018/12/22/world/africa/gupta-zuma-south-africa-corruption.html (accessed on March 28, 2020).

Pather, R. 2018. The state's case against the Guptas and co. *Mail & Gardian*, February 16, available at https://mg.co.za/article/2018-02-16-00-eight-in-court-for-milking-fiscus/ (accessed on March 28, 2020).

Pomerantz, K. 2019. The Story Behind TIME's Cover on Inequality in South Africa. *Time*, May 2, available at https://time.com/5581483/time-cover-south-africa/ (accessed on March 29, 2020).

Portfolio Committee on Public Enterprises. 2018. *Report of Public Enterprises Committee into Eskom Inquiry*. Pretoria: Portfolio Committee on Public Enterprises.

Reuters. 2019. South Africa withdraws corruption charges against Zuma's son. *Reuters*, January 24, available at https://www.reuters.com/article/us-safrica-zuma/south-africa-withdraws-corruption-charges-against-zumas-son-idUSKCN1PI0VG (accessed on June 11, 2020).

Rustomjee, Z. 1991. Capital flight under apartheid. *Transformation*, 15, 89–103.

SARB. 2016. Proposed joint tax and exchange control Special Voluntary Disclosure Program. Exchange Control Circular No. 6/2016.

SARB. 2019. Currency and Exchanges Guidelines for Business Entities, 2019-10-31 Pretoria: SARB (online).

SARS. 2006. SARS background briefing on tax amnesty for small business.

SARS. 2018. *South African Revenue Service—Annual Performance Plan 2017/18*. Pretoria: SARS (online).

SARS. 2019. *South African Revenue Service—Annual Report 2018/2019*. Pretoria: SARS (online).

Scott, K., and Pettersson, H. 2019. South Africa is the world's most unequal country. 25 years of freedom have failed to bridge the divide. *CNN*, May 10, available at https://www.cnn.com/2019/05/07/africa/south-africa-elections-inequality-intl/index.html (accessed on May 29, 2020).

Sethi, A., and Gopakumar, G. 2018. How Bank of Baroda's misadventures dragged it into South Africa's political crisis. *Hindustan Times*, February 6, available at https://www.hindustantimes.com/business-news/how-a-series-of-mistakes-by-bank-of-baroda-dragged-it-into-south-africa-s-political-crisis-ht-investigation/story-KZ8JRozaG0ToWrxbO0tbKN.html (accessed on June 17, 2020).

Sharife, K., and Joseph, J. 2018. India's Bank of Baroda Played a Key Role in South Africa's Gupta Scandal Organized Crime and Corruption. Organized Crime and Corruption Reporting Project (OCCRP), February 27, available at https://www.occrp.org/en/investigations/7696-india-s-bank-of-baroda-played-a-key-role-in-south-africa-s-gupta-scandal (accessed on January 16, 2020).

Smit, B.W., and Mocke, B.A. 1991. Capital flight from South Africa: Magnitude and causes. *South African Journal of Economics*, 59(2), 101–117.

Sole, S., and Comrie, S. 2017. How Brian Molefe "helped" Gupta Optimum Heist. *Politicsweb*, 16 May, available at https://www.politicsweb.co.za/news-and-analysis/how-brian-molefe-helped-gupta-optimum-heist—amabh (accessed on January 17, 2020).

South African Gauteng Division High Court. 2016. Case No: 22877/2018: Eskom hOldings Soc LTD vs. Mckinsey & Company Africa, Trillian Management Consulting, Trillian Capital Partners, National Director of Public Prosecutions and MMS Nxumalo N.O..

South African National Treasury. 1961. Exchange Control Regulations 1961 (as promulgated by Government Notice R.1111 of 1 December 1961 and amended up to Government Notice No. R.445 in Government Gazette No. 35430 of June 8, 2012) Pretoria: National Treasury.

South African National Treasury. 2003a. Exchange Control Amnesty and Amendment of Taxation Laws Act, 2003. Pretoria: National Treasury.

South African National Treasury. 2003b. Explanatory Memorandum on the Exchange Control Amnesty and Amendment of Taxation Laws Bill, 2003. Pretoria: National Treasury.

South African National Treasury. 2006. Small Business Tax Amnesty and Amendment of Taxation Laws Act, 2006. Pretoria: National Treasury.

South African National Treasury. 2018a. Final Report: Forensic Investigation into Various Allegations at Transnet And Eskom: Tender Number NT 022-2016 RFQ 026-2017. Pretoria: National Treasury.

South African National Treasury. 2018b. Minister's Speech at the SARS 2017/2018 preliminary revenue outcome announcement. Pretoria: National Treasury.

Stals, C. 1998. The changing face of exchange control and its impact on cross-border investment opportunities in South Africa. Address by the Governor of the South African ReserveBank, Dr. Chris Stals, at the Annual Australia/Southern Africa Business Council Meeting held in Sydney on 23/7/1998.

Steenkamp, T. 1996. Some aspects of corporate taxation in South Africa: The Katz Commission. *Economic Society of South Africa*, 64(1), 1–11.

Streak, J.C. 2004. The Gear legacy: Did Gear fail or move South Africa forward in development? *Development Southern Africa*, 21(2), 271–288.

Taylor, I. 2001. *Stuck in Middle GEAR: South Africa's Post-Apartheid Foreign Relations*. Westport, CT: Praeger.

Tuffias Sandberg. 2017. The latest on the SVDP. https://tuffiassandberg.co.za/the-latest-on-the-svdp/.

US Department of Interior. 2019. *US Geological Survey. 2015 Mineral Yearbook – South Africa* (Advance Release). Washington, DC: USGS, September.

van der Berg, S. 2009. Fiscal incidence of social spending in South Africa, 2006. Stellenbosch University: Department of Economics, Working Paper 10/2009.

van Rensburg, D. 2019. The great Samancor 'heist'. *Fin24*, 2 October, available at https://www.fin24.com/Companies/Mining/the-great-samancor-heist-20191002 (accessed on March 31, 2020).

Weeks, J. 1999. Stuck in low GEAR? Macroeconomic policy in South Africa, 1996–98. *Cambridge Journal of Economics*, 23(6), 795–811.

Winning, A. 2018. South African court authorizes freezing of $130 million in McKinsey case. *Business News*, January 15, available at https://www.reuters.com/article/us-safrica-politics-mckinsey/south-african-court-authorizes-freezing-of-130-million-in-mckinsey-case-source-idUSKBN1F500F (accessed on November 20, 2018).

Wood, E., and Moll, T. 1994. Capital flight from South Africa: Is under-invoicing exaggerated? *South African Journal of Economics*, 62(1), 17–28.

World Bank, UNDP, Statistics South Africa, and Department of Planning Monitoring and Evaluation. 2018. *Overcoming Poverty and Inequality in South Africa An Assessment of Drivers, Constraints and Opportunities*. Washington, DC: World Bank.

World Inequality Database,. https://wid.world/ (accessed on July 21, 2021).

Zucman, G. 2013. *The Hidden Wealth of Nations. The Scourge of Tax Havens*. Chicago, IL: Chicago University Press.

6

International Trade and Capital Flight

Challenges for Governance

Melvin D. Ayogu

Introduction

Poor governance is a binding constraint in the fight against capital flight and other illicit financial flows from Africa. Capital flight, in turn, undermines the efficacy of foreign aid as a tool for development. To further the goal of combating capital flight, and thus to enhance aid effectiveness, this chapter examines the double-edged role of governance. Because it can facilitate or deter capital flight, the question of how government wields its power is of critical importance.

This chapter focuses specifically on the governance of international trade and trade-related financial transactions. It demonstrates that the sword of governance has been wielded to cut predominantly one way—to facilitate capital flight—in key African countries.

The chapter argues that an important part of "getting governance right" is to redress existing practices in the management and oversight of international trade data that create wide scope for transgressors and institutionalized malpractices. The responsibility of governments for cross-border trade data quality and data transparency cannot be shirked. But because states and public officials are often complicit in illicit flows, the need for independent verification systems for trade and financial data cannot be overemphasized.

The economist Dani Rodrik has observed that the effects of policy reforms depend on the institutional context in which they are implemented. Experience has demonstrated, for instance, that trade liberalization policies "would not work if fiscal institutions were not in place to make up for lost trade revenue, capital markets did not allocate finance to expanding sectors, customs officials were not competent and honest enough" (Rodrik 2006). Similarly, foreign assistance will not work if public trustees can deftly commingle aid monies with domestic resources and then launder such monies in foreign jurisdictions where recovery of stolen public assets is extremely costly to pursue.

Melvin D. Ayogu, *International Trade and Capital Flight*. In: *On the Trail of Capital Flight from Africa*.
Edited by Léonce Ndikumana and James K. Boyce, Oxford University Press.
© Melvin D. Ayogu (2022). DOI: 10.1093/oso/9780198852728.003.0006

Institutions can be defined as the complex chemistry of formal rules, informal rules and enforcement characteristics that together form a society's incentive structure (North 1991, 2002). A society's incentive structure determines the manner in which people interact and the kinds of organizations which arise to seize opportunities created by the incentives. When the incentive structure encourages good governance, regimes become public-regarding. When it encourages poor governance, predation, lack of accountability and corruption thrive.

As an example of what can happen when institutions function perversely, *Vanguard*, a leading newspaper in Nigeria, reported in 2016 that the Federal Government was losing $775 million per year in foregone revenue from oil and gas cargoes "discharged at undesignated terminals." This amount would be equivalent to approximately 2.7% of the annual revenue of the Federal Government of Nigeria at the time. "Maritime experts," the report elaborated, "hold the opinion that all the Federal Government needed to do over the years to sustain collectable revenue inflow from transportation, berthing and cargo discharge of vessels was to enforce the policies that have been in existence for many years." Instead, some flout the rules with what one expert termed "impunity" (Vanguard 2016). This raises an obvious question: why would a government in need of development resources deprive itself of revenue in circumstances that are ostensibly within its control?

This chapter seeks to identify and understand how political, social, and economic arrangements (formal rules, norms/conventions) facilitate corruption in general, and capital flight in particular, among other ways by making it difficult to detect. The smoke and many mirrors of capital flight, and arguments from skeptics about whether it actually happens, have been most pronounced in connection with the commodities trade. Resolving controversies on this subject requires a better understanding of the rules of the game of international trade that shape this channel of capital flight and its tributaries.

Before delving further, a few remarks on institutions and the nexus of governance and capital flight are in order. Formal rules are created and enforced by political entities as part of the instruments of governance. Third parties rely on governments to ensure that agreements, once struck, are subsequently honored or enforced. Increasing specialization of economic activities and the attendant allocation of rights and responsibilities induce an additional set of complications.

As complex transactions—involving a variety of relationships, some personal and others impersonal, interacting across locations near, far, and remote—become a regular feature of trade, the development of equally complex enforcement mechanisms will be required. Already we can observe instances of this shift in the current approach to managing trade-related intellectual property (IP) rights. The evolution of rights management as a dominant business strategy, in contrast to the legalistic approach of granting exclusive rights to IP through patent, copyright, and trademark protection, has been driven by cost considerations, particularly the cost of enforcement. Capital flight and money laundering, too, involve complex

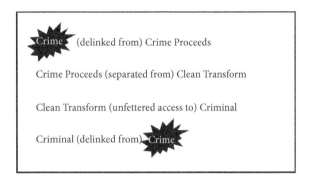

Fig. 6.1 The money laundering "value" proposition

transactions between a matrix of actors across the globe. In the criminal enterprise "value chain," depicted schematically in Figure 6.1, some of the personalities in the matrix often are known while others are unknown to some of the players.

Whereas third-party enforcement is the remit of government, what may be termed "first and second-party enforcements" are the norms of "appropriate behaviour" that constrain the conduct of the individual parties entering into a contract. Development of the appropriate norms is crucial because third-party enforcement is imperfect. This offers insight into why citizens can at times flagrantly disregard formal rules. From experience, they may have come to believe that they can, on average, get away with the violation because of the unreliable nature of the enforcement mechanisms. This also can help us to understand how insurgents can successfully wage a long-drawn out war of attrition on the state, sometimes laying to waste expensive and strategic infrastructure such as crude oil pipelines, factories or refineries. A case in point is Nigeria, where the unrest in the Niger Delta has frustrated many foreign oil exploration and production companies. Shell has made a major divestiture, while new investors are now more interested in deep sea operations offshore that are better insulated from the turmoil on land.

In complex exchanges involving dense networks, with costly third-party verification and subject to opportunism and cheating, as is typical of illicit financial flows, trust is crucial in facilitating transactions. In some cases, both formal and informal enforcement mechanisms may be in play, while in others informal mechanisms alone suffice. The position of the state as a monopolist of legitimate violence implies an unequal distribution of coercive power in the enforcement realm. As a result, individuals or groups have an incentive to try to hijack the government in order to determine how the "third-party" component of enforcement is exercised. Such corruption of government through corrosion of institutions is the grit of this study. The cases discussed illustrate the pervasiveness of the phenomenon of debasement, and its crucial role in capital flight from Africa.

Consider, for instance, the following statement from the South African Revenue Service (SARS), whose responsibilities include "record-keeping, verification, publication and analysis of trade data" (SARS 2017):

> Country code ZN is described as "Origin of Goods is Unknown." For purposes of better understanding, this has been renamed to "Gold, Petroleum and Other" as over 95% of this bubble is made up of gold. Gold due to legacy rules is treated as a country. You will therefore not be able to determine where the exports are going to [sic] or the imports are coming from. The aim is to rectify this, for gold specifically, as part of moving to the general system.

When a country whose number one traded commodity is gold has a rule (until recently, at least) that says we do not reveal movements in our international trade in gold, the temptations that such an arrangement present to would-be transgressors are immense.

Another curious rule allows South Africa to export and import with itself as the same Country of Origin (COO) and country of Destination (COD). These roundtrips create fertile ground for the concealment of illicit flows. In the corporate world, audits are used to verify sales figures in annual accounts and to ensure that they represent bona fide sales and not internal transfers. Disguising internal transfers as sales is akin to "cooking the books." Years ago, Al Dunlap, who at the time was the CEO of Sunbeam, was charged with accounting fraud by the US Securities and Exchange Commission for booking phony sales of electric blankets. An astute financial journalist, who thought it odd that the sales of electric blankets would be spiking in summertime, revealed these were internal transfers calculated to inflate the company's ostensible performance under his leadership (Byrne 1998; Norris 2001).

Applied to international trade transactions, what are data users to make of the balance of trade figures of a country that buys and sells to itself and books those transactions as "international trade"? Why was the recording of gold exports in South Africa not in accordance with established rules applied to other products? The wide latitude allowed when it comes to such official record keeping creates opportunities that some predictably exploit.

Similarly, in studies based on aggregated data at national levels, under-invoicing of exports and over-invoicing of imports accounts for a significant component of illicit cross-border flows (Ndikumana et al. 2015). This work has proven useful in drawing attention to a phenomenon that appears to be widespread in the Sub-Saharan region, prompting increased research efforts aimed at drilling down to the level of product types in individual countries. The analysis of such disaggregated trade data can help in uncovering some of the ways and means of capital flight as well as the institutional characteristics that shape how the practice plays out in different contexts within the region.

Asymmetries in Trade Data

Estimates of trade-related capital flight from Africa (Ndikumana et al. 2015) are based on the analysis of several internationally recognized conventional data sources, such as the Direction of Trade Statistics, the UN Comtrade, UNCTAD-stat, and the balance of payments accounts (BoP). The Direction of Trade Statistics is a database of the International Monetary Fund (IMF) that reports total imports and exports disaggregated by partner countries but not by product. UN Comtrade is the United Nations International Trade Statistics database. It contains detailed records both by product types and partner countries of imports and exports of goods crossing national borders, as reported by national statistical authorities, and "is considered to be the most comprehensive trade database available with more than 3 billion records."[1] UNCTADstat is a trade and development database that UNCTAD compiles, validates and processes based on a wide range of data collected from national and international sources.[2] The balance of payments (BoP) is a record of private and official transactions between the residents of a country and the rest of the world, including the exchange of goods and services as well as capital and unilateral transfers. The reporting format of BoP can vary across countries. Important BoP subaccounts are the current account (recording merchandise trade and services), the capital account (recording real and financial assets transactions), and the official settlements balance (recording foreign exchange transactions of the central bank).

These various databases enable trade misinvoicing to be estimated at the product level as well as at the aggregate level. A comparison is made between a country's recorded exports or imports to the imports or exports recorded by its trading partners, adjusting for the costs of freight and insurance. By aggregating across individual country-partners, a global estimate for the reference country can be obtained. A 2016 UNCTAD report views capital flight as largely responsible for the asymmetries in the Africa trade data.[3] This occurs when firms deliberately understate the value of their exports or overstate the value of their imports. In the case of exports, under-invoicing allows them to retain and conceal part of the foreign exchange earnings abroad; in the case of imports, over-invoicing allows them to remit foreign exchange overseas in excess of the actual cost of the imported goods, where the excess is retained and concealed from the country's authorities.

---

[1] United Nations, "About the data," available at https://comtrade.un.org/labs/dit-trade-vis/pages/about.html (accessed on July 30, 2019).

[2] For more, see "Statistics," available at https://unctad.org/en/Pages/statistics.aspx (accessed on July 30, 2019).

[3] Ndikumana (2016). Similarly, Ferrantino et al. (2012) conclude that capital flight explains a significant proportion of the asymmetries in the China-US trade.

"Mirror data" refers to circumstances in which two entities collect information on the same transactions. In a mirror dataset, information from one source in theory duplicates the information from the other source. Bilateral trade data is one such example. Generally, any two trading partners are presumed to collect identical information on their trade in goods and services in any given period. By using this idea of correspondence of mirror data to examine trade on a bilateral basis, researchers have sought to gain insights into the discrepancies that in some instances have been so large and persistent that they cannot be plausibly attributed merely to data recording errors.

Cumulative discrepancies between mirror data in international trade create global asymmetries in bilateral trade statistics, a phenomenon that has been a subject of concern worldwide. The European Union has been particularly concerned about the discrepancies in intra-European trade in services (also known as "invisibles" because they do not involve physical goods) (Figueira and Hussain 2006). The United States has been concerned with the sizable asymmetries in the bilateral merchandise trade data with China. Africa has been concerned about the large asymmetries in its primary commodities trade with the rest of the world. Aside from being concerned about their implications for capital flight, persistent asymmetries in mirror statistics calls into question the credibility of BoP statistics.

The common framework for reporting on balance of payments transactions set out in the IMF's *Balance of Payments Manual* is intended to ensure conceptual and methodological consistency. Diligent application of the framework across countries restricts the range of plausible explanations for bilateral trade asymmetries by excluding basic methodological differences. Nonetheless, the uniform practices recommended in the IMF Manual are still open to a degree of variance in interpretation and implementation. Such variations have generated competing hypotheses about the most likely explanations for the persistent methodical data asymmetries being recorded year after year.[4] These are discussed below, with examples of how some of the presumed factors play out in the African context.

Existing estimates of capital flight from Africa are likely to be conservative because of the near total absence of records on trade in services. Trade in services is a major component of foreign exchange movements because of the region's dependency on joint ventures in the extractive industries. These include engineering services, marine services, aviation, insurance and financial services, communications, computer and information services as well as royalties and license fees. Other missing items include miscellaneous business, professional and technical services, such as legal, accounting, management, consulting and public relations, advertising, market research, and research and development. As the African region

---

[4] For examples, see Figueira and Hussain (2006); Ferrantino et al. (2012); and Ndikumana and Boyce (Chapter 2 in this volume).

strives towards its expressed goal of economic diversification, the services sector will come to occupy a larger niche overall. At present, most of these excluded services are provided by relatively highly paid expatriates living in posh areas of the host countries often under tight security details. Yet the international trade in these services remains off the books.

The competing explanations for Africa's mirror-trade data asymmetries can be categorized into two major strands, namely the capital flight hypothesis and more innocuous alternatives. The latter strand maintains that asymmetries in mirror trade statistics are due to (a) non-deliberate shortcomings in the recording of trade transactions, (b) known and unknown diverse customs and practices at the primary sources where trading data are collected (metadata issues), and (c) habits that may appear to be deliberate obfuscation arrangements but in fact are simply administrative quirks. Various possibilities are outlined below.

Classification differences

On the innocuous end of the spectrum is the possibility that the same transaction may be reported accurately by both parties but classified differently. This would affect commodity-specific but not aggregate trade discrepancies. Several devices have been developed that function as conversion and correspondence tables to minimize such discrepancies at the product-level reconciliation. The *Harmonized Commodity Description and Coding System* introduced by the World Customs Organization classifies trade by types. The *Standard International Trade Classification* (SITC) maintained by the United Nations Statistical Commission, now in its fourth revision, is designed to assist in classifying transactions. Its supplement, *Broad Economic Categories*, also produced by the UN, provides a three-digit classification of transportable goods according to their main end use.

It is unlikely that primary commodities, which are Africa's predominant exports, are subject to this problem. The classifications of primary commodities are relatively clear cut. The items in question include crops such as cocoa beans, coffee beans, cut flowers, cashew nuts, and tobacco, and minerals such as diamonds, gold, silver, tantalum, tanzanite, platinum, crude oil, and natural gas. These types of merchandise do not fall in grey areas because of their complexity or amorphous nature.

Classification of destination or origin countries also can lead to discrepancies in bilateral data comparisons. Again, these should not result in aggregate discrepancies. The UN manual on trade classification offers examples:

> The partner "Areas NES (not elsewhere specified)" is used (a) for low value trade and (b) if the partner designation was unknown to the country or if an error

was made in the partner assignment. The reporting country does not send the UN details of the trading partner in these specific cases. Sometimes *reporters do this to protect company information… Due to confidentiality, countries may not report some of its detailed trade* [emphasis added]. For merchandise trade, this trade will—however—be included at the higher commodity level and in the total trade value for both goods and services.[5]

The timing of shipments can also lead to discrepancies: merchandise exported toward the end of one year may not be recorded as imports until the beginning of the next. If this were the sole reason for discrepancies, however, aggregation over several years would be expected to resolve the problem. It cannot explain asymmetries that persist over time or across products and partners.

Partner misattribution

Deliberate acts of false declaration of origin or destination by an importer or exporter or both parties can arise in order to benefit from trade policies, including duty reductions or tariff concessions, granted based on country of origin or destination. Misattribution can also facilitate smuggling or other forms of obfuscation that render difficult the task of asset tracing for purposes of freezing or confiscation of the proceeds of corruption and money laundering.

An interesting feature of the misattribution problem is that the rules of the game appear to have been shaped to give reporting authorities plausible deniability. Countries are granted considerable latitude on how to report transactions, notwithstanding the goal of harmonization. Expressing concern that the footloose criteria for partner attribution reduces the reliability of trade data, the UN Statistical Commission comments:

> For merchandise trade statistics, almost all countries report as partner country for imports the country of origin, which is determined by *the rules of origin established by each country* [emphasis added], and country of last known destination as the partner country for exports.[6]

Further complications arise from the transnational operations of multinational corporations engaged in global value chains.

---

[5] UN, "About the data," available at https://comtrade.un.org/labs/dit-trade-vis/pages/about.html (accessed on August 1, 2019).
[6] UN, International Trade Statistics Knowledgebase, "Bilateral asymmetries," available at https://unstats.un.org/unsd/tradekb/Knowledgebase/50657/Bilateral-asymmetries (accessed on August 1, 2019).

Driven in part, perhaps, by recent controversies following the unsettling implications of studies relying on trade data,[7] the UN's International Merchandise Trade
Statistics (IMTS) Expert Group has proposed that country of consignment be included in the data compilation manual as a possible partner attribution (ibid.) The
current rules allow the exporting country to record the country of consignment
as the "last known destination." In conjunction with each country establishing its
own rules of origin, this has created a wide berth for regimes so inclined to "cook
their books" to do so with plausible deniability. Under the rules proposed by IMTS,
the scope of plausible deniability is narrowed by specifying that a destination could
in fact be a transit point rather than an importing country. This can be viewed as
a strike against perfunctory reporting in the governance of international trade or
as a tacit acknowledgment of a potential channel of illegitimate conduct in international trade. Either way, it represents a positive step. Current initiatives from
UN Comtrade to upgrade its database to provide users "more information on the
nature of trade flows and partner-country attribution; symmetrical valuation of
imports and exports and more information on insurance and freight costs; as well
as more information on the nature of trade flows, especially re-exports, re-imports,
and goods for processing, and intra-firm trade" also reflect efforts to improve the
situation.[8]

Free ports

Free ports play an important role in anonymizing international trade analogous
to that of anonymizers in the world of virtual currencies (U.S. Federal Bureau of
Investigation 2012). They make the task of trade data reconciliation more difficult,
while increasing opportunities for trade-related capital flight. A free port is a place
where imported goods can be held tariff-free pending (a) re-export, (b) duty-paid
entry into the importing country, or (c) being processed without customs duties
prior to re-export. Existing free ports include the ports of Singapore, Hong Kong,
Dubai, Panama, and Amsterdam, the latter being Europe's leading entrepot. The
business of importing goods for re-export, with or without any value-added in the
free port itself, has grown enormously, particularly with the advent of container-
ization of cargoes. Indeed, the trade is now so well established that specialists have
emerged. They double as both importers and exporters acting as dealers within
certain shipping corridors. "Entrepot trade" as an established term in international
commerce speaks to the importance of this activity (see Box 6.1).

[7] E.g., UNCTAD (2016), Van Rensburg (2016).
[8] UN, "UN Comtrade upgrade plan 2018–2019," available at https://comtrade.un.org/data/doc/
UpgradePlan (accessed on August 1, 2019).

Box 6.1
Bitcoin and the role of freeports in Africa's commodity trade

---

What connects Bitcoins, entrepot trade, free ports and anonymizers? The answer, in a word, is *secrecy*.

Launched in 2009, Bitcoins are accounts (addresses) comprising unique strings of numbers and letters that represent units of the Bitcoin currency as well as uniquely identify the transactions. The transactions are not systematically linked to an entity. The "delink" feature endows it with some anonymity just as a freeport would confer to the ultimate destination of a shipment, seen from the viewpoint of the country of origin.

Even though traded under some level of anonymity, Bitcoin transactions are nonetheless transparent, in that they are publicly available in a shared transactions register. Strictly speaking, therefore, Bitcoin is semi-anonymous as certain aspects of the transactions are not hidden. So are entrepot trades if the parties report truthfully, fully, and timely.

The anonymity of cryptocurrencies can be enhanced further by using accessories designed to camouflage the source of a Bitcoin transaction and hence facilitate an extremely high level of anonymity. With such devices, the digital footprints—the originator-sender's instructions to the end user-recipient—are completely obfuscated. These tools and services collectively referred to as "anonymizers" make no pretensions as to their purpose.

Mixer, an advanced version of an anonymizer, obscures the chain of transactions on the blockchain (that is, on the up-to-date ledger containing encrypted records of all the previous transactions) by bundling them in the same Bitcoin address and transmitting them together in a manner that conceals the origin of the transaction (i.e., it creates the impression that they were sent from another address than the true origin). Another piece of sophisticated software in this repertoire of anonymizers is a tumbler that executes remittance instructions through complex protocols defying attempts to uniquely map virtual coin addresses to specific transactions.

To those versed in the global practices of multinational corporations, these concealment mechanisms should be reminiscent of the conduct of multinational corporations in the arena of commodity brokerage and secrecy jurisdictions. The analogy between Bitcoin and the role of freeports in Africa's commodity trade is evident.

When a country for various reasons is unable to trade directly with another foreign country, it is easy to see how entrepot trade can be a useful instrument. Say, for example, that Country A honors a regional sanction placed on country C, whereas country B is both a neutral party and an entrepot. Country A freely trades with B, and country C freely with B, as well. Then through the entrepot, A is enabled to trade with C indirectly and still maintain plausible deniability. If unchecked, entrepots can facilitate smuggling. Certificates of origin as well as declarations of destination can be forged by transgressors operating within such facilities. Clearly, the reporting protocols in place in the free ports and the nature of their activities are important factors in resolving the challenges of trade data reliability and making inferences based on information in the trade data.

For instance, entrepot trade in the free port of Amsterdam may help to explain the Netherland's large and systematic trade discrepancies in cocoa beans from Côte d'Ivoire. In contrast to the direction of discrepancies with most of its other trading partners, Côte d'Ivoire's exports to the Netherlands exhibit inflated invoicing (UNCTAD 2016). In other words, Côte d'Ivoire reports having sold more cocoa to the Netherlands than the latter reports importing. From the Ivorian perspective and in IMTS parlance, Netherlands is the country of "last known destination" of the beans from Abidjan. The Dutch story is particularly salient because trade in cocoa beans with the Netherlands accounts for over 30% of Ivorian trade in its most important commodity export.[9]

Trade in cocoa between Côte d'Ivoire and other trading partners apart from the Netherlands generally shows systematic underreporting, meaning that Côte d'Ivoire reports having sold less to those countries than their records acknowledge. This could be for purposes of capital flight. Or it could mean that the destination countries purchased some of the cocoa beans directly from Côte d'Ivoire and other quantities through third parties. Both practices are involved when the cocoa beans shipped to the entrepot are invoiced (and recorded in Côte d'Ivoire) at a below-market price and subsequently re-exported to their ultimate destination at their actual market price.

In attempting to unravel these discrepancies, French researcher Jean Merckaert (2020) finds that the Netherlands does not provide UN Comtrade with the complete trade statistics on entrepot trade and nothing on cocoa re-exports specifically. By choice, the Netherlands provides the UN with data on industrial exports and re-exports, but in an aggregated format that does not allow the components to be distinguished. This leaves to speculation as to why the country would provide the UN with data on industrial re-exports but not primary re-exports, as well as why these data are reported only in aggregated format. In this, the Dutch are exercising their option within the parameters of the IMTS 2010 convention. As previously noted, these sorts of anomalies in mirror data on trade are the focus of the current initiatives to upgrade the international reporting rules. At present, however, there seems to be sufficient latitude in the practice of entrepot

---

[9] Aside from trade reconciliation, reliable facts about a country's direction of trade are an important variable in international economic relations and foreign policy.

trade for opportunistic persons readily to find ways to turn free ports into a staging ground for illicit trade-related activities. Therefore, these locations serve as potential enablers of illicit financial flows.

Another insidious consequence of the activities of trading hubs is noteworthy. By obscuring information along certain segments of the value chain—for example, hiding the price at which a commodity is traded or the location to which it has gone—the countries that harbor trading hubs effectively deny primary commodity-producing countries the opportunity to optimize their diversification profile. Developing countries need to know the path values associated with all the segments in the global value chain through which their primary commodities are processed. These are crucial parameters in the industrial strategies of countries seeking to determine the best segments of the value chain at which to locate, based on their dynamic comparative advantages. Developing those advantages where they do not yet exist is a core goal of development planning. It would not be rocket science for national authorities to enter into an international agreement on trade reporting that mandates greater transparency.

The ethical conundrums of denying developing countries a clear view of global economic activities in which they have a significant stake are no different in the tree crops subsector as in the extractive industries subsector. Correspondingly, it can be argued that the same gusto with which concerned global citizens have pursued the "publish what you pay" initiatives in the extractive industries, including the efforts under the Extractive Industries Transparency Initiative, should be applied to tree crops as well.[10] Perhaps such an initiative could be called "Publish What You Take," or better yet, "Publish What You Take and Where it Goes."

Smuggling

Import smuggling leads to discrepancies in trade statistics when the value of the merchandise is recorded in the data of the exporting country but is unrecorded or undervalued in the data of the importing country. "Pure smuggling" refers to cases where goods escape recording altogether. "Technical smuggling" refers to cases where the importation is recorded but with understated quantities, prices, or both. The primary motive for both types of smuggling is to evade import duties or other trade restrictions.

Of course, smuggled goods must be paid for in full, just like any other imports. Payments for these goods are one type of illicit financial flow. They are distinct from capital flight, another subset of illicit financial flows, in that the funds are

---

[10] "Publish What You Pay" refers to initiatives that address the lack of transparency in transactions in primary commodities, particularly those vested in the state such as fuel minerals and solid minerals. The generally low degree of transparency in such dealings facilitates exploitation and theft of public resources by private entities and public officials.

used to pay for imports rather than stashed abroad. In balance-of-payments ter-minology, payments for smuggled imports belong in the current account whereas capital flight belongs in the capital account.[11]

Export smuggling likewise leads to discrepancies when the (full) value of the merchandise is recorded in the official books of the importing country but not the exporting country. Again, the primary motive is to evade duties or other restric-tions on trade. It is generally less prevalent than import smuggling for the simple reason that taxes on exports are less common than taxes on imports. Unlike import smuggling, export smuggling also can be a conduit for capital flight if the earnings are held abroad.

Smuggling, both pure and technical, can occur at both ends of the exchange link. Holding all else constant, if country A's border is relatively more tightly po-liced than country B's border, discrepancies in mirror trade statistics can be used to gauge the extent of smuggling into or out of country B. Differences in enforce-ment levels reflect differences in institutions. Using partner data as a benchmark in estimating the extent of smuggling and capital flight from trade data is consistent with the presumption of better functioning institutions in partner jurisdictions, typically those in industrialized nations.[12]

There can be a linkage between smuggling activity and free ports. If a good is successfully smuggled into a free port, or if a smuggler can operate in both the source country and an entrepot jurisdiction, the merchandise can be more easily re-exported to a destination country in its clean transform, that is, as non-smuggled merchandise originating either from the free port or, per forged documentation, from any feasibly contrived origin of choice.

Misinvoicing

Misinvoicing refers to falsification of the value of a trade by deliberately misreport-ing the price, quantity, or both in trade documents. Besides smuggling, important motives for misinvoicing include tax evasion, tariff evasion, or to circumvent quota restrictions as well as foreign exchange controls. Other illegitimate purposes in-clude enabling people to obtain money through false pretenses such as through false duty drawback, pre-financing of non-existent export trade and obtaining rebates for phantom exports (see Box 6.2).

---

[11] Note that the direction of import discrepancies due to smuggling is the opposite of those due to import under-invoicing for purposes of capital flight. The two offset each other and trading partner data comparisons can only tell us their net effect. In the measurement of capital flight, adjustments for import misinvoicing add to the BoP residual measure when under-invoicing exceeds smuggling and subtract from it when the reverse is true. For discussion, see Ndikumana and Boyce (Chapter 2 in this volume).

[12] This proposition is taken up subsequently in the discussion of oil and gas export trade in Nigeria.

Box 6.2
The Goldenberg Affair: Fraudulent Rebates for Phantom Exports

Africa's most infamous case of fraudulent manipulation of an export-incentive scheme was the "Goldenberg Affair" that roiled Kenya in the early 1990s. The details took 22 years to unravel and seemed to touch everyone who was anybody in Kenyan politics and key institutions of governance. One of the scheme's masterminds was the chief of the country's secret police, James Kanyotu, whose formal title was the Director of National Intelligence for the 27-year period from 1965 to 1992 (Bosire 2005). Three hundred and fifty people were identified as the recipients of "Goldenberg money" totaling more than 150 billion Kenyan shillings (a sum roughly equivalent to US$1.5 billion) (ibid.). In a country with a 2017 per capita income of 166,000 Kenyan shillings, this quantum was equivalent to the total average annual income of nearly one million Kenyans.[13]

Incorporated in July 1990 as a private limited liability company, Goldenberg International Limited ostensibly began exporting gold and diamond jewelry under the Local Manufacturers (Export Compensation) protocol which provided for the payment by the Customs and Excise Department of 20% export compensation to eligible exporters on the value of goods exported. The company obtained an additional 15% payment on its exports of gold and diamond jewelry. It was a lucrative arrangement: as a National Public Radio report put it, "For every $100 of foreign exchange that Goldenberg brought in, the Kenyan government would kick in an additional $35 in Kenyan shillings—a huge bonus."[14] The monies were paid from Treasury and treated as customs refund.

Over time, Goldenberg International Limited and its collaborator, Exchange Bank Limited, were paid export compensation until about 1994 when the scheme was uncovered. Questions were then raised about the legitimacy of the scheme and payments, including the fundamental question of whether or not gold and diamonds were in fact exported by Goldenberg International Limited. Ultimately, it was determined that the Goldenberg Affair was a case of subsidy for a phantom export.[15]

---

[13] Income per capita is from Economic Survey (2018), Kenya National Bureau of Statistics.
[14] Simon (2013).
[15] Additional accounts can be found at http://www.kenyalaw.org/Downloads_FreeCases/931–65.pdf (accessed on May 1, 2018).

When an exporter or importer falsifies documents in order to park money overseas illegally, the resulting capital flight fits within the meaning of money laundering as defined by US anti-money laundering statutes.[16] The structuring of the movement of funds is designed to avoid detection (transaction reporting). The circumvention of exchange control regulations—in the case of exports, the requirement to surrender export proceeds to domestic monetary authorities at the official exchange rate, and in the case of imports, the procurement of foreign exchange at the official rate in excess of the true value of the imported goods—is itself a crime tantamount to tax evasion. In the destination country, the payments disguise the provenance of the wealth. So, in addition to the predicate crime of falsification, there is that element of structuring of a monetary transaction whose purpose is concealment of the origin and nature of the money, or the nature of a trade to avoid transaction reporting. These are key elements in defining money laundering as "how one moves money and why."[17]

For the scheme to work, the counterparty at the other end of the transaction must agree to park the payment per the request of its trading partner. Clearly, this cooperation is a necessary part of the structuring of the transaction. It is doubtful that the counterparty will declare in the know-your-customer (KYC) component of its banking documentation that the lodgment is the unremitted export proceeds or excess import payments placed overseas by its partner to evade foreign exchange controls.[18] If scholars of illicit financial flows can easily see through these machinations, it would be naïve to presume that those who cultivate such alliances and repeatedly participate in such schemes are unaware of the design and purpose of the schemes; namely, moving funds to impede detection by law enforcement, and helping to disguise these funds as legitimate wealth.

Similarly, it would be problematic to accept the notion that states serving as entrepots, free ports or shipping hubs are entirely oblivious of their role in enabling potentially illicit financial flows. On the contrary, it is reasonable to suppose that these jurisdictions are sufficiently savvy to understand the roles of trading hubs in aiding and abetting trade misinvoicing and misattribution. They also know how to eliminate such facilitations, if they so wish. In this respect, trading hubs are to international trade much as secrecy jurisdictions are to international finance. Both facilitate capital flight and money laundering. Their formal and informal rules work to attract this kind of activity by means of embedded incentives. The visible hands of government are on the table, spread openly for all to see and for self-interested parties to self-select.

---

[16] U.S. Code §1956, "Laundering of monetary instruments," available at https://www.law .cornell.edu/uscode/text/18/1956 (accessed on July 21, 2021).

[17] Cuellar v. United States, 553 U.S. (2008), for example.

[18] KYC has become part of the mandatory requirements for financial institutions in demonstrating due diligence as part of Anti-Money Laundering AML/Countering Financing of Terrorism measures.

Transfer pricing

Transfer pricing—more accurately, transfer mispricing—refers to purposive self-misinvoicing by multinational firms operating across multiple jurisdictions with the objective of "cooking the books" to relocate profits to low-tax (or no-tax) jurisdictions (Kabala and Ndulo 2018). This phenomenon is distinct from capital flight. Insofar as the profits would have been repatriated in any case, transfer pricing reduces the government's tax revenue but not the country's stock of capital. We nonetheless discuss it here because transfer pricing and capital flight share some of the same attributes.

Unlike misinvoicing for capital flight, the extent of which can be gauged by observing discrepancies in trading partner mirror-data, misinvoicing for transfer pricing occurs identically on both sides of the transaction. Over-invoiced imports (e.g., for intellectual property rights or the intra-firm provision of other services) have, as their counterpart, over-invoiced exports from the exporting country; and similarly, under-invoiced exports (e.g., of minerals) are matched by under-invoiced imports in the books of the importing country. This means that transfer pricing is not included in conventional misinvoicing adjustments used in capital flight estimation.

Transfer pricing for purposes of tax avoidance or tax evasion (the difference between these terms hinges on the legality of the practice) is a problem in both developed and developing countries. There is a widespread impression, however, that it is more pervasive in developing countries, and there is an emerging body of evidence that supports this belief.[19] A recent study of South Africa also reported the striking finding that the practice is highly concentrated amongst the largest multinational firms: the top 10% of foreign-owned firms accounted for 98% of the country's total tax losses caused by profit shifting (Wier and Reynolds 2018).

Despite multiple initiatives to curtail abusive transfer pricing, the problem persists. One reason is the growth of intra-firm trade worldwide. When a firm with worldwide operations puts a price on goods or services provided by one subsidiary to another, who is to second-guess its judgment as to the "right" price? Estimates of the magnitude of mispricing typically rely on information on counterfactual "arms-length" prices, when this is available, but mobilizing the results of such comparisons for legal and enforcement purposes is not a straightforward task even when the formal rules are clear and strict. In reality, the rules often are neither, reflecting not only the weakness of governing institutions but also of the ability of powerful interests to shape the regulatory environments in which they operate. In seeking to play countries off against each other, multinational firms use their leverage to press not only for favorable rules but also for lower tax rates and for

---

[19] See, for example, Johannesen et al. (2017); and Janský and Palanský (2017).

tax exemptions. Even in the face of urgent needs for revenue, governments often accede to their demands.

Capital Flight and Trade: Non-Fuel Commodities

This section analyzes export and import procedures for non-fuel commodities, taking Nigeria as a case study. The following section does the same for fuel commodities. The goal is to illuminate the institutional foundations of capital flight, the way in which the structure of incentives influences the way in which the game is played. As this section demonstrates, the story is not just about innocuous statistical discrepancies, and the game is played across all sectors.

Export procedures

Primary commodities figure prominently in Africa's international trade. Table 6.1 presents resource intensity, defined as the ratio of primary exports to total exports, for African countries for which the pertinent data are available. In the majority of the 46 countries profiled, the ratio stands at more 50%. Crops are the most widespread of the tradeable primary commodities. They include traditional export crops such as cocoa, coffee, sugar, and cotton; cereals such as maize, wheat, sorghum, barely rye, oats, millet, and rice; oil crops such as palm oil, soybean, sunflower, rape seed, groundnut, sesame, and coconut; roots and tubers such as cassava, cocoyam, and yam; fruits and vegetables; and tobacco. Important solid minerals found in the continent include gold, silver, platinum, tanzanite, aluminum, palladium, diamond, manganese, cobalt, phosphate, bauxite, tin, tantalum, and tungsten.

Although less well-known than its petroleum resources, Nigeria produces a wide variety of solid minerals, most of them found in the Northern, Middle Belt and Western parts of Nigeria with concentration in Plateau State and Western States.[20] The formal rules for exporting non-fuel commodities from Nigeria are summarized in the flow charts shown in Figure 6.2a. The first step for a prospective exporter is to register with the Corporate Affairs Commission and subsequently with the Nigerian Export Promotion Council (NEPC). Provided the exporter meets the registration requirements, NEPC issues a certificate that the entity is now a recognized exporter in Nigeria.

---

[20] For details, see Nigerian government, "Nigeria Natural Resources," available at http://www .nigeria.gov.ng/index.php/2016-04-06-08-38-30/nigeria-natural-resources (accessed on August 1, 2019).

Table 6.1 Resource intensity in selected African economies

	Countries	Intensity ratio
1	Algeria	0.98
2	Angola	0.96
3	Benin	0.83
4	Botswana	0.16
5	Burkina Faso	0.73
6	Burundi	0.76
7	Cameroon	0.91
8	Cape Verde	0.41
9	Central African Republic	0.57
10	Chad	0.95
11	Cote d'Ivoire	0.80
12	Democratic Republic of Congo	0.59
13	Egypt	0.58
14	Equatorial Guinea	0.96
15	Ethiopia	0.84
16	Gabon	0.95
17	Gambia	0.66
18	Ghana	0.69
19	Guinea	0.78
20	Guinea-Bissau	0.96
21	Kenya	0.69
22	Lesotho	0.08
23	Madagascar	0.53
24	Malawi	0.88
25	Mali	0.52
26	Mauritania	0.91
27	Mauritius	0.29
28	Morocco	0.36
29	Mozambique	0.88
30	Namibia	0.53
31	Niger	0.62
32	Nigeria	0.98
33	Rwanda	0.86
34	Senegal	0.66
35	Seychelles	0.88
36	Sierra Leone	0.40
37	South Africa	0.45
38	Sudan	0.86
39	Swaziland	0.41
40	Tanzania	0.60

Continued

Table 6.1 *Continued*

	Countries	Intensity ratio
41	The Republic of Congo	0.92
42	Togo	0.63
43	Tunisia	0.23
44	Uganda	0.79
45	Zambia	0.85
46	Zimbabwe	0.69

Notes: Resource intensity is the ratio of primary exports to total exports. A high resource-intensity ratio is problematic because it indicates fragility regarding ability to finance development expenditure that requires availability of hard currencies. The period covered for the resource intensity data is from 1995 to 2013, with the exception of Tanzania for which the period is 1999 to 2013.
Source: UNCTAD data reported by Ayogu and Onyeka 2018.

Seventeen additional export certificates are on the menu at Step 5, depending on the product and the country of destination (see Table 6.2). Free ports and trading hubs are particularly significant for items 3 to 5, namely, certificates for cocoa levy, tariff concession for North-South trade, and export facilitation schemes for intra-regional trade. Securing the trade advantages promised in these schemes is based on declarations regarding origins and destinations of the commodities. These requirements can be readily gamed using the opportunities provided by trading hubs, as discussed above.

The export procedure for non-fuel minerals, as recounted in an interview with an operator experienced in both solid minerals and agricultural commodities, yields a parallel but different narrative.[21] Informal rules and norms complement the formal rules laid out above, shaping the underlying incentive structure. The exporter's goal is to retain the maximum possible proceeds from the export. In principle, a duly registered Nigerian exporter is required by law to surrender all export proceeds to his or her bank for conversion to domestic currency at the official exchange rate, which is invariably lower than the market rate.[22] This policy is viewed by exporters as a tax. Like other taxes, it is considered unduly burdensome in light of the poor delivery of public services and the perception of a high incidence of kleptocracy.

The rules also allow the exporter to deposit revenues into a foreign currency export revenue account (called a NXP account), from which the exporter can draw foreign currencies for specific approved purposes. Alternatively, having converted

[21] This account is based on an interview conducted in Lagos, Nigeria in 2018.
[22] The parallel market premium has averaged about 20% which also is the current markup over the official rate.

Table 6.2 Types of export certificates in Nigeria's export regime

Title of document	Use(s) of the document	Where obtainable
1. Exporters Registration Certificate	For Identification of Nigerian Exporter	Nigerian Export Promotion Council (NEPC)
2. Sanitary and Phytosanitary Certificate	Conditions for both exporting and importing countries to ensure safety in the handling of Agricultural product and natural resources free from diseases	Nigeria Agricultural Quarantine Services (NAQS)
3. ICCO-1 Certificate	It is a combined certificate of origin and declaration of value for cocoa levy	Federal Ministry of Industry, Trade and Investment, (FMITI) Produce Inspection Unit
4 GSP Form	For tariff concession for all countries involved in North-South trade	NACCIMA, NCS
5. ECOWAS TLS Certificate	For goods trade under the ECOWAS Trade Liberalization Scheme	NEPC, Ministry of foreign affairs and ECOWAS Secretariat
6. Form J	Clearance letter for the export of solid minerals	Federal ministry of solid minerals development and Nigerian mining corporation
7. Certificate of clearance from veterinary Health Services	Certificate of clearance from Veterinary Health Services	Department of Veterinary health services, Federal Ministry of agriculture
8. Certificate of clearance from national commission for museums and monuments	For exports of handicrafts and artefacts	National Commission for Museums and Monuments

Continued

Table 6.2 *Continued*

	Title of document	Use(s) of the document	Where obtainable
9.	Clearance from department of forestry	For exports of classified endangered wildlife species and wood products. Furniture and furniture components	Department of forestry, federal ministry of agriculture
10.	NXP Form	For commercial exports originating from Nigeria	CBN and Commercial Banks
11.	Non-commercial Exports (NCX) Form	For non-commercial exports	CBN and Commercial Banks
12.	NIMASA Form C series	For allocation of cargoes to shipping lines. It serves as cargo tracer and loading authorization to allotters.	NIMASA and commercial Banks
13.	Single Goods Declaration (SGD) Form C2C10	Gives details of consignments	NCS
14.	Certificate of quality for food, drugs and cosmetics	Certifies the quality of foods, drugs and cosmetics meant for exporters	NAFDAC
15.	Certificate of quality	For manufacturers only	SON
16.	Certificate of analysis and quality	To certify the quality of a product in question	Issued by manufacturers, processors or miners
17.	Certificate of quality and fumigation	To certify quality of raw agricultural commodities	Federal produce inspection service
18	Bill of lading and airway/roadway bill	Evidence of carriage of goods	Shipping company/transporter

Source: Nigerian Export Promotion Council, www.nepc.gov.ng.
Key: CBN=Central Bank of Nigeria, ECOWAS=Economic Community of West African States, NACCIMA=National Association of Chambers of Commerce Industry Mines and Agriculture, NCS=Nigeria Customs Service, NAFDAC=National Agency for Food and Drugs Administration and Control, NEPC=Nigeria Export Promotion Council, NIMASA=Nigerian Maritime Administration and Safety Agency, SON=Standard Organization of Nigeria.

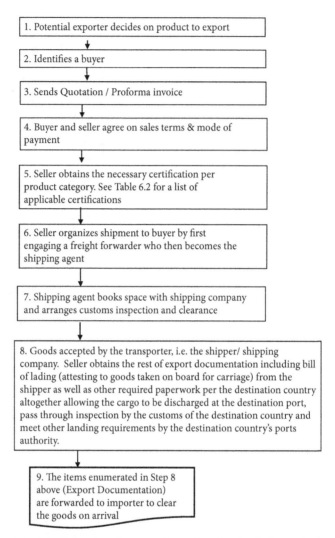

Fig. 6.2a Procedure for general merchandise (excluding oil and gas) exports in Nigeria

Note: The flow chart assumes that the exporter is licensed, meaning that all necessary requirements for issuing export license have been met and that the enterprise has a functional bank account.
Source: Narration based on the flow chart in Madu, O. (2015), "Trader Journey," mimeo, Multimix Academy, Lagos, Nigeria.

the export revenue to domestic currency at the official exchange rate, the exporter is supposed to be able to purchase foreign currency for approved purposes at the official rate, which is less expensive than the market rate. In practice, however, the experience of attempting to follow this procedure often proves frustrating, forcing many exporters to source funds outside the more attractive government rates.

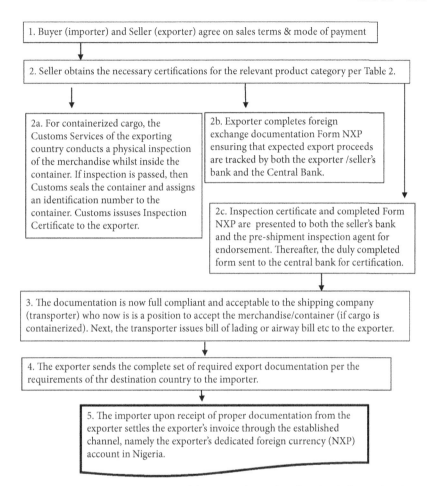

1. Buyer (importer) and Seller (exporter) agree on sales terms & mode of payment

2. Seller obtains the necessary certifications for the relevant product category per Table 2.

2a. For containerized cargo, the Customs Services of the exporting country conducts a physical inspection of the merchandise whilst inside the container. If inspection is passed, then Customs seals the container and assigns an identification number to the container. Customs issues Inspection Certificate to the exporter.

2b. Exporter completes foreign exchange documentation Form NXP ensuring that expected export proceeds are tracked by both the exporter /seller's bank and the Central Bank.

2c. Inspection certificate and completed Form NXP are presented to both the seller's bank and the pre-shipment inspection agent for endorsement. Thereafter, the duly completed form sent to the central bank for certification.

3. The documentation is now full compliant and acceptable to the shipping company (transporter) who now is is a position to accept the merchandise/container (if cargo is containerized). Next, the transporter issues bill of lading or airway bill etc to the exporter.

4. The exporter sends the complete set of required export documentation per the requirements of thr destination country to the importer.

5. The importer upon receipt of proper documentation from the exporter settles the exporter's invoice through the established channel, namely the exporter's dedicated foreign currency (NXP) account in Nigeria.

Fig. 6.2b Documentation required for general merchandise (excluding oil and gas) exports in Nigeria

The process for getting approval to purchase foreign currency at the preferred rate can be dilatory, and it is open to bribery and corruption.

The conduct of the exporters could be considered rational responses to the numerous challenges of doing business in this environment. Figure 6.2b is an augmented version of Figure 6.2a, with a focus on the money trail. In Step 1 the exporter selects a mode of payment that maximizes the likelihood of securing the expected export proceeds. This would be a mode that is sufficiently robust to address known and unforeseen contingencies.

Figure 6.2c depicts a process that games the steps shown in Figure 6.2b, so as to circumvent the constraints imposed by the formal rules. Because formal export channels are often cumbersome and slow, an exporter of merchandise with a short

1. **The Challenge :** For a majority of the merchandise under consideration, time-to-market is so much faster when transacting through the informal channels than through the formal channel. The time differential is said to exceed one month on average. For seasonal commodities, such a delay from transacting through formal channels imply potential revenue losses which, in conjunction with the foreign exchange loss on conversion of export revenue, reduces expected profit. The informal channel takes between 1–3 days to conclude, at least for charcoal and solid minerals. Formal export channels entail inspection and clearances from relevant agencies and ministries, often involving significant delays, leading to desperation, bribery and corruption.

Exporter-Recursive Solution to the Export Challenges

2. Rank probable safe havens for the expected export proceeds. Popular options include hiding some of the funds in the Republic of Benin, Togo, Ghana, Kenya, USA, UK and Switzerland. Current UK rules and regulation have been lately viewed as tough and pro Nigeria's anti-corruption measures, and Switzerland is perceived to have warmed up to mutual legal assistance with Nigeria thus also making it a less desirable jurisdiction for money laundering.

3. Conditional on options in Step 2, agree on terms of the sale and mode of transaction including preferred method of settlement: Misinvoicing, barter, or false declaration of merchandise? In a false declaration, for example, lead ore is declared whereas importer pays for platinum, the commodity that is actually shipped and received.

4. Follow the formal channel.

5. If so, then engage special freight forwarders. These special forwarding agents have cultivated relationships with customs and shipping companies that enable them to fast-track the process to bill of lading, bypassing Form NXP. Expedited services attract "non-documentation" premium.

6A. Fast-tracking the process in Step 5 may involve circumventing export inspection by bribing the authorities. This an especially attractive option when transporting low bulk, high value items such as gemstones. In such cases, shipments through courier companies are equally appealing. Some couriers may transport without a full suite of documentation. The core of the incentive—the value proposition—is to secure cross border shipment without complying with the Form NXP protocol. To the exporter, this means securing efficient commodity movement without the money trail.

6B. As an alternative to 6A, skip shipment entirely and instead transport the gemstones on board an airplane as a cabin baggage, booked in first class or business class. Arrive overseas destination and sell merchandise in any of the open markets such as Hatton Garden in London, UK; Antwerp, Belgium; Munich, Germany; Bangkok, Thailand; and Colombo, Sri Lanka.

Fig. 6.2c Exporter response to institutions (incentive structure) governing exports of general merchandise (excluding oil and gas) in Nigeria

shelf life will preselect the informal channel, and factor into the negotiated export price the premium from using the informal channel. Having decided to go the illicit route, an exporter's further consideration would be the destination of the proceeds, which also determines the mode of payment. Thus, in making the first decision in the chain depicted in Figure 6.2b, the exporter takes a panoramic view of the entire chain.

The routine described in Figure 6.2c is not hypothetical. In fact, the governments of some of the federated States of Nigeria and other interested parties have openly accused the Federal Government of Nigeria of "lacking the political will to implement mining [regulations] because of vested interests" (Folarin 2019). An estimated sum of one billion dollars is claimed to have been lost over three years by the Nigerian government due to gold smuggling, one of the many minerals conveniently falling under the government's blind spot (Folarin 2019).

The complexity of Nigeria's export protocols pale by comparison to the process for exporting goods from South Africa, and not to some faraway land such as New Zealand but to a neighboring African country which also belongs to the same customs union, the Southern African Development Community (SADC). An infographic account of the experience of a South African exporter, as reported by the Chief Executive of the Consumer Council of South Africa, is depicted in Ayogu (2019). South Africa's elaborate export protocol is presumably designed to safeguard expected export revenue of a country that cares very much about its fiscal circumstances, avoiding any potential leakages. The items of apparent interest to the authorities include rice, tea bags, mayonnaise, sugar, laundry detergent, dishwashing liquid, deodorant, milk, canned vegetables, maize meal, frozen fish, chicken, and fruit. A typical container load of an assortment of these items requires dozens of sets of documentation in hundreds of pages, carrying dozens of signatures of customs officials and dozens of custom stamps. For example, in the fiscal year ended June 2016, a total of 1262 shipments to Angola involved 64,362 sets of documents containing 758,462 pages. "Don't mess with South Africa's export revenue" is the clear message.

If this is so, then the question that must be asked is why would a country with such rigorous procedures for the export of tea bags, tomato ketchup, mayonnaise, and detergents treat its gold exports "as a country"? Besides its absurdity, why is there, in effect, a lower degree of diligence regarding records of exports of this particular commodity? Why does this not raise persistent questions within the society? Even if such treatment were thought to be rooted in the country's apartheid past, when evasion of trade sanctions could have been part of the motive, why have these "legacy rules" persisted long past 1994, when the new South Africa was born? The "bubble," as the state calls it, where users of trade data "will not be able to determine where the exports are going to or the imports are coming from," is comprised of "95% gold."[23] This unconventional administrative procedure raises more questions than it provides explanations of South Africa's recording protocols for international transactions.

Import procedures

In comparison with Nigeria's export requirements, its import protocol appears to be even more cumbersome. The process is described in detail in Tables 6.3 and 6.4. There are three salient points to note. The first is to recall that in the export

---

[23] SARS, "Explanations and notes," available at http://www.sars.gov.za/ClientSegments/Customs-Excise/Trade-Statistics/Pages/Explanations-and-Notes.aspx (accessed on August 1, 2019).

protocol described earlier, an important consideration for exporters is time-to-market, which can be subject to significant dilatory tactics in the formal channel, thus creating opportunities for alternative options to be attractive. Similarly, the threat of demurrage charges, levied by shipping firms when unloading of the cargo is delayed, given a cumbersome import process vulnerable to dilatory tactics, also creates opportunities for informal side payments, an example of what economists call "rent seeking." As the American legal scholar and behavioral economist Cass Sunstein (2019) has observed in a different context, "administrative burdens are an emphatically political choice" (Sunstein 2019).[24]

One way of boosting profits, as well as to recoup such informal "costs of doing/expediting business," is to reduce the duty payable by filing false declarations of the goods or their value (misinvoicing) and then bargaining over the distribution of the differential amongst the players.

The second point to note is the requirement for importers to apply for approval from the Central Bank for the purchase of foreign currency to settle the invoice. This leads to the practice of importers paying for "sawdust"—ghost (or overvalued) imports—as a means of relocating scarce hard currency overseas under false pretenses. This currency is obtained from the Central Bank at the official rate, which is more favorable than the market rate. Indeed, merely selling the currency thus obtained on the market would yield a tidy profit.

The third point is that there are two nodes in the customs clearance protocol at which a false declaration can, in principle, be detected. The first is at Step 15 in Table 6.3, where the risk channels are assigned and implemented. The other is at Step 26 of the sub-process described in Table 6.4 when the container is exiting the gate with the merchandise. Random inspection can detect a false declaration. A false declaration leading to a higher duty will trigger a Debit Note (DN) requiring the importer to pay additional charges. For our purposes, we are interested in whether such an adjustment will lead to a revision of the data captured at the Data Transmitting Interface (DTI) at Step 11 in Table 6.3. Our inquiries on this point elicited the information that ordinarily the DN is appended to the original set of import documentation, but whether the data revision is made is an open question.

The foregoing descriptions of the trade protocols in Nigeria and South Africa (the two largest economies in Africa) are meant to convey the nature of the environment governing the transactions summarized by official data on exports and imports. Additionally, they are meant to raise the level of appreciation of why it is challenging to secure the compliance of sovereign nations with rules of data reporting designed to harmonize the processes behind the data. If achieving

---

[24] Sunstein was referring to the U.S., where burdensome administrative procedures have been used, for example, to restrict voter registration. In other settings, the motives may have more to do with opportunities for pecuniary gain.

Table 6.3 Description of general merchandise import process in Nigeria

1	Importer identifies a supplier/exporter and agrees to deal.
2	Exporter sends pro forma invoice to importer. Importer arranges insurance accordingly.
3	Importer arranges payment: obtaining foreign exchange domestically; prepayment using an account overseas or enters into an international trade financing arrangement.
4	Importer opens a Form M on the Nigerian Trade Platform (Single Window) system. Form M and other applicable documentation are submitted to importer's bank.[1]
5	Bank reviews documentation for compliance. If validated then, submits the Form M to customs for approval.
6	Upon approval, importer authorizes the issuance of Letter of Credit if applicable and informs exporter to ship goods.
7	Exporter sends shipping document through her bank/ importer's correspondent bank for onward transmission to importer bank.
8	Bank forwards final shipping documents to customs for Pre-Arrival Assessment Report (PAAR).
9	Importer collects PAAR from bank and passes it to her clearing agent to work it through the clearing process for the release of the cargo (see Table 6.3 for details of the daunting clearing sub process).
10	Agent receives PAAR and confirms steamer or airline/transporter arrival and position of cargo.
11	Agent lodges Single Good Declaration (SGD) with the Data Transmitting Interface (DTI) which generates assessment notice indicating import duty to be paid.
12	Agent pays duty at a bank as indicated on the assessment notice and gets payment receipt from bank.
13	Agent returns to DTI café and inputs payment details which generates risk channel, that is, level of Government intervention.
14	Depending on the risk channel, the clearing agent follows the process for the risk channel generated for the transaction in question.
15	There are 5 risk channels namely Blue, Green, Yellow, Light Red and Deep Red.
16	Blue Channel is known as fast track for big manufacturers. They receive cargo at ship side and immediately relocate cargo to their warehouse. The company notifies the Post Clearance Unit of the Customs for inspection formalities which will be done at company/warehouse premises. Cargos are not touched until arrival of the Unit.
17	The green channel is for importers who have maintained a clean profile over the years. This channel allows this class of importers to take delivery of their consignments from the terminal after performing the shipping and terminal operator formalities. This may not always be the case as some transactions channeled to green are rerouted to Deep red.
18	The yellow channel indicates that a documentary check is required at the Customs Processing Center (CPC). The importer goes to the Query and Amendment seat at the C.P.C to confirm the details of the transaction as earlier declared and thereafter takes delivery of cargo once shipping and terminal formalities are completed.
19	The Light Red indicates that the shipment would go through a scanning process to confirm the nature of what is concealed as against what is declared.

Continued

Table 6.3 *Continued*

20	The Deep red channel indicates that a full physical examination would be done on the consignment.
21	Customs broker gets Exit Notice indicating formal release of cargo after due process.
22	The Exit Notice is required for Shipping line and terminal operator's release.
23	Customs broker gets a Debit Note which indicates the shipping charges and pays for charges at a bank.
24	The payment receipt, the Exit Notice and other documents in the SGD is used to obtain Shipping Release and Delivery Order. These documents are then taken to the terminal operator's office for settlement of terminal charges. Once payment is made and all documents attached, the terminal operator issues a Terminal Delivery Order (T.D.O) that is then used to move consignment out of the terminal and port.

[1] Form M is the template for an application for exchange control approval to purchase foreign currency from an authorized bank at the official rate much lower than the market rate that trades on average at 20% premium.
Sources: Author's compilation and verification of documents based on Madu, O (2015), "Trader Journey," mimeo, Multimix Academy, Lagos, Nigeria and information from http://nigerianports.gov. ng/import-export-guidelines-3/.

consistency across counterparties to the same transaction is difficult, the inferences and conclusions from official data rest on fragile foundations. This situation is presumably of serious concern to scholars and policymakers alike.

There are several takeaways from this fuzzy data terrain. First, a great deal more effort should be directed at clarifying, validating, and harmonizing international trade data. Second, some initiatives to improve trade data reporting are finally beginning to happen in this regard, as noted above.[25] Third, equally helpful would be the adoption of a more open-minded view regarding some of the more embarrassing perspectives on trade data discrepancies. Such a disposition may be constructive, leading to useful enhancements of data quality, particularly if suspected leaks in the current system are followed up, investigated, and found to exist. But progress along these lines cannot occur in an atmosphere of mutual distrust, automatic denials, self-serving arguments, and attempts to discredit unwelcome views.

Researchers working on Africa's development challenges conduct data-based empirical analysis to make inferences, including observations that African states tend to be fragile, dysfunctional, corrupt, and characterized by low growth, high

[25] The Automated System for Customs Data (ASYCUDA), developed by UNCTAD, is a specific example of efforts to improve the documentary procedures—process and control—in international trade. ASYCUDA is an integrated customs management system for international trade and transport operations in a modern automated environment, designed to improve security by streamlining procedures of cargo control, transit of goods and clearance of goods, and to help the fight against corruption by enhancing the transparency of transactions. See https://unctad.org/en/Pages/DTL/TTL/ASYCUDA-Programme.aspx (accessed on October 3, 2019).

Table 6.4 Description of general merchandise import clearing sub-process in Nigeria (Step 9 in Table 6.3)

1	The Declarant prepares the customs entry called Single Good Declaration (SGD). The SGD is a form in 8 copies that will be dispatched to various parties during the clearance process. The information on the SGD is captured at the Data Transmitting Interface (DTI) café. The declarant must have obtained a Risk Assessment Report (RAR) from Cotecana before preparing the Customs entry. The declarant also assesses his declaration. The assessment, based on the documentation of the import transaction, indicates the amount to be paid as duty by the declarant. The declarant prints assessment notice at DTI which carries all duties and taxes relating to customs release.
2	The declarant goes to the bank with the assessment notice and makes payment of the assessed value. Bank issues declarant Payment Acknowledgement sheet. The payment is electronically transmitted to the Customs system. The declarant then goes to CPC for consignment release.
3	NCS confirms payment at CPC and releases consignment by printing Exit note which is given to declarant.
4	Declarant takes original copy of B/L to shipping line for a copy of Debit Note or invoice which indicates the amount to be paid for shipping release after collection, the declarant goes to the bank and makes payment as reflected on Debit Note.
5	The declarant then takes the payment teller from bank and other documents listed above to the shipping line for a receipt and Delivery Order respectively.
6	Declarant takes Delivery Order, bill of lading and receipt of invoice to the office of the terminal operator for Payment Invoice which indicates how much is to be paid as Terminal charges.
7	The declarant goes to the bank for payment of terminal charges.
8	Declarant then takes bank teller along with other documents required for terminal release to terminal operator's office for collection of Terminal Delivery Order (TDO). Declarant gives TDO, letter of Authority and Identification card to driver to enter the port for loading of cargo.
9	Driver comes into the terminal to load and then drops the TDO at the terminal Operators office at the exit gate and collects Equipment Interchange Report (EIR). Steps 1 to 5 are similar for the Green channel.
10	Declarant goes to Terminal operators' office to book for physical examination at terminal.
11	Terminal Operator drops container at terminal for physical examination
12	Declarant goes for allocation of entry, collects examination form and confirms NCS officer assigned to undertake physical examination at terminal.
13	Assigned NCS officer for physical examination endorses examination form.
14	Declarant cuts container seal and invites other government agencies mandated to observe and confirm examination.
15	Examination agencies, in the presence of declarant, physically examine containers.
16	Declarant gets examination report from resident NCS officer.
17	Declarant takes examination report to Chief Examiner for endorsement.
18	Declarant takes examination report to Valuation Unit for endorsement.
19	Declarant takes examination report to Task Force for endorsement. Task Force at Terminal may refer declarant to Task Force main office for clarification before commencement of procedure.

Continued

Table 6.4 *Continued*

20	Declarant takes examination report to Officer-in-Charge (OC Terminal) for endorsement and release.
21	Declarant goes to NCS Resident officer for electronic transfer of release to Terminal Operator.
22	Declarant goes to terminal operator's office for Exit Note and then applies for TDO.
23	Declarant collects TDO, attaches all other documents and takes them to Enforcement Unit at Terminal for endorsement.
24	Declarant takes documents to the CIU office at Terminal for endorsement. CIU at Terminal may refer declarant to CPC for clarification before commencement of procedure.
25	Declarant takes all documents to Gate Control Unit at the gate for endorsement and collects Exit to leave the port.
26	If container is examined and found to contain under declared goods, Debit Note is raised by NCS for payment. Declarant continues with process after payment. However, if container is found to contain prohibited items, documents are held by NCS and transferred to Enforcement Unit for action.

Notes: The original source is O. Madu (2015), "Trader Journey," mimeo, Multimix Academy, Lagos, Nigeria, with modifications and updates by the author.

poverty, and high income inequality.[26] Yet few of those analyses ponder the conundrum in using the available data to assess outcomes without worrying about the quality of the data emerging from such arguably dysfunctional environments. It is as if, by some divine exception, data issues were immune from the influence of the constraining factors and development failures that are the subject of the analyses. How can all else fail except the reliability of the data used to determine the failure? The implication is that serious, concerted efforts to improve data quality should be a central item on development agendas.

Capital Flight and Trade: Fuels

Using UNCTAD data, primary commodities account for 98% of Nigeria's export revenue (see Table 6.1). Oil and gas dominate the country's exports.[27] Not surprisingly, the Federal Government of Nigeria has devoted much attention to the regulation and monitoring of the trade in fuel.[28] It is of great interest, therefore, to

[26] For perspectives on the Afro-pessimism literature, see Sender (1999).

[27] In 2016, oil and gas accounted for 92.3% of export revenue. Of the rest, agricultural commodities account for about 3% comprised mainly of cocoa beans, sesame seeds, and cashew nuts. See Central Bank of Nigeria 2017.

[28] In contrast, the non-fuel minerals have been left unattended by the Federal Government of Nigeria. This imbalance in attention on Nigeria's natural resource types has drawn pointed criticism from Nigeria's oil producing States, who accuse the Government of sharing the wealth from the south, where

ask how a barrel of Nigeria's oil moves from the point of extraction, the well head, to the point of sale (POS) where property rights are exchanged.

The paper trail

Three aspects of the upstream value chain—substance, displacement, and custody—are crucial for understanding the phenomena of pilfering, smuggling, and false declarations.

Substance refers to gradations in the quality of the crude oil that are reflected in their market price. These variations in quality are measured as API (American Petroleum Institute) gravity differentials. The two major categories are light and heavy crudes. Light crudes are preferred and command a higher price. Heavy crude oil contains more impurities which must be removed to produce the substance for which value will be exchanged. Primary processing at the wellhead separates oil from gas and water. Additional segregation can occur during bulk transportation in vessels prior to the cargo's arrival at the point of sale. The extent of segregation and evaporation depends on the duration of the carriage. Furthermore, temperature variations can induce natural separation of water and oil. For these reasons, readings taken at flow stations after primary processing can vary. The designation of oil as "export quality" instills some level of certainty in the determination of its quantity. Once crude oil is certified export quality, it is locked in for revenue accounting such that any further variation claims have to be established convincingly.

Displacement describes the flow path from wellhead to flow station to export terminal. Flowlines connect individual wells to the flow stations (where gas and water separation occurs), while pipelines connect the flow stations to the terminals. Export terminals are designated points of sale. "Bunkering" (the illegal pilfering of crude oil) can happen along any segment of the flow path from the wellhead to export terminal. The operators usually own the flowlines from wellhead to the flow stations. Some of the pipelines are owned and operated by the Nigerian Pipeline Development Corporation (NPDC), a subsidiary of the Nigerian National Petroleum Corporation (NNPC), while others are owned and operated by independent oil companies (IOCs). Following a wave of divestment of onshore assets by IOCs, ownership of some of the major pipelines were transferred to joint ventures between NPDC and indigenous companies that operate the pipelines.

Custody refers to chain-of-custody control protocols, the verification mechanisms attendant to the barrel of crude as it transits from wellhead to flow station to pipeline to export terminal or final point of sale. Where the standard fiscal meter

the oil and gas emanate, and leaving the revenue from non-fuel minerals largely mined in the north of the country to be monopolized by the producing States.

is not available at the export terminal, the out-turn, where the crude is trans-ferred to the purchaser, becomes the POS at which contractual export volumes are determined. Some offshore and deep-water production is stored on floating storage facilities and these are also designated as terminals for export.

Until the year 2000, the integrity of Nigeria's displacement and custody processes could not be guaranteed. "Monitoring" of activities basically was a mat-ter of accepting production numbers from the field rather than using fiscal meters to capture data on production and export-bound volumes at transfer points. Now meters installed at wellheads record the quantities transferred to flow stations for primary processing. The Department of Petroleum Resources (DPR) within the Ministry of Petroleum Resources is the industry regulator accountable for all mat-ters pertaining to crude quality, chain of custody and verification mechanisms. It is a DPR regulation that it be present at each out-turn.

Fiscal meters are installed at flow stations to record quantities after primary processing, prior to injection into the pipeline for transfer to the export storage terminal, pending sale. Evaporation and further separation while in transit means that for overseas sales, the volume may have changed materially from the volume at the export terminal. Revised volumes at point of sale would have to be verified on behalf of all parties. The buyer usually reports the final volume when transfer-ring the crude oil to the refineries. In some cases, DPR representatives are present to witness the verification of quantities.

Production from some offshore facilities flows to export terminals via pipelines, but in other cases the oil goes instead to floating storage facilities. In deep-water production facilities the wellhead lies at the seabed and flowlines and risers transport the crude oil to a floating production, storage and offtake platform (FPSO).[29] On the platform, water is removed, treated, and discharged—primary processing—and crude oil is stored. The fiscal meter on the FPSO records the quantities stored in tanks on the platform. Lockdown valves at each discharge point have tamper-proof seals and are under the watch of four independent overseers—Customs, the Department of Petroleum Resources, the operator, and an independent auditor. The keys to the locks are in the custody of the DPR and Customs, and they must be engaged simultaneously to release and open the valves.

The FPSO is a designated export facility. As such, it has defined exclusion perimeters under the protection of the state. The maritime exclusion zone is a five-kilometer radius protected by the Nigerian Navy and monitored from the FPSO. Daily production is reported and recorded. When a required export threshold is attained, application is then made to DPR for an offtake permit. On that basis, DPR assigns an allowable export volume with concurrent notification of the assign-ment to the Customs as well as to a subsidiary of NNPC, the Crude Oil Marketing

---

[29] Our account here is based on an interview on July 1, 2018 with Mr. Peter Oriaifo, CEO Erin Energy in Lagos, Nigeria, with editorial comments from Segun Omidele, and Chris Arima of Neconde Energy.

Department (COMD). It is the duty of COMD to obtain samples of all the crude oil produced to determine the blend as well as the reference sales price. DPR, the regulator, is present to conduct verification during transfer from the FPSO to the offtake tanker.

The oil company (vendor) pre-registers the pending transaction as well as the identity of the transporter. When the offtake vessel is 30 kilometers away from the terminal, the vendor is notified who in turn notifies the DPR and the port authorities to grant entry clearance to the offtake vessel. Additional oversight by the Nigerian Maritime and Safety Administration Agency (NIMASA) monitors all maritime traffic regarding vessel specifications, capacity and destination as well as compliance with safety regulations in Nigerian waters.

Leakages and non-transparency

The foregoing description of the chain of custody for tracking crude oil from extraction to POS confirms that the state can track the commodity with a view to verifying production and sales volumes. Whether it does so accurately is another matter. So-called "leakages"—unauthorized diversions of oil into private hands—occur from the wellhead to the terminal, with an assortment of players involved in a racket known as illegal bunkering. There are no reliable data on the scale of the phenomenon, but observers often place it at 10–20% of oil production, with some operators claiming even higher percentages.

Concerns have been expressed repeatedly about the lack of transparency and accountability in oil deals and the lack of credible repercussions for transgressions. These concerns extend beyond Nigeria and have found a collective voice in the Extractive Industries Transparency Initiative and the *Publish What You Pay* campaign.[30] Credible commitments to authentic verification schemes are key to restoring faith in future numbers.

The revenue realized from crude oil sales is a function of transaction prices as well as quantities sold. Opacity in either of the two dimensions renders the revenue figures dubious. Even if the quantities of oil sold were known with reasonable certainty, they tell little about total revenue because this magnitude depends on what the NNPC decides to disclose to whom and when and on the validity of that information.

Officials with the Central Bank of Nigeria say that data on crude oil revenue reported in the country's balance of payments accounts are based on unsubstantiated figures from the NNPC. The Central Bank accepts the data on an as-is basis, having no powers or instrumentality with which it can independently audit NNPC

---

[30] On the Extractive Industries Transparency Initiative, see https://eiti.org/ (accessed on August 1, 2019). On the Publish What You Pay campaign, see https://www.pwyp.org/ (accessed on August 1, 2019).

submissions.[31] But it should also be noted that the Department of Petroleum Resources is supposed to possess accurate data on export volumes and earned revenue. In theory, therefore, NNPC's data should be verifiable by reconciliation with that held by DPR.[32]

Numerous assessments of the NNPC have indicated that it may be the opaquest government institution in Nigeria. A 2014 study conducted by the Nigerian Natural Resource Charter and the Centre for Public Policy Alternatives characterized the NNPC as having "scarce or inadequate information, insufficient audits, and poor financial reporting standards," and concluded that "complexity and opacity in public revenue procedures have undermined oversight efforts by civil society actors."[33]

In 2014, the former Governor of the Central Bank of Nigeria, Sanusi Lamido Sanusi, declared that "NNPC has in violation of the law and constitution been diverting money from the Federation Account [the central government treasury], and involving itself in activities that warrant full investigation for more serious violations of the law" (Sanusi 2014). A subsequent forensic audit report by the international accounting firm PricewaterhouseCoopers (PwC) found an $18.5 billion gap between sales and cash remitted to the government in a 19-month period from January 2012 to July 2013, of which, according to Sanusi, about $12.5 billion appears to have been "diverted" (Sanusi 2015).

In her book, *Fighting Corruption is Dangerous*, former Finance Minister Ngozi Okonjo-Iweala writes that "the story of Nigeria's oil and gas sector is ugly":

> The impact of the sector has fallen far short of expectations because of inappropriate policies, inefficient and nontransparent institutions, corruption, capture by leaders, and rent-seeking internal and external elites. This makes the sector a minefield for anyone seeking transparency, accountability for revenue flows, or simply the honest and straightforward conduct of government business. Trying to block fraudulent oil marketers from access to government oil subsidies, pushing for accountability for revenues due to the Federation from the oil and gas sector, managing competing sectoral interests, and dealing with the noxious politics surrounding the sector have meant stepping on many powerful toes.

Dr. Okonjo-Iweala described her efforts to bring transparency and accountability to the sector as "probably one of the most stressful and dangerous tasks of my job as Finance Minister" (Okonjo-Iweala 2018, p. 54).

---

[31] Transcript of interview on July 9, 2018 with officials in the Statistics Department of the Central Bank of Nigeria.

[32] For data on natural gas, the unaudited information reported in the BoP is obtained from the Nigerian Liquified Natural Gas Limited. For other merchandise exports, the BoP data are obtained from customs services and licensed pre-shipment inspection agencies who by law are obligated to submit their data directly to the Central Bank.

[33] Natural Resource Charter and Center for Public Policy Alternatives (2014).

These observations are consistent with the conclusions reached by Nicolas Shaxson in an earlier analysis of efforts to improve transparency in Nigeria's oil and gas sector. He traced poor governance outcomes to two features of the "resource curse," the paradox that countries with abundant natural resource wealth tend to have worse development outcomes than countries with few resources. The first feature of such countries is that because the rulers get revenue from extractive companies rather than taxing their citizenry, the latter are disempowered; the second is that the revenues "foster the politics of patronage, involving fragmentation of society and the political system" (Shaxson 2009).

Concluding Remarks

First, a recap of the facts: Capital flight exists. Few would deny its existence, notwithstanding that some methods of identification remain contentious. This chapter has given examples and discussed some of the major controversies. There is also widespread recognition of, and concern about, asymmetries in mirror trade statistics as discussed here. Much of the debate in the literature on trade data asymmetries is about the extent to which they can be attributed to capital flight. The scale of discrepancies in some cases is such that if they indeed arise from capital flight, the implications are staggering and embarrassing. It defies comprehension as to how such systematic haemorrhaging can be allowed to persist in economies desperately seeking development capital. These tacit implications explain the sometimes-acrimonious nature of the debate. While not all asymmetries in mirror trade data can be ascribed to capital flight, there are persuasive reasons to seriously consider the likelihood that much of them can.

Poor data governance, both nationally and globally, has contributed to ambiguities surrounding the analysis of commodity-trade enabled capital flight. By fanning the flames of controversies around identifying capital flight, the weak state of data integrity effectively renders data governance itself an enabler of capital flight. The politicians who make the formal rules may also be interested parties in the game. Therefore, any credible data regime should consider independent verification systems and processes to mitigate conflicts of interest. To the extent that international agencies rely on national government agencies for data, such datasets are as reliable as the integrity of the primary sources that may or may not be self-interested players. But if states stand by their data, they should accept the valid conclusions therefrom.

The sustainability of capital flight depends on the relative ease with which "dirty money" obtained by illicit means can morph into clean money. Illegitimate wealth has the undesirable characteristic of being troublesome to spend. Money laundering thus is a necessary adjunct to dirty money, without which the pursuit of illegitimate wealth would cease to be a worthwhile venture. Money laundering is the gamut of steps by which illicit wealth is given the appearance of legitimacy so that the owner can enjoy it as if it were clean. This process is simplified in Figure 6.1, depicting the money laundering criminal enterprise proposition. Anti-money laundering (AML) measures refer to the repertoire of mechanisms by which society attempts to prevent criminals from having unfettered access to the clean transform of their money. Factors that weaken AML measures promote capital flight.

Capital flight has been ongoing for decades in Africa (Boyce and Ndikumana 2001). Institutionalizing capital flight and keeping it going for an appreciable period is likely to have entailed displacement of some existing opposing structures and blockage of new ones.[34] Good governance is inimical to capital flight, and poor governance is conducive to it. In other words, capital flight is antagonistic to proper institutions for good governance, instead promoting self-serving and expedient forms of governance. Capital flight can undermine an institution by altering its components, limiting its scope, diminishing its intensity, and thereby negating its efficacy. Thus weakened, the resulting institutions are able, and indeed intended, to accommodate capital flight and promote opportunistic crimes.

Here is how Mr. Femi Falana, a Senior Advocate of Nigeria and a distinguished human rights advocate has described the enabling environment for kleptocracy and its opportunistic complements in Nigeria:

Abacha's son was charged with stealing NGN463bn.[35] The case was in court for 14 years.... He said the immunity of his father should be extended to him. The Supreme Court said even if your father were still alive, he would have lost his immunity. But the objection was taken to court for 14 years. By the time they came back, the witnesses could no longer be found, the judge had been promoted, so you have to start de novo, and the case was withdrawn.

Today in England, if you file a motion that is meant to delay the case, you are disciplined by the law society.... But here, these are the lawyers that we are celebrating.

[Take] the case of James Ibori [former governor of Delta State accused of financial crimes]. Without a trial, he was discharged and acquitted. The judge carelessly forgot that the $15m seized from him when he wanted to bribe former [Economic and Financial Crimes Commission] Chairman Nuhu Ribadu was still there as an exhibit.

---

[34] For an out-of-Africa example of how institutions can be assailed, see McMillan and Zoido (2004).
[35] This sum is equivalent to approximately US$1.2 billion. Abacha's son refers to the son of the military ruler of Nigeria from 1993 to 1998, General Sani Abacha.

When the same man got to England, he pleaded guilty. You know why he pleaded guilty? When the lawyers saw his defence, they told him it was a sham, and they could not go on with the case. He asked if they could not file an appeal, and they told him, 'We don't do that here.' They told him that if they went on and he got convicted, he would get the highest punishment. But that is not the real problem. They told him they were afraid they would also lose their licence to practice law because they would be charged for wasting the resources of Her Majesty's court.

(quoted in Folarin 2019)

"To own the fight"

In December 2017, staff of Nigeria's EFCC staged an "anti-corruption walk" to mark International Anti-Corruption Day, calling on the Nigerian people "to take ownership of the fight against corruption" (Obi 2017). The call "to own the fight" is a plea for citizens to get involved. Institutions are the instrumentality for citizen engagement, the result of the complex chemistry between formal and informal rules that define a country's incentive structure. The formal rules originate from the state, and the informal rules are created by the people. As this study has shown, trade-related capital flight is rooted in the way in which governance has been bent to serve this purpose. Governance is neither self-implementing nor regenerative, meaning that it does not run itself or repair itself when broken. If the people do not get involved by investing in the task of governance through playing their roles, they may not experience good governance regardless of how sanguine their expectations are. The people will have to take charge and reshape governance by fixing institutions. This imperative is aptly captured in historical perspective by Roger Myerson in his Nobel Prize Lecture in 2007.

Economics began with Xenophon's "Oeconomicus" (c 360 BCE), in which Socrates interviews a model citizen who has two primary concerns. He goes out to his farm in the country to monitor and motivate his workers there. Then he goes back to the city, where his participation in various political institutions is essential for maintaining his rights to own this farm. Such concerns about agents' incentives and political institutions are also central in economic theory today. But they were not always.

(Myerson 2008)

A committed state will ensure that what occurs is adherence instead of malfeasance, action instead of inaction and dysfunction. It will respond diligently to whistle-blowers and credible informants, and cultivate intelligence rather than ignore the feedback or alarms from the public. When feedback is ignored, and the formal system is perceived as a sham, the public will not be motivated to feed the state with intelligence.

Establishing a functional public protector may be as much a necessary adjunct to good governance as money laundering is a necessary adjunct to capital flight. Establishment of prosecuting authorities for economic crimes no longer appears to be sufficient commitment to antigraft, especially when kleptocrats enjoy immunity from prosecution while in office. Furthermore, many of the anti-corruption agencies lose credibility as they become de facto instrumentalities of incumbents, employed deftly against opponents and skewing political competition by inducing opponents to defect to the ruling party to gain respite through prosecutorial discretion. Such carpet-crossing by politicians amplifies incumbency advantages and corrodes the political competition necessary for accountability and continued relevance of the electorate. In short, it corrodes democracy.

As of this writing, the initiative of UN Comtrade to provide users with more information does not appear to be moving at an encouraging pace. The initiative is a vital one, as it promises to provide details on the nature of trade flows and partner-country attribution, especially re-exports, re-imports, goods for processing, and intra-firm trade, thus allowing for better analysis of bilateral trade asymmetries. Regrettably, there are no specific member-states championing the initiative, a troubling situation given the entrenched interests in support of the status quo.

"Gold is a country," as declared by the South African authorities, is a poignant illustration of the possibility that what some observers see as mere data imperfections may in fact be manifestations of a calculated design. If so, why would the Government wish to change? The decision by the South African government to conflate gold exports categories, following the 2016 UNCTAD report, is an illustration of the widespread resistance to change and transparency. Why the extraordinary dispensation to this single commodity? Our analysis has clearly documented the fact that the problem is not only of defective rules and procedures, but also about rule violations that go unpenalized. Who is to enforce the rules *when the ghost buster is the ghost most of the time*?

Regarding the analogy between free ports and bank secrecy jurisdictions, the key question that must be asked is the scope of responsibility expected of the governments of countries that host these free ports. It is relevant to recall that Swiss banks would have resisted transparency reforms if the United States and Europe had not pressured Switzerland to reduce bank secrecy. So, who will pressure the governments of countries hosting opaque trading hubs to open up? Who is interested in pushing for timely implementation of the UN Comtrade data system upgrade? Put differently, who are the winners of the global criminal enterprises value chain? We know who the losers are.

There have been some notable achievements worldwide to increase accountability and reduce injury to commodity-dependent countries who are predominantly developing nations. The Extractive Industry Transparency Initiatives discussed above address accountability issues in fuels and minerals. The Kimberly Process

Certification Scheme to combat blood diamonds, in conjunction with subsequent US legislation, Dodd-Frank Section 1502 on conflict minerals, aims to address similar concerns in the solid-minerals subsector.[36] So far, there is no equivalent initiative for cash crops. The underlying theme in these initiatives is the importance of transparency of transactions and responsible corporate citizenship. It is time to demand that nations hosting trading hubs join the global responsibility movement by promoting transparency in international trade.

Acknowledgments

Valuable research assistance by Damilola Adeniran of the Center for Public Policy Alternatives (CPPA) Lagos is gratefully acknowledged, as is administrative support by Blessing Obiedere for the Nigeria component of the study. This research has benefitted from comments and guidance by industry experts and practitioners. Special thanks to Frank Edozie (Neconde Energy), Segun Omidele, Peter Owoeye (Bay Royal International), Peter Oriaifo (Erin Energy), Chris Arima (Neconde Energy), Leonard Ochueje (Central Bank of Nigeria), Obiora Madu (African Center for Supply Chain), Peter Onyia (Nigerian Customs), and Osita Mosanya (Nigerian Customs) for their valuable contributions. All errors and omissions are the author's responsibility, as are the views expressed here.

References

Ayogu, M.D., and Lewis, Z. 2011. Conflict Minerals: An Assessment of the Dodd-Frank Act, available at https://www.brookings.edu/.../conflict-minerals-an-assessment-of-the-dodd-frank-act/ (accessed on July 21, 2021).

Ayogu, M.D., and Onyeka, K. 2018. Are you being served? Governance and deprivation. *CWP # 181011— CPPA Studies on Inequality, Human Development and Economic Transformation*. http://cpparesearch.org/nu-en-pl/wp-content/uploads/2018/10/executive-summary_are-you-being-served.pdf (accessed on July 21, 2021).

Bosire, J.A. 2005. Report of the Judiciary Inquiry into the Goldenberg Affair, Republic of Kenya.

Boyce,J.K. and Ndikumana, L. 2001. Is Africa a Net Creditor? New Estimates of Capital Flight from Severely Indebted Sub-Saharan African Countries, 1970–1996. *Journal of Development Studies*, 38(2), 27–56.

Byrne, J. 1998. How Al Dunlap Self Destructed. *Bloomberg News*, July 6, available at https://www.bloomberg.com/news/articles/1998-07-05/how-al-dunlap-self-destructed (accessed on July 30 2019).

Central Bank of Nigeria. 2017. *Annual Report 2017*, available at https://www.cbn.gov.ng/Out/2018/RSD/CBN%202017%20ANNUAL%20REPORT_WEB.pdf (accessed on July 27, 2020).

---

[36] See Ayogu and Lewis (2011) for an elaboration of the conflict minerals legislation.

Child, K. 2017. Standard Bank may have to pay R51bn fine over forex. *Rand Daily Mail*, available at https://www.businesslive.co.za/rdm/business/2017-02-17-standard-bank-may-have-to-pay-r51-billion-fine-over-forex/ (accessed on July 21, 2021).

Ferrantino, M. J., Liu, X., and Wang, Z. 2012. Evasion behaviors of exporters and importers: Evidence from the US–China trade data discrepancy, *Journal of International Economics*, 86(1), 141–157.

Figueira, M-H., and Hussain, M. 2006. Asymmetries in EU current account data, *Working Paper and Studies 2006 Edition*, European Commission EUROSTAT, Luxembourg, November.

Folarin, S. 2019. Falana Laments Corruption in Judiciary, Seeks Reforms. *Punch*, available at https://punchng.com/falana-laments-corruption-in-judiciary-seeks-reform/ (accessed on July 27, 2020).

Janský, P., and Palanský, M. 2017. *Estimating the Scale of Profit Shifting and Tax Revenue Losses Related to Foreign Direct Investment*. Prague: Institute of Economic Studies.

Johannesen, N., Tørsløv, T., and Wier, L. 2017. Are less developed countries more exposed to multinational tax avoidance? Method and evidence from micro-data, Helsinki: WIDER, Working Paper 2016/10, revised version.

Kabala, E. and Ndulo, M. 2018. Transfer Mispricing in Africa: Contextual Issues. *Southern Africa Journal of Policy and Development*, 4(1), 16-28.

McMillan, J., and Zoido, P. 2004. How to subvert democracy: Montesinos in Peru. *Journal of Economic Perspectives*, 18(4), 69–92.

Madu, O. 2015. Trader Journey, mimeo, Multimix Academy, Lagos, Nigeria.

Merckaert, J. 2020. Bitter Chocolate: Capital Flight from Côte d'Ivoire. Amherst, MA: Political Economy Research Institute, Working Paper 517.

Myerson, R.B. 2008. Perspectives on mechanism design in economic theory. *American Economic Review*, 98(3), 586–603.

Natural Resource Charter and Center for Public Policy Alternatives. 2014. *Summary of the 2014 Benchmarking Report: Assessing the Governance of Nigeria's Petroleum Wealth*. Lagos: Center for Public Policy Alternatives.

Ndikumana, L. 2016. Trade misinvoicing in primary commodities in developing countries: the cases of Chile, Cote d'Ivoire, Nigeria, South Africa and Zambia. Geneva: UNCTAD.

Ndikumana, L., Boyce, J.K., and Ndiaye, A.S. 2015. Capital flight from Africa: Measurement and drivers. In S.I. Ajayi and L. Ndikumana (Eds.), *Capital Flight from Africa: Causes, Effects and Policy Issues*. Oxford: Oxford University.

Norris, F. 2001. S.E.C. Accuses Former Sunbeam Official of Fraud. *New York Times*, May 16.

North, D.C. 1991. Institutions. *The Journal of Economic Perspectives*, 5(1), 97–112.

North, D.C. 2002. Institutions. *The IMF Institute Courier*, 4.

Obi, P. 2017. Nigeria Facing Adverse Effects of Corruption – EFCC. *The Day* (Lagos), December 12, available at https://allafrica.com/stories/201712120226.html (accessed on July 24, 2019).

Okonjo-Iweala, N. 2018. *Fighting Corruption is Dangerous: The Story Behind the Headlines*. Cambridge, MA: MIT Press.

Public Eye. 2013. BD oil report triggers parliamentary investigations in Nigeria, available at https://www.publiceye.ch/en/media/press-release/bd_oil_report_triggers_parliamentary_investigation_in_nigeria/ (accessed on July 27, 2020).

Rodrik, D. 2006. Goodbye Washington Consensus, Hello Washington Confusion? A Review of World Bank's Economic Growth in the 1990s: Learning from a Decade of Reforms. *Journal of Economic Literature*, 44(4), 973–987.

Sanusi, S.L. 2014. How NNPC Illegally Diverted $20 Billion from the Federation Account. *Sahara Reporters*, February 5, available at http://saharareporters.com/2014/02/05/how-nnpc-illegally-diverted-20-billion-federation-account-cbn-governor-sanusi (accessed on July 22, 2019).

Sanusi, S.L 2015. Unanswered questions on Nigeria's missing oil revenue billions. *The Financial Times*, May 13, available at https://www.ft.com/content/e337c7a4-f4a2-11e4-8a42-00144feab7de (accessed on July 22, 2019).

SARS. 2017. Trade Statistics: Explanations and Notes, available at http://www.sars.gov.za/ClientSegments/Customs-Excise/Trade-Statistics/Pages/Explanations-and-Notes.aspx (accessed on August 22, 2019).

Sender, J. 1999. Africa's economic performance: Limitations of current consensus. *Journal of Economic Perspectives*, 13(3), 89–114.

Shaxson, N. 2009. *Nigeria's Extractive Industries Transparency Initiative. Just a Glorious Audit?* London: Chatham House.

Simon, J. 2013. How One Of Kenya's Biggest Scammers Ended Up On The Ballot. National Public Radio, April 17. Transcript available at https://www.npr.org/2013/04/17/177650616/how-one-of-kenyas-biggest-scammers-ended-up-on-the-ballot (accessed on October 9, 2019).

Sunstein, C.R. 2019. Wading Through the Sludge, *New York Review of Books*, April 4.

UNCTAD. 2016. Trade Misinvoicing in Primary Commodities in Developing Countries: The Cases of Chile, Côte D'Ivoire, Nigeria, South Africa and Zambia, Geneva: UNCTAD (December).

U.S. Federal Bureau of Investigation. 2012. Bitcoin Virtual Currency: Unique Features Present Distinct Challenges for Deterring Illicit Activity. Intelligence assessment, 24 April 24, 2012, available at https://www.wired.com/images_blogs/threatlevel/2012/05/Bitcoin-FBI.pdf (accessed on October 3, 2019).

Van Rensburg, D. 2016. How wrong the UN was on SA gold smuggling, *City Press*, available at https://www.news24.com/citypress/business/how-wrong-the-un-was-on-sa-gold-smuggling-20160729 (accessed on July 27, 2020).

Vanguard, 2016. FG loses 775.2m dollars on oil, gas cargoes discharged in undesignated terminals, available at https://www.vanguardngr.com/2016/05/fg-loses-775-2m-dollars-oil-gas-cargoes-discharged-undesignated-terminals-2/ (accessed on July 27, 2020).

Wier, L. and Reynolds, H. 2018. Big and 'Unprofitable': How 10% of Multinational Firms Do 98% of Profit Shifting. Helsinki: World Institute for Development Economics Research, Working Paper 2018/111, September.

7

Conclusions

Capital Flight in the World Economy

James K. Boyce and Léonce Ndikumana

In the make-believe world of the perfect neoclassical economy, capital flight from Sub-Saharan Africa would be a cruel irony. In a world of perfect markets, abnormally high profits would arise only as a reward for productivity-enhancing innovations, a temporary bonus while other producers catch up. In a world of perfect property rights, assets would change hands only through voluntary exchanges at mutually agreed prices. Floating alongside the perfect market would be the perfect state, impartially enforcing the rules and efficiently providing public goods and services. Natural resources, like oil, hard minerals, and fertile land, would be a sheer blessing, not a curse. Guided by the invisible hand of self-interest, capital would flow to investments wherever they yield the highest return, and hence from places where capital is relatively abundant to places where it is scarce.

The real world depicted in this book operates quite differently. Far from being perfect, markets often are riddled with imperfections. They routinely confer persistent excessive profits to those who wield control of choke points in the economy. Property rights are neither perfectly defined nor perfectly secure; instead powerful actors are guided, as if by an invisible hand, to opportunities for appropriation, capture, and outright theft. Governments are neither impartial nor efficient; propelled by the interplay between power and wealth, their central objectives morph from serving the public to serving the elite. Natural resources are a hunting ground for rapid wealth extraction and accumulation, and capital flows across borders are driven not by relative scarcity but by the relative secrecy available in offshore havens.

In this all-too-real world, capital flight from Africa and other "poor countries" across the world—more accurately, countries most of whose people are desperately poor—comes as no surprise. It is not ironic, simply cruel.

James K. Boyce and Léonce Ndikumana, *Conclusions*. In: *On the Trail of Capital Flight from Africa*. Edited by Léonce Ndikumana and James K. Boyce, Oxford University Press. © James K. Boyce and Léonce Ndikumana (2022). DOI: 10.1093/oso/9780198852728.003.0007

Understanding Capital Flight

The scale of capital flight from Africa is often large relative to the size of African economies. Measures of its overall magnitude, derived from forensic analysis of balance of payments and international trade statistics, indicate that annual out-flows from Angola, Côte d'Ivoire, and South Africa, for example, represent 3.3 to 5.3% of national income, and that cumulative capital flight greatly exceeds their total stock of external debt (see Chapter 2).

Measured capital flight here refers to foreign exchange outflows that are not recorded in the official accounts by virtue of their hidden transfer abroad. In this respect, these are illicit financial flows by definition. In addition to illicit cross-border transfer, capital flight is often illicit in other respects, too: due to illicit acquisition of the capital in the first place, and due to the concealment of income and income-producing assets from fiscal authorities.

In some instances, capital that was obtained illicitly is laundered at home before being transferred abroad, in which case the outflow may be officially recorded in the balance of payments accounts, escaping measures of capital flight. Moreover, some illicit flows bypass the country, as when bribes for the award of government contracts are paid into private offshore accounts of public officials. In such cases, the outflows are hidden in the prices in the contract and associated pay-ments. For these reasons, measured capital flight almost certainly understates the full magnitude of the phenomenon.

At the same time, not all flight capital is illicitly acquired. In some cases, in-dividuals may secretly send honestly obtained wealth abroad, fearing predation by kleptocratic rulers or impairment in value caused by inept management of the national economy. Sometimes researchers assume that such transfers account for most capital flight, invoking a "bad government, innocent victim" narrative that avoids probing into how flight capital was initially acquired.[1]

In this book our main focus has been on the flight of capital acquired illicitly as well as transferred by illicit means. Sometimes this involves activities that are ille-gal; others occur in the grey zone between what is legal and what is not. One of the prerogatives of ruling elites is to set the rules and bend them to personal advantage. "Illicit" here refers to wealth of dubious provenance, whether formally unlawful or not. It is possible, indeed likely, that in many countries illicitly acquired as-sets represent a substantial fraction of total capital flight. Econometric studies have shown that natural resources and external borrowing, two major sources of lootable foreign exchange, are robust predictors of the magnitude and timing of capital flight, a finding consistent with this view.[2] The fine-grained evidence

---

[1] See, for example, Khan and Haque (1985); and Collier et al. (2001, 2004).
[2] See, for example, Ndikumana and Boyce (2011a); Arezki et al. (2015); and Ndikumana and Sarr (2019).

presented in this book provides further support for this conclusion. Again and again, the authors describe how wealth plundered from African economies winds up stashed offshore.

The Resource Curse

The extraction of natural resources—hard minerals in South Africa, cocoa in Côte d'Ivoire, oil and diamonds in Angola—is deeply implicated in our case studies of capital flight. The resource curse that afflicts African economies includes not only the economic impact of natural resource exports on other tradable-goods sectors (the so-called "Dutch disease," whereby exchange rate appreciation renders import substitutes and other exports less competitive) but also the political impacts of resource wealth on governance.

In a land free of the resource curse, there often exists an unspoken contract between the government and the citizenry, an agreement robust enough to bind the polity together, however imperfectly honored. The citizens consent to paying taxes, and the state in turn delivers public goods and services.[3] The politics of the resource curse shreds this contract. The state relies for revenue not on the people but on natural resource extraction. No fiscal incentive compels it to care much about the provision of public goods and services to advance social welfare. Obtaining the bulk of its revenue from parastatal monopolies, export levies, signature bonuses and royalties, supplemented when needed by external loans, the state's main constituency becomes its foreign collaborators rather than its own citizens.

In her prize-winning book *Fire in the Lake*, historian Frances Fitzgerald (1973, p. 480) used a telling metaphor to describe the estrangement of the American-backed wartime regime in south Vietnam from the Vietnamese people: "The Saigon government," she wrote, "had turned over on its back to feed upon the Americans." Something similar can be said about the impact of the resource curse in Africa and elsewhere.

The stunting of the fiscal contract undermines not only the well-being of the citizenry but also the legitimacy of the state. To secure and maintain its grip on power, the ruling elite relies on clientelist patronage at best and overt violence at worst. Both exacerbate social cleavages that risk erupting into civil war.

In these circumstances there is a widespread sense of insecurity not only among ordinary people but on the part of the elite as well. Those in positions of power find it prudent to hedge against the possibility, if not inevitability, of an abrupt change in the political climate that would threaten their own privileges and fortunes. When feasible, assets at risk are moved offshore to safer havens.

---

[3] In an account of the formation of European states, Tilly (1992) emphasizes military protection as the key initial public service. For reviews of literature on the "fiscal contract," see Moore (2004) and Moore et al. (2018).

Plunder

While textbook neoclassical economics rules out plunder by assumption, Marxian economics often relegates it prematurely to the dustbin of history. Writing in the middle of the nineteenth century, Marx saw the pillage of Africa and other colonized territories as features of what he ironically called "the rosy dawn of the era of capitalist production," when plunder provided start-up capital for the industrial revolution in Europe.[4] In the capitalist era that followed, the main source of wealth and main locus of social tensions shifted to the exploitation of wage labor rather than direct appropriation of resources. In referring to the earlier period as the era of "original accumulation" (or "primitive accumulation"), Marx underestimated both how enduring the phenomenon of plunder would prove to be and how central it would remain to the functioning and malfunctioning of the world economy.

The defining feature of plunder is the acquisition of wealth by taking things rather than making them. Making grows the economic pie; taking is at best a zero-sum game. The plunderer's winnings come at the expense of those whose incomes are siphoned and assets robbed, and of future generations whose resources are depleted and life chances diminished. The net result is less than zero whenever the losses to the victims exceed the gains to the plunderers, as often happens, for example, when the losses come in the form of a financial crash or environmental degradation.[5]

Economists generally refer to plunder by a more anodyne term, "rent." Broadly speaking, rent is defined as "getting income not as a reward to creating wealth but by grabbing a larger share of the wealth that would otherwise have been produced" (Stiglitz 2013, pp. 39–40). Rent, so understood, refers to more than routine payments to landlords who own land or real estate; it encompasses payments to those who control markets, resources, and the state. Rent, in this sense, is another name for what was once called tribute.

This book offers plentiful examples of how plunder turns power into money. In Côte d'Ivoire, the world's top cacao producer, rent is extracted at choke points in the commodity chain that links hundreds of thousands of growers to hundreds of millions of chocolate consumers around the world. In South Africa, the siphoning of funds from the electric power sector by the Guptas and their allies illustrates what has come to be known as "state capture." In Angola, oil rents not only lavishly

---

[4] "The discovery of gold and silver in America, the extirpation, enslavement and entombment in mines of the indigenous population of that continent, the beginnings of the conquest and plunder of India, the conversion of Africa into a preserve for the commercial hunting of blackskins," wrote Marx in *Capital* (1976 [1867], p. 915). "These idyllic proceedings are the chief moments of primitive accumulation."

[5] On financial-sector impacts, see Stiglitz (2013) and Shaxson (2018). On environmental impacts, see Boyce (2007).

enriched a narrow elite but also entrenched their power in other key sectors, such as telecommunications and banking, even as the majority of Angolans lived in abject poverty.[6] In each case, ordinary people have paid tribute to the powerful.

In neoclassical development economics, where the concept of "rent-seeking" first came to the fore, the phenomenon is portrayed more or less exclusively as the perverse outcome of state interventions in the economy in general, and of protectionist trade policies in particular (Krueger 1974). This state-centric definition helped to prepare the ground for the liberalization agenda that began in the Reagan-Thatcher years, sometimes dubbed "neoliberalism," which sought to dismantle government regulation in the name of efficiency. But the equation of rent-seeking to state interventions missed the many ways that it is a pervasive feature of markets too. Contests over property rights and over the rents they generate are endemic in real-world economies; the fantastical premise that "initial endowments" simply fall from the sky, distributed like tokens at the beginning of a board game, is a peculiarity of neoclassical economic theory. Efforts to establish market power, up to and including outright monopoly, are as old as the market itself. As Adam Smith (1977 [1776], p. 144) famously observed in *The Wealth of Nations*, "People of the same trade seldom meet together, even for merriment and diversion, but the conversation ends in a conspiracy against the public, or in some contrivance to raise prices."

These realities cannot be banished by assumption or wished away. Nor can the need for states with all the messy politics that come with them. States are crucial to the functioning of every economy in the world, no matter how market-oriented. States are necessary to adjudicate contests over property rights, curtail private monopolies and "conspiracies against the public," protect the environment, and provide public goods and services. Like markets, they are always imperfect, and sometimes they fail outright. But they are an inescapable dimension of real-world economies.

In Africa and elsewhere, the ruling elites and their international collaborators rarely rely solely on either the state or the market for wealth and power. They operate in both spheres simultaneously, their position in one reinforcing their position in the other. In this respect the term "state capture" can be somewhat misleading, insofar as it posits the possibility of a state existing autonomously from the market, impartially enforcing the rules and looking out for the public interest. Such a state may be a laudable ideal, but it is far from a day-to-day reality anywhere in the world.

---

[6] Oil rent is the difference between the extraction cost and the world price. Comprehensive data on extraction costs are not available, but the average extraction cost (including both operational expenses and capital expenses) in Angola was reportedly $35/barrel in 2015. At the average world oil price of $80/barrel from 2010–2019, oil rent amounted on average to $45/barrel. Data from Statista (2015, 2021).

The divide in modern politics as to the best balance between the market and the state—the right favoring the market and the left the state—misses a more fundamental issue: the distribution of wealth and power. In a more oligarchic society, where wealth and power are concentrated in the hands of a few, the economy is unlikely to perform well for the majority of people regardless of the balance between market and state. In both spheres, plunder exacerbates inequality and crowds out productive activity. In a more democratic society, meaning a society in which wealth and power are widely diffused, the scope for plunder is diminished, and the market and the state are better able to advance broad-based economic well-being.

Transnational Networks

The nexus between plunder and capital flight is not purely an internal problem of African countries. Nor is it purely an international relationship in which an imperial power preys on faraway lands, as in earlier centuries. Rather it is a transnational phenomenon that spans national boundaries, operated by a network of individuals and institutions who are bound together by mutual benefit and convenience regardless of nationality.

The markets for bulk commodities like oil, hard minerals, and cacao are themselves transnational institutions of worldwide scope. Were it not for global demand, production of these commodities would be a minor feature of African economies. In principle, as economists have long insisted, international trade can lift living standards among all trading partners, much as in principle Africa's resource wealth should be a blessing for its people. In practice, however, there is a fateful disjuncture between textbook principles and real-world economies.

In exploiting the imperfections of markets and states, transnational plunder networks transform national borders from a constraint into a shield. The takers and their enablers move freely across borders, inhabiting a world of executive suites, gated communities, five-star hotels, first-class lounges, and private jets. In this world local cultures are glimpsed, if at all, only as artifacts displayed by interior decorators. At the same time, the networks gladly seize the advantages that borders can provide for concealing wealth from national authorities. Borders act as a semi-permeable membrane, allowing free movement of commodities, money, and people with the right credentials, but obstructing the reach of the rule of law. Far from an anomaly, in this world capital flight is a feature of business as usual.

The takers are aided and abetted by enablers: global banks and financial institutions, auditors and accounting firms, consulting firms, and lawyers for hire. The enablers, too, are essential parts of the transnational plunder networks, along with the corporate and government officials they serve, and they share commensurately in the loot.

Transnational plunder networks wield political influence everywhere they operate, which is to say just about everywhere. They use this influence to shield their dealings as much as possible from public scrutiny and from the rule of law. That is to say, they engage in not only the offensive game of looting but also a defensive game against opponents, played in countries on the receiving end of African capital flight as well as in the continent itself. It is a battle without end.

In the 1990s, for example, the OECD launched an effort to curtail the activities of tax havens in what Shaxson (2011, p. 193) called "the first serious and sustained intellectual assault on the secrecy jurisdictions in world history." Protracted negotiations led to a set of agreed recommendations on how to combat "harmful tax practices," including comprehensive reporting of information on transactions with tax havens. A counteroffensive was quickly mounted in the United States by a newly formed organization called the Center for Freedom and Prosperity, which unleashed a well-funded lobbying campaign in Congress and the press.

In this campaign the "innocent capital" trope was duly invoked. A conservative columnist warned in *The Washington Post* that the sharing of tax information would "hand a West African dictatorship a weapon for repression of its subjects seeking economic freedom in America."[7] This touching concern for the victims of repressive governments failed to acknowledge that unsavory regimes could be excluded from information sharing, just as they can be penalized by financial sanctions and trade restrictions. It also ignores the elephant in the room: the transnational plunder networks. "Who uses secrecy jurisdictions to protect their money and bolster their positions?" asks Shaxson (2011, p. 202). "The human rights activist screaming in the torturers' dungeons? The brave investigative journalist? The street protestor? Or the brutal kleptocratic tyrant oppressing them all? We all know the answer."

A turning point in this particular skirmish came in 2001 when the administration of George W. Bush took power. It promptly jettisoned the agreement, a move that US officials privately acknowledged "essentially guts the effort" (Milbank 2001). In explaining the US stance, Treasury Secretary Paul O'Neill complained that the exchange of offshore account information proposed by the OECD was "too broad" and "not in line with this administration's tax and economic priorities." A White House official put matters more bluntly: "Basically the US has very little to gain and it's a burden on our financial industry."[8]

US Senator Carl Levin, the tenacious chairman of the Senate Permanent Subcommittee on Investigations that held hearings on the matter, offered a contrary view, citing the role of secrecy jurisdictions in tax evasion by wealthy Americans:

[7] Robert Novak, "Global Tax Police," *Washington Post*, April 11, 2001. Reproduced as Exhibit 21 in *What is the U.S. Position on Offshore Tax Havens? Hearing Before the Permanent Subcommittee on Investigations of the Committee on Governmental Affairs, United States Senate*, July 18, 2001.

[8] O'Neill and the anonymous official are quoted in Milbank (2001). For more detailed accounts, see Easson (2004), Sharman (2006), and Sullivan (2007).

"Tax havens," he declared, "are waging economic warfare against the United States."[9]

In reality, of course, tax havens have very different impacts on differing segments of American society. "It is more accurate," Shaxson (2011, p. 200) remarks, "to say that they are helping a minority of Americans in their campaign against the working population." In this respect, Americans have much in common with Africans and with the peoples of other nations throughout the world.

Global Repercussions

The ill effects of transnational plunder networks are not limited to capital flight and tax evasion, and they are not confined to Africa and the developing countries. Like a systemic infection, the networks reach deep into host societies, not only stripping countries of resources and starving governments of revenue, but also elevating economic inequality, eroding social bonds of trust and empathy, and undermining the productive capacities of private enterprises as well as public institutions.

The elevated inequality resulting from plunder can be seen not only in the streets of Luanda, Abidjan, and Johannesburg, but also in New York, London, and other global metropoles. In world cities on the receiving end of hot money flows, the influx of capital pushes up real estate prices and residential rents, generating windfalls for the propertied while compelling working people to pay more for housing and live further from their places of employment.

The corrosive effects of transnational plunder networks on trust and empathy are evident not only in the indifference with which ruling elites gaze from their luxury vehicles upon the impoverished street people of African cities, but also in the casual disregard shown by ruling elites in the industrialized countries for the precarity and daily struggles of their lower-income compatriots. During the Covid-19 pandemic, journalist Masha Gessen (2020) witnessed in New York the "fundamental sense of division—of alienation—between the people who run things and the people who die," and likened the United States to a post-Soviet state where the elite lives in a separate universe from the rest of the country. What made possible the fumbling US response to the rapidly mounting death toll was the harsh reality that "we are not in this together." A hallmark of transnational plunder networks wherever they operate is that they cause elites to "turn over on their backs," in Frances Fitzgerald's phrase, to feed upon the takings.

The hollowing out of private enterprises, another repercussion, was exemplified in the collapse of Portugal's oldest banking dynasty, Banco Espírito Santo, in 2014,

---

[9] Quoted by Shaxson (2011, p. 200). The hearings were held that summer: *What is the U.S. Position on Offshore Tax Havens? Hearing Before the Permanent Subcommittee on Investigations of the Committee on Governmental Affairs, United States Senate*, July 18.

in the wake of the disclosure of massive uncovered loans made by its Angolan subsidiary.[10] Blowback from plunder in Africa has damaged public institutions elsewhere, too, as vividly shown by the "Elf affair" in which secret accounts of France's biggest oil company, Elf Aquitaine, were used to channel hidden cash payments to French political parties as well as African heads of state, and to fund lavish parties, mistresses, and villas. The modus operandi will be familiar to readers of this book: "Whenever Elf made a big acquisition or an investment in this period you find a middleman who sent a bill for a percentage commission, which was paid to an offshore account," a senior Elf official later explained. "Then the middleman returned most of the money to the person behind the fraud. It was classic, textbook embezzlement."[11] The transnational character of the scandal was underscored by French magistrate Eva Joly, who led the investigation: "I see so many resemblances, in France and abroad, between the corruption of the state and the mafias of various sorts," she wrote in her 2000 memoir: "The same networks, the same henchmen, the same banks, the same marble villas."[12]

In a wide-ranging study of past pandemics, *When Germs Travel*, historian Howard Markel (2005, p. 18) describes "the unintended consequences of not investing in the basic health care needs of the most impoverished citizens of the world," as drug-resistant strains of tuberculosis and other contagions spread across the globe. Capital flight is one reason for this underinvestment; elsewhere we have estimated that in the early 2000s, lower public health spending attributable to capital flight led to 77,000 excess infant deaths in Africa annually—a stark example of how private interests of ruling elites crowd out the public interest at the expense of the poor majority.[13] But the international transmission of infectious diseases is also an apt metaphor for the international transmission of the financial pathologies spawned by plunder. In both cases, the casualties extend worldwide.

Looking Ahead

The magnitude of capital flight from developing countries, and techniques to measure it, first emerged in the wake of the international debt crisis of the early 1980s, when it became evident that official statistics had greatly understated both external debt and capital outflows. At the time, however, discussion of capital flight in the so-called "international community"—the web of official international organizations including the Bretton Woods institutions, the United Nations,

---

[10] See Shaxson (in this volume); see also Engrácia Antunes (2019). In 2020, Portuguese prosecutors released a 4,100-page document accusing former BES chief executive Ricardo Espírito Santo Salgado and 17 of his colleagues of fraud, money laundering, market manipulation, and corruption (Wise 2020).

[11] Elf president Philippe S. Jaffre, quoted by Whitney (1999).

[12] Quoted by Ignatius (2002). On recent investigations of transnational corruption, see Bullough (2018), Burgis (2020), and Taub (2020).

[13] Ndikumana and Boyce (2011b, p. 83). See also Ortega et al. (2020).

and bilateral aid agencies—remained something of a taboo, a topic more often discussed *sotto voce* than raised in polite company. The Cold War was a major reason for this reticence, as concerns about financial malfeasance were brushed aside in the name of the rivalry between the Free World and the Soviet bloc. The refrain, "He may be a son of a bitch, but at least he's our son of a bitch," summed up the prevailing attitude to client regimes, no matter how corrupt or brutal their rule.

With the end of the Cold War, the bounds of acceptable discourse began to change. One indication of the new climate came in the early 1990s, when the IMF, African Development Bank, and World Bank cut off lending and other financial assistance to the flagrantly corrupt Mobutu regime in today's Democratic Republic of the Congo (Ndikumana and Boyce 1998).

In 2003, the United Nations General Assembly adopted the UN Convention against Corruption, the first and only international anti-corruption treaty, which among other things provides for mutual legal assistance in combating embezzlement, money laundering, and other corruption-related offenses.

In 2007, the World Bank and UN Office on Drugs and Crime launched the Stolen Asset Recovery (StAR) Initiative, which provides technical assistance in tracing and recovering looted wealth. In that same year, a conference hosted in Pretoria by the South African Reserve Bank brought together representatives of the Association of African Central Bank Governors, the African Development Bank, the Bank of England, the US Treasury, the World Bank and others for the first pan-African discussion of capital flight and steps to combat it (Ndikumana and Boyce 2011b, pp. 106–112).

In 2011, the Fourth Joint African Union Commission and United Nations Economic Commission for Africa Conference of African Ministers of Finance, Planning and Economic Development mandated the establishment of a High-Level Panel on Illicit Financial Flows from Africa. The mandate of the High-Level Panel, chaired by former South African president Thabo Mbeki, was to lead efforts in assessing the volume of illicit financial outflows and to coordinate policy debates in the continent and globally to address the problem.[14] As part of the 2030 Agenda for Sustainable Development, the United Nations (2015) committed to strengthening the framework for global efforts to combat illicit financial flows.[15]

These official actions were spurred and complemented by the sustained advocacy of civil society organizations, including Global Witness in London, Global Financial Integrity in Washington, Sherpa in Paris, and the transnational Tax Justice Network and International Consortium of Investigative Journalists. Civil society organizations in Africa, such as Tax Justice Network Africa, are actively

---

[14] The High-Level Panel published its first report in 2015 (UNECA 2015).
[15] See   https://www.unodc.org/documents/data-and-analysis/statistics/Drugs/IFF_framework_ and_
methodology.pdf (accessed on July 21, 2021).

contributing to raising awareness on illicit capital flows, tax evasion, and money laundering.

In 2014, more than a decade after the Bush administration sabotaged its previous effort to rein in tax havens, the OECD successfully launched a common reporting standard for automatic exchange of information among tax authorities (OECD 2017). Another indication of the changing international legal landscape came in 2020 with passage in the United States of the Anti-Money Laundering Act, containing measures to pierce the veil of secrecy surrounding the beneficial owners of shell companies.[16]

Thirty or 40 years ago, any of these initiatives on their own would have been virtually inconceivable. Together, they testify to how far global public opinion has moved and the international financial architecture has been reformed in the battle against transnational plunder networks.

There can be no guarantee that justice and the rule of law will ultimately prevail. The takers wield formidable wealth and influence, and they use it systematically in their quest to weaken rules, exploit loopholes, and evade the law. But neither is there any guarantee that the takers will continue to thrive in the financial shadows and underworld in the face of growing demands for transparency, accountability, and fairness.

Concealment, like hypocrisy, is the tribute that vice pays to virtue. As more and more becomes known about the predatory activities and harmful effects of transnational plunder networks, their room for maneuver becomes more constrained. Much has been accomplished, and much more remains to be done. It is our hope that this book will make a modest contribution to this effort.

References

Arezki, R., Rota-Graziosi, G., and Senbet, L.W. 2015. Natural resources and capital flight: A role for policy? In S.I. Ajayi and L. Ndikumana (Eds.). *Capital Flight from Africa: Causes, Effects and Policy Issues* (pp. 263–276). Oxford: Oxford University Press.

Boyce, J.K. 2007. Inequality and Environmental Protection. In J.M. Baland, P. Bardhan, and S. Bowles (Eds.), *Inequality, Collective Action, and Environmental Sustainability* (pp. 314–348). Princeton, NJ: Princeton University Press.

Bullough, O. 2018. *Moneyland: Why Thieves and Crooks Now Rule the World and How to Take it Back*. London: Profile Books.

Burgis, T. 2020. *Kleptopia: How Dirty Money Is Conquering the World*. New York: Harper.

---

[16] The act, which has been described as "the biggest anti-money laundering reform in a generation" (Monroe 2020), came after Senate hearings in which one of the bill's co-sponsors decried the role of the United States in enabling global corruption by allowing "looters" to shelter their ill-gotten gains, and the fact that "whole industries, American law firms, realtors, shell corporations, and financial services companies, cater to international crooks and kleptocrats" (Whitehouse 2019).

Collier, P., Hoeffler, A., and Pattillo, C. 2001. Flight capital as a portfolio choice. *The World Bank Economic Review*, 15(1), 55–80.

Collier, P., Hoeffler, A., and Pattillo, C. 2004. Africa's exodus: Capital flight and the brain drain as portfolio decisions. *Journal of African Economies*, 13(2), ii15–ii54.

Easson, A. 2004. Harmful tax competition: An evaluation of the OECD initiative. *Tax Notes International*, 34(10), 1037–1077.

Engrácia Antunes, J. 2019. Banco Espírito Santo: Anatomy of a banking scandal in Portugal. In D. Busch, G. Ferrarini, and G. Van Solinge (Eds.), *Governance of Financial Institutions*. Oxford: Oxford University Press, 23.01–23.29.

Fitzgerald, F. 1973. *Fire in the Lake: The Vietnamese and the Americans in Vietnam*. New York: Vintage Books.

Gessen, M. 2020. Why America Feels Like a Post-Soviet State. *New Yorker*, July 31.

Ignatius, D. 2002. True Crime: The Scent of French Scandal. *Legal Affairs*, May/June. Available at https://www.legalaffairs.org/issues/May-June-2002/story_ignatius_mayjun2002.html (accessed on March 29, 2021).

Khan, M.S., and Ul Haque, N. 1985. Foreign borrowing and capital flight: A formal analysis. *IMF Staff Papers*, 32(4), 606–628.

Krueger, A. 1974. The political economy of the rent-seeking society. *American Economic Review*, 64(3), 291–303.

Markel, H. 2005. *When Germs Travel*. New York: Vintage.

Marx, K. 1976 [1867]. *Capital*, Volume 1. London: Penguin.

Milbank, D. 2001. US to Abandon Crackdown on Tax Havens. *Washington Post*, May 11.

Monroe, B. 2020. After overwhelmingly hurdling Congress, "biggest AML reform in a generation," breaker of beneficial ownership chains now in hands of President. Association of Certified Financial Crime Specialists, December 11. Available at https://www.acfcs.org/after-overwhelmingly-hurdling-congress-biggest-aml-reform-in-a-generation-breaker-of-beneficial-ownership-chains-now-in-hands-of-president/ (accessed on January 11, 2021).

Moore, M. 2004. Revenues, state formation, and the quality of governance in developing countries. *International Political Science Review*, 25(3), 297–314.

Moore, M., Prichard, W., and Fjeldstad, O.H. 2018. *Taxing Africa: Coercion, Reform and Development*. London: Zed Books.

Ndikumana, L., and Boyce, J.K. 1998. Congo's odious debt: External borrowing and capital flight in Zaire. *Development and Change*, 29(2), 195–217.

Ndikumana, L., and Boyce, J.K. 2011a. Capital flight from Sub-Saharan Africa: Linkages with external borrowing and policy options. *International Review of Applied Economics*, 25(2), 149–170.

Ndikumana, L., and Boyce, J.K. 2011b. *Africa's Odious Debts: How Foreign Loans and Capital Flight Bled a Continent*. London: Zed Books.

Ndikumana, L., and Sarr, M. 2019. Capital flight, foreign direct investment and natural resources in Africa. *Resources Policy*, 63(101427).

OECD. 2017. *Standard for Automatic Exchange of Financial Account Information in Tax Matters*, 2nd edn. Paris: OECD.

Ortega, B., Sanjuán, J., and Casquero, A. 2020. Illicit financial flows and the provision of child and maternal health services in low and middle-income countries. *BMC International Health and Human Rights*, 20(15). Available at https://doi.org/10.1186/s12914-020-00236-w (accessed on July 21, 2021).

Sharman, J.C. 2006. *Havens in a Storm: The Struggle for Global Tax Regulation*. Ithaca, NY: Cornell University Press.

Shaxson, N. 2011. *Treasure Islands: Tax Havens and the Men Who Stole the World*. London: Random House.

Shaxson, N. 2018. *The Finance Curse: How Global Finance Is Making Us All Poorer*. London: Bodley Head.

Smith, A. 1977. [1776]. *The Wealth of Nations*. Chicago, IL: University of Chicago Press.

Statista. 2015. Average cost to produce one barrel of oil in top oil producing countries worldwide in 2015. Available at https://www.statista.com/statistics/597669/cost-breakdown-of-producing-one-barrel-of-oil-in-the-worlds-leading-oil-producing-countries/ (accessed on March 22, 2021).

Statista. 2021. Average annual Brent crude oil price from 1976 to 2021. Available at https://www.statista.com/statistics/262860/uk-brent-crude-oil-price-changes-since-1976/ (accessed on March 22, 2021).

Stiglitz, J. 2013. *The Price of Inequality: How Today's Divided Society Endangers Our Future*. New York: W.W. Norton.

Sullivan, M.A. 2007. Lessons from the Last War on Tax Havens. *Tax Notes*, July 30.

Taub, J. 2020. *Big Dirty Money: The Shocking Injustice and Unseen Cost of White Collar Crime*. New York: Viking.

Tilly, C. 1992. *Coercion, Capital and European States, A.D. 990–1992*. New York: Wiley.

United Nations. 2015. *The 2030 Agenda for Sustainable Development*. New York: United Nations.

United Nations Economic Commission on Africa (UNECA). 2015. Illicit Financial Flows: Report of the High-Level Panel on Illicit Financial Flows from Africa. In *Report Commissioned by the AU/ECA Conference of Ministers of Finance*. Addis Ababa, Ethiopia: UNECA.

Whitehouse, S. 2019. Whitehouse Remarks in Judiciary on Combating Kleptocracy. Washington, DC: Office of Senator Sheldon Whitehouse, June 19. Available at https://www.whitehouse.senate.gov/news/speeches/whitehouse-remarks-in-judiciary-on-combating-kleptocracy (accessed on March 31, 2021).

Whitney, C. 1999. A seamy French tale of sex, politics, and an oil company's lost millions. *New York Times*, February 11.

Wise, P. 2020. Prosecutors accuse ex-chief over collapse of Banco Espírito Santo. *Financial Times*, July 15.

Index

Printed and bound by CPI Group (UK) Ltd, Croydon, CR0 4YY